The Early Stuart Church, 1603–1642

The Early Stuart Church, 1603–1642

EDITED BY

KENNETH FINCHAM

Stanford University Press
Stanford, California
1993

Stanford University Press
Stanford, California
Editorial matter, Introduction © 1993 Kenneth Fincham;
    Chapter 1 © 1993 Kenneth Fincham and Peter Lake;
    Chapter 2 © 1993 Nicholas Tyacke; Chapter 3 © 1993
    Kenneth Fincham; Chapter 4 © 1993 John Fielding;
    Chapter 5 © 1993 Judith Maltby; Chapter 6 © 1993
    Andrew Foster; Chapter 7 © 1993 Peter Lake;
    Chapter 8 © 1993 Anthony Milton; Chapter 9
    © 1993 Peter White
Originating publisher The Macmillan Press Ltd,
    Hampshire, England
First published in the U. S. A. by
    Stanford University Press
Printed in Hong Kong
ISBN 0-8047-2196-3
LC 92-83917
This book is printed on acid-free paper.

Contents

Preface

I have enjoyed editing this collection of essays. In part this is because early Stuart religious history is so lively a subject, and during the lengthy gestation of this book much new work has appeared, which has provided (in most cases!) occasion for reflection and reconsideration. In part also it is because my fellow-contributors have been so co-operative, listening to my suggestions and exhortations with exemplary forbearance, and then in every case beating me to the finishing-post. I am especially grateful to those amongst them who here offer a taste of their forthcoming monographs; to Peter White, for again entering the lists against the Tyackeian consensus (if it exists!); and to Peter Lake, for agreeing, at the last moment, to revamp and extend a collaborative venture of a few years ago. It is also a pleasure to acknowledge the expertise and patience, in about equal measure, of the Macmillan team, above all Vanessa Graham and Sue Cope.

The essays which follow offer new thoughts and evidence on both familiar and relatively uncharted territory; there are some omissions – notably on the Catholic community, on which we must await the important research of Michael Questier – but the aim has been to examine a number of central themes across the forty years before 1642. The extent to which we have fulfilled this aim I leave to the tender mercies of the reviewers.

14.iv.92

K.F.

This book is dedicated to Alison, Liz and Sandy with love and affection.

Introduction

KENNETH FINCHAM

THE search for the causes of the English Civil War has always dominated early Stuart religious history. This is a pity. For there is much else to be learnt about English society, culture and politics from a study of the doctrine, controversies, institutional concerns, private initiatives and pastoral practices of the Church between 1603 and 1642. The Church itself consisted not merely of a privileged clerical corporation, with its own elected assemblies, courts and property, but also the congregation of lay believers, many of them vocal, assertive and critical, whose religious aspirations had to be satisfied or shaped. The Church's teaching aimed, as the word religion means, 'to bind together' society with a common set of beliefs, so its government was too important to be left to clergymen; yet as a key ideological agent for the crown, the Church's pulpits were platforms for criticism as well as compliment. So powerful was its authority and influence, that the early Stuart Church became a battleground for rival visions of English society, fought out at court, in Parliament and in the parishes of early Stuart England.

Such diverse functions prompt certain questions. What was the character of monarchical control over the Church under James I and Charles I? Did their rule see the triumph of a century of protestant evangelism? Which forces promoted, and which subverted, the unity of English protestantism? These questions, among many others, are addressed in this collection of essays. The volume aims to nudge the current historiographical debate away from an obsessive preoccupation with one doctrine – predestination – and towards an appreciation of a range of contentious issues: conformity, order, worship, clerical authority and wealth, even attitudes towards the Church's own past. This introduction provides some thoughts on these themes, as well as a review of the contemporary civil war among historians of the early Stuart Church. These scholarly disagreements continue in the essays which follow, most notably in Chapter 9, where Peter White challenges the assumptions and arguments of several fellow-contributors.

II

Almost everyone in early Stuart England desired religious unity, but on whose terms? Developments and conflict after 1603 have their immediate origins in the protracted Reformation process of mid sixteenth-century England. Of immense significance for the future was the fact that protestantism was only one of a number of formative influences on the reformed Church of England which took settled form in 1559; so too were political convenience, tactical compromises and institutional inertia. The Church retained its Catholic structure of bishops, cathedrals and Church courts; the Book of Common Prayer contained some traditional offices and ceremonies; and Elizabeth I, herself a moderate protestant, was determined to preside over a genuinely national Church which could incorporate Church papists and nominal conformists along- side advanced protestants. Further institutional reform was there- fore blocked. The diversity of continental protestant teaching and the ambiguity of official formularies (the Prayer Book, Homilies and Articles of Religion) also implied a certain plurality of theological perspective from the earliest years of the reign. In 1564 Elizabeth attended a Cambridge disputation between Andrew Perne and Matthew Hutton. The two clashed violently over central issues such as the relationship between scripture and the Church, and the status of Rome – to Perne, the apostolic mother of Christianity, to Hutton, the seat of Antichrist. Neither divine was formally censured, and it is as significant for the character of the Elizabethan Church that Perne remained Master of Peterhouse, as that Hutton ended as Archbishop of York. The state Church that both served was a bastion of social and political order as well as a missionary organis- ation, and friction between these two roles was invariably resolved by the queen in favour of the former. Thus in 1577 she suppressed prophesying meetings, notwithstanding their role in promoting a preaching ministry, in the belief that they were vulnerable to presby-terian infiltration. Evangelism could not be allowed to threaten monarchical government of the Church. Controversy was the pre-dictable result of a Church characterised by religious pluralism, continuities from the pre-Reformation past, political interference and lack of further reform. Vigorous arguments took place over the Church's government, doctrine, ceremonies and relations with other Churches, debates which ran deep into the seventeenth century.[1]

What patterns emerge from a study of religious divisions in the early Stuart Church? In the 1950s and 1960s a favoured model to explain these tensions was the clash of two antagonistic groups, Anglicans and puritans, the forces of conservatism pitched against the progressives. Anglicans represented the ecclesiastical authorities – supreme governor, bishops, Church officials and conformist clergy and laity – and were all dedicated to the defence of the *status quo;* and among their number were John Jewel, Archbishop Whitgift, Richard Hooker and William Laud. Opposed to them were the puritans, those more zealous protestants committed to further reform, subversive of received authority and the engineers of the 'puritan revolution' of 1640–60.[2] On this view, crown and bishops made repeated attempts to curb puritanism, especially as rep-resented by Archbishops Whitgift in the 1580s, Bancroft in the 1600s and Laud in the 1630s. Why then were Laud's policies so much more controversial? Here great weight is attached not just to Laud's intemperate zeal, but also to the appointment of George Abbot to succeed Bancroft as Archbishop of Canterbury in 1611. Instead of appointing a successor in the same tradition (Andrewes or Overall), James I allegedly bowed to pressure from his favourite, the Earl of Dunbar, and chose Abbot, a churchman obsessed with popery but indulgent towards puritans. Thus during Abbot's 22 years in office the pass was sold to the puritans, and only on his death in 1633 could William Laud attempt to reimpose neglected discipline and ceremonies. His government provoked a puritan backlash, and after 1640 both he and the episcopal order were eliminated.[3]

Neither the model of Anglican versus puritan, nor this interpre-tation now seem satisfactory. To conceive of two exclusive groups across an eighty-year period (1559–1642) is to ignore evidence for change and fresh challenges, to which rival solutions were proposed. Moreover, 'Anglican' is an anachronistic tag: bar a few separatists, all English protestants were 'Anglican' before 1642, members of an inclusive national Church; and to label any one group 'Anglican' is to imply that they alone represented the 'true' pre-war Church of England. In fact, the struggle between rival groups for control of the Church before 1640 means the term 'Anglican' is best confined to the period after 1642, to categorise those who remained loyal to the Prayer Book and episcopacy in an era of persecution, to be swelled by other protestants in the 1660s who rejected Dissent.[4] Equally, puritans have been dethroned as a coherent opposition. While Patrick Collinson has identified an organised group of committed presbyterians within the Elizabethan Church, it is also evident that puritan influence was pervasive. Its word-centred piety, and relentless activism for a reformed Church and society, purified of corruption and sin, is now found to have influenced courtiers, privy councillors and senior churchmen including, it has been suggested, Elizabeth I's last Archbishop of York, Matthew Hutton. That *doyen* of puritan writers, William Perkins, had his funeral sermon preached by one future bishop, his writings defended by another.[5]

Nor does the appointment of Abbot as archbishop seem to be such a watershed. Not only is it the case that he was nominated by his predecessor Archbishop Bancroft; but there is little sign that puritanism revived after 1611. Instead, we find Abbot enforcing clerical subscription to canon 36 of 1604 and continuing Bancroft's work to protect the income of the parochial clergy. Nor should we accept the assumption that archbishops ruled the Church.[6] In fact, the formulation and implementation of policy involved crown, bishops and councillors, as well as archbishops; and, as Fincham and Lake observe in Chapter 1, both James and Charles were active supreme governors. Nevertheless, as we shall see, this general interpretation of Anglican and puritan has been recently revived to counter the arguments offered by Nicholas Tyacke since the 1970s.

So influential and controversial has Tyacke's argument been that it repays careful investigation. In a famous article of 1973, enlarged as a book in 1987, Tyacke proposed that most clergymen and a majority of the more educated laity were Calvinists, who accepted absolute and double predestination. God had ordained some to salvation and some to reprobation, and human action could not influence, let alone alter, the divine will. The theses in the divinity faculties of the two universities and the publications of the press demonstrated this Calvinist dominance. The shared doctrine of predestination blunted the differences between puritans and more moderate Calvinists over Church government and ceremonies, and helped stabilise the reformed Church. However, the emergence of the Arminians in the 1590s challenged this stability. Arminians denied the Calvinist teaching on predestination, arguing instead for divine grace freely available in the sacraments and for salvation as fore-ordained in the light of human will. Arminians rose to prominence under James I but did not enjoy real influence over policy until the accession of Charles I. From the late 1620s Calvinist teaching was proscribed, and a novel ceremonialism and sacramentalism introduced, which provoked a violent reaction after Charles I was forced to call the Long Parliament in November 1640. On this view, therefore, Arminians not puritans were the novel and destabilising force, 1625 not 1610–11 is the crucial turning-point in the government of the early Stuart Church.[7]

Patrick Collinson has given powerful support to this interpretation by adding a vital diocesan dimension. He argues for the increasingly widespread observance in the Elizabethan and Jacobean Church of 'Grindalian episcopacy'. This was a style of government practised by Calvinist bishops which overlooked divisive issues of nonconformity in favour of the common endeavour of bishop and puritan to spread the gospel and resist Roman Catholicism, activity which by the 1620s had promoted genuine stability and had largely erased Elizabethan polarities between puritans and anti-puritans. This harmony was destroyed in the 1630s by the imposition of 'an alien and innovative' policy of Arminianism.[8]

Although many scholars have broadly endorsed Tyacke's general argument, others have censured it on a variety of grounds. He has been accused of replacing one crude polarity (Anglicans and puritans) with another (Arminians and Calvinists); of assimilating Jacobean puritans into mainstream Calvinism to the extent that they have become an endangered species; of confusing doctrinal views on grace with liturgical and disciplinary preferences; and of giving unwarranted emphasis to predestination in the range of theological disputes and arguments. The fullest criticism has come from George Bernard, Christopher Hill, Kevin Sharpe and Peter White.[9] All four deny there was 'a rise of Arminianism', and see Charles I and Laud enforcing thoroughly conservative aims of obedience, order and uniformity just as previous monarchs, and most of their archbishops, had done before them. Though their emphasis differs, all

four appear to be reviving the earlier model of the protracted struggle between the authorities and nonconformists, in other words,
between Anglicans and puritans. Peter White in Chapter 9 of this
volume sees the English Church as distinct in its liturgy, polity and
doctrine, and committed across the two reigns of James and Charles
to a *via media* between Roman corruption and the challenge from
puritans and separatists. The only novelty of the 1630s was the
vigour with which policy was enforced, and Charles's own partisan
favour to churchmen. The strength of these claims and counter-
claims, by Tyacke, White and others will be tested in the analysis
which follows; suffice it to say here, that Tyacke's achievement has
been to put theological issues back at the centre of our analysis.[10]

III

What follows is an attempt to build on the insights of Tyacke and
Collinson, while moving on from the controversy over predestination to investigate the full range of issues confronting early Stuart
protestants. Clearly much turns on the religious categories we
employ to anatomise English protestantism. One answer is to conceive of educated protestant opinion as a spectrum, as proposed by
Peter White in Chapter 9, yet he warns that 'both conservative
and radical protestantism were heterogeneous' and that 'doctrinal
preference did not necessarily correspond with liturgical taste'. The
difficulty with this latter statement is that for many contemporaries,
as well as for historians, these links seem evident and substantial.
Thus in the 1630s we find both the Calvinist Samuel Ward and
the anti-Calvinist Robert Shelford acknowledging the link between
Arminianism and ceremonial piety.[11]
   We may use the notion of a spectrum in a different way, to
identify four broad groupings among educated protestants during
James I's reign: radical puritans, moderate puritans, conformist
Calvinists and anti-Calvinists. None of these categories is watertight,
but each reflects a common position on the related issues of doctrine,
piety and conformity. At one end we can locate a puritanism characterised by demands for ecclesiastical reform and a commitment to
an intense word-centred piety. Requests for sweeping changes to
the Church's formularies, discipline and ministry were largely
blocked at the Hampton Court Conference of 1604, but they were

followed by repeated attempts in early Stuart Parliaments (1604–10, 1614, 1625, 1626 and 1628) to modify clerical subscription. In 1628 the proposal was supported by John Pym, Francis Rous, Sir Nathaniel Rich, Christopher Sherland and other moderate puritan MPs, and their arguments also disclose dissatisfaction with the Prayer Book. In this light, the Parliaments of 1621 and 1624, which contained no bills to ease subscription, were quite exceptional; and since subscription was enforced throughout this period, the renewed demands after 1625 to modify it probably indicate the hope that a new monarch would prove more amenable than the last – as we know, something of a miscalculation! This fairly constant pressure for institutional reform qualifies Sir Geoffrey Elton's remark that 'Puritanism has no continuous history' as well as the over-optimistic view that the reforming sting of puritanism had largely been drawn by the accommodating climate of the Jacobean Church.[12]

Tyacke has recently identified among these reformers a 'radical puritan continuum' stretching from 1604 to 1640. They included prominent London aldermen as well as divines such as Arthur Hildersham and John Dod, who lost their livings in 1606–7 for refusing to subscribe. Theories of congregationalism, the heir of Elizabethan presbyterianism, were advanced against the order of bishops, and in the later 1620s these circles had close connections with the Feoffees for Impropriations. Clear links can be traced between these radicals and sympathetic moderate puritans and indeed some conformist Calvinists: thus James Ussher, future Archbishop of Armagh, spent the day of Prince Henry's funeral in 1612 at a private fast with John Dod and Ezechiel Culverwell, both deprived ministers. Such links are important in explaining the effective organisation that puritans displayed in their push for godly reformation once the Long Parliament of 1640 had opened.[13]

The radicals' brethren, the moderate puritans, were partial conformists within the Jacobean Church. Clergy among them offered a token subscription in return for the opportunity to preach the gospel and supplement parish services with the round of fasts, household prayers, psalm-singing and sermon-repetition, all extra-legal rather than illegal manifestations of that 'voluntary religion' which Collinson has sensitively evoked. Typical of their number was the prolific author Richard Bernard, who reluctantly conformed in 1608 and established a flourishing preaching practice in eastern Somerset under the indulgent eyes of successive Jacobean bishops, only falling foul of the ecclesiastical authorities in the 1630s. Such puritans were Calvinist in doctrine, their piety centred on the sermon, scripture and self-examination, their holy-day the sabbath. The round of edificational and charitable works performed on Sundays by strict sabbatarians gave the day an almost sacramental stature as a conduit of divine grace. Although many protestants supported strict discipline on Sundays, from the 1590s puritan writers were arguing that the fourth commandment ('Remember the sabbath day, to keep it holy') was entirely moral, and tensions arose from the practical implications of that theological perception.[14] Puritans' piety was also animated by the search for assurance of their status as elected saints, which has been labelled 'experimental predestinarianism'. This was a theological current that encouraged a blurring between the visible godly and the invisible elect, making external behaviour the sign of election, and led some down the path of questioning an inclusive national Church that mixed the wheat with the chaff, the elect with the reprobate.[15]

Although Calvinist conformists accepted the doctrine of predestination, most did not draw on the 'experimental' tradition. Instead, they were acutely aware of the pitfalls of the doctrine, which might promote despair or antinomianism (release from moral law), and attempted to reconcile God's arbitrary decrees with both the general promises made in scripture, and repeated in the Prayer Book, as well as the pastoral needs of a national Church ministering to all. Significant differences of emphasis and minor modifications of doctrine distinguished their position from the 'experimental' perspective. For 'credal' Calvinists argued that the elect were unknowable in this life; many, including Archbishops Hutton and Bancroft, warned against presumptuous spiritual security, to check the dangers inherent in the belief that the elect could never fall from grace; they somewhat softened the decree of reprobation with the suggestion that it occurred after, not before, the fall of Adam; and some advanced a hypothetical universalist view of the atonement, that Christ had died for all, even if all would not be saved. A typical moderate Calvinist was Arthur Lake, a Jacobean Bishop of Bath and Wells, who argued that prolonged speculation on the doctrine of predestination was not pastorally profitable, and informed his Somerset ordinands that 'in a minister's commission, grace is universal'. Many Calvinist laity, with a less refined grasp of doctrine, may have also gravitated towards this general position as a satisfactory accommodation between their religious beliefs and social realities. In short, we should not conceive of English Calvinism as a set of rigid propositions, unresponsive to pastoral needs in the parishes.[16]

Both puritans and conformist Calvinists also shared a common opposition to the Church of Rome, though here again there was a series of divergent views. As Anthony Milton argues in Chapter 8, almost all accepted the pope as Antichrist, though some rejected all Roman teachings and traced the ancestry of the reformed Church of England to heretical underground groups in medieval Christendom; others could maintain the descent of the episcopal office from apostolic times. This second argument had the advantage of justifying the government of the Church, and conformist pressures could lead a figure such as Archbishop Abbot to adopt the second position without renouncing the first. Similarly, Calvinists could disagree about the precise dangers posed by popery: Abbot's fervent anti-popery contrasts with the moderate position of Bishop Lake, who saw Rome as a Church in error rather than the mystical Babylon.[17] Finally, a commitment to evangelism also drew many Calvinists and puritans together: in Chapter 3 Fincham shows how Jacobean bishops and puritans co-operated in extending the preaching ministry.

As conformists, these Calvinists also upheld the formularies and government of the Church, and the supreme governor's authority to determine rites and discipline, and often maintained the *ius divinum* (divine right) status of episcopacy. It is hard, however, to identify many enthusiastic ceremonialists among them, apart from Bishop John Williams; and though it is true that in the 1630s Calvinist bishops can be found enforcing official ceremonies, this was a matter of public duty rather than personal preference. John Davenant, Calvinist Bishop of Salisbury was a vigorous enforcer of Laudian altar policy, but he also complained privately of this new ceremonialism.[18] We urgently need more studies of such conformist Calvinists, who are usually lost sight of between the more visible extremes of puritan and Arminian. Current studies, however, suggest that we should resist confusing their sympathy for puritans with similarity, for the view of each group on government, ceremony and the implications of predestinarian doctrine remained distinct. Thus it appears that the dominant religious culture of the Jacobean

Church was not puritanism so much as the active alliance of conformist Calvinists and puritans.[19]

Finally, there was a developing anti-Calvinist interest, critical of
Calvinist teaching on grace, its sermon-centred piety and its obsessive aversion to the Roman Church. Instead, anti-Calvinists advocated a vision of decorous public worship based around a strict
observance of the Prayer Book and canons, in which divine grace
through prayer and sacraments were available to the entire Christian community, participating in an inclusive national Church primarily defined by its unbroken episcopal succession through the
ages. The first coherent exposition of this position was by Richard
Hooker, writing in the 1590s, although other divines, notably Lancelot Andrewes, were advancing similar ideas from the pulpit.[20] This
cluster of concerns, here described as 'anti-Calvinist', is often also
called 'Laudian' or 'Arminian'. None of these three terms is entirely
satisfactory. To label this movement 'Laudian' ignores the fact that
most of these ideas were first articulated by others in the 1590s,
when Laud was only in his twenties; while 'Arminian' may give too
central a significance to predestination for Laud and many of his
allies. In an important clarification of his position, Tyacke argues
in Chapter 2 that Laud was more concerned with sacramentalism
than Arminianism; moreover, 'Arminianism' is an awkward term
to apply to a number of prominent supporters of Laud in the 1630s,
such as Bishops Piers and Dee, whose views on grace are obscure.
The objection to 'anti-Calvinism' is that it may imply a negative
gloss on what was a positive programme for reform. Nevertheless,
it does remind us that in origin the movement was primarily reactive
against a dominant Calvinism, defined in terms of doctrine and
piety, rather than representing a clear tradition going back to the
1550s; in Chapter 2 Tyacke traces Laud's evolution from an early
Calvinist phase, and a similar progression can be observed for
Hooker, Andrewes, Neile, Howson and others.[21] Indeed, it is difficult to construct an unbroken genealogy of anti-Calvinists from the
1550s to the 1590s. One obvious link would be Perne, Master of
Peterhouse from 1554 to 1589, but his influence seems tenuous,
except over the ritualist Robert Shelford; more promisingly, Diar-
maid MacCulloch had established connections between anti-puritans and Suffolk Catholic gentry in the 1580s, but how typical this
was remains unclear.[22] Given that each of these labels – Laudian,
Arminian and anti-Calvinist – is imperfect, each is deployed by

different contributors in Chapters 1–4 and 6–7 to refer to the same set of religious ideals, first codified in the 1590s and the inspiration for change in the 1630s.

Here then are four main groupings, representing conventional clusters of attitudes rather than factional interests on the divisive issues of conformity, piety and doctrine in the Jacobean Church. Another point of friction was resurgent clericalism, which by turning laity against clergy cut across the positions identified above. If anti-clericalism was one product of the Reformation, then a renewed clericalism turns out to be another. As Andrew Foster demonstrates in Chapter 6, the fortunes of the clerical estate improved dramatically on the accession of James I, the monarch who wished to be remembered as 'a true lover of the Church'. As a result bishops resumed their traditional role as councillors and intimates of the crown, clergy were appointed as J.P.s and this new confidence led to a novel assertiveness – over the divine right of tithes, for example – and open criticism of lay interference in ecclesiastical affairs. The defence of clerical rights drew together divines such as the Calvinist Carleton and the anti-Calvinist Richard Montagu, though the two were to fall out in 1625–6 over the doctrine of grace.[23] The revival of clericalism began in 1603, rather than 1625 as historians have usually implied. Lay criticism remained fairly muted until after the accession of Charles I, which means we cannot explain hostility to Laudian rule as primarily opposition to clergy occupying high secular office.

It is difficult, therefore, to accept the view of the Jacobean Church as a stable and harmonious body. Rather, it was riven with friction and disagreement. Fincham and Lake in Chapter 1 chart the growing rivalry between Calvinist and anti-Calvinist bishops at court, especially after the appointment of Abbot as Archbishop of Canterbury in 1611. Abbot is usually portrayed as an indulgent governor, but towards anti-Calvinists he was consistently aggressive and divisive. John Fielding (Chapter 4) shows how these theological divisions also emerged in Peterborough diocese over issues of conformity and sabbatarianism. However, Peterborough was peculiarly polarised, perhaps owing to an entrenched puritan community clashing with an anti-Calvinist episcopal administration of unusual longevity; elsewhere, especially in the second half of the reign, the differences between puritans and their opponents were rarely rehearsed, something which Fincham in Chapter 3 attributes to the restraining hand of James I. Nevertheless, the deprivation of puritan ministers in 1604–9, and the criticism of Jacobean diplomacy from puritans and some Calvinists in 1618–23 caused much acrimony and controversy. At parochial level, too, there is abundant evidence of friction between reforming puritans and their defiant neighbours, clashes which David Underdown has characterised as 'cultural conflict'.[24]

We may enquire, therefore, how the Jacobean Church managed to contain these internal tensions and rivalries. One powerful force for unity, as Fincham and Lake make clear, was James I himself. Dedicated to unity among obedient protestants, and seeing real political advantage in patronising rival groups of churchmen, James demanded minimal conformity from puritans, attempted to contain disputes between Calvinists and anti-Calvinists, offered favour to churchmen while avoiding excessive provocation to laymen, and urged those looking for advancement to defend the royal supremacy and episcopacy as divine and complementary institutions. The strength of his Church lay in the incorporation of diverse and competitive threads in English protestantism, and its acceptance of the ambiguities of official formularies which could produce rival readings of the English reformed tradition. For much of his reign, James I has claims to be regarded as the 'common and ameliorating bond' who could favour both the Calvinist James Montagu and the anti-Calvinist Lancelot Andrewes, who was a patron of preaching yet questioned excessive preaching, who castigated puritanism but tolerated moderate puritans, who could denounce the pope as Antichrist and yet seek confessional unity.[25]

Important as royal policy and patronage was in a monarchical Church, three other factors were also working for unity. One was the broad hostility to Rome, whether aimed against its politics or theology, which promoted general protestant solidarity; in the words of Thomas Holland, Regius Professor of Divinity at Oxford, 'Love God and hate popery'.[26] Two other concerns drew together moderate puritans and conformist Calvinists: a common devotion to spread the gospel, and a shared acceptance of the core doctrine of predestination. All three received official encouragement for much of James's reign; all three were to be shattered in the 1630s. It is clear, however, that by the early 1620s Jacobean unity was becoming brittle. Not merely had James's indulgence towards moderate puritans deepened the convictions of anti-Calvinists that disorder in the Church was worsening, and that remedies needed to be strengthened; his patronage had also transformed anti-Calvinists from an inchoate and marginal group into a formidable coterie at the centre of power, so that the role of the supreme governor as arbiter between rival groups became all the more essential and delicate. Finally, the disputes generated by the Thirty Years' War exposed the strains within English protestantism, between an articulate puritanism and an increasingly confident anti-Calvinism.

IV

Five of the essays in this volume suggest that the anti-Calvinist interest triumphed in the later 1620s and then implemented policies which marked a significant break with the past. The political events of the 1620s are fundamental for understanding this process. The sustained agitation against the Spanish Match, conducted in the pulpit and the press by moderate puritans and some conformist Calvinists, drove James I towards anti-Calvinist churchmen who supported his foreign diplomacy and accepted the propriety of a Catholic marriage. His hostility to puritans was expressed to one of their number, John Yates, in 1624: 'puritans dissolved Parliaments, perturbed his affairs and he would make his kingdom too hot for us'. Charles I inherited this suspicion of a popular puritan conspiracy against the crown, which seemed to be confirmed by the series of disastrous parliamentary sessions of 1625–9, and he too turned to anti-Calvinist churchmen, who shared his fear of puritan disorder and his preference for the solemnity of divine worship.[27]

Several historians such as Bernard, Hill, Sharpe – as well as Peter White in this volume – maintain that official policy in the 1630s represented traditional conformist concerns of obedience and order against unruly puritans and lax clergy and laity.[28] The chapters by Fielding, Fincham, Lake and Tyacke directly challenge this view; instead, they see the dominant protestant tradition of the previous sixty years under official attack from a relatively new and less central strand of English protestantism. Caroline policy did represent a new departure, even if many of its elements have clear antecedents, as Fincham and Lake observe in Chapter 1. For example, the desire to enhance the wealth, resources and status of the clerical estate considerably predated 1625; but it was now allied with a new emphasis on the ministry as a sacramental priesthood rather than a preaching order and enjoying the political backing of a supreme governor less concerned than James had been to placate lay susceptibilities. Charles I, in Peter White's vivid phrase, was 'more cleric than king'. Tyacke elsewhere has shown how explicit Calvinist preaching and publishing on predestination, which had suffered little hindrance under James I, was prohibited under the Declaration of November 1628 forbidding controversy.[29] Here, Peter Lake (Chapter 7) explores the positive ideals of the 'Laudian style' on reverent worship, a sacrificing priesthood and the holiness of God's house, views which had been formulated in the 1590s by Hooker, Andrewes and others but which had not hitherto inspired official policy. Caroline reforms in the 1630s were directed against a puritanism enlarged to include Calvinist doctrine and puritan piety as well as ceremonial nonconformity. This caused a marked shift in the priorities of diocesan government, which Fincham explores in Chapter 3. The official hostility to incessant preaching and the attack on sabbatarianism reversed the dominant practice of the Jacobean authorities, while Caroline discipline combined old *and* new conformity, as one contemporary put it.[30] Not only were the ceremonial provisions of the canons of 1604 systematically enforced for the first time; new requirements were also introduced, principally the relocation of the communion table at the east end of churches, protected by a rail. Religious images, traditionally condemned as idols by protestant reformers and hitherto confined to the Chapel Royal and private chapels such as Holyrood and Robert Cecil's Hatfield, now began to proliferate in collegiate and parish churches.[31]

Attitudes towards the Church of Rome, and the understanding of the English Church's own history, were also changing. As Anthony Milton shows in Chapter 8, Laud and some of his associates rejected the Foxeian apocalyptic interpretation of Christian history and denied the pope to be Antichrist, Rome to be Babylon, the ancestors of protestants to be a succession of true believers in a sea of popery. Instead, they argued for continuity with the pre-Reformation Catholic Church through an institutional succession of bishops, and acknowledged Rome to be a true though corrupt Church. James I had talked of confessional unity; but these divines were distinctive for their positive celebration of pre-Reformation practices, and their

respect for Rome and concomitant suspicion of non-episcopal protestant Churches abroad.[32]

A variety of factors inspired these changes. The fears that moderate Calvinists voiced about the potential dangers of rigid predestinarianism were enlarged by anti-Calvinists; Laud, Buckeridge and
Andrewes could claim that Calvinist doctrine was incompatible
with civil government, preaching and ministry. Peter Lake has
argued that Hooker's presentation of anti-Calvinist piety emerged,
in part at least, from the need to refute the presbyterian vision of
a Church dominated by the godly; and the concern to vindicate a
genuinely national Church, and the availability of neglected ritualism in the Prayer Book, were both powerful impulses long after
Hooker's death. It was also widely held by these divines that puritan
practices provoked protestant division and apostasy to Rome: as
Charles I succinctly put it, 'the neglect of punishing puritans breeds
papists'. Moreover, anti-Calvinist divines felt vulnerable to the
taunts of Roman writers that English protestantism was characterised by disunity, irreverence and laxity.[33] Puritan agitation over the
Spanish Match and the turbulent Parliaments of the 1620s convinced others of the veracity of a puritan conspiracy against the
crown. As Fincham and Lake suggest (Chapter 1), Caroline
religious policy fitted into a broader political style emphasising the
advancement of order, obedience and uniformity through ceremonial means. What cannot be proved is that Laud and his allies
were consciously following in the footsteps of Whitgift and Bancroft,
as Tyacke's critics have suggested. Rather, the prevalent view seems
to have been that the English Church had been corrupted by false
practice and inept government from the middle years of Elizabeth's
reign.[34]

The result was a polarised Church. Caroline clericalism offended
not just many Calvinists but others such as Viscount Falkland, who
feared an attempt to subjugate the laity to the clergy.[35] Official
restrictions on Calvinist teaching were extremely alarming to puritan opinion, who saw true doctrine as the central mark of a true
church. They were also deeply troubled at the attack on sabbath
observance, which in the words of William Gouge put 'a knife to
the throat of religion' since it threatened 'the very life of piety' as
many puritans conceived it.[36] Nor could they easily express their
views in print. Tyacke has outlined the shift in official attitudes
after 1625 against Calvinist writing on predestination; similarly, at

least four books in defence of sabbatarianism were written in the 1630s, but were only published in England in 1641, after the collapse of the Personal Rule.[37] As the puritan John Vicars wrote privately in 1636:

> Manuscripts are now the best help God's people have to vindicate the truth, printing being nowadays prohibited to them, especially if their writings have any least tang or tincture of opposition to Arminianism yea or even to popery itself.

Of course Caroline censorship was never wholly effective or consistent: until 1637 it was possible to republish previously licensed works; while the simple tactic of resubmitting a manuscript could pay off. *The Cure of Hurtfull Cares and Feares*, a tract by the puritan Thomas Pierson, was refused publication in 1634 on the grounds that 'there is no need for it', but it was licensed two years later by one of Laud's chaplains. In short, a recent claim that 'books of all complexions were published in the 1630s' oversimplifies a complicated situation.[38] It is also significant that precious few anti-Calvinist works on sacramental piety were published in the reign of James I, further evidence of the marginal character of anti-Calvinism, but in the changed climate of the 1630s many works appeared defending the new ritualism. The authors of these works are analysed by Fincham in Chapter 3, their arguments by Lake in Chapter 7.

Thus many of the forces promoting unity in the Jacobean Church were dissolved in the 1630s. The discouragement of preaching, the hostility to Calvinist divinity and nonconformity, as well as divergent attitudes to Catholicism, caused a realignment of protestant groupings. Many conformist Calvinists felt pulled in two directions: to remain united with their moderate puritan brethren, or else fall in line behind the authorities. A few were radicalised, such as Cornelius Burgess. Others conformed but with little enthusiasm for aspects of Caroline policy. Thus Bishop Hall of Exeter later recalled that during the 1630s he had enforced 'anciently received orders' but avoided 'new impositions', a claim largely borne out by the diocesan records, but at the cost of facing accusations of leniency.[39] The reaction of an Oxfordshire parson, Thomas Wyatt, must have been common among conformist Calvinists: he outwardly conformed, while expressing his unease in his diary. In it he was critical of the Caroline controversialist Peter Heylyn ('he careth not who fall so he may rise, a busy brain') and the ritualist John Cosin ('a popish and superstitious fellow') and dismayed by bishops such as Wren (who 'did most importunously trouble the ministers of his diocese about altars and old rites').[40] Yet, as we have seen, many conformist Calvinists had already distanced themselves from the 'experimental' tradition of puritan piety, and accepted that concentration on the doctrine of grace was not desirable, so the ban on predestinarian teaching would not have been wholly unwelcome. It has been suggested that the desire not to split a common front against Rome best explains the co-operation of many Calvinist conformists with the Caroline regime; pressures for obedience and career considerations cannot have been wholly absent either. In Robert Sanderson's case, it seems likely that his recruitment reflected his own developed anti-puritanism, stirred by the practices of John Cotton's gathered congregation at Boston in Lincolnshire. There must have been many others who also united behind a traditional fear of puritan extremism.[41]

Nor was this constituency shunned by the centre. Though very few Calvinists were promoted to the episcopate, and Bishops Hall, Davenant and Morton were all treated with some suspicion, nevertheless Calvinists such as Davenant continued to preach regularly at court, and the royal chaplains included other Calvinists such as John Prideaux, John Hacket and Sanderson, whose selection was no doubt intended to vindicate the Caroline claim to occupy the middle ground of English protestantism.[42] As Peter White observes (Chapter 9), Laud and others still proclaimed the virtues of the *via media*, though White does not accept that the centre had shifted since the accession of Charles. Similarly, as John Fielding demonstrates below, in Peterborough diocese successive reforming bishops – Piers, Dee and Towers – tried to detach Calvinists such as Lord Montagu from local puritan opposition through concessions over preaching. Such tactics were particularly appropriate in view of the strong puritan community in Northamptonshire, but they may well have been attempted in other dioceses.

V

Does this concentration on religious division encourage us to discount the positive achievements of these years? The early Stuart

Church saw the culmination of over fifty years of protestant evangelism: the increasing influx of graduates into the ministry, the steady rise in numbers of licensed preachers, the publication of a vast range of protestant catechisms, pocket-sized bibles and prayer books, the slow but steady improvement in literacy levels across society, the leadership provided by a largely resident and pastorally-minded episcopate, and the discipline enforced by Church courts which were reasonably respected and fairly effective, all this, some scholars have suggested, made protestantism bite. Standards were rising and with them expectations.[43]

Yet some historians of popular religion have seen no cause for congratulation. Sir Keith Thomas has argued that protestantism had little appeal to much of the population, and those who grasped some protestant doctrine blended it with age-old superstitions.[44] Another pessimist is Christopher Haigh, who sees profound resistance among the semi-literate majority of the people to a faith centred on the word, propagated by divisive puritan preachers and accompanied by an assault on traditional pastimes and festivities in the name of moral reformation.[45] Of course it is the size rather than the existence of this conservative element which is important, an awkward fact since the sources for precise quantification of religious opinion in this period hardly exist. That said, it may well be that Haigh is unduly influenced by the exceptionally slow impact of protestantism in Tudor Lancashire. Martin Ingram has concluded from a study of rural Wiltshire that 'some degree of unspectacular orthodoxy' best characterises the piety of most early Stuart parishioners; similarly, a recent examination of an urban community, Southwark, has established regular observances of baptism, communion and the churching of women right up to the civil war. We shall explore the religious meaning of conformity later. It is also the case that historians know much about disruptive ministers but little about their pastorally-sensitive colleagues since secular and ecclesiastical courts were there to investigate complaints, not to hand out awards. Yet the persistent discussion of effective pastoral practice in protestant sermons and ministerial manuals implies not just a problem but the attempt to redress it.[46]

Protestant hostility to traditional culture has attached widespread attention. A celebrated study of Terling (Essex) by Drs Wrightson and Levine sees village society becoming increasingly polarised by the end of the sixteenth century in response to demographic expansion, economic changes and new cultural and religious standards. Puritan zeal and economic pressures drove parish notables to impose a programme of moral reform on their social inferiors. Bastardy, bridal pregnancies, alehouses, Sunday sports as well as dancing were the targets of this 'culture of discipline', an argument which has subsequently been extended by Dr Hunt to the whole county of Essex, and by Professor Underdown to the south-west of England.[47] Underdown has also identified a rival response to the process of economic and cultural stratification, in direct challenge to puritan aspirations: namely, a reinvigoration of traditional festivities and institutions such as church-ales and local games in order to promote a hierarchical, harmonious and unified society. This revival won official backing, best expressed in the Book of Sports of 1618, reissued in 1633, which sanctioned Sunday recreations. Underdown's suggestion of two rival conceptions of community fits well with other evidence of Laudian hostility to puritan divisiveness between godly and ungodly; as Lake argues in Chapter 7, the encouragement of Sunday sports was part of a wider vision of social unity, in which the sacred rituals were performed in church, the profane rituals thereafter on the village green.

Several features of this broad interpretation have been challenged. First, the close identification of puritans with the 'better sort' has been questioned by parish studies in Wiltshire, Essex and East Sussex, where religious and moral differences split society vertically rather than horizontally.[48] Delinquents were very often the young rather than the poor.[49] In Chapter 5, Judith Maltby offers an analysis of the social composition of signatories to petitions of 1641–2 in defence of the Prayer Book and bishops. Here again, support for the traditional order appears to be spread evenly from the poor up to parish notables and officeholders.

Secondly, to what extent was puritanism the chief inspiration for moral reform? From a study of Keevil (Wiltshire), Ingram has argued that economic pressures alone can account for tougher treatment of bastardy and bridal pregnancy, and Wrightson himself has shown that the fear of disorder, harsher attitudes towards the poor and the desire to conserve barley in periods of dearth, as well as religious attitudes, accounts for the suppression of alehouses.[50] Much Parliamentary legislation and the disciplinary work of the Church courts indicates that the reformation of manners was scarcely a puritan prerogative: an anti-puritan such as Robert Sanderson was also a committed opponent of popular recreations and drunkenness, while Archbishop Laud tried to impose strict moral discipline in Oxford University during the 1630s. Naturally, motives and objectives often clashed: Laud's support for Sunday recreations contrasts with the rigid sabbatarianism of many puritan activists; and while Laud could regard dearth as sometimes man-made, puritans such as Sir William Masham attributed it to divine judgement.[51] Nevertheless, both Laud and his opponents projected themselves as agents of moral and social order. Both were most effective when they could mobilise a wider body of opinion which did not share their ideological perspectives. In the 1630s hostility to sabbatarianism allowed the Caroline regime to strike a popular chord in its defence of lawful recreations; conversely puritans enlisted popular anti-popery in their stand against the feared subversion of law and religion on the eve of the Civil War.[52]

There has also been a tendency to treat the 'profane multitude' of puritan criticism as irredeemably irreligious, though the evidence points more to a rejection of puritan piety rather than Christian teaching itself.[53] Others, at last, have begun to examine popular religion in its own terms. Dr Watt's study of cheap print demonstrates the important place that religion possessed in popular culture. Poor households would display painted cloths of biblical subjects, while religious verses commonly adorned the walls of alehouses. The contents of godly ballads and the penny godly suggests that protestant teaching modified, rather than eliminated, pre-Reformation piety: traditional concern with death and judgement appeared alongside more central protestant themes such as repentance and salvation through faith.[54] How accurate a guide this may be to popular religious understanding remains an open question.

Perhaps the most important and provocative discussion of popular conformity has come from Dr Haigh, who has identified a conformist element in many congregations, whom he labels 'parish Anglicans'. These were former Catholics left high and dry by the failure of the Catholic mission in the 1570s and 1580s, who fell into conformity with the protestant Church, centring their religious practice on those ceremonies and rites in the Prayer Book which reminded them of the faith of their childhood. Here was a constituency which pressed for ritual to be observed, and although Haigh's published work has not ventured beyond 1603, he suggests that a later generation of these parish Anglicans formed a natural bedrock of parochial support for Laud in the 1630s.[55] Judith Maltby examines aspects of this argument in Chapter 5. She contends that by the beginning of the seventeenth century these conformists were not Church papists but 'Prayer Book' protestants, devoted to the offices and piety of the Book of Common Prayer. This attachment, as John Morrill has argued, was to persist in the hostile environment of the 1640s.[56] Maltby challenges Haigh's view that these conformists welcomed Laudian changes, pointing to the condemnation of recent corruptions in petitions drawn up in defence of the liturgy and bishops in 1641–2. Old conformity (such as Prayer Book ceremonies) they welcomed, but not new conformity, such as altar policy, unsanctioned by law or tradition. This interpretation is all the more interesting since it has been claimed, from evidence not yet published, that the rapid, widespread compliance over the altar policy suggests genuine enthusiasm for the change.[57]

VI

Reactions to Caroline rule differed very widely. The encouragement of Sunday sports and the revival of ritualism enjoyed some parochial appeal; groups of clergy across the country preached and wrote in favour of the new ceremonialism, and some members of the educated laity also welcomed these changes, support which Fincham briefly explores in Chapter 3. Both deserve further research if we are to understand fully the forces united behind the new religious order in the 1630s. As we have noted, discontent among puritans and some conformist Calvinists is also quite evident, but it did little to undermine royal authority. The Personal Rule collapsed as a consequence of the Scottish crisis, although once the opportunity had been created for change, the puritan platform for thorough reformation became a potent force in English politics. Until 1642, however, the number of principled sectarians remained very small, and most puritans attempted to preserve the concept of a national Church. So for all our talk of polarisation under Archbishop Laud, it appears that protestant fragmentation in the 1640s, leading ultimately to the dissenters, was a direct consequence not of the 1630s but of the political crisis after 1642.

The precise contribution of religion to the coming of Civil War is open to debate. Certainly, the recent emphasis on its dynamic contribution is in good measure because 'the rise of Arminianism' provides a plausible explanation for revisionists who deny the significance, or existence, of long-term clashes over secular ideologies.[58] There is no doubt that religion was a central element in the crisis of 1640–2: the intervention of Scotland and Ireland in English politics makes little sense without reference to religion, and Professor Russell has indicated how religious allegiance helped to determine the choice of sides when war occurred, which of course is not the same thing as why war occurred.[59]

The primacy of religion clearly did drive some, such as Sir Robert Harley, to take up arms;[60] yet for many others, the interdependence of political, religious and social perceptions makes such attributions inappropriate. Dr Smith has recently argued for the integration of political and religious order in the outlook of that moderate royalist, the fourth Earl of Dorset.[61] It is also striking how the conspiracy theories of both sides linked questions of politics with religion; as Fielding argues in Chapter 4, Parliamentarians in Northamptonshire were very often the puritans who had opposed Caroline reforms in both Church and state during the Personal Rule as symptoms of a creeping popery; conversely, Lord Montagu, a Calvinist and erstwhile patron of puritans, was moved by respect for legitimate authority and order in state and Church to join the king. The fear of popular tumult in 1641–2 also helped to rally support for the royalists.[62] As for Charles I himself, he was fighting for the recovery of an adequate revenue, and for an untrammelled authority as supreme governor in an episcopalian Church as much as anything else. 'No bishop, no king' was a cherished principle for Charles as it had been for his father, since both accepted that episcopal government of the Church underpinned monarchical rule in the state. Hard-headed political demands, not theological dogma, drove Charles to war.[63] In short, religion may have been the central discourse of 1642, yet we must acknowledge that it embodied and mediated a host of secular concerns and values.

To understand religion's integrative role in 1642 leads us back to the pre-war Church, to its authority, practices and tensions; and also forward to this collection of essays which, we believe, places these problems in focus.

1. The Ecclesiastical Policies of James I and Charles I

KENNETH FINCHAM and PETER LAKE

I

Recent scholarship has tended to contrast the acumen and flexibility of James I with the ineptitude and rigidity of his son Charles I, whose shortcomings are regarded as perhaps the most obvious cause of the Civil War.[1] This interpretation has been most marked in religious history, with Charles's government held responsible for both the final destruction of the Calvinist dominance of the English Church and the triumph of Arminianism, which created tensions powerful enough to destabilise politics and lay the ground for war. In some accounts, the villain of the piece is not Charles I but William Laud, whose doctrinaire policies and irascible rule proved disastrous for himself and the Stuart monarchy.[2]

Of late, there has been a reaction against such views. There was no 'rise of Arminianism', merely the pursuit of traditional conformist aims – order, uniformity and obedience – with unusual zeal. Many of the personnel (such as Laud) who rose to power under Charles had been preferred under James and many of the policies of the 1630s had been set out in the canons of 1604. Moreover, the architect of policy was Charles, and Laud just his master-mason helping to construct a genuine Caroline Church.[3]

So some recent literature invites us to make a simple choice between continuity and change. Simple, but false. We shall suggest that Caroline policies and priorities make sense only in the ideological and political context of James I's reign. Hardly any of the ideas translated into policy under Charles were intellectually novel or even new to the court by 1625. Again, almost all the leading lights of the Caroline regime had enjoyed royal favour under James. The two monarchs also shared many central ideals and prejudices. Both regarded monarchy and episcopacy as divinely-ordained and complementary offices intended to promote true religion and punish sin. Each proclaimed their devotion to unity, and presented their policy as a *via media* between the two poles of popery and puritanism, the political dangers of which both were determined to emasculate. Each was also more conciliatory towards Rome and English Catholics than many of their protestant subjects. Notwithstanding these continuities, the Caroline synthesis which emerged was recognisably different from what had gone before.

Both the style and content of Caroline ecclesiastical policy represents a distinct shift from the aims and assumptions of the Jacobean establishment. James I had attempted to construct a unified Church based on a small number of key doctrines, in which advancement was open to a wide range of protestant opinion and from which only a minority of extreme puritans and papists were to be excluded. A Jacobean style of ambiguity and compromise quickly emerged as the king mediated between rival groups of English protestants and adopted a series of rhetorical postures which were often contradictory: James was both the champion of protestant Europe against Rome and the irenic diplomat, indulgent towards moderate puritans yet fearful of puritan subversion, the patron of preaching and the resolute enemy of contentious preachers. While movement between these positions allowed James to harmonise conflicting interests at home and abroad, it also left him open to manipulation as political circumstances altered. Charles I, by contrast, regarded the Jacobean achievement of unity as illusory, for it had undermined uniformity of worship and doctrine and permitted the emergence of a popular puritan threat to monarchy. Vigilant government in Church and state was necessary to cauterise this malignancy. Consequently order and obedience, authority and deference, replaced flexibility and accommodation as the hallmarks of Caroline policy. All this, too, has important parallels with the secular political culture of the two courts.

II

James I believed that two groups, puritans and Catholics, challenged his authority as a Christian prince and towards each he
developed a similar policy of detaching moderate from radical
elements.[4] Moderates were to be incorporated into his refurbished
Church while radicals faced repression or expulsion. Let us take
each group in turn. James is justly famous for his strident denunci-
ations of puritanism, and ridicule of puritan practices pepper his
career.[5] Such uncompromising remarks were often qualified by, and
held in tension with, other more nuanced views of the same issues.
James's strategy towards puritans was first enacted at the Hampton
Court Conference of January 1604, but we find its assumptions
already outlined in the revised preface to the 1603 edition of *Basilikon Doron*, printed in England within days of his accession to the
throne. There the king had defined puritans in political terms as
Anabaptists, sectaries, rigid presbyterians and all who challenged
royal authority. To these he promised unyielding opposition. Yet
this hostility did not extend to all nonconformists, many of whom
were obedient subjects:

> I protest upon mine honour, I mean it not generally of all
> preachers or others, that like better of the single form of policy
> in our Church [of Scotland], than of the many ceremonies in the
> Church of England; that are persuaded that their bishops smell
> of a papal supremacy, that the surplice, the cornered cap and
> such like are the outward badges of popish errors. No, I am so
> far from being contentious in these things (which for my own
> part I ever esteemed as indifferent) as I do equally love and
> honour the learned and grave men of either of these opinions.

Here was a key statement of royal intent, widely read at the time
and often cited by puritans and conformists long after 1603.[6] This
clear distinction between radicals and moderates also reoccurs in
James I's speeches and actions throughout his reign: repression for
the radicals was balanced by the promise of reform and favour to
those who were prepared to express their case for further reformation in the language of expediency, while accepting that the
issues themselves were indifferent.

At the Conference, which opened on 14 January 1604, James

offered concessions to win over moderates to his new protestant consensus. Thus he promised to reform a number of long-standing abuses in the Church: among others, pluralism was to be limited, the preaching ministry strengthened, the law of excommunication revised, minor features of the Prayer Book amended, and a new translation of the Bible undertaken. The price to pay for these reforms was conformity in an episcopalian Church. The king rejected puritan complaints against the discipline and ceremonies of the Church, and underlined his complete hostility to any form of presbyterianism by twice stating his famous maxim, 'no bishop, no king'. Instead, he demanded that all clergymen acknowledge his temporal and spiritual supremacy, as well as the scriptural warrant for the Prayer Book, the degrees of bishop, priest and deacon, and the Articles of Religion. In other words, subscription was required to Archbishop Whitgift's Three Articles of 1583, which were shortly afterwards adopted as canon 36 of 1604. Those moderate puritans who subscribed ceased, in James's eyes, to be puritans, since they had renounced subversive disobedience to the royal command. This explains why James was prepared to compromise over the enforcement of ceremonies, such as the use of the surplice, so long as the legality of his ecclesiastical polity were accepted. Thus at the Conference he promised a period of grace to nonconformist clergy in Lancashire; similarly, in the long run, subscription and not strict ceremonial conformity was the means used to pursue the royal ideals of peace and unity.[7] Throughout his reign James was to be much more interested in extracting proof of loyalty and obedience than in the small print of regular conformity. In this, as we shall see, he was very different from his son.

The drive for Jacobean order after the Conference resulted in the deprivation of about eighty beneficed ministers, the majority of whom were ousted in the early months of 1605. Archbishop Bancroft had taken up the king's distinction of moderates and radicals in his circular of 22 December 1604, when he required the bishops only to remove those ministers who refused both subscription and ceremonial conformity. James would have preferred full conformity, but in practice was prepared to settle for less provided he obtained some obedience from querulous puritan consciences. The campaign for conformity he regarded as a necessary step to establish genuine unity, and thereafter remained hostile to intransigent nonconformists. In Star Chamber in 1607 a Kentish minister was degraded, fined and had his ears cropped for libelling episcopal government. In May 1611 bishops were ordered to win round any nonconformist clergy 'or else remove them and that with convenient speed'. Over the next decade, James admonished several bishops who permitted deprived clergymen to resume their ministry without first subscribing. However, those puritans who showed a willingness to compromise received preferential treatment. When John Cotton of Boston was reported to James I for nonconformist practices, he escaped deprivation by agreeing to confer over the ceremonies with his diocesan, Williams of Lincoln.[8] This episode perfectly encapsulates James's policy: puritans he defined as those who defied royal authority, so that accommodation was possible even with those such as Cotton who compromised to the limited extent of attending talks on conformity. James's abrasive anti-puritan rhetoric needs to be seen in the context of its practical application in cases such as this.

Some of the reforms offered in return for conformity were implemented over the next decade. The Prayer Book underwent minor textual amendment, and the Authorised Version of the Bible eventually appeared in 1611. In order to remove the twin evils of pluralism and nonresidence, Bancroft endeavoured to secure a Parliamentary statute to restore impropriated tithes to vicars and curates, but his proposals were wrecked on the rocks of vested economic interests among the laity. James, however, remained publicly committed to the ideal of an effective preaching ministry, and in a series of instructions between 1605 and 1611 ordered bishops to proceed against non-residents and force pluralists to employ preaching curates. In 1610 he also repeated his willingness to reform the abuses of excommunication provided some suitable scheme were submitted. Clearly James's activities as an ecclesiastical reformer were not confined to a burst of activity at the beginning of his reign, as some historians have suggested.[9]

How successful was the king's policy in enticing moderate puritans to stay within his refurbished Church? The pattern of deprivations after 1604 can be better explained by reference to local circumstances and the scruples of individual clergy than to any Jacobean theory. Nevertheless, his policy bore fruit in the long run. Presbyterian pretensions among the clergy largely disappeared and reluctant conformists were won round to the Jacobean settlement. This had much to do with James's sponsoring of anti-papal polemic, his own rising reputation as a godly prince and his patronage of evangelical Calvinists. Among the bishops he promoted were many zealous preachers, including two Archbishops, Abbot of Canterbury and Matthew of York; and royal patronage even extended to puritans such as John Preston, who became a chaplain to Prince Charles and was offered a bishopric in 1624.[10] In the middle years of his reign James presided over a settled Church from which the political radicalism of puritanism had ostensibly been removed.

III

James's desire for unity and his appeal to moderate opinion also extended to Catholics. The king did not share the view of many protestants that papists erred over beliefs central to the faith. Instead he distinguished between core Catholic doctrines to be held *de fide* and other issues on which debate and disagreement were acceptable among Christian brethren. This allowed James to argue that the Church of Rome, though vitiated with serious errors of belief and practice, still remained a true Church since it professed the crucial doctrines of the Trinity and the Incarnation. Such a view underpinned his plans to reunite Christendom, based on the authority of scripture and the practice of the primitive Church and effected through a general council of princes. His appeal to the pope in 1603-5 to convene such a council proved fruitless. Such an attitude also sanctioned leniency towards English Catholics as well as his assertion of the essential equivalence of the popish and puritan threats.

Thus James played down doctrinal differences and reserved his criticism for papal claims to supremacy and the power to depose secular rulers. It was on this issue, of course, that the menace of popery and puritanism coincided. To James, the pope's status as Antichrist was based on his claim to depose princes. If the pope dropped this assertion, the king implied he might not be Antichrist after all. In 1612 James told the Spanish ambassador that he had only 'written in his books that the pope was Antichrist' because of his claims 'in deposing and setting up kings at his will'.[11]

Such ambiguous views gave the king maximum room for manoeuvre with papists, at home and abroad. It also meant his more moderate protestant subjects could emphasise his irenic intentions towards Rome, while their more anti-popish colleagues could use his sponsorship of anti-papal writings and his denunciation of the pope as Antichrist to cast him in the role as champion of international protestantism. Whatever short-term political advantages this may have brought, when James refused to predicate his foreign policy on the need for an anti-popish crusade against Spain after 1618, many of his subjects were distressed by his apparent failure to live up to his own rhetoric.

These perceptions provided a potent justification for James's habitual distinction between radical and moderate papists. Among the ranks of radicals he numbered Catholic clergy and lay apostates from protestantism who accepted both the papal deposing power and the assurance that rebellions against the enemies of Rome were meritorious to salvation. More moderate spirits, born and bred as Catholics, were offered not toleration but tolerance. The Oath of Allegiance of 1606 was his formal offer to such moderate papists to accommodate themselves to the Jacobean regime by affirming their civil obedience and by repudiating the deposing power of the papacy. According to the king, the intention was 'to make a separation between so many of my subjects, who although they were otherwise popishly affected, yet retained in their hearts the print of their natural duty to their sovereign; and those who . . . thought diversity of religion a safe pretext for all kinds of treasons and rebellions against their sovereign'. Although in practice the oath was only fitfully enforced in the provinces, in theory it remained for James the touchstone of Catholic loyalty and moderation.[12]

James's policy had a limited impression on the fortunes of English Catholics. The financial penalties for recusancy continued to be exacted on many Catholics who had taken the oath; and events such as the assassination of Henri IV of France in 1610 precipitated a widespread drive against recusancy, undertaken with explicit royal backing. The most tangible evidence of royal policy in operation lay in the presence of many crypto-Catholics at the Jacobean court, including the Earl of Northampton, Edward Lord Wotton and Sir George Calvert. As Northampton had stated in 1606, the highest preferments were now attainable for those Catholics prepared to conform.[13]

The origins of Jacobean policy towards English puritans and Catholics clearly lie in Scotland. There James had learnt to distinguish between strands of presbyterian opinion in order to reassert his own authority against the militants led by Melville, especially in 1596–1600. The slow restoration of diocesan episcopacy was only possible because James was able to carry with him an important portion of protestant opinion. Indeed, the influential preface to *Basilikon Doron* was written in the light of his Scottish experience, even if one eye was directed to England. As for Catholicism, he attempted to rule the north through the Catholic earls, most notably Huntley, from whom he repeatedly sought nominal conformity, and kept links open with the international Catholic community through figures such as the exiled Catholic Archbishop of Glasgow. The effects in England were the Jacobean categories of moderate and radical, and the entry into government of crypto-Catholics such as Northampton. Yet Jacobean policy also formalised and embodied certain trends in Elizabethan government. The failure of the undifferentiated assault on puritans in 1583–4 had taught the queen and Whitgift to concentrate their attack on the more marginal and radical element, the presbyterians, who were silenced through Star Chamber in 1589–91. Equally, the Elizabethan regime was willing to use Catholic loyalists as an example to their co-religionists; thus among the commissioners at the trial of Mary Queen of Scots we find the Catholic peers Viscount Montagu and Lord Lumley. Bancroft's intrigues with the Catholic appellants in 1601–2 during the Archpriest controversy was an attempt to promote Catholic division and explore the possibility of neutralising the political dangers of Catholic priests, although in November 1602 the government broke off its links and accused the appellants of disloyalty and disobedience.[14] Despite these piecemeal precedents, before 1603 there was little sign of any consistent conception or pursuit of an even-handed policy towards puritans and Catholics.

IV

In the interests of religious unity, and for the success of his policy, James had to incorporate a wide range of theological opinion into his ecclesiastical establishment. For the policy towards puritans he needed evangelical Calvinists who were committed to a preaching ministry and an episcopal Church. For his Catholic policy he needed protestants who were sympathetic to his irenic attitude towards Rome. Few divines combined both perspectives. Evangelical Calvinists such as George Abbot opposed any tolerance to mod-

erate Catholics, while churchmen such as Richard Neile, who supported this latter policy, were no friends to godly preachers.

It is no surprise, therefore, that the king employed a broad spectrum of theological opinion in royal projects. Among the fifty-four
translators of the Authorised Version of the Bible were staunch
Calvinists, such as Thomas Ravis and Samuel Ward, anti-Calvinists
such as John Overall and Richard Thomson, and two puritan
delegates to Hampton Court, Lawrence Chaderton and John Rainolds. The king also ensured that a similar plurality of views flourished among his bench of bishops. Though traditional accounts
have attributed the selection of bishops to the intervention of
important patrons, such as Salisbury and Buckingham, James, like
Charles I, exercised a direct and informed control over appointments. Abbot, for example, won the see of Canterbury in 1611 not
simply because he secured the backing of Dunbar, but because he
was a tough opponent of popery, the political dangers of which
bulked large in James's mind following the murder of Henri IV the
previous summer.[15]

How did James I justify this range of religious opinion in the
heart of his church? The explanation lies in his belief in Christian
unity, based on a very limited number of crucial Catholic doctrines.
It is apparent that Jacobean divines agreed on what the king took
to be the essential pillars of Christian doctrinal truth; and in royal
projects such as the Oath of Allegiance controversy or the translation of the Bible, the king can be seen organising divines of
divergent opinions around his position as a reforming Christian
prince invested with a divine authority to govern the Church, supported by the apostolic order of bishops. These were the essential
issues for James, and disagreements among his churchmen were
acceptable because they involved those secondary issues on which
true Christians might differ. There is good evidence that, for James,
the theology of grace was one such issue. So long as private doubts
did not erupt into unseemly and disorderly altercation, James was
prepared to allow a certain variety of opinion. This was the policy
he urged on the United Provinces in 1610, and only when such a
course proved impossible to sustain and religious divisions seemed
to threaten political unity did James openly support the Calvinist
cause at the Synod of Dort.[16]

It would hardly be plausible to attribute this support solely to
political circumstances. On the contrary, ample evidence suggests

that James subscribed to a moderate Calvinist position on the theology of grace. From his favourable response to John Rainolds's desire for clarification of Article 17 in 1604 to his stance at Dort, the king publicly supported Calvinists against anti-Calvinists. In England theological propriety might allow divergences of private opinion, but the demands of political and ecclesiastical order would not allow open dispute, so the king suppressed public expression of anti-Calvinist theology. James, for example, knew of Lancelot Andrewes's liberal opinions on the theology of grace, but enjoined him to silence. Andrewes acquiesced in this demand, resorting to private correspondence with leading Dutch Remonstrants and allowing himself biting asides against Calvinists in his sermons before the king. He grew to great favour with James, not on account of his anti-Calvinism but for his rare gifts of eloquence and erudition.[17] His friendship with the king was entirely in accordance with the secondary status that James gave to predestination.

Unsurprisingly, the incorporation of a wide range of theological opinion produced much factional and personal rivalry at court. In the middle years of the reign a loose coalition of Calvinist bishops and councillors including Abbot of Canterbury, Bishops John King and James Montagu, Lord Chancellor Ellesmere and Edward Lord Zouche opposed the influence of crypto-Catholics such as the Earl of Northampton and the rising influence of anti-Calvinists led by Bishops Neile, Andrewes, Buckeridge and Overall. Between 1611 and 1614 Northampton and Abbot repeatedly clashed over the treatment of Catholics, as Abbot's recommendation of severity was opposed by Northampton.[18] The most sustained conflict, however, occurred between rival groups of bishops.

At stake between Calvinists and anti-Calvinists was much more than conflicting views of the theology of grace. Each was offering the king a different vision of the English Church. Calvinists wanted the preaching mission to be strengthened, Catholics to be persecuted and anti-Calvinists harried into conformity or apostasy. Anti-Calvinists, in turn, tried to persuade the king that Calvinists had corrupted English protestantism: the liturgy was neglected in favour of excessive preaching, while nonconformity and disorder flourished. In other words, James had available to him two coherent alternatives to his policy of conciliating moderate puritans and papists, but throughout his reign chose not to adopt either and thereby forfeit the unity he had so laboriously constructed.

Naturally, the rivalry between Calvinists and anti-Calvinists turned on the attempt to manipulate James's stated fears of popery and puritanism. In 1610–11 Abbot tried to block Laud's candidature for the presidency of St John's College, Oxford with the charge of popery, which he repeated against Laud and Howson in hearings before the king in 1615. Howson, in turn, insinuated to James that Abbot and other leading Calvinists were 'puritan bishops', a line of argument that at the time, at least, James would not accept. Similarly, from the pulpit Andrewes linked criticism of the Spanish Match and Calvinist predestinarian teaching as two aspects of the same puritan presumption, a shaft clearly aimed at Abbot and other Calvinist opponents of the marriage. James was well aware of these differences and enjoyed his role as a godly prince mediating between them. Significantly, he retained his independent stance by refusing to side decisively with one group. Thus in the hearing between Howson and Abbot in 1615, James cleared Howson of popery but also warned him to preach more often against Rome. Howson complied with this order, and three years later received a bishopric.[19]

Such an impulse to divide and rule was not confined to religious policy. It was a basic element in James's kingcraft, which had been formed and formulated in Scotland, where he had spent much time trying to escape from the controlling influence of contending noble and religious factions. Keith Brown has noted that Jacobean policy in the 1590s revolved around the tension between the council led by the administrator Maitland, the bedchamber led by his favourite Esme Stewart and a regime in the localities founded on the power of the conformist Catholic Huntley. This anticipates his English government: a council led by the administrator Cecil, but counterbalanced by the crypto-Catholic Northampton, and a bedchamber filled with Scots and led by his two favourites Carr and Buckingham.[20] England was not the cradle, but the consummation, of Jacobean policy.

V

The perplexing issues raised by the outbreak of the Thirty Years' War in 1618 were powerful enough to shatter the religious unity that James had so carefully fostered. Many protestants, including

Archbishop Abbot, interpreted the conflict as an apocalyptic struggle between the forces of good and those of Antichrist, and urged
that England intervene on behalf of its beleaguered protestant brethren abroad. James rejected this view. He denied both that Stuart
dynastic interests compelled him to support the claim of his son-
in-law Frederick V to the throne of Bohemia and that the resulting
conflict in central Europe was a confessional strife. His solution,
instead, was diplomatic negotiations and an intensified pursuit of
the match between Prince Charles and the Spanish Infanta in the
hopes of bringing the two sides together. However, the failure of
Jacobean mediation, protestant defeats abroad and the prospect of
the Spanish Match at home collectively seemed to many English
protestants to presage the triumph of Catholicism.

As a consequence James faced much hostile criticism from the
pulpit and press, which he attempted to quieten through proclamations, confinement of offenders and eventually in 1622 a set of
Directions to Preachers to avoid discussing matters of state.[21] Worse,
for James, was the fact that some of this opposition came from
senior figures in the Church. They included several royal chaplains,
as well as Dean Sutcliffe of Exeter, Archdeacon Hakewill of Surrey
and George Abbot, Archbishop of Canterbury. Abbot, for example,
had arranged for a tract against the marriage to be presented to
Prince Charles in 1621; he spoke up against toleration for Catholics
under the marriage treaty; and in 1623 there appeared a letter to
James, ostensibly from the archbishop, which condemned the
match. Although Abbot privately denied the authorship, he did not
publicly repudiate its contents, since he was in broad agreement
with its anti-Spanish sentiments.[22]

The public outcry against the match awoke James's latent fears
of puritanism. For much of the reign he had chiefly defined puritanism in terms of conformity, and had controlled it, or so he believed,
through the use of subscription. This no longer seemed an adequate
response as ministers denounced royal policy from the pulpit. Moreover, the crisis over foreign policy exposed a glaring contradiction
between the king's ecclesiastical and foreign policies. Both were
founded on his cherished image of *Rex Pacificus* and were now mutually exclusive. Though James had succeeded in reducing tension
over ceremonies and conformity, he had not contained the virulent
antipapal edge of English protestantism. Indeed, with uncompromising anti-Catholics such as Abbot inside his own Privy Council,

James's vaunted distinction between 'moderates' and 'radicals' seemed increasingly redundant. On his own terms the king had palpably failed to contain the threat of puritanism. As a result, James became a victim of his own rhetoric. Events seemed to be calling into question the assumptions and structures with which he had contained puritanism. In 1615 James had said there was no such thing as a puritan bishop, but by the early 1620s, with Abbot's example before him, he was not so sure. Protest against the match allowed the rhetorical initiative to pass to anti-Calvinist divines who were at their happiest and most influential in invoking a popular puritan conspiracy. Were they right, James mused, that his policy of incorporation had created a fifth-column of conforming but potentially subversive puritans within the church? If public opposition and popular preaching against royal policy did indeed constitute puritanism, then clearly such puritans infested his whole Church from top to bottom.

So the chief beneficiaries of this crisis in royal policy were anti-Calvinist churchmen, who supported James's hispanophile diplomacy and railed against puritan subversion.[23] By the early 1620s the anti-Calvinist court lobby was significantly strengthened, with Andrewes at Winchester, Montaigne at London and Laud at last elevated to the episcopate. Death also removed the Calvinist Bishops James Montagu and John King, while Abbot's opposition to the match had sharply reduced his influence. Equally, James was now susceptible to a redefinition of puritans which would accord more closely with his present predicament. This Richard Montagu attempted to supply in his two books, *A New Gagg for an Old Goose* and *Appello Caesarem* in 1624–5, aided and abetted by prominent anti-Calvinist bishops. In *A New Gagg* Montagu dramatically reduced the points of difference separating the English and Roman churches, and redefined puritanism as doctrinal Calvinism. If the English Church was to retain a credible claim to apostolic Catholicity, then James I should distance himself from doctrinal Calvinism and its concomitant hostility to Rome. This position had certain attractions for the king, currently being pushed into a confessional conflict he abhorred under pressure from his son, the Duke of Buckingham and a rabidly anti-papal House of Commons. Montagu's provocative message received a hostile reception among Calvinists, but not from the king, who merely asked him to clarify his position. Montagu responded with *Appello Caesarem*, a still more inflammatory assimilation of Calvinism with subversive puritanism, which the king ordered to be printed.[24] As this response demonstrates, the threats from puritanism and popery were not merely rhetorical tools but also real phobias for James I, which on occasion meant that the royal manipulator could be manipulated. The murder of Henri IV of France in 1610 had panicked James into aggressive moves against English Catholics and into choosing George Abbot as Archbishop of Canterbury; by the early 1620s it was the puritans who now menaced James, who awoke in terror one morning in 1623 on hearing gunfire.[25] No wonder he found Montagu's message so seductive.

James's death in March 1625 robs us of the chance to see how far he had been wholly converted to Montagu's line and how far this was just another manoeuvre to distance himself from the war policy advocated by Charles and Buckingham. Though Jacobean policy toward puritans had been undermined, it is not the case that the king had abandoned it. Moderate puritans enjoyed peace in the dioceses until after his death; and in June 1624, while commending the activities of Bishop Harsnett against disorderly popular lecturers, he publicly warned him against prosecuting lecturers 'that are conformittants'. Outward conformity, as ever, was James's concern. By this date, with the collapse of the Spanish Match, the Directions to Preachers of 1622 were also generally ignored.[26] As we shall see, the decisive shift occurred after James's death.

VI

Charles I was taciturn, where his father had been positively loquacious. James's whole style of kingship had turned on his capacity to catch his subjects and foreigners in a web of words. The same was never true for his son. His speeches to Parliament were short, and many royal declarations were written by the king's servants and merely amended by Charles, who confessed that he 'found it better to be a cobbler than a shoemaker'.[27] To gauge Charles's opinions, much must be inferred from what he did or from what was said in his name or at his behest. This difficulty, as we shall see, has led some historians to belittle, and others to exaggerate, his role in the formulation of ecclesiastical policy.

Over the long term, however, there is little doubt where Charles's religious sympathies lay. Anti-Calvinists who had prospered in the last years of his father's reign now received a more exclusive royal patronage. Thus Laud, who had never fully enjoyed James's trust, quickly won great favour with Charles. He was chosen by Charles to preach before Parliament in 1625 and 1626, and to preside at the coronation in the place of his disgraced rival, John Williams. On Lancelot Andrewes's death in September 1626, Laud became Dean of the Chapel Royal and was promised the reversion of Canterbury. The king's religious preferences were made quite clear with his appointment of Laud and Neile to the Privy Council in April 1627 and his preferment of Richard Montagu to first a chaplaincy and then a bishopric in the face of Parliamentary criticism.[28]

Within a month of James's death, Charles sought the advice of Andrewes on ecclesiastical issues, especially over the vexed matter of predestination. In April 1626 he commissioned Laud, Harsnett and Morton to undertake a wide-ranging review of ecclesiastical matters, and rebuked his episcopate for not standing up for the Church, whose interests he was anxious to promote, a clear sign of the new king's aggressive clericalism. A Proclamation of June 1626 attempted to settle doctrinal disputes over predestination, in which Charles belatedly acted on the advice of five anti-Calvinist bishops, and prohibited further discussion by preaching or writing.[29] From the outset of his reign, therefore, Charles showed every sign of wishing to resettle the affairs of his Church and enhance the status and independence of his clergy. In doing so, he relied primarily on the advice and support of the anti-Calvinist faction at his father's court.

Indeed, anti-Calvinist churchmen dominated the lists of episcopal appointments and promotions between 1625 and 1641. By 1633 four out of five key sees – Canterbury, York, London and Winchester – were controlled by anti-Calvinists. The exception was Durham, itself newly modelled by Neile and John Cosin, but governed after 1632 by Thomas Morton. Such exceptions were few in number: Joseph Hall to Exeter in 1627, Barnaby Potter to Carlisle in 1629 and Morton to Durham are the only obvious examples of Calvinist promotions between 1625 and 1641. Prominent Calvinists who were eligible for elevation – John Prideaux, Ralph Brownrig or Richard Holdsworth – had to wait until the changed circumstances of 1641. Equally telling is the fact that, contrary to his father's practice, Charles's chosen clerical intimates in the 1630s were *all* opponents

of Calvinism and proponents of the new ritualism: his Privy Coun-
cillors (Laud, Neile, Harsnett and Juxon), his deans of the Chapel
Royal (Laud, Juxon and Wren), his clerks of the closet (Neile,
Juxon, Wren and Steward) and his royal almoners (White and
Curle).[30]

Here, then, is an emphatic shift from the Jacobean balance of
ecclesiastical power. Calvinists were not completely excluded from
royal favour or preferment. Hall, Davenant and Prideaux all continued to preach at court and Robert Sanderson, a staunch conformist but no anti-Calvinist, emerged late in the 1630s as a prominent
court preacher.[31] But there could be no doubt which style of churchmanship was in the ascendant.

VII

How quickly did Charles's religious preferences manifest themselves? As a number of scholars have pointed out, the evidence for
the years 1625–9 is ambiguous. Thus the York House Conference,
sometimes misrepresented as the Caroline equivalent of the
Hampton Court Conference, turns out to be held at the insistence
of leading lay Calvinists and to have ended rather inconclusively.
For Calvinists looking for a ringing reaffirmation of orthodoxy as
they understood it, ambiguity here was as good as defeat. Yet as
Sheila Lambert has rightly observed, Richard Montagu himself was
far more unsure of support from Charles than he had been from
James.[32] So too was Laud, writing despondently of Montagu's prospects in 1626: 'methinks I see a cloud arising and threatening the
Church of England'. Later in the decade, Montagu was widely
reported to have renounced his attack on the five points of Dort,
and his controversial *Appello Caesarem* was suppressed by royal proclamation. In February 1629 Laud apparently preached against
popery and Arminianism, and the House of Commons were told
that both Laud and Neile had been on their knees before the
Privy Council denying that they were Arminians. Even after the
Proclamation of 1626, well-connected preachers such as Henry
Leslie continued to preach and print court sermons taking a broadly
Calvinist line on the points at issue. In the Parliament of 1628 Laud
and Neile took a backseat as Archbishop Abbot was recalled from
suspension to play a prominent part in condemning Manwaring

and to help in compiling the royal Declaration of November 1628 against contentious preaching on predestination.[33]

All this evidence needs to be placed in a specific political context. Charles was committed to a war against Spain in alliance with prominent anti-Spanish peers and some of the leading anti-popish elements in the House of Commons. Montagu had every right to be concerned. For however much Charles may have sympathised with his religious values, the logic of the king's position made overt patronage of anti-Calvinists very dangerous indeed. Desperate for Parliamentary supply and support of the most godly M.P.s, Charles's political agenda pointed to the abandonment of Montagu. In this light, what is surprising is Charles's determination to protect and promote Montagu rather than succumb to political expediency. So long as Charles was at war the policy of appeasing parliamentary opinion was always before him, pushed by moderate councillors who were unhappy with the 'new counsels' in Church and state. This surely accounts for the appointment of Hall to Exeter in 1627, or the court preaching of Leslie, both backed by powerful councillors such as the Herberts with intimate links with the godly in and outside Parliament.[34] Charles, of course, would not sacrifice Laud, Neile or Montagu but was prepared to contemplate limited concessions. Here is surely an early example of that Caroline syndrome identified by Conrad Russell: the king's willingness to adopt, for pragmatic reasons, a course of action designed by its originators to herald a genuine change of policy while neither understanding nor assenting to such a shift. Once all hope of parliamentary supply had gone the situation changed very quickly. One of the early victims was Bishop Davenant, who in March 1630 preached a court sermon on the theology of election, only to be censured by Harsnett in front of the Privy Council.[35] The opportunity for Calvinist expositions of the controverted points of predestination at court, opened by the exigencies of the political situation in the mid-twenties, was now closed.

This is not to suggest that the king's Declaration against contentious preaching was consciously used as a weapon to silence Calvinists and give anti-Calvinists free rein. Thus at Woodstock in 1631 Charles reiterated that the Declaration was to be observed by both sides.[36] Yet the practical application of the terms of the Declaration inevitably depended on the theological presuppositions of the interpreter, so that anti-Calvinist assumptions did colour the enforcement of the Declaration at court. Charles and Laud were happy to hear views which fitted their own understanding of what was fair and reasonable. This would explain a remarkable collection of sermons preached by Robert Skinner before the king throughout the 1630s. Skinner deployed the Caroline rhetoric of mystery and moderation, of awed silence and restraint before the sheer incomprehensible majesty of the divine will. Charles was praised for saving England from the continental fate of religious conflict by issuing and enforcing his Declaration. Yet in the same sermons, all given in the king's presence, Skinner was able to brand doctrines central to contemporary Calvinist orthodoxy – a conception of God's will and providence as absolute and unconditional, perseverance, a limited notion of the atonement – as antipathetic to all Christian truth and piety, and to replace them with Arminian doctrines on the same issues, stressing the conditionality of God's will, the doctrine of election from foreseen faith and reprobation for foreseen sin. Skinner clearly believed that he was obeying the royal Declaration, and his regular appearances at court and his elevation to the episcopate in 1637 imply that his efforts met with a certain royal approval. In contrast, Calvinist preachers such as Prideaux were reduced to sniping from the pulpit. In his court sermons Prideaux muttered darkly about the threats to orthodoxy from a list of heresies which included Pelagianism and Socinianism in close proximity. Yet he made no attempt to discuss the crucial doctrinal issues. In view of Prideaux's known views and printed works, where he equated both heresies with Arminianism, such seemingly innocuous statements were unmistakable to the practised ear.[37] Calvinist divinity at the Caroline court was clearly at a low ebb when a Regius Professor of Divinity at Oxford had to resort to such coded language.

VIII

In the years after 1629, freed from the need to appease parliamentary opinion, Charles was able to turn religious preferences into policy. Parliamentary criticism of royal favour towards anti-Calvinists prompted an instruction of April 1629, through the bishops, to punish preachers who suggested there was 'any innovation or alteration in religion' and to encourage those who taught political obedience and uncontroversial divinity. In May bishops without court or household offices were ordered back to their dioceses to take personal charge of their sees. Both orders were incorporated into the royal Instructions of December 1629. Resident bishops were to protect their temporalities, police the pulpits, enforce the royal Declaration against controversial preaching, encourage prayers and catechising and impose conformity on lecturers. A proclamation two months earlier also urged the repair of parish churches and chapels.[38]

Further changes followed within weeks of Laud's appointment to Canterbury in September 1633. In October the Jacobean Book of Sports was reissued to check sabbatarian excesses, and a month later the king threw his authority behind an altarwise table placed at the east end of the church in the St Gregory's case. Charles also sponsored various attempts to exalt the status and financial independence of the clergy. As Christopher Hill has demonstrated, royal initiatives to preserve episcopal estates and augment the revenue of both parish clergy and bishops were expressed in a number of instructions and legal cases throughout the decade. Charles himself took an intense personal interest in the endeavours of London clergy to increase their tithe revenue, regularly presiding at hearings. The king was always concerned to free the clergy from lay control and unlike his father was also prepared to appoint clergy as magistrates in city corporations, and to back various cathedral canons in their disputes with mayors and aldermen who processed inside their cathedral with the sword and mace of office held aloft, symbolising their claim of jurisdiction over the close. The same desire to vindicate property rights and the independence of the clergy informed the Scottish Act of Revocation of 1625, and the eventual resistance from the covenanters was described by Charles as a conspiracy of factious and grasping lay interests, alienated by the king's concern for his clergy.[39]

Taken individually few of these measures were without precedent. The Book of Sports had been compiled by James I, the altarwise position could claim some warrant from the practice of the Chapel Royal and certain cathedrals, while clerical dependence on the laity had alarmed Elizabethan conformists such as Bancroft and Hooker. Taken collectively and properly enforced, however, they represented an hostility to any form of ceremonial laxity, to Calvinist preaching, sabbatarianism and the word-centred piety of the godly which was a world away from conformity as construed and enforced by James I.

The Jacobean attempt to separate moderate and radical puritan opinion was dead and buried. Instead, these new ideals of order and uniformity closely mirrored Charles's own preferences and practice.

According to Sir Philip Warwick, servant to Charles I in the 1640s, 'Bishop Andrewes, Laud and Hooker were this Prince's three great authors', and the writings of all three anti-Calvinists were recommended by Charles to his daughter on the eve of his execution. The king was also an ardent ritualist, bowing towards the altar on entering church and having rails round both the altar and the font in the Chapel Royal. His annotations on a draft of the Scottish Prayer Book underline his desire for correct liturgical practice: the times when priest and people should stand were carefully spelt out, and Charles inserted a prayer for saints as exemplars, insisting that the prefix S or SS be used. Ministers should also be referred to as priests, for they were a sacramental as much as a preaching order.[40] The architectural setting for the beauty of holiness was another royal concern. Cathedrals, as mother churches of each diocese, should exemplify the dignity and holiness of God's temples. At Durham in 1633 Charles ordered that 'certain mean tenements' near the cathedral be demolished; while the interior of the cathedral should not be cluttered either with moveable seats (as at Durham, York and elsewhere) or a chapter-house, which offended Charles on a visit to Winchester in 1636.[41]

The implication of this reforming zeal was a marked discontent and indeed discontinuity with the immediate past of the English Church, and at times Charles himself talked explicitly about his own sense of his reign as a new beginning. On his view, 'the uniformity, devotion and holy order' of divine service had been neglected since the last years of the sixteenth century, a neglect which he attributed to puritan scruples and episcopal laxity. His own model of an ordered Church looked back not to the canons of 1604 but to the early years of Elizabeth I, who had 'perfected' the English Reformation. In 1629 he even toyed with reviving the Elizabethan Injunctions of 1559.[42]

Here was a careful stance between reform and tradition, enabling Charles to reconcile his defence of Christian laws and doctrine that approximated most closely to the primitive Church with his desire to clean out the augean stables of a Church long defiled by neglect and faction. It was exploited by apologists for the regime, anxious to refute puritan charges of illegality and innovation. Charles was compared, in his own hearing, to Old Testament kings such as Zerubbabel who had rebuilt the Temple and David who had restored piety.[43] Perhaps the most forceful use of the king's own example came from Peter Heylyn in his defence of Caroline altar policy. Heylyn presented an image of a pious monarch, whose devotions and actions embody a vision of the beauty of holiness:

> When did you ever find a king that did so affect Church work or that hath more endeavoured to advance that decency and comeliness in the performance of divine offices which God expecteth and requires than his sacred majesty? . . . His majesty's religious carriage in the house of God and due observance of those orders which the law requires in common people is a more excellent sermon upon that text than ever you yet preached on any.

Heylyn went on to praise Charles's restoration of St Paul's as an example for other patrons to follow, and his practice while on progress to attend parish churches and there 'set a copy to his people how to perform all true humility and religious observations in the house of God'. The book was commissioned by Charles and it is inconceivable that these remarks did not carry the king's approval.[44] Charles, we may infer, wanted the ecclesiastical policy of the Personal Rule grounded on his own will and example.

Caroline methods of making and promulgating policy show the same tendency. Most policy initiatives took the form of proclamations, instructions and orders in council. Charles's preferred method was a royal hearing, in which both sides submitted to his arbitration, and after the rival counsels had been heard, the supreme governor would pronounce his binding judgement. Such hearings included not just the St Gregory's case of 1633 but also various disputes at Oxford University settled by the king at Woodstock in 1631, Laud's claim to visit both universities in 1636, and the intended resolution, in the clergy's favour, of the long-running tithe dispute in London. Unlike Jacobean hearings, where all sides emerged with some consolation, Caroline disputes were to be resolved not fudged, and in each case there were clear winners and losers.

These hearings exemplify Charles's dynamic conception of his supremacy, as the fount and interpreter of ecclesiastical law. In

Charles's view, the supreme governor in consultation with his clergy had effected the Reformation and could legally initiate further change. Parliament, he believed, had merely ratified the breach with Rome. Thus Charles could introduce into Scotland an Ordinal, Book of Canons and Prayer Book after consultation with a select band of Scottish bishops, bypassing the General Assembly, rather than packing it, as his father had done. His status as God's lieutenant on earth Charles took quite literally. The importance he attached to touching for the king's evil as proof of his semi-divine status is telling evidence of this. While James had rather cynically agreed to observe the rite, Charles invested much importance in it, and probably touched regularly throughout the 1630s. In 1638 he had the ceremony depicted on the cover of a Prayer Book presented for use at Garter ceremonies, accompanying an incensing angel and representations of preaching and the baptismal rite.[45]

It is no surprise, then, that Charles believed his ecclesiastical powers to be very extensive. It is also true that he was relatively untroubled by the restraints of common and statute law which could pose difficulties in secular politics, most famously in his attempt to punish Eliot and other parliamentary leaders in 1629–30. Where statute law did limit him, Charles showed characteristic impatience, even pique. At a hearing during the London tithe dispute, Charles chided the city aldermen when they cited an Henrician statute which bolstered their case. They were, he claimed, siding with the letter of the law against the spirit, the spirit, of course, as discerned by Charles. Heylyn's claim over the altar that 'the king's chapel . . . or the king's practice in his chapel maybe and is the best interpreter' of the 'rubrics, laws and canons of the Church' has, on this evidence, a ring of Caroline authenticity about it. Thus in 1640 Charles could ignore precedent and (with judicial approval) allow Convocation to sit long after the dissolution of the Short Parliament.[46]

IX

What then of Archbishop Laud, once credited with masterminding religious policy in the 1630s? Is Dr Sharpe right to see him simply as the king's good servant?[47] In a personal monarchy, where much business was conducted by word of mouth, it is notoriously difficult to attribute final responsibility for policy to either king or minister.

The situation is doubly difficult in the case of Charles and Laud. On the one hand, Laud was justifiably paranoid about the activities of his enemies in Parliament, court and Church, following intense persecution from Calvinists earlier in his career. Throughout the 1630s he systematically tried to cover his tracks, and secured direct royal authority for all major decisions. Thus in 1633 the Book of Sports was reissued on Charles's written mandate; three years later so too were alterations to what became the Scottish Prayer Book: 'I gave the Archbishop of Canterbury command to make the alterations expressed in this book, and to fit a liturgy for the Church of Scotland', Charles wrote in the annotated Prayer Book.[48] Laud's remorseless search for plausible deniability was triumphantly achieved at his trial, though it could not save him. For his part, Charles I had virtually no use for the conventional monarchical wisdom that allowed the sovereign to lay the blame for unpopular policies on his councillors. Charles evidently believed that the most easy and honourable way for him to secure the compliance of his subjects was to leave them in no doubt that official policies and demands were his own. This was a political technique he had perfected with Buckingham in the 1620s and he persisted with it with Laud (and others) in the 1630s. As a result it is almost impossible to tell precisely who was doing what in the formulation of ecclesiastical policy. Even well-informed observers seem to have been confused. Laud himself drily observed to Wentworth that Charles liked to appear to be the originator of policy, and yet on other occasions complained that he could only serve the king as well as the king would allow him. Panzani, the resident papal agent, thought that Charles was irresolute and was manipulated by Laud.[49]

In fact, the relationship is best understood as a partnership, held together by a common view of the world, of order and threats to order, but mediated through their rather different personalities and relationship to power. Like any partnership, each needed the other. Most obviously Laud needed Charles to overcome opposition in the court, Parliament and country. In January 1637 Laud requested the assistance of a higher court than High Commission against Bastwick, Burton and Prynne, and five months later the three were tried and convicted in Star Chamber. But Charles needed Laud to translate royal impulses and preferences into policy. Indeed, he needed and used Laud (amongst others) to turn royal thoughts into words. Moreover, Charles lacked a detailed understanding of ecclesiastical administration and relied on Laud to turn commands into action. This is apparent from Charles's annotations on the annual reports from his bishops submitted by Laud for his inspection. On the disrepair of Rochester Cathedral, Charles commented that 'this must be remedied one way or another'. When Laud complained of a new lectureship at Huntingdon in which the lay patrons claimed the right to hire and fire the lecturer, Charles reacted firmly. 'I will have no priest have any necessity of a lay dependency. Wherefore I command you to show me the way to overthrow this.' Laud wrote to the local bishop, citing the king's displeasure, and ordered that either the lay patrons confine themselves to nominating a lecturer or else abandon the lectureship.[50]

This exchange represents a perfect example of the symbiotic relationship between archbishop and monarch. Ostensibly, the yearly reports from each bishop, summarised for royal inspection by Laud himself, gave Charles the chance to intervene directly in the affairs of his Church. In fact, they also allowed Laud to bring various issues to the king's attention and, initially at least, to control the terms in which they were viewed. When in 1638 Richard Montagu, newly ensconced as Bishop of Norwich, informed Laud that he was reluctant to force the laity to receive communion at the rails, Laud referred the matter to the king. But as he did so he also provided Charles with a lengthy defence of the practice and duly received the royal authority for its continuation in Norwich.[51]

At other times Laud had to work harder for his view to prevail. During the St Gregory's case in 1633, Charles seemed momentarily prepared to allow the minister and churchwardens to remove the communion table from the east end into the chancel at communion times. Laud, however, intervened with the observation that the parishioners were puritan nonconformists who would always follow their own devices and desires. This point evidently struck home, since in the final judgement no mention was made of moving the table from its altarwise position. Again at Hampton Court in June 1636 Charles upheld Laud's power to visit the universities as inherent in his metropolitical authority. Counsel for Cambridge University opposed the claim, most effectively on the grounds that it would give Laud a concurrent jurisdiction independent of the crown. At this Charles told the Archbishop that if this was the case he 'must then write Wolsey's style, *Ego et Rex meus*'. Laud had to fall on his knees, plead that he was the king's humble subject and only desired 'to curb sedition', an affirmation which in the lexicon of Caroline debate was unanswerable.[52]

These occasions represent something more than the successful manipulation of a credulous king by a wily servant. In these exchanges we are surely watching a practised double act, in which Laud was able to win the day because he had learnt, over a long period, the rhetorical formulas, the buzz-words and bugbears, against which Charles was certain to react. All depended on those shared aims and assumptions which united king and archbishop. In the end both got what they wanted: Laud could parade himself as the king's loyal servant, and receive royal directions to back up his own orders, while Charles was able to exert, vindicate and display his own authority over the Church; additionally, the interests of order and the beauty of holiness, as both men defined them, were being served.

X

What has been sketched above can also be seen as part and parcel of a wider Caroline style in Church and state. For from the mid 1620s Charles became increasingly obsessed with threats to order in Church and state. Faced with political crisis and the collapse of a war effort that had begun so promisingly in 1624 with parliamentary approval, Charles had recourse to the very conspiracy theory of popular puritanism which his father had endorsed in the last years of his reign. Charles and several anti-Calvinists equated the popular challenge through the House of Commons with the puritan threat in the Church. To remove such subversive elements, Charles embarked on a reform of the commonwealth, first through reform of court and Church and then through use of the court, Chapel Royal and cathedrals as images of good government, virtue and decorum for the emulation of the wider nation. Caroline reform of the court was based on the restoration of ritual and ceremonial decorum, on distance and reverence before the regal presence. The royal marriage was deployed as an image or epitome of good government, and the masques celebrated the dispersal of the unruly humours and disordered impulses of the anti-masque by the mere appearance and gaze of the king. As Ben Jonson lamented, in the masques of the 1630s the elements of visual imagery and display came to predominate over the dramatic text.[53] Where James had sought to win over his subjects and ensnare his enemies through his command of language, Charles turned to visual symbolism and outward ceremony as an intrinsically more effective and less disturbing means of communication between ruler and ruled.[54]

The links between these secular practices and Caroline styles of piety and churchmanship are obvious. In both Church and state Charles sought to impose order and decorum on his subjects, to suppress dispute and inculcate unity and obedience through the repetition of the ceremonies of order, hierarchy and worship. The parallel between the awe and reverence due to God and the king was repeatedly exploited by Caroline apologists in comparisons of Church, chancel and altar with court, presence chamber and chair of state; comparisons used to legitimate Caroline values in the Church and to expound the beneficient effects of those values in secular politics.[55]

Charles's dispatch of the gentry home to the country to keep order and hospitality in their locality was paralleled by his dismissal of the bishops from court to their sees. Episcopacy and magistracy were to co-operate to unify the social order and to expel the dissident, puritan elements in Church and state, and both were to account for their actions in regular reports to the centre. The two pillars of Caroline order, the aristocracy and the episcopate, met practically and ceremonially at court and the Privy Council; and the interdependence of Church and state was perfectly summarised, as Peter Heylyn observed, at the Garter ceremonies, that order of Christian knights named after St George, both soldier and martyr for Christ, and presided over by Charles, both king and priest.[56]

XI

The Caroline style in Church and state, though derived from Jacobean precedents, emerged in the 1630s as quite distinct. Not merely were Jacobean elements rearranged, but they were also sometimes reformulated. While both monarchs acknowledged the divine status of bishops, to Charles bishops alone could confer orders, which effectively unchurched most continental protestant communities. While both recognised the threat from popery and puritanism, Charles did not construct a policy on the equivalence of this threat, being chiefly exercised by the dangers of puritanism. Thus the Jacobean Oath of Allegiance, framed against Catholics, was in Charles's view an excellent check on puritans.[57] Each monarch was also interested in establishing religious unity in his three kingdoms. James VI and I sought 'congruence' through Calvinist episcopalianism in multiple kingdoms; Charles, in contrast, attempted a uniformity of practice, taking a Caroline Anglicanism as his model simply because he held that it came 'nearest to the purity of the primitive doctrine and discipline'.[58] The difficulties he subsequently faced were the result less of a 'British Problem' than hostility to anti-Calvinism in three kingdoms. The choice with which we started, the choice between continuity and change is, as ever, no choice at all.

2. Archbishop Laud

NICHOLAS TYACKE

I

William Laud deserves to rank among the greatest archbishops of Canterbury since the Reformation. Indeed one is hard pressed to think of others in the same league, save the obvious Thomas Cranmer. But to say this does not necessarily imply approval. Rather it acknowledges the fact that both men made a major contribution to the future of the English Church. Although Cranmer was burnt to death as a heretic and Laud was executed for treason, their respective legacies lived on. In the case of Laud the time lag was greater, yet just as the Elizabethan Church owed much to Cranmer so did the Restoration Church to Laud. Thus commentators in the 1660s were clear that it was the religious supporters of Laud and not his opponents who had won through. Whereas in the early seventeenth century 'the current of the Church of England ran the Calvinist way' now 'Arminianism' is 'received amongst our clergy', as are similar innovations: 'the communion table set altarwise', when 'it ought to be in the body of the church', and 'bowing' practised towards it.[1] This hostile evaluation, made by Sir Thomas Littleton during a parliamentary debate in March 1668, serves to indicate, albeit in shorthand form, some of the longer-term consequences of the 'Laudian' movement for both doctrine and worship. Our concern in this essay, however, is with the beginnings of that story and more specifically the contribution made by Laud himself.

While Archbishop Laud has never lacked for biographers, the modern historiography begins in 1940. Since then the pendulum has swung from the frankly materialistic interpretation of Hugh Trevor-Roper to the psychological portrait painted recently by Charles Carlton. Writing against the background of the 1930s,

Trevor-Roper defined religion as 'the ideal expression of a particular social and political organisation' and saw Laud as the religious representative of those elements in society opposed to the forces of nascent capitalism. For Carlton, by contrast, the key to Laud lies in his 'insecurity', arising from his allegedly 'humble origins' and supposed homosexuality. Meanwhile, to others, Laud remains the epitome of 'Anglicanism'. All three of these interpretations, not least the last mentioned, depart fairly radically from seventeenth-century assessments. Moreover, they ring their changes on the same basic body of evidence.[2]

On the face of it, the sources for the study of Laud are both abundant and accessible; the nineteenth-century edition of his collected works runs to seven volumes and there are literally thousands of references to him in the published calendars of *State Papers Domestic*. Closer inspection, however, reveals a less satisfactory situation. Only a fairly small proportion of this material is concerned with religious as opposed to administrative matters. Furthermore, there is virtually nothing at all before the second decade of the seventeenth century. Laud was born in 1573, and this means that his formative years are very difficult to reconstruct. Hence the heavy reliance by historians on the near-contemporary life of Laud, written by Peter Heylyn and first published in 1668. (Heylyn was twenty-seven years younger than Laud, but had worked quite closely with him during the 1630s.) It is Heylyn, for example, who supplies the details of Laud's early clashes with his fellow Oxford theologians at the turn of the century. Clearly there is a possibility that our view of Laud has been unduly coloured by Heylyn, who may have read his own later preoccupations into the record.

This type of criticism also applies to the historical background, as sketched by Heylyn in his biography and elsewhere. Laud is depicted as struggling almost single-handedly against a dominant Calvinism in Oxford and in the English Church more generally *circa* 1600: 'two or three' in the face of an 'army'. Heylyn is quite clear that Laud was effectively a revolutionary, overturning what had become the religious *status quo*. But, according to Heylyn, Laud had right on his side. In this scenario Laud, unlike most of his contemporaries, was true to the Elizabethan settlement of religion. For, so the argument runs, only during the later sixteenth century was the English Church swamped by a rising tide of Calvinism. Heylyn stresses that he is not simply talking about the Elizabethan puritan challenge to the Prayer Book and the bishops, but something much more pervasive. By 'Calvinism' he means the type of teaching, on subjects like predestination, contained within the pages of John Calvin's famous book – *The Institution of Christian Religion*.[3]

Arguably, however, far from later historians paying too much attention to Heylyn, and thus misconstruing Laud's role, they have on the contrary failed to take sufficiently seriously what he says. Certainly the current picture of Laud tends to be one of an ecclesiastical administrator rather than a theologian, highly efficient but no innovator. Yet it, in turn, has created a problem of interpretation, because if Laud was such an ordinary ecclesiastic why did his archiepiscopate prove so controversial? Various strategies have been evolved to meet this difficulty. Firstly there has been an attempt to shift attention away from Archbishop Laud to King Charles I. Laud, it is said, was simply obeying orders, and the initiative for change was that of the king. But if the direct evidence for Laud's religious views is less than abundant that for Charles is almost non-existent, and to substitute the one for the other solves nothing. Alternatively there is the argument that little central direction existed and thus Laud cannot be held responsible for the innovatory religious policies of individual bishops. Nevertheless this anarchic view of the 1630s remains unconvincing, particularly given the activities of Laud's own officials.[4]

Again it has been claimed that Laud was the victim of a puritan backlash, due to his attempt to take up the task of ecclesiastical reconstruction left uncompleted by Archbishop Bancroft in 1610. Here the blame is attached to Laud's immediate predecessor at Canterbury – Archbishop George Abbot, who at worst was himself a puritan and at best was a lax administrator. For over twenty years (1611–33), this version has it, Abbot let things slide; conformity was only intermittently enforced and nothing done to improve the financial lot of the parish clergy. This, however, is a very partial reading both of Heylyn and of the historical record, abolishing as it does any real difference between Laud and most of his predecessors at Canterbury, and making Abbot not Laud the true exception. Undoubtedly the churchmanship of Archbishop Abbot had its idiosyncratic features, notably his virulent anti-Catholicism, although there is little sign that the death of Archbishop Bancroft led to a resurgence of puritanism. Nor were efforts abandoned under Abbot to solve the economic problems of the English Church.[5]

Moreover the logical implication of Heylyn's view of Laud, as an isolated opponent of Calvinism, is that not only Archbishop Abbot but also Archbishop Bancroft and Archbishop Whitgift, not to mention Archbishop Grindal and perhaps Archbishop Parker too, were all Calvinists. The evidence suggests that this was indeed the case, and that the mature theology of Laud differed from that of his predecessors at Canterbury from at least Grindal onwards. Investigation of official university teachings and the licensed publications of the printing press also substantiates the claim about Calvinist dominance.[6]

Confidence in Heylyn's grasp of the overall pattern of English religious developments in the later sixteenth century does not, of course, obviate the need for further research into the career of Laud, especially the early phase. Heylyn's Laud, apart from the supposed influence of his tutor John Buckeridge, at St John's College, Oxford, comes essentially out of an intellectual vacuum. Laud himself, however, does provide one further clue, noting in his diary the fact of his ordination as deacon and priest, in 1601, by Bishop John Young of Rochester. On its own this would be without significance, since the bishopric of Oxford was vacant at the time. Nevertheless another tradition, recorded by David Lloyd in his *Memoires* of 1668, has Bishop Young prophesying of Laud that, 'if he lived, he would be an instrument of restoring the Church from the narrow and private principles of modern times, to the more free, large and public sentiments of the purest and first ages', because 'finding his study raised above the systems and opinions of the [present] age' and 'upon the nobler foundations of the fathers, councils and ecclesiastical historians'.[7]

We might still dismiss this simply as embroidery after the event, were it not that Bishop Young was also a long-standing critic of the Calvinist theology of grace. Preaching before Queen Elizabeth, in 1576, Young had spoken of the 'profane curiosity' of those who moved 'unnecessary questions' about 'election' and 'reprobation'. Furthermore there are some traces of a Rochester connection of like-minded St John's College men. Laud's Oxford tutor Buckeridge was a prebendary of Rochester, during the 1590s, while another former St John's College fellow, Henry Bearblock, was vicar of Strood next door to Rochester. Bearblock and Buckeridge can be found acting together in 1602 against the puritan William Bradshaw, who at the time was lecturer at Chatham. Bradshaw responded by criticising in turn the religious teaching of Bearblock. Thus he characterised his sermons as being 'full of charity towards adulterers, drunkards, blasphemers and other sinners that swarm in the Church', and 'none that hear you but they are God's faithfull children . . . though they be foul, grievous sinners, yet they are repentant and God's mercy belongs unto them; that no man is without sin, but the best and holiest is unclean'. At issue here seemingly were divergent views of the original sin of Adam and its consequences for mankind generally. Could all Christians aspire to Heaven, as Bearblock implied, or was this the prerogative only of a predestined minority of elect saints who were not like ordinary mortals? As a puritan Bradshaw was particularly concerned to distinguish the godly from the rest, although he apparently recognised an anti-Calvinist tendency in Bearblock's preaching that many in ecclesiastical authority would also have found offensive.[8]

In a published work of four years later (1606), Bradshaw went on to accuse some conformist members of the Church of England of a recent falling away from what 'heretofore hath been constantly and generally held by our Church'. Instead they now teach 'things which have been accounted and are in truth popish or Lutheran errors, viz. touching general grace and the death of Christ for every particular person, against particular election and reprobation, for images in churches . . . , that the pope is not Antichrist . . . , also the necessity of baptism [and] auricular confession'. (Interestingly the official reply to Bradshaw denied all these charges.) The most likely target of his remarks was certain Cambridge theologians who, during the 1590s, mounted an abortive counter-attack against the dominant Calvinists.[9] Bradshaw had been a fellow of Sidney Sussex College at the time. But he may in addition have been alluding to his more recent encounter with the Oxonians from St John's College. Much later Laud was to recall how shocked he had been by a book published in 1605, which claimed that the pope was as certainly Antichrist as Jesus Christ was the son of God. Laud had also caused a furore in 1604 at Oxford when, for one of his bachelor's theses in divinity, he maintained the necessity of baptism, and he certainly came to hold most of the other views itemised by Bradshaw.[10]

The likelihood is that the religion of Laud reflects, in part, the ethos of his particular Oxford college. St John's was a Roman Catholic foundation, dating from the reign of Queen Mary. The

Catholic founder, a merchant called Thomas White, continued to oversee the college until his death in 1567. As late as 1573 five fellows, including the future Jesuit Edmund Campion, defected to Rome. 'Owing to this exodus', it has been said, the university authorities 'were suspicious of the religion of all the members of the college'. Similarly, for us historians, the nature of the protestantism of those others who continued in the Church of England remains in some doubt. But unlike the Marian parish priests who conformed under Elizabeth, their combinations of old and new largely dying with them, a college environment could provide some continuity of religious beliefs. This is not, however, to imply that Laud's tutor Buckeridge was a crypto-Catholic. For Buckeridge entered St John's in 1578, five years after the Catholic exodus and one year after the arrival of Bearblock.[11]

Yet we may surmise that the protestantism of many of the fellowship owed comparatively little to the thought of continental reformers. Although the Thirty-nine Articles – the English confession of faith – clearly denied a number of central Roman Catholic teachings, such as purgatory and transubstantiation, the Elizabethan Prayer Book still lent itself to a variety of possible interpretations on many other doctrinal issues. Moreover during the second half of the sixteenth century the continental followers of Luther and Calvin were becoming increasingly estranged from one another. In these circumstances the existence of a measure of English resistance to Calvinism is unsurprising. At the same time these years saw a reviving interest in the early Christian writers or Church fathers, as they are known. The Greek fathers especially provided a powerful court of appeal from certain aspects of modern protestantism. Hence the significance of the following passage from the earliest extant publication of John Buckeridge. Preaching against Scottish presbyterianism in 1606, he said that 'in a reformation [of the Church] we should conform ourselves . . . to the rule of the ancient scriptures, apostles and fathers: Chrysostom, Nazianzen, Basil, Ambrose, Jerome, Augustine, Gregory and the like, rather than after the new cut of those who have not above the life of a man on their backs, sixty or seventy years'. This perhaps sounds innocuous enough until we recall the grave reservations entertained by some Elizabethan bishops about the orthodoxy of the Greek fathers, notably Chrysostom, on the subject of predestination.[12]

II

William Laud went up to Oxford in 1589, and was the only child of a substantial Reading clothier. When his father died in 1594 he left money and stock worth £1,200, as well as three properties. The widow, who died in 1600, had a life interest in half of the estate. Her brother Sir William Webb was a lord mayor of London, who bequeathed his nephew William Laud £100 in 1599. All of which is difficult to reconcile with the notion of 'humble origins'. On the contrary, Laud was unusual among his fellow clergy both as regards his means and his connections.[13] Nor is it at all clear that his sexuality was significant for his career. But why did he go to university, rather than into business? The fact that his half-brother William Robinson also became a clergyman suggests that parental wishes were important here. As we have noted, there is a tendency among historians to see Laud as primarily an administrator – a bureaucrat whose holy orders were necessary to his career. Yet if this was his ambition he set about it in a very odd way. Within only a few years of ordination Laud had become embroiled in religious controversy at Oxford. Far from attracting the favourable attention of superiors, it could be argued that this endangered his early prospects. Because Laud chose not to publish his views in print this has obscured the truth that he first appeared on the public stage as a controversial *theologian*.

Laud seems very early to have developed an extremely exalted view of episcopacy, both as divinely instituted and an essential mark of the true Church. The effect of this was to redress the denominational balance in favour of Roman Catholicism, at the expense of the protestant non-episcopal Churches. It was also apparently the original occasion of Laud's clash with George Abbot, the future archbishop, who like many other English protestants derived the historical succession of the true Church partly via various medieval heretical groups. According to Laud, the English Church stemmed from that of Rome – the transition only occurring at the Reformation. These rival theories had particular practical application when it came to foreign policy, clergy of Abbot's stamp believing in a pan-protestant cause and looking askance at any alliance with a Catholic power. Furthermore the true radicalism of Laud's views on episcopacy has eluded historians. For the claim that bishops were *iure divino* was something of a Jacobean commonplace. But Laud went much further, arguing that 'only a bishop can confer orders'. This was one of his Oxford doctoral theses in 1608 and the effect was to unchurch most European and also Scottish protestants, denying as it did the legitimacy of their clergy.[14]

We should not, however, assume that the ideas of the mature Laud were all fully fledged by the time of his ordination. Nor is Buckeridge likely to have been the sole intellectual influence on him. During the 1630s, Laud was to comment on the damage done to students by too early exposure to Calvin's *Institution*, and his remarks may be partly autobiographical – for there is evidence that he himself went through a Calvinist phase. Central for understanding the intellectual development of Laud are his surviving manuscript annotations to a three-volume set of Cardinal Bellarmine's *Disputationes*, published between 1596 and 1599. These annotations have never been properly studied and present considerable problems of interpretation. They include entries made as late as 1618. On the other hand some are probably much earlier. Of greatest interest here is Laud's comment on a section where Bellarmine maintains, against Calvin, that faith once had can be lost. Laud notes, in support of Calvin, that 'the regenerate' cannot fall into final impenitency. The implication of this remark is that Laud originally accepted the Calvinist doctrine of double and absolute predestination, because the unregenerate are by definition incapable of salvation. It also helps to explain how he was able to become chaplain in 1603 to the Calvinist, not to say puritan, Earl of Devon.[15]

Devon died three years later in disgrace for having married the divorced Lady Penelope Rich, her first husband still living, which was in breach of canon law. Laud had performed the marriage ceremony and was thus implicated in the scandal. Again, his annotations on Bellarmine indicate the religious reasons with which he justified his action. The ensuing débâcle, however, looks to have precipitated an intellectual crisis, leading Laud fundamentally to rethink his theological position. Two years later, in 1608, he became chaplain to Bishop Richard Neile, and this relationship was to prove very important for his subsequent career. Neile had considerable influence at court, as clerk of the closet; moreover he too looks to have broken with an earlier Calvinism. By 1615 Laud definitely had come to be identified as an anti-Calvinist. Clearly Neile and Laud were both ambitious men, although it was not only the fruits of office which they wanted. Laud especially sought power with a

particular end in mind, namely to translate into practice his ideal
of the kind of organisation the Church of England should be. This
vision included a wealthier Church and one more independent of
the laity, to be achieved by an even closer alliance with the monarchy than already existed. The example held forth is that of King
David in the Old Testament. Meanwhile, according to Laud, priests
continue to live in a 'mean' condition and the Church lies 'basely',
both the victims of 'sacrilege'.[16]

Laud elaborated on this conception in a number of surviving
sermons from the 1620s. A recurrent theme is that of the 'unity' of
Jerusalem, the ancient temple and city standing for the English
Church and state. 'Commonwealth and Church', he preached in
1621, 'are collective bodies made up of many into one, and both so
near allied that the one, the Church, can never subsist but in the
other, the Commonwealth, nay so near that the same men, which
in a temporal respect make the Commonwealth do in a spiritual
make the Church'. Laud goes on quite explicitly to blur the distinction, made famous by St Augustine, between 'grace' and 'nature',
the city of God and that of the world. There was little or no room
in this scheme for a godly elite distinct from earthly hierarchies.
The Church was, or ought to be, the nation at prayer and according
to set forms, worship being built around the sacrament of holy
communion rather than preaching.[17]

One of these sermons also sheds very important light on the
position of Laud vis à vis what, in the aftermath of the Synod of
Dort in 1619, we can call Arminianism. (At Dort the Dutch Arminians, who rejected Calvinist teaching on predestination, were condemned by an international gathering which included English representatives.) Preaching before King James in March 1622, Laud
ventured some remarks on the question of individual 'assurance' or
certainty of salvation. He chose his words carefully, in expounding
the second part of his text: 'Because the king [David] trusteth in
the Lord, and in the mercy of the most High, he shall not miscarry'
(Psalms 21, 7). According to Laud, these words are not to be
understood in an 'absolute' sense. There is a 'double condition',
involving on David's part a 'religious heart to God that cannot but
trust in Him', and on God's part a 'merciful providence' which
'knows not how to forsake till it be forsaken, if it do then'. The
safest course is to rely on God's mercy, 'for that holds firm when
men break'. Yet mercy 'will not profit any man that doth not believe

and trust in it'. At a time when Calvinism still passed for orthodoxy and King James had as yet given no public signal to the contrary, Laud was obliged to tread warily. Nevertheless he does raise the possibility of God's *forsaking* David, and therefore of the non-perseverance even of the elect, while covering himself with the additional statement that faith and hope are 'due only' to God's mercy.[18]

That, however, is far from exhausting the relevance of this sermon of 1622 by Laud. For in the same section which discusses Christian assurance he cites approvingly a passage on free will from the *Collationes* of John Cassian. By the seventeenth century Cassian was notorious as the founder of what is called Semi-Pelagianism – a theological half-way house between Augustine and Pelagius on the subject of predestination and free will, elaborated during the first decades of the fifth century. Cassian had been ordained by Chrysostom and drew intellectually on the Greek fathers, in combating the thoroughgoing predestinarian teaching of Augustine against the Pelagians. Never formally condemned, Cassian remained a vital source for anyone who wished to break away from the Augustinianism of the protestant Reformation. Semi-Pelagianism is in fact an early Christian equivalent of Arminianism.[19]

We do not know when Laud first read Cassian or the extent to which he agreed with him, although the library of St John's College, Oxford, acquired a copy of the *Collationes* in 1608.[20] Yet for Laud to cite Cassian, in such a doctrinal context, when preaching before the king appears a remarkable piece of boldness, and suggests that he was confident of support. Certainly the sermon was subsequently printed by royal command, and that August James I issued Directions prohibiting all 'popular' preaching about the pros and cons of predestination. It has been convincingly argued that in these last years of his reign James, partly for political reasons, was moving away from his previous support of the Calvinists.[21] As for Laud, his sermon of 1622 constitutes a declaration of Arminian sympathies.

Laud had become a bishop in 1621, but only of St David's. Not until 1633, aged sixty, was he in a position as archbishop fully to apply his ideas at national level. It would be something of an exaggeration to describe the first two decades of the seventeenth century as the wilderness years of Laud. He did become head of his Oxford college, in 1611, and Dean of Gloucester, in 1616. These were, however, years of relative obscurity, which also partly explains the lack of surviving evidence. One of the earliest episodes which can be documented independently of Heylyn is Laud's intervention at Gloucester Cathedral, as newly appointed dean. On arrival there he found the communion table positioned in the middle of the choir, and in early 1617 ordered that it be placed altarwise at the east end. There were a variety of cathedral practices at the time, although this initiative by Laud implies a very uncalvinist view of the eucharist or holy communion, as a source of grace to all receivers. Indeed he was later to describe the altar as 'the greatest place of God's residence upon earth'. The year 1617 also saw the altarwise repositioning of the communion table at Durham Cathedral, where his patron Neile was bishop. Again at about the same time Laud's old tutor and mentor John Buckeridge, now a bishop, apparently commissioned a remarkable new chalice for his private chapel. This chalice survives, having been bequeathed by Buckeridge to St John's College, Oxford, and has been dated on the basis of the maker's mark. Modelled on the design of pre-Reformation chalices, it also depicts Christ as the 'good shepherd' – the sheep on his shoulders representing a sinner gone astray. Under Queen Elizabeth most chalices had been melted down and turned into communion cups. Buckeridge's chalice is the earliest extant example of a subsequent renaissance, the actual image of the good shepherd deriving from early Christian sources.[22]

Very much more was involved here than simply aesthetic considerations. This is clear both from a discourse on kneeling at communion, published by Buckeridge in 1618, and from his surviving will of 1631. Buckeridge describes himself in this latter document as the 'most unworthy Bishop of Ely', beseeching God to 'wash me thoroughly in the blood of thy son . . . and though my sins be as crimson yet let it please thee to make them as white as snow'. This is a highly unusual will for the period, and it certainly does not mean that Buckeridge had led an especially immoral life. There are echoes here of the teaching of Henry Bearblock in the 1590s – 'no man is without sin, but the best and holiest is unclean', and also of Buckeridge's own discourse, where he describes prospective communicants as 'vile and base . . . mortal and sinful' and invokes the image of the prodigal son. Traces too of this attitude can be found in the will made by Laud in 1644, where he calls himself 'a most prodigal son' and speaks of his 'many great and grievous transgressions'.[23] Calvinist wills of the period tend to be very different, the testators confidently affirming their belief that they are elect saints and often with no reference at all to personal sinfulness. By contrast in the anti-Calvinist economy of salvation, now being evolved by Buckeridge, Laud and their like, the sacrament of holy communion played a crucial role. Salvation came via the grace which it conferred, penitent sinners being washed by the blood of Christ.

The same association of ideas can be found present in Laud's volume of private devotions. Especially striking is the eucharistic section, where Laud prays before receiving the elements of bread and wine:

> O Lord, I am thy son, thy most unkind, prodigal, run-away son, yet thy son . . . O Lord, in thy grace I return to thee; and though I have eaten draff with all the unclean swine in the world, in my hungry absence from thee, yet now Lord, upon my humble return to thee, give me I beseech thee the bread of life, the body and blood of my Saviour.

Having received the sacrament of holy communion, Laud concludes: 'enrich me with all those graces which come from that precious body and blood, even till I be possessed of eternal life in Christ'.[24] Herein lies the remedy for sin, as opposed to an arbitrary decree of divine election. Such views are also a very important dimension to the ceremonial changes characteristic of the 1630s, when Laud was actually in the saddle.

Behind Laud and Buckeridge, however, stands another English religious figure – that of Lancelot Andrewes. When Andrewes died in September 1626, Laud described him as 'the great light of the Christian world'. Preaching at the funeral, Buckeridge said 'I loved and honoured him for above thirty years space'. He and Laud were appointed by Charles I to edit the collected sermons of Andrewes, which appeared as a handsome folio volume in 1629 and with a dedication to the king. The third edition, of 1635, also includes an analytical subject index. Some of these index entries provide important pointers to the thinking of Andrewes and, by extension, that of his editors. 'Eucharist . . . the conduit-pipe of grace', 'Grace offered to all', 'Perseverance and falling back', 'Prayer . . . the chief part of God's service', 'Reprobation not absolute' and 'Sermons . . . not the chief exercise of religion'.[25]

Andrewes was an anti-Calvinist veteran of the 1590s. Yet his central role has been obscured by the misdating of a key sermon preached before Queen Elizabeth, at Hampton Court, on 6 March 1595. This sermon relates to the predestinarian controversy at Cambridge University, where Andrewes was Master of Pembroke Hall. On the text 'Remember Lot's wife' (Luke 17, 32), it was not published until 1629 but repays close study. The wife of Lot is described as an example of 'imperseverant and relapsing righteous persons'. Andrewes distinguishes between 'two sorts', the one 'in state of sin that are wrong' and the other 'in state of grace that are well, if so they can keep them'. For the latter are always in danger of turning back, like Lot's wife, and finally perishing. Perseverance is, of course, the coping stone of Calvinist predestinarian teaching, the crown laid up for God's elect. But the clear message of Andrewes in 1595 was that no one can rest safe.[26]

It may well be significant that this is the only extant sermon of Andrewes which treats at length of perseverance or any related predestinarian theme and, as we have said, it remained unpublished in his lifetime. Was he warned off the subject? Certainly that happened to him under King James. Nevertheless, in the wake of the religious crisis at Cambridge, Andrewes ventured some further private comments. Among other things, he stated that 'almost all' the fathers maintained that the decree of election was due to 'faith foreseen'. Therefore according to them election, like reprobation, was not absolute. Instead, both were conditional. Andrewes did not 'dare', so he wrote, to 'condemn' this view. But anti-Calvinist teaching on the theology of grace was only part of his legacy. Andrewes also possessed a chalice, 'having on the outside of the bowl Christ with the lost sheep on his shoulders', which sounds identical to that later bequeathed by Buckeridge to St John's College, Oxford. In his will Andrewes spoke of himself as a 'most wretched and unworthy sinner', to some extent anticipating Buckeridge and Laud. Similarly his collection of private devotions includes a eucharistic prayer reminiscent of that used by Laud, and in this case taken from Chrysostom.

As thou didst not repel even the harlot like me, the sinner, coming to thee and touching thee; as thou didst not abhor her filthy mouth and polluted, . . . in like sort vouchsafe to accept me withal the inveterate, miserable, the singular great sinner to the touch and partaking of the immaculate, awful, quickening and saving mysteries of thine allholy body and precious blood.[27]

Both prayers abolish any real distinction between election and reprobation, all mankind being plunged into an abyss of habitual sin and from which the only escape is via the eucharistic sacrifice. They also, in effect, restore a section of the Roman Catholic Missal omitted from the English Prayer Book, which must seriously qualify any attempt to portray English Arminians as merely latter-day Edwardian protestants.[28]

We have dwelt on Andrewes because Laud and his circle regarded him as an intellectual father figure. Indeed the thinking of Andrewes underlies many of the more salient religious developments of the 1630s. Although he passed through a number of bishoprics and ended up a Privy Councillor, only at the very end of the reign of James I did the views of Andrewes come to pose a major threat to Calvinist hegemony. Probably Andrewes achieved the height of his effective influence under the new king, Charles I, and during the last eighteen months of his life. Hence it is significant that Laud was promised the succession to the archbishopric of Canterbury, by Charles, in October 1626 – the month after the death of Andrewes.[29]

III

According to one tradition Laud was elevated to the episcopate, in 1621, thanks to the royal favourite Buckingham. Alternatively, he may have owed his promotion to the growing influence at court of his backers among the bishops. Either way, Laud's becoming Bishop of St David's needs to be understood against the changing political background of the time. The Thirty Years' War had broken out three years earlier, and King James was anxious to avoid direct military involvement. As a consequence he sought to counterbalance the Calvinist war party at home, by promoting clergy such as Laud. It was a case of peace, and possible toleration of Catholic recusants, against war in the name of the true, Calvinist religion. Whatever Buckingham's role in the initial promotion of Laud, the latter rapidly established a key position in the Buckingham household. This seems to have come about due to the religious wavering of Buckingham's mother, who was tempted to turn Catholic. Her conversion would have been politically embarrassing, and Laud's own brand of moderate protestantism was required to prevent it. In the process, Laud became the chaplain and confidant of Buckingham in 1622. This was also the occasion of Laud's major published work, the conference with Fisher the Jesuit about the claims of the Roman Catholic Church to religious obedience. Laud conceded that Rome was 'a true Church in essence', although 'corrupt and tainted'. But because of the limited terms of reference of this debate, it tells us little about his wider thought. None the less he did include a quotation from St Jerome to the effect that a Church could not exist without bishops.[30]

Despite this court employment, Laud seemingly failed to win the complete trust of King James. Promotion from St David's only came in 1626. Indeed his career in national politics did not fully take off until 1627 when he became a Privy Councillor, King Charles having come to the throne two years earlier. Moreover Laud always remained first and foremost an ecclesiastic, and comparisons with Cardinal Wolsey or the contemporary Richelieu are misplaced. It was the churchmanship of Laud which primarily attracted the new king. Charles I, like Laud, apparently came to regard Calvinism as fundamentally subversive of the institutional structures of state as well as Church. As early as 1625, Laud can be found claiming that the 'fatal' teachings of Calvinism nullified the 'practice of piety and obedience'; the overweening confidence of the self-styled elect was equally destructive of 'external ministry' in the Church and 'civil government in the commonwealth'.[31]

There was no necessary conflict, however, between Calvinism and divine right monarchy, and what probably tipped the balance was the religious aversion of Charles to this type of Christian evangelism. As we have remarked, he promised Laud Canterbury in 1626 – when the Calvinist Abbot still had seven years to live. That June saw the issue of a royal Proclamation banning the subject of predestination from press and pulpit, in the name of the 'peace and quiet' of the English Church. This was elaborated during late 1628, in a Declaration prefacing a reissue of the Thirty-nine Articles. The impact was felt immediately at Cambridge University, and rather more gradually elsewhere. A precedent, of course, had been established here by the Jacobean Directions to Preachers in 1622, although these had proved largely inoperative. But a ban on all predestinarian teaching was something which anti-Calvinists like Andrewes had also sought back in the 1590s. Then, as now, Calvinists complained that this penalised orthodoxy. Like them, we should not necessarily take the proclaimed peacemakers at face value. To forbid a body of established teaching, because of some opposition to it, is in fact a classic means of altering the *status quo*. Public opposition to Calvinism at this date was mainly confined to the writings of Richard Montagu, who in his *A New Gagg* of 1624 and *Appello Caesarem* of 1625 had gone much further than the remarks of Laud in 1622. Yet behind Montagu was a powerful body of backers, who included Andrewes as well as Laud, Buckeridge and Neile. They in turn successfully pleaded his cause with Buckingham and Charles.[32]

According to Laud, Calvinist theology made of God 'the most unreasonable tyrant in the world' and was also deeply divisive. As he said in 1626, 'divide the minds of men about their hope of salvation in Christ and tell me what unity there will be'. In July 1628 Laud was promoted to the bishopric of London, which gave him a potentially key position in the operation of press censorship – especially of religious books. Laud also vetted in advance the sermons preached at Paul's Cross, the most public pulpit in the land. Here it can be shown that from mid 1628 Calvinist sermons disappeared, and by the following year were being replaced by Arminian ones. Particularly interesting in this connection is Laud's answer to the resolution of the House of Commons, in January 1629, against Arminianism. The Commons had avowed for truth the 'sense' of the Thirty-nine Articles which 'by the general and current exposition of the writers of our Church hath been delivered unto us'. Laud did not attempt to deny that the tenor of 'current' teaching was opposed to Arminianism. But he noted that this was only a 'probable' argument as regards the true nature of English Church teaching. For 'the current exposition of the fathers themselves hath sometimes missed the sense of the Church'. He added that 'consent of writers . . . may, and perhaps do, go against the literal sense' of the Thirty-nine Articles. Consent to an 'article, or canon, is to itself'.[33]

The same year, 1629, Laud had a hand in regulating religious lecturers, at a national level, and in turning afternoon sermons into catechisings. The purpose of lectureships was to provide sermons, and they were often held by clergy with conscientious scruples about conforming. One object of the new Instructions was to remove this puritan loophole, by making lecturers read the Prayer Book service before preaching. This policy, like other aspects of the Caroline religious programme, had been foreshadowed in the last few years of King James. It was now revived and extended, the moving spirit apparently being Archbishop Harsnett of York – the senior surviving Arminian cleric. The fact of Harsnett's involvement underlines the collective responsibility of the anti-Calvinist leadership for religious alterations under Charles I. Discussions also took place between Laud and Charles, in December 1629, about revising the Elizabethan Injunctions of 1559. In this connection a document was drawn up comparing them with the Jacobean canons of 1604. Two particular failings in the canons were highlighted, concerning control of printing and the location of the communion table in churches. On this latter topic, the author concluded 'it were to be wished it would please His Majesty by some declaration to take away the scruple which some nowadays make of the placing of the communion table'. Here indeed we seem to have the genesis of the altar policy of the 1630s.[34]

At this point it is necessary to clarify further the relationship between Calvinism and puritanism. Puritans were generally Calvinists, but only a minority of Calvinists were puritans in a nonconformist sense. Thus during the 1620s the Archbishops of Canterbury, York and Armagh were all Calvinists. To call George Abbot, Toby Matthew and James Ussher 'puritan' archbishops would be inappropriate. They were not saboteurs, working to undermine the English Church. Nevertheless Calvinism had provided a shared frame of reference for conformists and nonconformists alike, which was now being dissolved. This is the context of the winding up in the early 1630s of the Feoffees for Impropriations: a group of puritan-minded clergy and laity who had begun to buy up impropriated tithes in order to increase the stipends of preachers. Laud was convinced that a puritan 'plot' was afoot, 'to overthrow the Church government', although in earlier days it would probably not have been so regarded. Rightly or wrongly, Laud felt unable to harness the enthusiasm of the Feoffees to his own plans for augmenting clerical incomes. The issue was partly one of control, a major objection being that much of the money was earmarked for unbeneficed lecturers. There is also a theological aspect to this, because of the Calvinist stress on sermons.[35]

The full impact of religious change, however, was only felt after Laud became archbishop in 1633. The first few months of his primacy saw both the start of a campaign against strict Sunday observance and a royal ruling in favour of the altarwise position of communion tables. The former involved a reissue of the Jacobean Book of Sports of 1618, which had never been strictly enforced. Whereas during the Elizabethan and Jacobean periods sabbatarianism had increasingly become part of English religious life, from 1633 there was a sustained attempt to reverse the process. One of the arguments adduced in favour was that on Sunday Christians celebrate the fact that Christ died for all mankind without exception and not just the elect. But there was no simple correlation of attitudes here, some notable Calvinists also being opposed to sabbatarianism. At the same time the Book proved a serious stumbling block to puritans. On the subject of altars Laud and Neile, the latter recently appointed Archbishop of York, had made their views known as early as 1617. Now, however, began the systematic application of the cathedral model at parish level. The start was signalled by the case of St Gregory's-by-St Paul's, in London, which King Charles himself adjudicated in November 1633. The king found in favour of the St Paul's Cathedral authorities and against the parishioners, ordering that the communion table should remain in its new position at the east end of the chancel. Apropos the question whether the moving spirit here was Laud or Charles, the strict answer is neither since we know that Archbishop Neile had already begun converting parish communion tables in the northern province some months previously.[36]

Yet there can be no serious doubt that Laud wholeheartedly supported the altar policy. During 1634 he commenced a metropolitical visitation of the province of Canterbury, and issued instructions to his vicar-general, Sir Nathaniel Brent, in favour of 'the railing in, the setting up at the east end the communion table and the receiving thereat'. Laud, it is true, favoured persuasion rather than coercion, which served to differentiate his position from that of Arminian zealots like Bishop Matthew Wren.[37] The aim, however, was the same, namely to remodel communion practice throughout England. Laud assumed that a majority of parish churches at the start of the 1630s did not have their communion tables placed altarwise. The subsequent change was probably for many people the most obvious and symbolic religious act of the Caroline regime.

It is also clear from the history of his chancellorship of Oxford University that Laud advocated the custom of bowing towards the altar. Both this and the altarwise position of communion tables were to be embodied in the canons of 1640.[38]

Many altars and chancels were further embellished at this time, with pictures of the crucifixion. Decency, order and ecclesiastical status were all factors. But so too was a greatly enhanced view of the importance of the eucharist itself, as the fount of 'eternal life in Christ'. Such 'immaculate, awful, quickening and saving mysteries' almost demanded setting apart in a holy of holies – railed in at the east end of churches. This profound shift of emphasis also spelt redundancy for Calvinist teaching on predestination. By 1632 Calvinism had been silenced at both Oxford and Cambridge Universities. The following year, 1633, the succession of Laud to Canterbury saw a marked tightening of press censorship. Both his own chaplains and those of his protégé Bishop William Juxon of London can be shown to have taken their function as licensers seriously, and at the expense of Calvinists. Conversely, they permitted the publication of Arminian theological views. Neverthless this was essentially secondary to the sacramental reorientation of English religious life now occurring.[39] Certainly in the longer term the future lay with the party of Laud. What however temporarily halted them in their tracks was the political collapse of the Caroline regime, in 1640, following on the Scottish rebellion.

The ostensible cause of the revolt in Scotland was the new Prayer Book of 1637, although Laud claimed that religion merely served as a subterfuge. He also denied direct responsibility for the Scottish Prayer Book, while admitting to approving strongly of its content. Laud said he would have preferred the Scots to have adopted the existing English Prayer Book, as more conducive to uniformity between the three kingdoms. While we may accept this, the sacramental thrust of the new liturgy is none the less extremely revealing. One of the most important departures from that of England concerned the communion service, where the words of administration simply follow those of the first Edwardian Prayer Book: 'the body of our Lord Jesus Christ, which was given for thee', and 'the blood of our Lord Jesus Christ, which was shed for thee, preserve thy body and soul unto everlasting life'. This altered the Elizabethan formula which had subjoined the significantly different wording of the second Edwardian Prayer Book. The initiative here was apparently that of Bishop James Wedderburn of Dunblane, who argued that 'the words which are added since, "take, eat, in remembrance etc.", may seem to relish somewhat of the Zwinglian tenet that the sacrament is a bare sign taken in remembrance of Christ's passion'. Nothing must be allowed to detract from the saving reality of the 'body' and 'blood' of Christ in the eucharist.[40]

'All reformation that is good and orderly takes away nothing from the old but that which is faulty and erroneous'.[41] So Laud generalised from the making of the Scottish Prayer Book. Others, of course, saw such alterations as 'innovation'. Not only the chief executive, Laud was also a leading architect of religious change during the 1630s – working in close alliance with both King Charles and in some cases over-enthusiastic subordinates. From 1633 onwards Laud at Canterbury, Neile at York and Juxon at London oversaw a coherent reform programme centring on doctrine and worship. The intellectual roots ran back to the Elizabethan period, but only came to fruition under Charles I. Eclipsed in the mid-seventeenth century, the movement was to re-emerge at the Restoration as a major directing force.

3. Episcopal Government, 1603–1640

KENNETH FINCHAM

I

It has become customary to contrast the peaceful and settled Church of James I with the divided and turbulent Church of his son, Charles I. The accession of a new monarch in 1625 saw, it is claimed, the adoption of new, aggressive policies towards puritan nonconformists, which wrecked the carefully constructed Jacobean balance between rival interests. Yet we lack a thorough study of diocesan government across the two reigns with which to measure the changes and continuities of these years in the localities, a fact which has allowed a recent commentator to claim that there was nothing novel about episcopal rule for much of the 1630s.[1]

This essay offers a broad survey of the changing practice and image of episcopal government in the dioceses of early Stuart England. While each see posed different problems for its bishop, his administration was also shaped by the wider influences of the national protestant Church and supervision from an active pair of supreme governors. Diocesan studies have their place, but our concern here is with the precious truths that reside in generalities. For an investigation of the objectives and temper of episcopal rule *does* show a marked contrast between the two reigns, indicative of the altered pattern of preferment by the crown as well as the changed agenda that bishops were required to observe. At work, too, was a shift in the dominant image of the bishop from that of preaching pastor to that of disciplinarian. The activities of both benches of bishops earned praise as well as censure from different groups of clergy and laity; indeed, the popularity of some Caroline reforms should not be obscured by the ostensibly unanimous condemnation of Laud at the opening of the Long Parliament.

II

Ninety-two bishops occupied the twenty-seven English and Welsh sees between 1603 and 1640. New appointees were selected by the crown, after consultation with leading lay and clerical advisers. Both James I and Charles I generally chose their bishops carefully, usually preferring to appoint royal chaplains whom they already knew.[2] While James elevated numerous Calvinists and anti-Calvinists, his son Charles was more partisan. The influential sees went to anti-Calvinists such as Laud and Neile, with very few evangelical Calvinists being promoted after 1625, Bishops Hall, Potter and Morton being the obvious exceptions.

A new bishop's theological views was only one of a number of formative influences on his administration. The concerns of central government, the expectations of local society and above all the character of the diocese all made their mark. Thus bishops of Chester were much exercised by the poverty of their temporalities and the entrenched position of local Catholics, neither of which was so pressing for bishops of Ely, who, in turn, had the unusual responsibility of administering a secular liberty, the Isle of Ely. Devolved ecclesiastical authority in dioceses such as Lincoln or Norwich contrasted with the centralised control available to bishops of Chichester and Gloucester. Working within these local variations, every bishop had to tackle nationwide problems: the challenge from puritan and Catholic nonconformists, the moral and spiritual conduct of the laity, and the economic and pastoral difficulties of the parochial ministry. All also faced periodic demands for action or information from the centre. Our interest here is with the balance bishops struck between these various competing claims on their time.

The charge of episcopal negligence, once championed by Hugh Trevor-Roper, need not detain us long. Although the loss of administrative records, or brief tenure of office, means that we have little detailed information about the government of well over half of the bishops, it is clear from extant evidence that most were reasonably energetic rulers. The majority resided in their sees, presided at visitation, sometimes sat in their consistory courts to enforce ecclesiastical discipline, and almost invariably assembled a team of diocesan lawyers and officials who were responsive to their wishes. This is as true for the bishops of James I as it is for their Caroline successors, so the issue here is not one of diligence but of aims and achievements.[3]

Perhaps the pre-eminent aim at the opening of the seventeenth century was to strengthen the ministry. The Elizabethan ambition for an educated and active preaching ministry was only beginning to be realised by 1603, and many Jacobean bishops, in their turn, placed their shoulder to the pastoral wheel. Certainly some of this activity was prompted by higher authority. At the Hampton Court Conference James I had committed himself to furthering the preaching ministry, and central directives in 1605 (from Bancroft) and in 1610 (from James himself) aimed to satisfy parliamentary grievances by enforcing canonical requirements for clerical residence and weekly parochial sermons.[4] But many bishops did not need to be prodded into action. On visitation in 1611, Bishop Barlow urged the Lincolnshire clergy that 'if they would but diligently study the English books of divinity that are now in print, they might do much good in God's Church'. He then proceeded to cross-examine several ministers accused of misconduct, especially drunkenness, warning some to appear before him at a later date. James Montagu at Bath and Wells sent his non-preaching clergy to local lectures, with their notebooks in hand. Others went further: Ravis of London, Abbot of Canterbury, Bennett of Hereford and Lake of Bath and Wells adopted Elizabethan schemes of vocational training for poorly-educated ministers to encourage them to qualify for preaching licences. Visitation preachers took up this problem, and thundered against their lazy or scandalous brethren. Unless we reform ourselves, warned Samuel Crook at Bath in 1612, we cannot hope to reform our flock. At Barnstaple in 1616 Richard Carpenter deplored the persistence of ministers who 'have not such tolerable knowledge and skill as their place and office requireth'.[5]

Care was also taken over recruitment: Andrewes, Lake, Morton and others took advantage of rising educational standards to reject unsuitable candidates for ordination. Several bishops in outlying areas such as Carlisle and Bangor used their patronage and university connections to attract preaching graduates into their dioceses. Both laity and clergy became accustomed to see their bishop in the pulpit, whether in the cathredral, on visitation or occasionally 'in combination' with local lecturers. Very few Jacobean bishops resident in their sees let such preaching opportunities slip by.[6]

A handful of Calvinist bishops made evangelism the dominant mark of their government. In this group we find Archbishops Abbot and Matthew and Bishops Bennett, King, Lake, Morton and Robinson. Each was a diligent preacher, patronised a preaching ministry and worked closely with local puritan ministers to advance the gospel. Lake was intimate with the puritan preaching circle of east Somerset; Matthew's senior chaplain John Favour organised the famous preaching exercise at Halifax in the West Riding; and Bennett backed the efforts of Thomas Pierson to evangelise northern Herefordshire. Matthew was right to proclaim the Jacobean era as 'this flourishing time of the gospel'.[7]

Episcopal supervision also extended over the laity. Their spiritual and moral failings dominated consistory business, with which bishops were fairly regularly involved. Particular offences such as recusancy and the misconduct of the gentry were often referred directly to the diocesan. Thus in 1614 the charge that Sir Bartholomew Mitchell had fathered a child of his maid was investigated by Bishop Montagu in the privacy of his palace, rather than in the cathedral. Some bishops waged campaigns through their consistories: Lake was a tough opponent of incestuous crime, Harsnett periodically lashed out at sabbath-breakers, and Andrewes enforced the proper provision of utensils and furnishings for communion. A few bishops devoted much time to court business, preferring to sit themselves than delegate to their subordinates. Bishop Carleton of Chichester, for example, attended over ninety meetings of the Chichester consistory between 1620 and 1627, an impressive tally in view of his other commitments, as bishop, local magistrate and lord of Parliament.[8] Two Caroline priorities – the maintenance of Church fabric and the compilation of ecclesiastical terriers – in fact have important Jacobean antecedents. The repair of Church structure was primarily entrusted to archdeacons and deans under canon 86 of 1604, but in a number of dioceses – Chichester, Gloucester, Peterborough and Durham – the episcopal administration lent a helping hand. Ecclesiastical terriers, which recorded the lands of the parish Church, were the first line of defence against lay encroachments. Although canon 87 of 1604 required each parish to compile a terrier, it was not regularly enforced until Archbishop Abbot's metropolitical visitations in the years after 1612.[9] Diocesan records, therefore, explode the myth of a Jacobean Church staffed by a negligent episcopate and in urgent need of thorough reform.

Nor was puritan nonconformity ignored. Throughout his reign James I regulated puritan nonconformity with the tool of subscription rather than that of ceremonial conformity. In other words, he demanded formal acceptance of the government, liturgy and doctrine of the Church, but did not require that controversial ceremonies, such as the use of the surplice, be constantly observed. This strategy was novel: under Elizabeth I, both subscription to Whitgift's Three Articles and ceremonial conformity had been haphazardly enforced.[10] It was also quite distinct from the preference of Charles I for subscription and full ceremonial conformity.

For James was keen to construct a broad and unified Church which could incorporate the different styles of divinity within English protestantism. At the Hampton Court Conference in January 1604, James rejected puritan requests to modify the ceremonies and government of the Church, and determined on subscription to regulate nonconformity. Later that year Archbishop Whitgift's Three Articles of 1583 were adopted as canon 36 which required every minister to accept the royal supremacy and the legality of the Prayer Book, the Ordinal and the Thirty-nine Articles of Religion. As James observed, subscription was necessary 'in every well governed Church' for the preservation of peace, and as a device 'to discern the affections of persons, whether quiet or turbulent'. The willingness to subscribe would distinguish moderates who would remain obedient notwithstanding their dislike of certain ceremonies from radicals who rejected the formularies and government of the Church. Subscription was enforced from the winter of 1604–5. Archbishop Bancroft of Canterbury instructed his bishops to eject beneficed ministers who would neither subscribe nor practise the ceremonies, but to spare any who might be won round in due course. Over the next five years between seventy-three and eighty-three beneficed ministers lost their livings, while an unknown number of curates and lecturers had their licences withdrawn.[11]

Conciliatory gestures by some puritan clergymen and the intervention of powerful patrons helped to minimise the number of deprivations. But it is also clear that several bishops such as Hutton of York and Rudd of St David's questioned the expediency of the campaign, fearing the Church could ill afford to lose the services of so many nonconformist preachers. The slightest hint of conformity saved many puritans. It is no surprise that Hutton removed only four ministers in a diocese of nearly eight hundred parishes. However, those ousted in 1604–9 were usually barred from resuming their ministry without first subscribing, and Bishops Barlow, Dove, Morton and Bridgeman were all reprimanded by the king at various times for indulgence towards non-subscribing ministers.[12]

For the rest of the reign subscription was also exacted from ordinands entering the ministry and from clergymen seeking institution to livings or licences to preach or hold a curacy. On only a handful of occasions were ministers allowed to evade part or all of canon 36. Archbishop Tobias Matthew did allow Alexander Cooke, deprived of his ministry in 1605, to become vicar of Leeds in 1615 without first subscribing. But this was an exceptional case, the result of Matthew's esteem for Cooke's pastoral gifts, and elsewhere the archbishop regularly turned away clergymen who would not fully subscribe.[13]

Less attention was paid to ceremonial conformity. Churchwardens' presentments against ministers who failed to observe ceremonies in the Prayer Book and canons, such as wearing the surplice, had been numerous in 1604–6 but quickly fell away. At Gloucester, for example, thirty nonconformist clergymen had been identified in 1605, but only four were reported in 1610, and four more in 1613. Although the authorities might periodically recommend ceremonial conformity – as in London diocese on a visitation in 1615 – most puritans were left undisturbed unless they drew attention to themselves by publicly challenging the ceremonies.[14] Under James I, therefore, subscription but not strict ceremonial conformity was enforced by the episcopate. Why one without the other? The king would have preferred the rites and ceremonies to be observed but he was prepared to accommodate moderate puritans once they had assented to the liturgy and polity of the Church by their subscription. Such an indulgent approach won the approval of most of James's bishops. For a few it meant a quiet life, avoiding disagreeable clashes with local puritan squires, but for many it presented an opportunity to pursue the evangelical mission of the Church in partnership with puritan preachers.

In view of the favour extended to moderate puritans, and the encouragement of preaching from the crown and many prelates, it is no surprise that these years saw the consolidation of the image of bishop as a preaching pastor. This model, furnished by scripture and burnished by humanism, presented the bishop as a benign and paternal leader, committed to furthering the gospel through personal preaching and patronage. So dominant was this model that we find it deployed in episcopal biographies, dedicatory epistles and sermons preached at the consecration of bishops, and it seems to have influenced the rule of many evangelical Calvinists on the Jacobean bench, including the Abbot brothers, Babington, Lake, Matthew, Morton, Montagu and Parry.[15] This model of episcopal government, however, came under attack from a small but influential group of divines.

For the minority of anti-Calvinists among the episcopate became deeply critical of the Jacobean polity. The fateful brew of Calvinist divinity, puritan practices and lay rapacity had, they claimed, produced false teaching, irreverence and clerical poverty. Much as they applauded James I's general support for Church interests, these divines looked for the restoration of the revenues and political authority of the clerical estate. They also deplored the fervent evangelism of so many clergy, and the cosy accommodation of moderate puritans. In sermons before the king, Bishops Andrewes and Buckeridge urged James I to change course. Andrewes attacked the contemporary devotion to preaching and claimed that sacraments, ceremonies and prayer were all neglected. Buckeridge pleaded for the enforcement of ceremonial order, though he conceded that James preferred a policy of 'love and patience' to one of confrontation. Both feared that the English Reformation had replaced superstition with profanity and both wished, like their disciple Laud, to return the English Church to its 'first Reformation' of the mid-sixteenth century. Moreover, they declared that royal policy had not checked the puritan menace. Radical puritans of presbyterian views remained in the English Church, even at Oxford University, claimed Andrewes and Howson; while subscription had not removed opponents of the ceremonies. Harsnett coined the phrase 'conformable puritans' to describe those who subscribed but held the ceremonies to be unlawful. In the 1630s puritan clergymen were to be constantly rebuked for breaking their subscription. False teaching and irreverence thrived as the episcopate ignored ceremonial conformity and concentrated on evangelism, in the process, according to John Cosin, reducing Christian faith to knowledge: know your catechism, listen to sermons and you will be saved. Evangelical bishops and a complacent monarch had allegedly sold the pass to the puritans. Cosin, like Bishops Andrewes and Barlow before him, proclaimed that government and discipline, not preaching, should be the prime concern of the episcopate.[16]

James I resisted this alternative programme of order and uniformity. Even in the face of intense puritan criticism of his foreign policy in 1618–23, the king contented himself with tightening his control over the pulpits, but would not sanction further moves against nonconformists. Until 1625, thus, subscription rather than full ceremonial conformity was enforced.

Anti-Calvinist bishops did register their dissatisfaction in a number of ways. Their articles of enquiry issued on visitation expressed great hostility to puritan practices. While Archbishops Abbot and Matthew asked if the surplice was 'commonly' or 'usually' used, Bishops Overall, Harsnett and Neile enquired if the minister wore the surplice 'always and at every time both morning and evening . . . and doth he never omit to wear the same?' Barlow, Neile and Harsnett curbed the number of lectureships in their dioceses; flagrant nonconformist practices were checked, so that the mayor and aldermen of Coventry, for example, found themselves in 1611 reported to the king by Bishop Neile for refusing to kneel at the receipt of communion; while in 1617, the desire for greater reverence led Laud, as Dean of Gloucester, to move the communion table to the east end of the cathedral and to require the canons to bow towards it, and in 1620 his patron Neile permitted a stone altar to be erected in Durham Cathedral.[17] These amounted to only minor victories, however, and the rigorous imposition of ceremonial order had to wait until after 1625.

III

Anti-Calvinist ideas prospered after the accession of Charles I. The call for strict discipline was embraced by the new king, whose aesthetic preferences for order and reverence were sharpened by his fears of a puritan conspiracy in Church and state. The instructions given by Nathaniel Brent, Archbishop Laud's vicar-general, in metropolitical visitations in twenty dioceses between 1634 and 1637 express the priorities of the Caroline regime.[18] First, full liturgical and ceremonial conformity was enforced. Ministers were to read divine service in its entirety with no omissions and hold services on Wednesdays and Fridays as the Prayer Book stipulated. Proper clerical attire was essential: this meant 'constantly' wearing the surplice during services, and outside Church 'never' failing to use a canonical cloak, that symbol of the priestly caste. A premium was placed on reverent conduct during services: parishioners should bow at the name of Jesus and stand at the creed and gospels, as canon 18 stated. Most significant of all, the communion table was ordered to be 'set at the upper end of the chancel north and south and a rail before it or round about it'. Reception of communion at the rails was to be encouraged.

Secondly, preaching was to be carefully monitored. Official concern at ill-regulated sermons and lectureships had already been voiced in the royal Instructions of 1629, which stated that catechising must replace Sunday afternoon sermons in parishes, that only 'grave and orthodox' ministers be permitted to join combination lectures, and that lecturers be persuaded to accept benefices. Brent reminded preachers of these instructions, told them to reduce the length of their sermons, and urged them to preach regularly on the theme of political obedience to the crown. Finally, churchyards were to be cleared, and terriers of ecclesiastical property compiled.

Was Laud here simply enforcing existing ecclesiastical regulations? There were clear precedents for most of his actions, a fact which apologists for the reforms naturally emphasised. At Dorchester in 1635 Brent told the assembled clergy that Laud was ordering no more than had been required since the Reformation, although he did not add that it had rarely been enforced. Likewise he defended the erection of altar rails on grounds of decency and order, 'to keep off dogs and to free it from all other pollutions'. Similarly, Charles I claimed that the canons of 1640 merely authorised ancient, if neglected, rites and ceremonies.[19] These protestations of conservatism were no doubt intended to silence critics and win over waverers, and may well represent Charles I's own convictions. Yet an alternative view is that several of these changes were innovatory, and the whole programme of reform admits a different ideological reading.

First, certain changes went beyond the Prayer Book and canons. Laud defended the new position of the communion table with reference to the Elizabethan Injunctions of 1559. He regularly quoted its first section, that 'the holy table' should be 'set in the place where the altar stood' but ignored the next clause permitting it to be moved elsewhere in the chancel at the time of communion.

Neither the Injunctions of 1559 nor the canons of 1604 envisaged rails or the reception of communion there. Laud encouraged both. Thus in December 1637 we find his vicar-general Nathaniel Brent ordering the churchwardens of St James's Dover:

> to advance and remove up their communion table to the same east or upper end and before it to build and place a decent rail cross the same quire or chancel for the communicants accommodated with some convenient thing to kneel upon to come unto, and receive the blessed sacrament at the hands of the minister in the time of the celebration keeping himself within the same rail, according as it was by him (Brent) given in charge to the minister and churchwardens throughout the diocese at the last ordinary visitation.

Similarly, when Bishop Richard Montagu queried the practice of receiving at the rails, Laud advised Charles I that the 'bishop continue it and look carefully to it'. Such evidence makes it hard to accept the claim of Dr Davies that neither in Canterbury diocese nor elsewhere did Laud ever encourage the practice of reception at the rails, though it is perfectly true that the archbishop could be circumspect about compelling parishioners to receive there.[20] Canon 7 of 1640 gave retrospective warranty for the altar policy, although some latitude was permitted about reception at the rails. It also recommended bowing towards the east end on entering and leaving Church, a ceremony urged by Laud and several other bishops in the 1630s at a time when it had no canonical basis, although it was the customary practice in the Chapel Royal and in a number of cathedrals such as Wells.[21]

The tight regulation of preaching and the attack on sabbatarian teaching also represented a sharp break with prevalent practice in the later Elizabethan and Jacobean Churches. Although James I's Directions to Preachers (1622) anticipated some features of his son's Instructions of 1629, the Caroline suspicion of lecturing and excessive preaching marked the triumph of the views of anti-Calvinist churchmen such as Harsnett and Neile over the more typical favour which had been extended to preachers by many Jacobean bishops, led by Abbot of Canterbury and Matthew of York. Nor is any Caroline bishop known to have revived those vocational training schemes favoured under Elizabeth and James in order to enhance the preaching strength of the clergy, for the evangelical impulse was now to be contained. As Laud observed, government now was 'more noble and necessary' than preaching.[22] The pronounced antipathy to sabbatarianism was also novel. James I's Book of Sports had been issued in 1618 but only one bishop, Godwin of Hereford, showed much enthusiasm for enforcing it. On its republication in 1633 ministers were required to read the Book from the pulpits, a test of obedience used to detect refractory nonconformists, and a large number were temporarily suspended, and a few deprived, for their refusal to comply. Charles I commissioned official defences of the policy from Peter Heylyn and Francis White, and defences of sabbatarianism could not be printed until 1641.[23]

It is also plausible to interpret these changes as the implementation of anti-Calvinist ideals proposed by Jacobean divines such as Andrewes and Buckeridge. Their vision of an orderly and reverent piety, squarely based on prayers and sacraments rather than preaching, accompanying the elimination of nonconformist practices and beliefs, was certainly the major inspiration for Caroline reforms. As noted elsewhere in this volume, Caroline court prelates in the 1630s were *all* anti-Calvinists. Their speeches and writings make it plain that new ideals underpinned the enforcement of traditional (though neglected) rites and ceremonies. Laud, for example, in his defence of altar policy admitted that although the positioning of the communion table was a matter indifferent, the altar was 'the greatest place of God's residence upon earth . . . yea, greater than the pulpit', a statement which epitomised his reverence for sacramental grace. Similarly Wren saw the English Church as corrupted by foreign doctrines from the early years of Elizabeth so that 'we are now well nigh fallen into an hatred of the true worship and into contempt of all things divine and holy'.[24] Outside the court, it is true that the theological views of several active Caroline bishops (Piers, Dee and Towers) are unclear. Nevertheless, anti-Calvinist beliefs were held by a number of their colleagues, among them Richard Montagu, Augustine Lindsell and Robert Skinner.

Let us take Skinner of Bristol (1637–41) as an example. Although very few diocesan sermons or 'charges' survive for the Caroline episcopate, we possess two by Skinner. Both were delivered in 1637 and each expresses hostility to Calvinist teaching and puritan practices. The first, a visitation charge to the Dorset clergy, warned the ministry to observe 'sound doctrine and wholesome discipline'. Among the modern authors he recommended for study were Hooker and Andrewes, the founding-fathers of anti-Calvinist piety. Preaching should also be profitable, and Skinner condemned the disregard by some Calvinists of the baptismal rite in favour of 'real baptism', the conversion experience. Ministers were to preach Christ crucified to all their flock, 'without extenuating the grace of God' available to any penitent sinner. Skinner had in mind the tendency of some Calvinist ministers to distinguish between godly and ungodly in their congregation, which in their view corresponded to elect and reprobate. The ministry were then exhorted to honour their subscription to the doctrine and discipline of the English Church 'without hypocritical dissimulation or Jesuitical equivocation'.

The same year Skinner preached a sermon at Bristol originally delivered before Charles I in 1632. In it he attacked the Calvinist doctrine of perseverance, that none can fall once they have attained grace, arguing instead that once sanctified we do have the option to accept or reject divine grace. He scorned Calvinists who rested secure in their presumed election, in the mistaken belief that 'all are tied up by an absolute decree and a fatal necessity and so can do no more'. Why then did St Paul bother to exhort us to gain grace? He also satirised the presumption and hypocrisy of some Calvinists who would not abandon a member of their selected group of godly, whatever he did:

> Neither drunkenness nor gluttony nor fraud nor lying nor slandering nor railing nor reviling nor (I had almost said) rebellion can cast him out of their calendar of saints; still a child of grace and one of God's dear servants for all this.

Instead, Skinner argued that we must express our grace by our good works, which includes the reverent worship of God through humble devotion, kneeling and adoration in church where God does 'abundantly manifest his grace and mercy and saving power'.[25] Skinner's derision of Calvinist excesses, and his exultation of ritual, exemplifies the new understanding invested in Caroline reforms by anti-Calvinist churchmen. His sermons also prove that at least one member of the diocesan episcopate was proclaiming these new ideals in his see. There is no reason to suppose he was the only one.

How far was Caroline policy observed by the bench of bishops?

Visitation articles provide one clue. A comparison with Jacobean articles shows that sets for the 1630s displayed a greater concern with nonconformist practices, often enquired minutely into the conduct of preachers and lecturers, demanded that canonical habits be worn, and that the laity worship with reverence.[26] Consistory court records in most dioceses show that some enforcement of ceremonial conformity now accompanied clerical subscription to canon 36. No longer were the authorities satisfied with the Jacobean requirement of formal obedience; and whereas once a puritan divine such as Richard Bernard had enjoyed some indulgence in view of his preaching and pastoral gifts, now, as Dee of Peterborough observed, 'no man's learning and piety shall excuse . . . his unconformity'.[27]

Bernard's career exemplifies the changing fortunes of nonconformists in the early Stuart Church. Although Bernard had lost his living of Worksop in 1605 for refusing to subscribe, he was wooed back into the ministry by Archbishop Matthew, at the price of subscribing, and thereafter his minor infringements of the ceremonies were tolerated first by Matthew, and later in Somerset by Bishops James Montagu and Arthur Lake. In 1617 he was presented before Wells consistory court for failing to wear his graduate hood, in contravention of canon 58, but the case was dropped when Bernard claimed he had Lake's warrant for this. No wonder that in 1621 he publicly praised Lake as 'a blessed bishop, a very man of God'. The climate changed with the arrival of William Piers as bishop in 1632. In October 1634 Bernard was before Piers accused of a long list of nonconformist practices. Piers made his opposition to puritan divinity very clear: Bernard was forbidden to continue his longstanding practice of repeating the sermon and questioning the congregation on what they had heard; he was to cease catechising the young and ignorant in the middle of prayers, despite the plea that Bishop Lake had permitted this; he was to follow the exact questions and answers in the Prayer Book catechism and not enlarge on them; and he was to display greater reverence in Church, remove his hat in prayer time, and genuflect on entering Church. An inscription in praise of the sabbath was to be erased. Bernard himself was a strong supporter of sabbatarianism, and wrote a tract in the 1630s attacking official policy, although it could not be published until 1641. He was also unsympathetic to the altar policy, and in 1636 was accused of tampering with the newly-positioned communion table.[28]

Not all nonconformists faced such difficulties. Puritan ministers in Warwickshire, for example, under the jurisdiction of either Thornborough of Worcester or Wright of Coventry and Lichfield did not suffer rigorous supervision. But the atmosphere of confrontation elsewhere certainly alarmed Warwickshire puritans: and Laud's rule in London, Wren's in Norwich or Neile's at York, for instance, certainly justified these fears of imminent persecution. Here the net was cast not just for rigid nonconformists but also 'conformable puritans' whose outward observance was not matched by genuine acceptance of the ceremonies. Brent's reports back to Laud are full of the difficulties of trapping such clergymen.[29]

Perhaps no more than thirty nonconformist ministers lost their livings in the 1630s. This relatively small number should not conceal the firm and sustained pressure for conformity. Many zealous Caroline bishops such as Neile and Piers avoided depriving any ministers, but instead made extensive use of the weapons of suspension and excommunication. In 1634, for example, Piers excommunicated two Somerset clergymen for refusing to read the Book of Sports, and did not absolve them until 1638.[30] Neile's tough stance encouraged several ministers to resign and depart for the Dutch Republic or the New World. This was often welcomed by the authorities. When William Bridge fled abroad to escape punishment from Bishop Wren, Charles I commented 'Let him go; we are well rid of him'. In January 1637 the Privy Council even debated ways of encouraging extremists to emigrate.[31]

The tightening control over lectureships and sermons took many forms. At Bath and Wells Piers suppressed numerous lectureships (though he later reinstated one, at Taunton), and ensured that catechising replaced Sunday afternoon preaching. At Norwich, Wren permitted only beneficed ministers to serve as lecturers, to put 'a straighter tie' on them 'to observe and justify the rites and ceremonies which the Church enjoineth'. The godly preaching circle of Thomas Dugard suffered little trouble from Bishop Thornborough, though he did replace the Stratford-upon-Avon lecturer with a minister beneficed in his diocese, in accordance with the Instructions of 1629.[32] At Exeter, Hall encouraged lecturers provided they displayed a minimal degree of conformity. Neile's remarkable performance of only licensing thirteen preachers in his eight years as Archbishop of York was not typical of the bench. Both Wren and Piers granted large numbers of preaching licences (in Piers' case, as many as his evangelical predecessor, Lake) since they saw edifying sermons exhorting obedience and conformity as an important antidote to puritanism. Many of Wren's licences went to ritualists such as Richard Drake and John Nowell, both committed opponents of nonconformity. The men Wren wished to bar from the pulpit were puritans, 'the faction of assurance and undoubted salvation' as his chancellor put it.[33]

Too many accounts of the 1630s rest on the well-documented activities of Wren, Piers and Neile. Who were the other zealous reformers? One was Curle of Winchester, who on visitation required parochial reports on the observance of the royal Instructions on preaching, and suspended at least fourteen ministers for refusing to read the Book of Sports. His patronage went to such figures as John Oliver, domestic chaplain to Archbishop Laud, and William Page, his own chaplain and author of a book enjoining bowing at the name of Jesus. Curle encouraged reverence in divine service, recommending the practice of the Chapel Royal, 'so God may be worshipped not only in holiness, but in the beauty of holiness'.[34] Another reformer was John Bancroft of Oxford, who demanded from ordination candidates their views on the altar policy and Book of Sports. He too suspended three ministers for refusing to read the Book of Sports, and suppressed several lectureships. Among these was a combination lecture at Woodstock, licensed by his predecessor Richard Corbet, who had also joined its preaching roster.[35] As John Fielding demonstrates below, Bishops Dee and Towers of Peterborough were also committed supporters of the new programme: Towers, like Richard Montagu, held that the rails defined 'a holy sanctuary' which the laity should not enter, and he advocated bowing towards the altar. Equally, there were a few anti-Calvinist bishops who were less aggressive. A clear example is Richard Corbet, Bishop of Oxford then Norwich, perhaps a more enthusiastic satirist than disciplinarian. Although Corbet condemned contentious preaching and commended the new ceremonialism, his mild government at Norwich came under attack in 1635–6 both from Laud's visitors and his successor there, Matthew Wren.[36]

It is well-established that several Calvinist bishops were unhappy with these ceremonial changes. Both Davenant of Salisbury and Hall of Exeter privately criticised the new ritualism, while Hall and Morton of Durham were spied on by Laud's agents.[37] Let us pursue

Hall's episcopate as a case-study. As Bishop of Exeter (1627–41), Hall used his court of audience as an effective disciplinary tool. His targets, however, were not puritans so much as the customary moral failings of the laity and clergy. Throughout the 1630s he admonished brawling, drunken and scandalous clergy, heard parochial disputes over rates and the annual perambulation, and settled cases of marital discord. His visitation charge of 1631 attacked schismatics rather than puritans, and he enforced the royal Instructions of 1629 with a light hand. During the 1630s lectures flourished at Chudleigh, Plymouth, Penzance and elsewhere.[38] Some parishes did erect an altar-rail following Laud's metropolitical visitation of 1634, but the policy was never rigorously imposed by Hall, and to judge from churchwardens' accounts, a significant number of Devon churches did not possess a rail by 1640. Indicative of Hall's approach was the fact that in 1636 he surveyed the fabric and furnishings of parish churches, but the condition of the paving, seats and stonework were his concern, rather than the location of the communion table.[39]

The range of Hall's activities should not surprise us, for throughout the 1630s nonconformity was only one of a number of issues on the episcopal agenda. Another was the protection of clerical property and possessions. Bishops were ordered to husband their resources, and much greater attention was now paid to the restoration of parochial church fabric, a concern which united Calvinists such as Hall and Morton with anti-Calvinists such as Neile and Richard Montagu. All also backed the compilation of ecclesiastical terriers, with the active encouragement of Archbishop Laud; while the detection and correction of errant clergy and laity by Hall was matched elsewhere. Drunkenness among the clergy, for example, was a problem occasionally noted by Laud's agents, and was publicly condemned by, among others, Richard Montagu of Norwich. 'I must confess', he declared in 1639, 'the laws are not strict enough for such malefactors, but if such men come under my fingers, what extremity law will afford they are like to find.'[40]

Did the image of episcopacy alter in line with the new priorities and practices of the 1630s? Certain Calvinist bishops, such as Joseph Hall, still pursued the Jacobean model of the bishop as preaching pastor, an image which he had vigorously commended in a Convocation sermon of 1621. Hall did preach in his diocese (though curiously *not* on visitation) and practised the courtesy and tolerance associated with that churchmanship. He regularly referred to 'my fellow-ministers' and 'my worthy brethren of the clergy', and addressed the inhabitants of Exeter as his 'loving neighbours and friends'.[41] Another who followed the same image was Robert Wright, Bishop of Bristol (1623–32) then Coventry and Lichfield (1632–43).

Wright is usually depicted as a dozy diocesan and covetous landlord, but he was also anxious to imitate the Jacobean model. He was certainly a regular diocesan preacher, and in 1642 referred proudly to his 'fifty-eight years painful and successful preaching of the gospel of Christ'. Like Archbishop Abbot, and Jewel before him, Wright wished 'to end my days' in the pulpit. In one sermon, preached on visitation at Shrewsbury in 1634, Wright promised to win over his audience by the mildness of Christian love rather than the force of his own authority, a classic statement of paternal rather than punitive leadership. His demeanour evidently won friends: on his translation to Coventry and Lichfield, he received a gift of plate from the Corporation of Bristol 'as a testimony of love and affection'.[42] Hall and Wright's government demonstrates the enduring appeal of the image of preaching pastor in the hostile climate of the 1630s, and it was precisely this style of rule which many had in mind in 1640–1 when they called for a return to the Church of King James and Queen Elizabeth, a call common to future episcopalians such as Thomas Warmstry and future presbyterians such as John Ley. Both looked for a revival of 'fatherly, not despotical' government exercised with Christian compassion and humility, and they repeated the Jacobean truism that the chief episcopal duty was 'the preaching of the word, making more account of the canons which concern the substance, than the ceremonies of their calling', in other words enforcing residence and preaching rather than ritual.[43]

In the 1630s, however, a rival model of the bishop as disciplinarian was gaining ground. Symptomatic of this shift was the sermon preached at the consecration of Bishop Towers at Lambeth Palace in 1639. The preacher, Peter Heylyn, portrayed the Church as endangered by 'factious and perverse preachers' who challenged ecclesiastical order and political stability by labelling bishops as innovators and agents of Rome. He called on the bishops before him, as soldiers and physicians, to crush dissent and restore the health of society.[44] Here was an image which mirrored the renewed episcopal concern with order and conformity, and Heylyn's silence

on the bishop's preaching responsibilities paralleled the reluctance
of many Caroline bishops to preach regularly in their sees, a con-
scious rebuttal of that evangelical Calvinism which had animated so
many of their Jacobean predecessors. As Piers proclaimed, regular
preaching may have been necessary in the infancy of the reformed
Church, 'yet now there was no such need'. So we find few anti-
Calvinist bishops in the pulpit during visitations or at the consecration of new churches. Laud virtually gave up preaching after his
elevation to Canterbury; Neile is not known to have preached once
in his eight years at York; while Wren later admitted that he had
never preached in either of his two dioceses.[45] Wren, Piers and Laud
also earned a reputation for abrasive government, but some of their
colleagues were more circumspect. Samuel Ward, the puritan town
preacher at Ipswich, received courteous treatment from Richard
Corbet, while Richard Montagu extended the hand of friendship to
his former adversary, the Calvinist John Yates: 'You are welcome
to me if I be welcome to you . . . I shall ever expect you when you
come to town'.[46] Such gestures must have considerably softened the
strident image of the bishop as disciplinarian.

IV

What, then, of the popularity of episcopal rule between 1603 and
1642? The theme may seem risible, in view of the abolition of the
order in the 1640s. Yet much contemporary opinion was not hostile
to bishops. Throughout these years there was an insatiable demand
from the laity for 'bishopping', or confirmation, which could turn
visitations into popular progresses.[47] Only some puritans stood aside
and condemned this 'popish' rite. There is also plenty of evidence
that by the later years of James I's reign the episcopate had regained
some of the public esteem it had lost during the sixteenth century.
The evangelical bent of many bishops satisfied both Calvinists and
puritans, the latter being also appeased by the official connivance
over ceremonial conformity. Royal favour towards certain court
bishops, in the hard currency of privy councillorships, further
enhanced the standing of the whole order.

More controversial, perhaps, is the suggestion that Caroline
reforms also found a constituency. This of course did not include
most puritan clergy and laity, who were deeply disturbed by official

policy in the 1630s, which seemed to portend a return to Rome. Laud and Neile were especially vilified: in a commonplace book belonging to the circle of the Earl of Warwick, against the phrase 'venerable bishop' is the entry: 'not Laud or Neile'. Such contemporary sentiments make sense of the violent attack on Laud and his associates in the opening months of the Long Parliament. Conformist Calvinists such as Robert Sanderson or Dean Young of Winchester, who cannot be properly labelled puritan, were divided in their attitude to the new order. The range of their reactions, and the official gestures to accommodate them, is a fascinating and neglected topic which cannot be discussed here.[48] Others were openly enthusiastic. Nicholas Tyacke's pioneering work on anti-Calvinist laity such as William, Lord Maynard or Sir Richard Dyott is one suggestive pointer. There were certainly many others with a taste for devout worship and ritualism. One was Viscount Scudamore, the restorer of Abbey Dore and staunch friend of Laud; another was Lieutenant Hammond, whose travel journals in 1634–5 record his appetite for the beauty of holiness, and a third was Sir Roger Twysden, who thoroughly approved of the distribution of communion at the rail.[49]

The renewed emphasis on reverence and order also found allies among many parochial clergy in the 1630s, evident from both printed works and diocesan records. At Norwich in 1636 Bishop Wren had little difficulty selecting fifty-eight divines to act as 'standing commissioners' to enforce discipline once the visitation was over. In other sees, visitation sermons, those barometers of diocesan life, reveal a considerable number of ministers defending the enforcement of ceremony and exhorting the necessity of obedience, discipline and reverence, themes which were sometimes explored at greater length in theological treatises. Among these divines were Edward Boughen, once chaplain to Bishop Howson and in the 1630s parson of Woodchurch in Kent; John Browning, once chaplain to Andrewes and by 1634 chaplain to Lord Maynard; John Elborow, beneficed in London; the Surrey minister William Hardwicke; William Sherley of Dorset; the poet William Strode; a Cambridgeshire incumbent, John Swan; and Richard Tedder of Norfolk. In every diocese it is possible to identify fervent clerical supporters of the new order. The title of Hardwicke's visitation sermon of 1638, *Conformity with Piety requisite in God's Service* exemplifies the concerns of many of these clergy. Other ministers, such as Henry Ancketyll of Mells (Somerset) or Boughen in Kent pressed the ceremonies on their parishioners and reported offenders to the authorities.[50]

The fact that over half of Wren's commissioners were Elizabethan or Jacobean ordinands demonstrates that Caroline reforms appealed to an older as well as a new generation of ministers. The strength of puritan nonconformity in Norwich diocese may have long repelled many of these commissioners; similarly, the new climate of the 1630s permitted long-standing critics of Calvinist teaching to air their views: Robert Shelford, one of Wren's commissioners, could thus publish his controversial *Five Pious and Learned Discourses* in 1635. The new emphasis on the dignity of the priesthood may have won over others. But Wren's supporters also included several divines once content with the Jacobean polity. One was Fulke Robarts, formerly a member of the godly preaching circle at Norwich, and another was Thomas Goad, once chaplain to Archbishop Abbot and champion of Calvinist orthodoxy. Both appear to have been convinced that puritanism did represent a genuine threat to the integrity of the English Church.[51] This whole area needs more thorough research; suffice it to say that the strong backing given to Caroline reforms by the long-established parochial clergy indicates that anti-Calvinism was not just concocted in the universities, but also articulated some cherished ideals of many rank and file churchmen and laity. Attitudes to official policy in the 1630s cannot be gauged solely from the unopposed impeachment of Laud in Parliament in late 1640; indeed, at that time it may well be that Laud's friends in both houses were keeping their powder dry for the anticipated and more serious challenge to existing ceremonies and government.

V

This essay has emphasised the continuities as well as changes in episcopal rule across the reigns of James and Charles. Both benches of bishops addressed endemic problems of nonconformity, misconduct by both clergy and laity, and the material conditions of the Church. In both reigns we can find bishops uncomfortable with official policy, discreetly modifying the impact of royal orders. Yet there was also a marked change of direction in the years after . 1625, as the Jacobean connivance at ceremonial nonconformity was abandoned in favour of a drive for order and reverent worship. The ideal of the preaching prelate fell into official disrepute, and vocational training schemes for the parish clergy were shelved. Much higher priority was now attached to protecting the lands and revenues of the clerical estate. Bishops even had to account for their stewardship with annual reports to their metropolitan, in contrast to James I's less systematic methods of monitoring his episcopate. Reports were not always returned, altar rails not everywhere erected, nor lectureships universally monitored, yet the change in official policy had a discernible impact across the dioceses in the 1630s. The cost for Bishop Hall of perpetuating Jacobean ideals was repeated allegations at court of his remiss government. This altered atmosphere is captured well in visitation sermons. While those in James I's reign regularly discussed problems of pastoral ministry, in the 1630s they invariably centred on obedience and conformity. Indeed, often the preachers themselves drew attention to the change in royal policy, as typified by the observation of Humphrey Sydenham, preaching at a Somerset visitation in 1636:[52]

> Authority . . . hath been long time asleep, begins to rub her eyes again; and Aaron's rod which seem'd in our latter times to droop and wither, doth at length blossom and bud afresh; canons, constitutions, decrees which were formerly without soul or motion (oh blessed be the religious care of an incomparable sovereign, a powerful metropolitan, and by them here an active diocesan) have recover'd a new life and vegetation. Ceremonies, harmless ceremonies . . . have gotten their former lustre and state again.

4. Arminianism in the Localities: Peterborough Diocese, 1603–1642

JOHN FIELDING

I

Religion is once more regarded by historians as a direct cause of the Civil War. It is the Arminians and their leader, William Laud, who are now portrayed as the revolutionary element, not the puritans. By means of the support of their royal sponsor, Charles I, this clique of theological innovators was able to stage an ecclesiastical coup after 1625, the success of which outlawed Calvinist theology, the previous orthodoxy, and paved the way for a wholesale reorientation of the liturgy and ecclesiology of the Church of England in the 1630s. This 'revolution' provoked a conservative, puritan backlash in the 1640s which resulted in the disestablishment of the Church altogether. The impression received from such accounts is that the religious causes of the Civil War can be traced back only as far as the beginning of Charles I's reign. In contrast, James I's reign is portrayed as a period of consensus on Calvinist predestinarian theology and of relative ecclesiastical peace, largely free of the controversies which were to occur in his son's reign. The outbreak of these disputes is explained solely in terms of Charles's political decision to support Arminianism. The prehistory of Arminianism remains rather obscure, which might lead to the conclusion that Arminian views appeared from nowhere in the 1620s after being previously held only by one or two bishops and university dons.[1]

The evidence from Peterborough diocese contradicts the description of James's reign as a time of tranquillity in Church affairs with protestants unified by a simple adherence to Calvinist theology. In what follows it will be argued that the Jacobean period was one of religious conflict between the two camps – Arminian and puritan – who were divided on a range of issues and not solely on the vexed question of predestination, and whose positions represented completely different views of true religion. During James's reign the puritans generally came off better under a Calvinist king whose policies were irenic in intent. In Charles I's reign, whose secular ideas coincided with the religious aims of the Arminians, the pendulum swung the other way. Yet here again some reappraisal is needed. Even during the height of Arminian power in the 1630s the issue between them and their opponents was never simply, nor indeed primarily, predestination, but involved a different outlook on religion. Hence the efforts of Peterborough bishops of that decade, which enjoyed some success, to use the issue of authority to woo moderate Calvinists into acceptance of the changes, or at least into silence on the subject. Finally, it will be argued that there existed a correlation, on the eve of the outbreak of Civil War, between the views of true religion described and attitudes to political developments.

II

From the first years of the century Peterborough, which comprised the counties of Northamptonshire and Rutland, contained two mutually antagonistic groups which subscribed to quite different opinions regarding the nature of true religion. The puritans believed in an activist or 'experimental' brand of predestinarianism which theoretically allowed for the identification of the elect in this life. This theology was the blue-print for a system of practical divinity which emphasised evangelical preaching as the foremost means of drawing out the community of the godly from the mass of the ungodly. This community, which some identified with the visible church, was distinguishable from the rest of society by its acceptance and practice of scriptural values and, most obviously, by its preference for unofficial forms of collective piety – household devotions and private fasts – as well as for a rich diet of sermons.[2] In stark contrast, the proto-Arminians were anti-Calvinists whose ideas represented a deliberate alternative to the divinity described above, unlike those of more conventional conformists like Archbishop Whitgift. For him, disciplinarian conformism was simply a means to bolster political and social stability: it did not possess any religious value. Although a Calvinist by personal belief, this theology was not the basis of his ecclesiastical policy. The Arminians, however, invested conformity with a positive significance. Denying the selective grace of predestination, they emphasised the grace available to all who took part in those ordinances of the Church which were deemed holy – first among which were the sacraments – while denigrating the whole system of divinity organised around evangelical preaching and a personal response to the message of scripture as irrelevant to salvation and socially subversive. The Christian community or visible church was, on this view, defined as all those who expressed outward belief by obedient participation in the worship organised by the Church.[3]

The sources of sponsorship for the clergymen who subscribed to these views were quite different. Unlike the puritans, whose careers revolved around lively preaching ministries which would often include serving their turn at one of the combination lectures at Northampton, Kettering or Daventry, the Arminians' power base was in the Church court structure. Through the patronage of Thomas Dove, bishop of the diocese 1601–30, a group of Arminians belonging to Richard Neile's circle was able to establish itself. Dove appointed John Buckeridge Archdeacon of Northampton but both men tended to leave the responsibility for diocesan government firmly in the hands of their deputies, Richard Butler and later John Lambe; these men quickly put themselves at the head of an Arminian party which included David Owen and Robert Sibthorpe. This common religious allegiance was perhaps the result of shared experiences at university. From the later sixteenth century onwards the higher Peterborough diocesan officials tended to be clients of Lord Burghley, who lived near the cathedral town, and graduates of his college of St John's, Cambridge. Here, during the Calvinist mastership of William Whitaker (1587–95), a conformist group had developed among the fellows. Neile, himself a client of Burghley's son, the Earl of Salisbury, had been a friend and contemporary there of Lambe and Butler at a time when, after the death of Whitaker, an anti-Calvinist reaction was taking place. Two of the deans of Peterborough in this period – John Palmer and Richard Clayton – were Burghley clients who had opposed Whitaker, and Clayton, as Master of the college after Whitaker, brought conformists back into favour. Other Peterborough Arminians connected to

St John's include Francis Dee (bishop in 1634), who attended after Whitaker's death, and William Beale, a Church court officer who was an Arminian Master of the college after 1634. The Arminians did not have the same access enjoyed by the Calvinists to the vast stock of lay-controlled patronage of benefices; this varied from the single benefices owned by the multitude of puritan gentry in the upland communities of south-west Northamptonshire to the sponsorship of magnate dynasties in the north of the diocese. They were forced to rely instead on patronage from within the hierarchy (Lambe, Neile and other sympathetic bishops such as William Laud), although significant penetration of patronage came only through their increased influence at court in the late 1620s, when they achieved greater access to the mass of royal patronage. Where lay patronage of Arminians did occur it tended to come from men connected to the court; hence the support of the Comptons, Earls of Northampton, for David Owen, John Towers (bishop in 1639) and Peter Hausted. The Arminians were similarly reliant on court contacts, as we shall see, when it came to political survival.[4]

Ample evidence has been adduced to prove the domination of the Jacobean Church by formal Calvinist doctrine, and this fact muted the Arminian challenge. Controversy arose not over predestination but over the no less crucial matters of public worship and the status of Sunday. The ambiguity of James I's policies meant that he gave active support to moderate Calvinists and also (later in his reign) to Arminians, both of whose services he required at various times. As we shall see, the hostility between Arminians and puritans was difficult to pacify even during the reign of a king dedicated to containing them both within a unified Church.

III

The first visible division came at the beginning of James's reign, when the puritans revived their political demands for a further reformation of the Church. The campaign was coordinated by the London minister, Stephen Egerton, but Northamptonshire clergymen played an active part, in 1603 petitioning James I for a reformation 'according to the rule of God's holy word' to restore 'the doctrine and discipline' of Christ. The puritans envisaged a partnership of gentry and clergy to promote, by political means, a programme of reform which had both positive and negative aspects. The first involved the creation of a godly preaching ministry by the provision of a 'Moses in every parish'. In tandem with this, there was to be a sweeping away of the remnants of popery, especially of such practices as the use of the sign of the cross in baptism and the wearing of the surplice. Such usages were to be abolished or, at least, not enforced as compulsory.[5]

The strength of the Northamptonshire campaign was reinforced by Bishop Dove's appointment as his deputy of the proto-Arminian, Richard Butler, a man who seemed to embody the puritans' fears for the doctrine and discipline of the Church. Butler's divinity was anti-Calvinist: in 1610 he preached a court sermon against justification by faith alone which was condemned as popish even by Archbishop Bancroft. Predestined grace was replaced by that conferred by the sacraments, and Butler was on record as having stated the necessity of baptism to salvation. Furthermore, he joined with his fellow Church court official, David Owen, in presenting for preaching false doctrine Thomas Randleson, Owen's purtian nonconformist curate, who had preached at one baptism that 'though baptism was necessary yet it was not necessary unto salvation, that they were popish preachers that taught that children were not ordinarily saved without baptism'. If this commitment to the positive, religious value of conformity was a hallmark of Arminianism, so also was the definition of the visible church as those participating in its worship. Accordingly, Butler attempted in 1603 to enforce as compulsory a wide range of Prayer Book ceremonies, many of which the puritans deemed popish, in what his enemies claimed was the most stringent enforcement of conformity since before the Reformation. Ministers were threatened with suspension from their livings if they did not use the sign of the cross in baptism, always use the surplice, order their congregations to receive the communion kneeling (and do so themselves) and practise the churching of women after childbirth. As a result of Butler's initiative many ministers were harassed for nonconformity, including his old enemy, Robert Catelin, vicar of All Saints' parish, Northampton. In response Catelin, a key figure in the local puritan campaign, wrote to Stephen Egerton proposing that the puritans demand the opportunity to convince the bishop that the views of his deputy were erroneous. Failing this, a disputation between the parties was to be arranged, the outcome of which was to be decided by mutually agreed moderators. If it was concluded that Butler's doctrine was indeed erroneous and popish, then he should be removed from his position in the Church courts and deprived of his benefice.[6]

No such opportunity was forthcoming and in 1604 Butler's drive for conformity received official backing in the form of a royal order that ceremonial conformity be everywhere enforced. The crisis which followed is eloquent testimony to the way in which James I's policy allowed two such mutually contradictory and hostile elements to flourish within the same Church. On the one hand, the king gave orders to deprive only immovably radical puritans, who both refused to conform and to subscribe to all three of Whitgift's Articles of 1583, while holding out the prospect of preferment to moderates who would renounce presbyterianism and conform. Dove obeyed the order to allow nonconformists time to discuss their scruples by holding a public disputation at Peterborough in which he claimed to have persuaded many of the 'factious ministers' to conform. The Church court records confirm that, although twenty-nine ministers were suspended, thirteen were not deprived, of which at least eight were allowed to escape with a very open-ended promise to discuss their objections. That sixteen still resisted until deprivation (eighteen percent of the national total and more than in any other diocese) is suggestive not only of the strength of puritanism in the area but also of the perceived immediacy of the threat of Arminianism there.[7]

The ambiguity of James's policy is revealed in his response to the aftermath of the crisis. The puritan J.P.s – Sir Edward Montagu, Sir Richard and Sir Valentine Knightley – presented to the king and council a petition signed by forty-five Northamptonshire gentlemen begging that the deprivation of the ministers, all of whom were 'faithful preachers' who had 'confuted papism, repressed Brownism' and 'beaten down sin and impiety powerfully', be reversed. The response reflects James's susceptibility to an identification of radical puritan nonconformity with presbyterianism and a threat to his throne. In James's eyes the petition was tantamount to rebellion. Refusing to submit, Montagu was removed from the commission of the peace, as was Sir Francis Hastings who had drawn up the petition, the lord chancellor describing it as 'mutinous, seditious, malicious, factious, tending to rebellion by the combination of many hands against law'. A letter from John Lambe to Richard Neile only days after the petitioners' punishment is revealing of the way

Arminians shored up their own position by both stressing their own obedience and playing on the king's fears of puritan extremism. Lambe dismissed current rumours in Northampton, which predicted a St Bartholomew's type massacre by papists, as the attempts of puritan agitators to whip up further disobedience and nonconformity among the lower orders. In this way, claimed Lambe, the 'simple puritan' was convinced that 'he stands alone against the cruelty of the papists, for God, for religion and for his own life'. In contrast to the authorities in most other dioceses Butler, as Archdeacon of Northampton 1611–12 and Lambe, as chancellor of the diocese after 1615, repeatedly tried to resurrect conformity as an issue. James's continued dislike of puritan nonconformity allowed Butler in 1611 to pursue his old enemy, Robert Catelin, who had escaped deprivation in 1605 through the support of the Corporation of Northampton. In 1614 Catelin was again in trouble with the king, probably reported this time by Neile. Dove was informed that James wished Catelin to use 'perpetual conformity, that the people of that town may no longer be borne with in their refractory disposition'.[8] At times like these the Arminians could still utilise the king's hostility towards nonconformity, but it was to be the 1630s before the necessary royal backing was forthcoming to really make conformity the issue.

The second major religious division of the reign became visible over the subject of the sabbath. John Lambe was chancellor of the diocese after 1615, Bishop Dove having retreated into retirement after the crisis of 1604–5, and from the first it was clear he opposed the traditional idea of a Sunday sabbath. The issue again revealed the two quite different views of religion held by Arminians and puritans. The Arminian policy was intended to enforce respect for the feast days commanded by the holy Church and, once more, to emphasise the positive religious value of its worship. This aim dictated what was permissible on the holy days. Thus, parishioners were presented for any activity which prevented their attendance at prayers. In 1616 Lambe complained of the desuetude of the Christmas holiday by puritans at Northampton: 'where the holidays are most neglected, and so much so that on Christmas Day last, myself saw 1000 at the sermon at the great church of All Saints in the forenoon and not 40 at divine service in the afternoon. And on St. Thomas day last, 100 or 200 shops were kept open and few or none at church'. Lambe pursued one 'puritan' shopkeeper in particular for opening on Christmas Day and angrily described the man's entrance into church 'in all his old clothes, and a very foul band, all dirty and in most sordid manner, of purpose in scorn and disgrace of that feast'.[9]

In contrast, the puritans subscribed to the notion of a Sunday sabbath which was scriptural in origin, while ignoring saints' days, which many regarded as too reminiscent of popery. The sabbath was central to the puritan world-view in that the observance thereof – either by private individuals or by godly magistrates ordering its usage – was regarded as virtually infallible proof of one's elect status. Accordingly, Robert Bolton, a client of Sir Edward Montagu, laid odds of 'a thousand to one, a constant keeper of the sabbath is sound-hearted towards God: and as great odds, a common sabbath-breaker [is] a stranger to the power of grace'. Sunday was regarded as the sharpest focus for that process of the formation of a community of true believers separate from the world. On that day, more than on any other, the professor displayed his calling by refusing the sinful blandishments of conventional sociability and engaging instead in the holy ordinances of sermon-hearing, praying and conversing with the other saints. This was the message of *The Society of Saints* (1630), a collection of sermons by Sir Edward Montagu's chaplain, Joseph Bentham, some of which were preached in the 1620s. Here Bentham supported the sabbatarian position that the entire day be kept free of all but godly activities but especially of sports and dances, which were inherently sinful: 'where lawful labours and profitable works are forbidden as unlawful, there lustful and wanton actions of sports and delights much more ... which are never so strictly commanded only sparingly permitted'. In short, the issue of the sabbath revealed, once more, the two differing attitudes towards the Christian community either as an inclusive body based on participation in public worship or as an exclusive grouping of proven true believers.[10]

This was the background to the issue in 1618 of the so-called Book of Sports, which legalised most pastimes (except bear baiting and plays) so long as they followed evening prayers. The intention of the king may have been to create peace by means of a compromise between the views of Catholics, who wished to indulge in sports, and zealous protestants, who supported a twenty-four hour sabbath. In Peterborough the effect was just the opposite of what was intended. The issue of the declaration sparked off a dispute between the puritans and their enemies: in the Northampton parish where the Arminian, Robert Sibthorpe, was vicar, one puritan woman was presented for scolding some youths she caught practising sports with the words 'they might choose whether the king should hang them for not obeying him or the devil burn them for so breaking the sabbath' and for going on to say about the Book that 'she does not think it lawful, let others do what they list'.[11]

The clearest division came when puritan J.P.s led by Sir Edward Montagu and Sir Thomas Brooke reacted against the sudden proliferation of festive events caused by the Book's issue. In July 1618 they wrote to the constables of Grafton Underwood, whose town feast was imminent, stressing the sabbatarian part of the Book (that they present those who used recreations before the end of prayers) and invoking the clause which stated that, when prayers were over, parishioners were to retire to their own parishes to use such recreations or be punished as rogues. By this the justices were referring to a group of musicians who had already been sent for from nearby parishes. Lastly, the unlicensed selling of ale was forbidden. The conformist attitude found its champion in John Williams, parson of the town who, although a Calvinist in doctrine, was for the moment an ally of the Arminians. The patron of John Lambe and the client of Lord Keeper Bacon, Williams had recently become a J.P. of the *quorum*. He was a supporter of Sunday sports who had campaigned for them at court in the previous year with Bishop Richard Neile. Sending for Montagu's warrant, he publicly contradicted it in the churchyard. He allowed the music and the selling of unlicensed ale to go ahead and taunted the puritan J.P.s: 'am I not justice of the peace of the *quorum*, doctor and parson of the town? Therefore never a precise justice of them all shall have anything to do in my town without me'. By this stage the dispute had become a *cause célèbre*; as one observer wrote, 'all men's mouths are full of it'. Northamptonshire opinion divided along factional lines: Sir Thomas Crewe, Sir John Pickering and Sir Arthur Throckmorton expressed support for Montagu. Williams's friend, Sir Francis Fane, who was trying to set up an alternative faction among the gentry to the godly clique that dominated county politics, joined Sir John Isham in backing the conformist position. Despite solid local gentry support, and the backing of the assize judges, Montagu and his followers failed to perceive the sympathy at court for Williams's actions. Throckmorton wrote to Montagu asserting that

Williams would gain little credit for his opposition to them 'wherein it had been meeter for his ministry rather to have suffered'. Events showed them to be mistaken. Montagu's overtures to his brother Henry and to Attorney General Sir Henry Yelverton (a puritan neighbour) yielded little result and he found Sir Henry Hobart, judge of common pleas, 'but cold in it'. All this is suggestive of the atmosphere at court; despite all Montagu's efforts nothing further was heard of the puritans' attempts to impose their own interpretation on the Book of Sports, and Williams's views seem to have carried the day.[12]

The result of royal policy was to stir up factionalism between the existing religious groupings in the diocese. However, in the absence of any unequivocal royal sponsorship of the Arminians, the Calvinists were able to organise and articulate effective opposition to the policies of Lambe and Williams. In 1616 members of the Corporation of Northampton, who had been harassed by Lambe over nonconformity as well as the question of the sabbath, gained Sir Edward Montagu's aid in forwarding a list of complaints against the chancellor to the assize judge, Sir Edward Coke. According to his biographer, it was John Williams who saved Lambe by referring the charges to himself and by prevailing on his contacts at Cambridge University to grant Lambe a doctorate. Having been thus foiled, the aldermen (again with Montagu's support) submitted a list of grievances, charging Lambe with persecuting them in the Church courts over the Christmas holidays and other matters, to the 1621 Parliament. Again, Williams (now lord keeper) stepped in to save Lambe by persuading Sir Edward Sackville, chairman of the committee of grievances, to disregard the charges. This does not seem to have been entirely successful, but Williams's intervention ensured Lambe's access to the king who, after reading his letter of self-justification, saved him from his enemies by knighting him. By utilising his court influence Lambe survived, though there was to be no repetition of his policies of 1615–21 in the remainder of his chancellorship to 1629. Yet in terms of policy, if not personnel, Montagu's party won a signal victory; their Sabbath Bill, which forbade sports even after evening prayer, was read in 1621. The early dissolution of that year prevented it from receiving the royal assent, but it became statute in 1625, effectively eclipsing the Book of Sports until 1633.[13]

James I's ecclesiastical policy allowed both of the mutually hostile religious groupings in Peterborough diocese to flourish and, in the case of the Book of Sports, actually excited that hostility. He had won over the vast majority of Calvinist clergy to conformity, but his fear of radical puritanism also permitted the Arminians to survive, especially after the reaction to the Spanish Match in 1621 seemed to confirm his fears. Lambe's self-defence in 1621 was that he was setting about the eradication of puritan disobedience and that his enemies had been 'set . . . on by greater persons in the county that, through me, aim at your majesty's ecclesiastical jurisdiction'. This was the situation as it stood in the diocese when in 1625 James was succeeded by a king who, in contrast, pursued a more partisan ecclesiastical policy.[14]

IV

Not before the 1630s, however, did the promotion of a sympathetic archbishop afford the Peterborough diocesan officials the opportunity to reorientate the Church in an Arminian direction while marginalising the divinity of their enemies. Mirroring the national changes, the 1630s saw the promotion of more active Arminian incumbents to the see of Peterborough after Dove's death in 1630. William Piers (1630–2) and Augustine Lindsell (1633) were cautious in their approach but Francis Dee (1634–8) and John Towers (1639–49) embarked on a radical programme of liturgical and ecclesiological reorganisation. Lambe was no longer chancellor of the diocese after 1629 but he kept in close contact with his old colleagues as a high commissioner and as dean of the Court of Arches, the most important appellate court in the southern archdiocese.

The concept of a holy visible church, and of a Christian community defined as participation in the sacraments of that Church, is concisely expressed in the writing of the Peterborough Arminian, John Pocklington. What, according to him, distinguished the community of true Christians from heretics was that 'those had churches and places of abode, but these had none, but were stragglers and had their communion in corners . . . the eucharist cannot be received among heretics for the elements must be consecrated . . . this heretics could not do, because they had neither altar nor church'. The visible church was invested with a positive holiness by dint of its continuation of the Church of the apostles. This holiness resided in the hierarchy and was conferred upon the altar, or the church itself, by the ceremony of consecration. Such ideas were behind Bishop Dee's visitation article ordering all to bow when entering or leaving church, and behind his and Bishop Towers' articles forbidding profanation of the church yard (which their deputies described as 'so holy a place') by any secular activity whatsoever. If God was more present in a consecrated church than in the outside world, he was most present at the altar, especially during the sacraments. Pocklington described the railed-in area around the altar as the *'sanctum sanctorum'* and the altar itself as worthy of reverence 'in regard to the presence of our saviour, whose chair of state it is upon earth'. This vision of a sacrament-centred divinity involved an increased emphasis on the sacerdotal rather than the preaching role of the clergy. Only priests, wrote Pocklington, could enter the 'holy of holies' and receive the sacrament there. Laymen were forbidden, and this included the king. A perceived divine immanence in this part of the church is also displayed in Sibthorpe's remark, made at All Saints, Northampton, after removing seats which stood further to the east than the communion table, that 'it was not fit that any sit above God almighty'. These views lay behind the elaborate reverence famously shown to church and altar by the Arminians. Peter Hausted's parishioners claimed he 'bowed almost down to the ground at his entering the chancel, and again in the middle thereof and when he comes to the first of the three steps which ascends up to the altar, and bows in the like manner three several times . . . at his returning'. A renewed stress was also placed on the necessity of that other crucial sacrament, baptism. Bishops Piers and Lindsell ordered that there be no delay in baptising sick children. Lindsell forbade the puritan practice of baptising in bowls and Dee followed this up by ordering fonts to be repaired, which were 'always' to be used and basins 'never'.[15] The task facing the Arminians was to create the holy altars and churches which were so crucial to their ideal of a true church.

In his 1634 visitation articles (which are the earliest example of their type yet discovered) Dee ruled that tables be 'placed conveniently at the east end of the chancel' and 'cancelled in'. By ordering that tables stand thus permanently, Dee was making a clean break with former injunctions on the subject, which envisaged a table placed anywhere in the church for communion. The policy was not followed in isolation. The bishop probably took his cue from Archbishop Laud's similar instruction for his metropolitical visitation in the same year which was, in turn, based on the 1633 precedent of the Privy Council's ruling regarding the parish of St Gregory in London. Despite Dee's enthusiasm, the enforcement of the policy depended on the willingness of local churchwardens to report faults; as a result enforcement was sporadic before 1637.[16]

In that year Dee ordered that the altar, and the ceremonies associated with it, be placed at the centre of parochial observance. He commissioned a survey of parishes in the western half of the diocese, which was carried out by hand-chosen officials led by Robert Sibthorpe and Samuel Clarke. A railed altar was to be created in every parish; every minister was to administer the communion at the rails and every parishioner was to receive there, kneeling. It was urged that ministers celebrate communion more often; communion at monthly intervals was recommended. Bishop Towers placed these requirements in his printed visitation articles of 1639. The mechanism of the survey permitted the authorities a far greater efficiency in the detection of faults but the crucial element in the success of the altar policy in the diocese was their control of the central courts. When the churchwardens of All Saints', Northampton refused to rail the communion table, Samuel Clarke excommunicated them. Lambe, as dean of the Court of Arches, supported Clarke's verdict and even though the Court of Delegates overturned Clarke's judgement, Lambe and Clarke still forced the wardens to comply by pursuing a case against them in the court of High Commission. This was to become a familiar pattern. Charles Chauncy was pursued by Laud and High Commission from a Hertfordshire benefice to his living of Marston St Lawrence in Northamptonshire. In both places he refused to set the communion table altarwise and was accordingly suspended from his office in 1634. Chauncy, a client of the puritan magnate, Viscount Saye and Sele, promised Laud to conform but he was never comfortable and emigrated to New England shortly afterwards. Ministers who refused to practise the new type of communion, like Thomas Ball of All Saints' Northampton, and Miles Burkit of Pattishall, were also punished. Burkit was charged in High Commission with encouraging his churchwardens to remove the table from the rails at the Easter communion, the most important of the year, and for refusing to bow towards the altar when Jesus's name was mentioned in the service. As a result, he was suspended from practising his office in 1638 and not reinstated until 1640 despite signing a promise to Lambe of conformity in the future. Pressure like this was able to overcome even puritan recalcitrance, and contributed to Dee's success in altar creation. A failure rate of thirty per cent (in the more puritan half of the diocese) compared favourably with one of seventy for William Piers's diocese of Bath and Wells for the previous year.[17]

The church restoration campaign was intended to make holy altars and churches reflect their potent holiness, and that of the sacraments performed there, and to enforce conformity to an ordered and uniform practice of worship. Examples of clerical enthusiasm for the concept of the 'beauty of holiness' include Robert Sibthorpe's hiring a painter to adorn the altar rails with gold stars at his parish of Burton Latimer, and Richard Crompton's creation of a railed stone altar at St Sepulchre in Northampton. The clearest example of laymen subscribing to such notions is that of Sir Robert Bannastre, father-in-law of the Arminian, Lord William Maynard, and a member of the board of the green cloth under James I. After 1626 he set about restoring his parish church of Passenham. The interior walls were painted with the figures of the prophets and evangelists. Most significant, however, were the portrayals of Nicodemus and Joseph of Arimathaea which flanked the altar. The clear purpose was to focus the attention from the forerunners of Christ to His spiritual presence at the altar itself. To reflect the holiness of the sacraments, communion utensils were upgraded. Dee ordered that every parish buy a silver plate for the bread and a silver chalice from which to drink the wine. The survey showed that this ran clean contrary to current practice which was simply to use any jugs, bottles and plates which came to hand. Lastly, the survey of 1637 reflected the Arminians' obsession with order. Pages of minutely detailed instructions stipulated three feet as the standard height for every pew in the diocese. This involved the cutting down of at least one hundred and twenty high pews owned by the aristocracy and gentry, which was the cause of much resentment. Chancels were cleared of seats and pews arranged in neat rows pointing towards the east end of the church. Order was thereby added to uniformity in worship and the parish church was to become the Arminian paradigm of a properly organised kingdom.[18]

The Arminians' enjoyment of powerful support in the 1630s made possible the imposition of the ceremonial observances at the core of their practical divinity. Yet, even in this decade, committed

Arminians, with their well-known antipathy to preaching as well as to the more obvious forms of puritan religiosity, were a small minority when compared with the mass of evangelical Calvinists, who had formed the backbone of the Jacobean Church. This predicament still made a head-on confrontation with predestination and evangelical divinity unfeasible. Furthermore, it was unnecessary, since the existence of a basic agreement on the essentials of Calvinist doctrine did not imply a homogeneity of opinion on the relevance and application of that doctrine. The Arminians knew that by preventing predestination itself from becoming the issue, they could use the legitimacy provided by their official backing to divide the Calvinist ranks over the issue of conformity. The re-issue of the Book of Sports in 1633 is a clear instance of this. There was great support for the Sunday sabbath in Northamptonshire, as we have seen in 1618, and if the estimation of Nicholas Estwick, Lord Montagu's chaplain, was accurate, then nearly twenty per cent of the ministers in the county disliked the Book. Significantly, this level of opposition did not materialise – only eight ministers openly refused to read it. The virtue of the Book was no longer the question; royal backing made the issue whether the Book's offence to religion was serious enough to warrant disobedience to royal authority.[19]

In return for conformity, ministers who maintained silence on the subject of predestination, in line with the various royal orders to that effect, would be allowed to enjoy freedom to preach, albeit a form of preaching now firmly subordinated to the set forms of public worship. Thus the authorities were able to push the Church in a more Arminian direction, while gaining a measure of support for their policies. Bishop Piers in 1631 restricted the personnel of the Kettering lecture to a list of ministers approved by himself, a list headed by Sibthorpe. Lecturers were to read morning service in surplice and hood before their sermon, and were to avoid controversial subjects in line with the royal orders. 'Inconformable factious strangers' were barred. This was probably an attempt to win over the moderate puritan, Edward, Lord Montagu, who was the chief sponsor of the lecture. Three of the permitted clergy were his clients (one was his chaplain, Joseph Bentham) and several of the other ministers were moderate Calvinists. The return of unlicensed nonconformists after this date, who preached in opposition to the policies of the 1630s, resulted in the lecture's disestablishment at some time prior to 1636. Dee wrote to Montagu denying any part in the event and he may indeed have regretted offending moderate opinion. The policy met with less success when it was applied to the Northampton lecture. Charles I's instructions of 1633 restricted the personnel of such lectures to orthodox, local divines and yet Robert Woodford's diary clearly illustrates that such vocal dissenters from the Laudian regime as James Cranford and William Castle were openly preaching in the period 1637–40. The reason for the lecture's escaping Kettering's fate would seem to be that the Corporation, which sponsored the lecture, had hoodwinked the authorities into believing that it was read only by the vicar, Thomas Ball. Ball was himself a vocal opponent of Laudianism, and was punished in 1634 for broaching forbidden matters in his sermons. The impression is that the other aspect of the 1629 orders, the conversion of afternoon sermons to catechism classes, was more often obeyed. At first, nonconformist ministers like Miles Burkit or Charles Chauncy were presented for using the wrong catechism or for preaching after catechising, but refusal to catechise was rare. By 1639 Towers, with Laud's approval, was allowing ministers to preach after their classes so long as they preached on the same subjects raised by the catechism.[20]

Dee and Towers both made efforts to appeal to moderate Calvinist opinion. Dee invited Edward Reynolds, a moderate with wide godly connections, to preach the sermon at Daventry in the course of his second triennial visitation. Reynolds urged his clerical audience, for the sake of their flocks, to refrain from discussing predestination and to use ceremonial conformity at all times. The most comprehensively conformist lecture was to be erected on the orders of Sir John Lambe and Bishop Towers in 1639 at Brackley, where Sibthorpe was the incumbent. The mayor and aldermen seem to have held conformist views. They supported Sibthorpe in his opposition to the sabbatarian zeal of the local J.P. John Crewe, who tried to expel a group of musicians from the town as vagrants. At the same time, they wished to enjoy the variety of sermons provided by a combination lecture. Like Piers, Towers allowed them to do so by erecting a combination of fifteen preachers approved by himself (headed by Sibthorpe), but Towers' proposal was more structured to subordinate preaching to praying. Before the sermon the lecturer was obliged to read the morning service and the communion service (this latter at the communion table); both were to be performed in surplice and hood. After the sermon (which was not to exceed one hour) the minister was to return to the communion table to read one or two of the collects and then bless and dismiss the congregation, who were to observe full ceremonial conformity throughout. There can be no clearer indication of the role accorded preaching by the Arminians. Nevertheless, it was successful in answering moderate demand for preaching while excluding the enemies of the Arminians from the pulpit.[21]

The Arminians' obsession with uniformity and obedience in religion had a clear counterpart in the 'new counsels' which came to the fore at court in the later 1620s. Robert Sibthorpe's underpinning of the absolutist notions behind the Forced Loan of 1627 is well known; above all he stressed the subject's duty to pay exactions levied by a divine-right monarch. Samuel Clarke, his colleague in the Church courts, was active in the collection of this prerogative tax. The nonconformist puritan threat to true religion was, in these men's eyes, matched by the secular puritan threat to the monarchy. In the 1630s Sibthorpe regarded all resistance to prerogative measures, such as the Ship Money tax, as the symptoms of a puritan conspiracy to overthrow the crown. As with the religious issue, the Arminians used the direct involvement of royal authority to divide opinion. Sibthorpe brought a Star Chamber suit against Thomas Bacon, lord of the manor at his parish, accusing him of conspiring with other 'English puritans' such as Richard Knightley and the sheriff, Sir John Dryden, to sabotage the Ship Money levy. One local clergyman, Thomas Harrison, made similar allegations against Sir Richard Hutton shortly after his verdict in favour of John Hampden. Harrison, who was presented to his living by Archbishop Laud, accused Hutton of treason for this verdict, stating that the orthodox opinion was that 'whatsoever the king in his conscience may require, we ought to yield'. He was heavily punished, but his actions at least indicate what sort of opinions were perceived as orthodox at this time. Finally, Sibthorpe's view of the Scottish resistance to the attempted royal imposition of a new Prayer Book as the culmination of a puritan conspiracy, chimes well with the official attitude expressed by Charles in a proclamation of 1639, which denounced the Scots as traitors to the crown. Sibthorpe wrote to Lambe that he hoped the rumours of peace proved true 'for otherwise I and such as I am (that I may not say you) must expect little peace . . . if *Bellum Episcopale* as they say some style it

be not ended, and *Rebellio Puritanica* for so I know it may be truly
styled, be not subdued'.[22]

V

The Arminians' official backing in the 1630s altered the reaction of
non-Arminians to these policies and enabled the authorities to
divide the Calvinist ranks on the issue of conformity. As in James's
reign, the subjects of ceremonies and the sabbath revealed fundamentally different ideas about the nature and role of the visible
church. There was a consensus among moderate and radical Calvinists that the public worship and festivals of the Church, which were
basically pre-Reformation in character, were devoid of any positive
religious significance and might therefore be left up to the Church
itself, whose role was perceived negatively, as the organiser of non-
essentials. However, to the radicals the Arminians' enforcement of
these irrelevant practices as compulsory undermined predestination
by implying the necessity to salvation of the worship ordered by a
holy church. The holiness accorded the church and its sacraments
usurped the holiness of the visible saints: 'when God's people meet
together in any place, He is spiritually present with them not with
respect to the place, but to the persons'. This comment was made
by Daniel Cawdrey, vicar of Great Billing, in his reply to the
Arminian apology of John Pocklington. He went on to denounce
the Arminian concept of a holy visible church. That the 'power of
dispensing grace is in the Church's consecration' was 'manifestly
false'; after the communion the 'consecrated elements lose their
holiness and return to their common nature and use, much more
does the table lose its holiness, if it had any'. Hence also the
comments of the puritan diarist, Robert Woodford, who described
Laudian ceremony as 'popery, idolatry, superstition and profaneness' and who prayed that God would bring down those divines
who sought to 'defile thy ordinances with base human inventions'.
Cawdrey also denounced the holiness invested in the Church's feast
days, which almost 'thrust out the holiness of the Lord's Day'.
Ministers who held such views tended to refuse to conform in the
1630s. Cawdrey, Thomas Ball, Andrew Perne and John Baynard
were all preaching that popery was spreading throughout the land;
furthermore, Cawdrey, Ball and Charles Chauncy refused to

celebrate the communion at the altar rails, and a petition circulated among the clergy of the Wellingborough area in support of this nonconformity. In addition, Ball, Perne and Baynard refused to read the Book of Sports. Sir Richard Samwell is a rare case of a member of the gentry being accused of favouring nonconformity; he was charged in High Commission with inciting the disobedience of the churchwardens of his parish to the altar policy. Resistance came to a head in 1639 when J.P.s meeting at the Assizes publicly condemned the primary visitation articles of Bishop Towers, which were the first printed articles for the diocese ordering all parishioners to receive the communion at the altar rails.[23]

The authority behind the policies of the 1630s caused moderate Calvinists, such as the group of clerics associated with Edward, Lord Montagu, to draw away from their more radical colleagues. Such men included Joseph Bentham and Nicholas Estwick, who were Montagu's clients and among the clergy licensed by Bishop Piers to preach at Kettering after 1631 and Edward Reynolds, who enjoyed a variety of Calvinist contacts. Conformity was justified by the indifferent nature of the ceremonies, which might therefore be practised without scruple. These men subscribed to a highly deferential notion of order, in which dissent by the socially inferior was regarded as placing the whole social fabric in danger, a view which was quite different from that of the radicals for whom such a concept of order was meaningless in a society where popery was so rampant. Similar moderate attitudes emerged over the re-issue of the Book of Sports in 1633. Even to moderates the sabbath, unlike ceremonies, was not an indifferent matter. The king's direct authorising of the Book, however, obliged every minister to obey. Nicholas Estwick wrote to Samuel Ward, the moderate Calvinist Master of Sidney Sussex College, Cambridge, who supported his opinion that ministers might read the Book while secretly reserving the right to regard its contents as unlawful: 'if men cannot publish anything without sin, which pleases not themselves, I suppose this scrupulosity would lay the foundation of disorder and confusion both in the Church and commonwealth'.[24]

In this dispute between moderate and radical Calvinists over concepts of order, the issue of predestination was almost irrelevant. Even on the moderate side ministers disagreed over the importance of the doctrine. Joseph Bentham was an evangelical Calvinist who, even in 1635, published overtly predestinarian sermons aimed at creating a division between the visibly godly and ungodly. And yet on the subject of conformity he took the same line as Reynolds, for whom predestination was clearly a secondary doctrine. In his visitation address Reynolds accepted the Arminian desire for silence on the subject on the grounds that while agreement persisted on 'fundamental truths' ministers ought to 'silence our disputes in matters merely notional and curious, which have no necessary influence into faith and godly living'.[25]

Religious affairs cannot be explored in a vacuum as distinct from other political developments, since the issue of conformity played a significant role in deciding political allegiance on the eve of the outbreak of Civil War. In Northamptonshire resistance to prerogative taxation tended to be identified with puritanism and support for the thesis of the Grand Remonstrance of 1641, which described the history of the previous sixteen years in terms of a gradually unfolding popish plot to undermine true religion and the liberties of the subject as protected by free Parliaments. The Northamptonshire petition in support of the Remonstrance was headed by Francis Nicolls and John Sawyer who had been pursued by Sir John Lambe for instigating a private fast at Kettering in support of the Scots and in opposition to the new, more conformist canons of 1640. A host of puritan clergy, including Thomas Ball and Daniel Cawdrey, had attended. Nicolls and Ball had both resisted payment of the Forced Loan. The list also included Richard Knightley who (like his father) was associated with the Parliamentary group of John Pym, which had been warning of a popish threat to Church and state since the later 1620s. Knightley senior had refused to pay the loan and had been accused of conspiring to hinder the Ship Money tax. Religious nonconformists like Sir Richard Samwell and George Catesby refused to pay the Loan and Catesby also rejected demands for Ship Money. The complete popish conspiracy theory was also held by men of lesser social status like Robert Woodford who, by the later 1630s, was playing the blame firmly on the shoulders of Laud, the bishops and the court and even describing Charles I as 'unconverted' to true religion.[26] This conspiracy theory was the opposite pole to the Arminian notion of an anti-monarchical conspiracy by puritans and the lower orders, which Charles must crush. Espousing this thesis with particular intensity, the radical Calvinists were able (after 1640) to carry along more moderate parliamentary opinion to banish the machinery of prerogative rule and eventually to abolish episcopacy and raise arms against Charles. Conversely, many moderate Calvinists, such as Montagu and the clerical circle patronised by him, were prepared to trust Charles's initial concessions as genuine and regarded further questioning of royal motives by the lower orders as seditious. It was the issue of order raised by the implications of nonconformity to the policies of the late 1620s onwards – both secular and religious – which separated Montagu the royalist from his erstwhile puritan colleagues, who became Parliamentarians.

VI

The evidence for Peterborough diocese tends to argue against the concept of a Jacobean tranquillity shattered only by the meteoric rise of a novel Arminianism after 1625. It also contradicts any simplistic notion of a Calvinist consensus based on a common adherence to the predestinarian theology of grace. Arminianism was the theological right wing of a broader range of divinity practised generally by men with predestinarian views, but who accorded that theology a varying degree of relevance for their practical churchmanship. Committed Arminians might be in a minority, but there clearly existed a conformist constituency which shared their fears of puritan populism. Arminians co-existed within the Jacobean Church with a variety of conformist divines as well as with puritan enemies whose ideas for the further reformation of the Church were diametrically opposed to their own. A longer perspective seems possible on the religious causes of the Civil War. The disestablishment of the institutional Church in the 1640s and the purge of ungodly ministers now appears as the logical escalation of the conflict between Arminians and puritans which had begun in 1603 with the latter's attempts to expel Richard Butler. This is not to remove all significance from the succession of Charles I, but rather to trace the conflict back to the tentatively balanced heterogeneity of the Jacobean Church. It was difficult enough to maintain ecclesiastical peace in the reign of a king who was dedicated to preserving the various religious elements within a unified Church, but whose own policies did not always produce the intended effect. In the reign of his more partisan son, who was not so impartial, it proved impossible.

5. 'By this Book': Parishioners, the Prayer Book and the Established Church

JUDITH MALTBY

> Moreover, by this book are priests to administer the sacraments, by this book to church their women, by this book to visit and housle the sick, by this book to bury the dead, by this book to keep their rogation, to say certain psalms and prayers over the corn and grass, certain gospels at crossways, etc. This book is good at all assaies [on every occasion]; it is the only book of the world.
>
> Henry Barrow, *A Brief Discoverie*, 1590.[1]

I

The protestant separatist Henry Barrow, assessing the religious health of the people after the Reformation, censured English parishioners for their over-attachment to the rites and ceremonies of the reformed Church of England. Historians, by contrast, have largely ignored the conformist element within the established Church. A generation of local studies inspired by Patrick Collinson's magisterial *Elizabethan Puritan Movement* (1967) have concentrated on those who failed to conform to the national Church, including Roman Catholics and protestant separatists, but above all on nonconformist puritans who remained within the Church but refused to conform to many of its lawful practices. No doubt this is primarily a matter of sources: as John Morrill has rightly commented, 'religious commitment is best observed in conditions of persecution'. In the all too elusive world of the early Stuart parish, individuals who failed to conform and were prosecuted for it, left behind more evidence of their activities than those who did conform. But a less respectable reason may also be suggested. Much of the work on religion at the local level rests on the belief that nonconformists took their faith more seriously than men and women who conformed to the lawful worship of the Church of England. It is not the intention here to challenge the view that puritanism is best understood as an active and legitimate strand within the established Church, but rather to endorse it. Such a view provides the necessary corrective to the 'Anglican vs. puritan' antithesis which has so bedevilled our understanding of early modern English Christianity. Rather, the assumption challenged here is that 'puritanism' had a monopoly on all that could be considered genuine, vigorous or successful in the Church of England: the flattering view that the godly present of themselves, that 'perception, realistic enough, that as sincere and genuine rather than merely conformable protestants they were thin on the ground'.[2] Identification of 'successful' movements in contemporary Christianity, or in the history of the Church, is a notoriously subjective exercise.

Meanwhile, many social historians, following Keith Thomas' *Religion and the Decline of Magic* (1971), hold a general view that conformity had little or no impact on the lives of ordinary people. For the mass of the population, especially the poor, any contest between the underworld of magic and folk religion and Christian orthodoxy led to the latter's quick retreat from the field. England was a society of 'two cultures' – popular and elite – and they were relatively self-contained with little cross-fertilisation. As Keith Wrightson has remarked: 'the truly godly commonly found themselves in a minority. For many of their neighbours church attendance remained a gathering of neighbours rather than an intensely spiritual experience'. Among much social history, as in the field of ecclesiastical history, the verdict of the self-validating 'godly' on the quality of the religious experiences of those outside their fellowship, 'the multitude', has been too readily accepted. Between those interested only in the puritan agenda for the Church, and those assuming the lack of importance of conventional religion in the lives of ordinary women and men, the question of the importance of the conforming majority has scarcely been raised.[3]

An exception must be made for work of Christopher Haigh. He has broken rank with the dominant interest in puritanism and attempted a more integrated view of English Christianity. He has questioned the effectiveness of preaching as the best instrument for inculcating sophisticated protestant theology among the people and drawn our attention to the role of liturgy as a means of imparting, through repeated words and actions, the basic tenets of the reformers. More recently he has argued: 'In some parishes the opponents of the godly were clearly the profane, but those who defended ceremonies against the godly can hardly be called "the ungodly".' Dr Haigh's analysis of 'parish Anglicans' (the term he prefers) takes some far more controversial turns, however. He has suggested that parochial support for the lawful liturgy and cere-monies directed by the rubrics of the Book of Common Prayer should be seen as residing in a constituency abandoned to their fate by the failure of the Roman Catholic mission priests. These men and women are rather unhappily but memorably described by him as the 'spiritual leftovers of Elizabethan England'. The continued authorisation and use of some pre-Reformation practices no more invalidates the label 'protestant' in England than it does for many areas of the Lutheran Reformation where, by Genevan standards of reform, an unjustified number of pre-Reformation ceremonies were retained as well. Dr Haigh, like many of the historians he is critical of, allows 'Geneva' to fix the goal posts of protestantism.

Even more doubtful is his assertion that these 'spiritual leftovers' formed the natural constituency for the controversial Laudian inno-vations of the 1630s. It seems reasonable to conclude that such Prayer Book protestants did provide local backing for drives for liturgical conformity under Archbishops Whitgift and Bancroft, for example. After all, quite often, the fact we know about the presence of nonconformity is due to the diligence of the supporters of the Prayer Book through the presentations they made in ecclesiastical courts. But it shall be argued here that rather than forming a natural constituency for Laudianism, the descendants of these 'spiritual leftovers' helped to provide opposition to Laudian reforms: the policy of Thorough was perceived by them as an attack on parochial Prayer Book protestantism.[4]

II

In 1604 fifteen articles were addressed to Bishop Richard Vaughan of Chester by parishioners at Manchester against their curate Ralph Kirk. Among other charges, it was alleged that Kirk had failed to wear the surplice, use the cross in baptism and administer communion according to the canons. We might be tempted to regard this as simply an example of pressure from the authorities for presentments resulting in a detailed series of accusations. In fact, closer inspection reveals much about the parishioners' own beliefs and concerns. Several of them wanted the sign of the cross to be made over baptised infants and 'pestered' Kirk to do this. So much so, that he started to insult the parents: 'he asketh them whether they will have a black, a red, or blue, or a headless cross and such other contemptuous words'. He was clearly no wit. Others were angry that Kirk had attempted to eliminate lay participation at morning prayer as directed by the Prayer Book.

> For the manner of morning prayer whereas divers of the parish, who have been used to help the parish clerk, to read verse for verse [i.e. to make the responses] with the curate for forty years last past and more. . . . The said Ralph Kirk hath of late times not permitted them to do so.

The parishioners claimed that Kirk had received a special monition from the chancellor of the diocese, ordering him to allow the people to make the accustomed and set responses of the Prayer Book service. Not only did Kirk fail to conform to the order but it would appear that the spark which escalated the conflict to the level of formal legal proceedings was precisely Kirk's behaviour on this point. The collegiate Church at Manchester has been described as a conservative institution; its fellows in particular were slow to adapt to religious changes of the mid-Tudor period. In 1571, one fellow attempted to make the Prayer Book eucharist as much like the pre-Reformation mass as he could. Have we therefore discovered some of Dr Haigh's 'spiritual leftovers'? I think not. The laity were rarely expected to make the Latin responses in the medieval mass; that they should was, for English Christians, an innovation of Archbishop Cranmer's liturgical reforms.[5]

The evidence from Manchester in 1604 of an informed and articu-

late group of conformist laity, demanding worship according to the
Book of Common Prayer and willing to go to law to discipline their
minister, is a pattern we find repeated elsewhere time and again.
It is clear that many parishioners wanted the set order of prayers
observed. William Hieron of Hemingby in Lincolnshire omitted set
prayers and even rejected the idea of them, 'being as he [sees] . . .
them a few dead lines', complained the articles against him presented towards the end of the sixteenth century. In 1602 the churchwardens of Kimcoate, Leicestershire presented their minister for
not reading the whole of the Common Prayer: 'in many things he
breaketh the order of the Church and the Book of Common Prayer'.
Parishioners at Husband's Bosworth wanted the entire Prayer Book
service and complained in 1603 that the curate Mr Hall was not
reading the whole service, which indicates that at least some of the
laity there knew what the order of the service should be. In 1639
parishioners in Tarporley, Cheshire, could tell that their curate
John Jones was omitting the Ten Commandments from the communion service 'and other parts of divine service contrary to law
and to the contentment of your ordinary and scandal of well affected
people'. In fact, not only did some laity know what the order of
service should be, but some of them brought their own books to
follow it in. In 1590 Thomas Daynes, vicar of Flixton in Suffolk
was deprived of his living in the consistory court in a case in which
all the witnesses against him were parishioners. In addition to his
predictable failure to use the sign of the cross in baptism, allow
godparents, wear the surplice, church women, or pray for the queen
as supreme governor of the Church of England, he rebuked his flock
and called them 'papists and atheists' for bringing their Prayer
Books to church in order to see if he was observing the lawful
services. Daynes declared from the pulpit that 'his parishioners
were papists and that they would rather . . . hear mass . . . than to
hear the word of God truly preached'. He reproved his congregation
'for looking in their books' and said 'that they which would have
service said according to the Book of Common Prayer are papists
and atheists'. Knowledge of the liturgy and the desire for it to
be properly performed was not exclusively a concern of pre-
Reformation churchgoers or Roman Catholics.[6]

It is worth considering whether the attitudes revealed in these
cases reflect more accurately the preferences of 'church papists' than
'Prayer Book Anglicans'. Professor Collinson has recently argued for

the former interpretation; that objections to puritan practices came from semi-conforming Catholics as a way presumably to antagonise their godly ministers. The conservatism of the Manchester clergy early in Elizabeth's reign has already been remarked upon. There were, however, numerous presentments for protestant nonconformity in Manchester and its dependent chapelries throughout our period. The choice of a protestant liturgy does seem a curious weapon for 'church papists' to use; early in Elizabeth's reign conservatives in Manchester did their best to undermine the new Prayer Book. The vicar of Flixton, of course, claimed his accusers were papists but we should exercise some restraint in readily accepting his version of events. 'Church papists' who not only attended the parish church but made use of the ecclesiastical courts and owned their own copies of the Book of Common Prayer seem an improbable combination. Smearing one's opponents with the damaging stain of popery, whether sincerely or as a deliberate libel, was hardly unknown in the early seventeenth century. Although he was accused of many things, few historians accept the charge against Archbishop Laud of crypto-popery made by some contemporaries. The Earl of Clarendon's observation that some of the so-called 'Calvinian faction' called 'every man they do not love, papist' is a warning worth bearing in mind.[7]

General support for the lawful liturgy also extended to the central sacramental acts of the Christian religion and its rites of passage. Repeated complaints were voiced about the failure to administer communion. In 1628 the inhabitants of the chapel of Bruera in Cheshire alleged that through the neglect of their minister they were being excluded from the sacramental life of the Church. The sincerity of the chapelry inhabitants about their desire to receive the communion was verified by one Edward Haydocke. He deposed that he had served the cure for many years for an annual stipend of £5. He read divine service and arranged yearly at Easter for another minister in priest's orders to celebrate the eucharist, 'this deponent being but a deacon'. The inhabitants of Bruera chapelry, according to their deacon of many years, *did* repair to receive the sacrament. So their feeling of being deprived seems to be genuine, rather than acting as a pretext to persecute an unpopular local clergyman.[8]

Not only is there evidence that the laity wanted communion services, but they often wanted to communicate themselves and in a certain manner. Feelings could run high on this matter, as Bishop Thomas Morton of Chester observed in 1618, 'some will receive the sacrament at the hands only of the conformable, and some only of unconformable' ministers. Historians of local studies, however, have placed so much emphasis on either the priest who withheld the sacrament from parishioners who knelt, or members of the laity who refused to kneel at all, that the existence of parishioners who insisted on kneeling in the face of clerical criticism has been essentially ignored. William Hieron, for example, had such retrogrades in his flock, who complained that 'he hath refused to minister the communion to such as kneel until he hath lifted them up with his hands and then delivered them the sacrament'. He also railed against those who knelt at the Lord's Prayer. In the early 1640s, the parishioners of Tarporley battled with their rector Nathaniel Lancaster and his curate John Jones, through the Church courts, Quarter Sessions and by petitioning the king and the House of Lords. In their petition to the king, forty-five subscribers complained that Lancaster and Jones:

> called your petitioners dogs . . . in the pulpit who will not be conformable to his orders, nor will he suffer any of the parishioners to receive the communion at the feast of Easter, neither will they according to the ancient order of our Church of England prescribed in the Book of Common Prayer.

Lancaster also used an unlawful catechism and refused to admit any (including adults and especially 'old persons') to communion who refused to be instructed by an unauthorised catechism. When one John Walley petitioned against Lancaster in Quarter Sessions, he lamented the passing of 'many orders and customs which we have had in former times . . . [and are] now taken from us'. One of these customs was receiving at the communion rails: 'the rails before our communion table are cast aside'. It would be mistaken, however, to see this as an expression of 'popular Laudianism' as described by Dr Haigh. A plan for Tarporley Church dating from perhaps 1613 shows that the holy table stood behind rails even then, but was free-standing in the chancel. The distinction between approved rails that had existed before the onset of Laudian innovations and 'popish' rails imposed by the policy of Thorough was one made by contemporaries and endorsed in legal decisions in the House of Lords in the early 1640s.[9]

There is evidence that visiting the sick with communion was still desired after the Reformation. On one occasion a number of parishioners at Hemingby in Lincolnshire sent for Hieron on behalf of a bedridden man who desired 'to reserve the sacrament for the strengthening of his faith'. The vicar responded to this request by saying 'let him live by the strength of the last [communion], I do not mean to make a popish matter of it'. One of the 'many orders and customs which we have in former times' to be taken away by Nathaniel Lancaster at Tarporley, complained layman John Walley, was that there was now 'no visiting of the sick, nor any communion to them.' This was a far cry from what George Herbert advised in ministering to the sick or distressed. The country parson 'fails not to afford his best comforts, and rather goes to them than sends for the afflicted, though they can, and otherwise ought to come to him'. In ministering to the sick, Herbert urged the use of auricular confession, admonitions to charitable works and the administration of the eucharistic sacrament, stressing how 'comfortable and sovereign a medicine it is to all sin-sick souls, what strength and joy and peace it administers against all temptations, even to death itself'. Some parish priests and laypeople did match Herbert's high standards. A case from St Bridget's parish in Chester in 1612 tells of a minister, Mr Evans, encouraging a parishioner recovering from a long illness, Thomas Marsland, to prepare himself to attend holy communion the following day. If he was still too ill to come to church, however, the priest offered to bring communion to his house. Marsland was reluctant to take the sacrament 'for there was some thing [that] troubled him in [his] mind'. Evans expressed perfectly proper Prayer Book protestantism: the minister giving warning of holy communion so that preparation can be made by the communicants as well as a willingness to visit the sick with the sacrament. Marsland, too, responded in a way thought proper for a layperson by the Prayer Book, that those too troubled in their conscience to receive holy communion should seek out a 'discreet and learned minister of God's Word' for pastoral advice.[10]

Conforming parishioners also wanted baptism, and like holy communion, they often wanted it performed lawfully. The rector of Folkingham had by his prolonged absences, complained the churchwardens, caused grief to some parents and exposed their children to danger. While Hoskins was away, parents were forced to walk two miles to the next parish in order to have their infants baptised, 'to their parents' grief and danger and peril to their infants'. This same charge was made against Lancaster and Jones in Tarporley: parents of young children complained that they were forced to travel several miles to a neighbouring parish in order to procure infant baptism or baptism with the Prayer Book ceremonies.[11]

Parental grief and anger could be great when a child died unbaptised. Conflict of this sort had a long history at Bunbury in Cheshire. In 1611 the vicar Richard Rowe was presented, not only for not making the sign of the cross in baptism, but that he 'refuses to baptise any but on the sabbath or holy day although it be in danger of death'. In 1626, it was charged against John Swan:

> that you have . . . divers times or at least once . . . refused to baptise one or more child or children being in danger of death although you had notice of the same, in so much that they have died without that holy sacrament of baptism from you.

The long suffering parishioners of Ellington in Huntingdonshire accused their parson Anthony Armitage in 1602 of refusing to baptise a child on a week day, which later died unbaptised.

> [Armitage] did refuse to baptise the child . . . in the week day, being made privy by the said Morley [the father] and other ancient women of the parish that the child was very weak and in peril of death, in so much the child died without baptism to the great grief of the parents.

The refusal to baptise on a week day is often seen by historians as an indication of puritan sentiments in a minister, reflecting the desire to discourage any magical connotations that the ceremony might have left to their 'semi-pagan' or 'crypto-papist' congregations. The model conformist parson George Herbert supported the view that baptism was ideally a *public* not a *private* sacrament. However, under such conditions as described concerning Francis Morley's child, Herbert, as a pastor, made exception – as did the Common Prayer Book.

> The pastors and curates shall oft admonish the people that they

defer not baptism of infants any longer than the Sunday or other holy day next after the child be born, unless upon a great and reasonable cause be declared to the curate, and by him approved. And also they shall warn them, that without great cause and necessity they baptize not children at home in their houses.

Rowe and Swan may well have been acting from one sort of theological conviction. But was Anthony Armitage's action – or lack of it – the result of conviction or negligence? We do not know. It has been maintained that to puritan clergy baptism did not convey grace but marked admission to the congregation of Christ; to such clergy the death of an unbaptised child 'was not a catastrophe'. It is suggested here that to some parents the death of their unbaptised child was 'a catastrophe'; the Church court records testify to the 'great grief of the parents'.[12]

If omitting the sign of the cross in the baptismal rite can be taken as evidence of puritanism, may not reiterated insistence by individuals upon the ritual be taken as evidence that some parishioners desired the lawful ceremonies prescribed in the Prayer Book?[13] The parishioners of Anthony Armitage complained that he omitted the sign of the cross as well as the set prayer that went with the action. All the deponents in this case, who had information to contribute on this particular, confirmed it. Tempers apparently ran hot on this question. A yeoman, Richard Price, related that his child had been one of those the vicar had refused to cross 'and this deponent found fault with it'. Francis Morley, the father of the child who had died without baptism, described the disagreement between Armitage and Price more strongly and said they were 'at controversy because Armitage . . . would not sign it with the sign of the cross'. Perhaps Morley and Price felt the same as George Herbert, and thought 'the ceremony not only innocent, but reverend'.[14]

Prayer Book protestants wanted their dead buried properly, reverently and with the rites authorised by the established Church. In the various sets of articles arising out of the disputes at Tarporley, there are several concerned with proper burial. It was complained that Lancaster would not 'execute the holy order of the Church in burial'. He would not meet the corpse at the churchyard gate, nor permit mourners to come into the church, nor 'prayer among the congregation that come with the dead' – all ceremonies directed by the Prayer Book rubrics. Lancaster even struck a man as he tolled a bell for a passing soul, as had been directed in visitation articles for the diocese. John Swan of Bunbury also refused to meet the corpse at the churchyard gate, or use the Prayer Book rite.

> Neither did you meet the said corpse [and bring it] into the churchyard and church, nor read the usual prayers and service (appointed for the burial of the dead) when you went to accompany the same to the grave, but only carried the service book under your arm.

At the neglected chapelry of Bruera (1628), it was complained that no provision for decent burial had been made by the vicar of St Oswald's.[15]

Improperly conducted funerals were a point of great contentiousness between parishioners at Ellington in Huntingdonshire and the minister Anthony Armitage. They felt that the vicar did not 'perform his duty in the burial of the dead'. Only the previous Saturday before these articles were preferred, Armitage had gone to Huntingdon at the time arranged for the funeral of Mary Hale. He did not return until dusk, having kept the mourners and 'the whole parish also' apprehensively waiting for two hours inside the church, where they had moved to await their pastor's arrival. When he returned, Armitage refused to say the service until the people had moved the corpse outside; though by then it was so late 'that he could scarce see to read prayers', complained one parishioner. Once hustled out of the church (according to the Prayer Book the burial service should begin outside in the churchyard), the frustrated mourners apparently decided to bury their neighbour properly and carried her body all the way back to the churchyard gate where, again according to the Prayer Book's rubrics, the officiating priest was required to meet the corpse. But Armitage, the subscribers lamented, refused at any time to meet the body at the churchyard gate and the burial of their neighbour Mary Hale was no exception.[16]

The evidence for Armitage's shocking behaviour at the funeral of Mary Hale is largely supported in the depositions of witnesses made in this case. Several deponents claimed that once the vicar had finally arrived, he had refused to 'read prayers' before the actual interment; probably meaning that he left out the part of the service which was to be read by the priest as the body was moved from the churchyard to the grave. The tailor John Tall added that Armitage had also refused 'to meet the corpse of one Richard Gates his wife late of Ellington deceased'. Parishioners also saw the duty of presiding at holy burial as one most desirably exercised by some-one in holy orders; indeed this is what the Prayer Book directed. John Tall had such additional cause for grievance with Armitage, besides the vicar's treatment of his neighbour's deceased wife. Tall's child and the child of a neighbour Christopher Brit, were buried by the Parish clerk, even though Armitage was resident in Ellington.

> [Armitage] being at home his self, but [he] appointed the clerk of the parish to put them into the earth very undecently and undutifully, contrary to the order of the Book of Common Prayer.

At Macclesfield in 1604 the curate had been illegally dismissed by the mayor and replaced by one Francis Jackson who was not only a nonconformist but also, it was claimed, not even ordained.

> [Jackson has taken upon himself] to exercise the office of the minister or curate there, wherein the said Francis Jackson being a mere layman, hath taken upon him publicly to read divine service [and] to bury the dead. . . .

Jackson was not thought a 'sufficient' minister by the inhabitants of Macclesfield because he was not in holy orders.[17]

Cases such as these raise some serious doubts about descriptions of attitudes towards death in early modern England. It has been argued that the rejection of ceremonies at funerals was not just a 'puritan' concern but becoming standard among many 'orthodox Anglicans' as well by 1640. Keith Thomas describes a growing indifference towards the dead in post-Reformation England among the 'truly religious', due to the protestant doctrine of election.

> Whereas medieval Catholics had believed that God would let souls linger in purgatory if no masses were said for them, the protestant doctrine meant that each generation could be indiffer-ent to the spiritual fate of its predecessor. . . . This implied an altogether more atomistic conception of the relationship which members of society stood to each other.

The 'problem' that the preciser sort of protestants perceived with the religious inclinations of their neighbours was not, in fact, one of indifference towards Prayer Book ceremonies and folk customs at funerals. The separatist Henry Barrow strongly condemned the enthusiasm of the common people for the funeral ceremonies contained in the Prayer Book. Indeed the detailed list of ritual transgressions which the Tarporley parishioners complained of for burials of kin and neighbours by their ministers; the dogged persistence with which the parishioners of Ellington carried about the body of their dead neighbour Mary Hale in an attempt to secure the lawful and conformable ceremonies due her; the anger and discomfort expressed by the fathers, John Tall and Christopher Brit over the irreverent interments of their children; or the concern at Macclesfield that Christian burial was an office best performed by a clerk in holy orders; suggest that they failed to hold an 'altogether more atomistic conception' of their relationships to each other in the family and the village community. Moreover, it appears that these parishioners were expressing that very 'solidarity' with their neighbours which has been linked to the 'hotter sort of protestant'.[18]

It is worth noting that an absent feature of these cases, and most court cases concerning overtly religious matters, is any hint as to what understanding of grace was held by the participants. People certainly objected to being labelled unregenerate from the pulpit by their clergy, as was the case with the parishioners of William Hieron of Hemingby, whom he likened to 'thieves in gaol'.

> ... and in the pulpit [Hieron] divideth his auditory thus, having one or two that he thinketh assent his novelties. He pointeth unto them, I speak to you regenerate, and turning his body, countenance and hand to the rest of the parishioners he sayeth, I speak to you also.

That the people of Hemingby objected to Hieron's remarks is hardly surprising, regardless whether they as individuals chose to emphasise divine initiative or human response as the key to salvation. Whether laypeople who presented their clergy for nonconformity were more likely to be Calvinist or Arminian seems to me to be an unanswerable question: the evidence for any direct connection does not exist. There is no doubt, especially in the early decades of the seventeenth century, that in Parliament and the universities differences over how grace operates in the world were hotly disputed. In the parish, however, the *hows* of worship, perhaps more than the *whys* of worship, were what concerned many laypeople, and perhaps even most clergy as well. It would be as mistaken to see such an attitude as shallow or unsophisticated as to paint the theological debates in the universities and Whitehall as obscure or elitist. It may mean that disagreements over the outward expressions of religious belief have a clarity and immediacy for the life of a community absent in many soteriological debates. 'Faith apart from works', after all, 'is dead' (James 2.17).[19]

III

Church court records provide one source for understanding Prayer Book protestantism; a second source are the petitions, nearly two dozen in number, produced in support of the liturgy and episcopacy between 1640 and 1642. The growing perception that the Church of England was 'in danger' is a marked feature of conformist thought on the eve of the Civil War. The Short and Long Parliaments provided a two-fold opportunity for the airing of grievances in religious and civil matters, as well as the means to seek their redress. Perhaps it is surprising in retrospect but the early months of the Long Parliament witnessed a degree of unity on religious matters. It was a shared hostility to Thorough, however, which provided the sense of unity of purpose; once the destruction of the Laudian ascendancy over the English Church was underway, cracks began quickly to appear. The series of Root and Branch petitions against episcopacy and proposals in the House of Commons of radical change in the government and worship of the Church of England rallied conformist protestants in defence of the lawful liturgy.[20] Their petitions provide little support for Dr Haigh's view that they had welcomed the ceremonial innovations of Archbishop Laud in the 1630s. Huntingdonshire conformists, for example, agreed that recent corruptions had been allowed in the Church but suspected that many of the petitions calling for reform 'under [the] colour of removing some innovation, lately crept into the Church and worship of God, and reforming some abuses in the ecclesiastical courts' intended rather the destruction of the reformed Church of England.

[These petitions] which we conceiving and fearing not so much to aim at the taking away of the said innovations, and reformation of abuses, as tending to an absolute innovation of Church government and subversion of that order and form of divine service, which hath happily continued among us, ever since the Reformation of Religion.

Petitioners from Somerset agreed and called for the 'condign punishment' of those responsible for introducing recent corruptions into the government and worship of the established Church.[21] In contrast both to the Laudians and to the rooters, the conformist petitioners looked favourably back to the 'Church of Elizabeth and James', rejecting innovations of the 1630s and proposals for reform in 1640–2 alike.

Pro-Church petitions were sometimes the result of proddings and encouragement by an M.P. who used the petition to back his support of the established Church in Westminster, which may have been the case with Sir Ralph Hopton in Somerset. Conversely, as in Herefordshire and Cornwall, the unreceptiveness of a county's representatives could spur conformists in the provinces to petition as a way of circumventing their obstructive or apathetic M.P. and making their views known. Great importance was placed by the Commons' leaders of all complexions on the role of petitions.[22]

The gentry appear to have dominated the drafting and organising of petitions. Assizes and Quarter Sessions – the natural gathering places of a county's elites – formed the obvious places for the hatching of petitions. This is well illustrated in Gloucestershire, Cornwall, Kent and Somerset, for example.[23] Furthermore, although the pro-Church petitions obviously shared common concerns, by and large these are expressed with individuality, indicating local rather than centralised composition. This is in marked contrast to the Root and Branch petitions which were often formularic and followed a lead set by interests in Westminster. The textual similarity of the Root and Branch petitions was ironically noted by the royalist poet Abraham Cowley: 'Petitions next for every town they frame,/To be restor'd to those from whom they came,/The same style all and the same sense does pen,/Alas, they allow set forms of prayer to men'. In some cases there is no evidence to suggest that Root and Branch petitions were ever circulated in the county before being presented in Westminster. The most obvious instance of this was in Cheshire where the rooters simply doubled the numbers claimed by the petition for upholding episcopacy. Divisions in county communities over the future of the religious settlement often followed older established lines of rivalry between leading families, as in Cheshire, Herefordshire and Nottinghamshire. But mutual concern over the future of the Church of England could also occasion the laying aside of old differences, as in the case of the alliance of two former election rivals, Sir Roger Twysden and Sir Edward Dering in Kent.[24]

As striking as the evidence for the local composition of and initiative for the pro-Church petitions, is the fact that the prime movers and drafters were overwhelmingly members of the laity. The clergy have left little evidence of their involvement in the initial stages. Parochial ministers in particular, however, did play an important role in 'getting hands'; the crucial next stage in a petition's life, as in Devon, Suffolk, Lincolnshire and Cheshire. Bearing in mind the dominant role of the laity in the conformist petitions, the level of support for the clergy expressed in them is all the more striking. Several petitions included calls for the better financial provision for parochial clergy, cathedrals and universities. The importance of preaching was sometimes linked with the importance of the sacramental ministry: a juxtaposition which should warn us against creating simple antitheses. Gloucestershire conformists strongly endorsed the Book of Common Prayer and episcopal government but maintained that no one should 'be enjoined to frequent his own parish church [unless] . . . there be in it a . . . preaching minister'. Equally the level of positive support for the clergy – though never at the abrogation of the laity's responsibilities – should urge us to a more nuanced consideration of the complex relations between clergy and laity than the treatment of 'anti-clericalism' as a historical phenomenon has often allowed.[25]

Support for the Prayer Book was expressed with varying intensity and for a variety of reasons in the pro-Church petitions. Some petitions, stressing obedience to the law, called for the enforcement of conformity to the lawful liturgy and ceremonies until Parliament should make legal provision otherwise. Dissent in religion was, after all, disobedience from the law. But the clause often used, 'until such alteration be made' might just as well reflect confidence that Parliament would uphold the Elizabethan settlement, rather than a thoroughgoing erastianism. People in the provinces in 1641–42 had even less notion about where reform was heading than did Members in Westminster. It seems clear that many M.P.s in 1641 did not support radical reform of the national Church. Concern for the fate of the Prayer Book 'swayed a majority of the House by the end of August, and was strong enough to move men as zealous as William Strode, Serjeant Wilde and John Crewe' away from the Parliamentary cause.[26]

But the Book of Common Prayer was also defended on far less expedient grounds. Some petitions, like those from Staffordshire and Huntingdonshire presented the liturgy as the chief force for engendering the Reformation in the previous century. In this view the Prayer Book provided the spiritual equivalent for the nation of regular exercise and a balanced diet: its continued use ensured a 'continuous reformation' and kept the Church of England 'healthy'; its regular use was the greatest guarantee of a Church free from popery and schismatic heresies. Petitioners for the Church expressed as well the conviction that the Prayer Book even aided their worship of God. Cheshire conformists thought the Book of Common Prayer was viewed by the people

> with such general content, [and] received by all the laity, that scarce any family or person that can read, but are furnished with the Books of Common Prayer; in the conscionable use whereof, many Christian hearts have found unspeakable joy and comfort; wherein the famous Church of England our dear mother hath just cause to glory: and may she long flourish in the practice of so blessed a liturgy.

The fact that conformists could attach 'sacred value' to their worship was reinforced by the sense of outrage expressed when Prayer Book services were profaned or interrupted. Petitioners from Cornwall condemned 'irreverent vilifiers of God's house', while from Southwark some conformists complained of the 'insolent carriage' of some clergy and laity during the time of divine service:

> some [of them] calling the doctrine and discipline of our Church cursed, others refusing to read the Book of Common Prayer, enjoined by statutes, others calling it popish, others behaving themselves most unreverently at those prayers, or standing with-

out the church till they be done, refusing to join with the congregation, in those prayers.

A sense of anger at the violation of sacred time and sacred place is expressed in a number of pro-Church petitions. Such behaviour in church was described by the Cheshire petitioners as 'sacrilegious violences . . . upon divers churches'.[27] That the word 'sacrilege' was used is surely significant and telling. The fact that some contemporaries were unable to recognise any 'sacred value' in Prayer Book worship does not mean that we cannot now recognise such feelings among men and women who did conform.

IV

It is now appropriate to turn to one of the most difficult questions concerning support for the lawful liturgy and polity of the Church of England: what can be said, if anything, about the different sections of society from which the established Church attracted loyalty and even, perhaps, affection? Or, as opponents maintained, were supporters and subscribers for the Church most often drawn from 'gullible labourers': '. . . hedgers at the hedge, ploughmen at the plough, threshers in the barns'?[28]

Material from Church court cases of the sort already discussed do provide occasional impressionistic evidence of the social spread of adherents of Prayer Book protestantism; the wide range of persons who could and did organise to present clergy who failed to perform their ministerial obligations faithfully according to the Book of Common Prayer. Legal proceedings were initiated and supported from individuals across a wide sweep of the social spectrum: from gentlemen and yeomen to husbandmen and day labourers; women and men; those who could sign their names and those who made their marks. The active supporters of the proceedings on behalf of the much put upon parishioners of Anthony Armitage in Ellington, Huntingdonshire ranged widely in terms of their social standing. Thirteen of the deponents against their minister included one gentleman, one yeoman, two labourers (one of whom was a woman), three tailors, one draper, three husbandmen, one 'sheerman' and one whose occupation was unstated. Seven or eight of them, that is over half, made their marks at the end of their depositions.[29]

Court material such as that discussed above and evidence provided by the subscribers to the Cheshire petition for the Prayer Book suggests that support for the Church of Elizabeth and James came from a cross section of English society. It was not 'determined' by social or economic standing.

Although a great many petitions were produced in 1640–2 in support of the Book of Common Prayer and episcopacy, few survive with the schedules of subscribers. Not only did Cheshire produce two pro-Church petitions, one for episcopacy in February 1641 and one for the Prayer Book in December 1641, but the schedules of subscribers for both survive, providing roughly six thousand names for the former and nine thousand names for the latter.[30] These schedules of names, when compared with economic documents relating to the same locality, provide an almost unique opportunity to build a profile of the social and economic composition of supporters of the established Church. The subscribers to the petition for the Prayer Book will be examined here, as they relate directly to the concerns of this essay.

There is not space here to describe in detail the methodological concerns underpinning the analysis. In the end, it was possible to match five of the sixty-three identifiable localities to complimentary extant church rates for the years 1640–2. The choice of the five communities was dictated entirely by the serendipity of identification and survival of church rates and subsidy returns. Happily, however, the five communities – Tilston, Frodsham, Wilmslow, Marbury and Middlewich – provide a reasonable geographic spread across the county.[31]

An obvious question to ask is what proportion the subscribers to the Common Prayer petition formed out of the overall adult male population in the five localities? The rate of subscription varied from 69% for Wilmslow to 27% for both Frodsham and Tilston; Wilmslow was in fact the only community in which the rate of subscription among adult males reached over 50%. How many of the subscribers were eligible to pay the church rates? Using data from 1640–2 the results range from 49% of subscribers in Tilston to just 18% in Frodsham. In all five communities less than half of the subscribers were economically significant enough to contribute to one of the humblest forms of taxation in the early seventeenth century, the church rates.

Another revealing source for the economic and social standing of subscribers are the subsidies imposed by central government on localities throughout the period of the Personal Rule. However, these subsidies were even more elitist than Ship Money, affecting only the most substantial members of the gentry and they throw a light on a handful of the most economically and socially substantial of the potential subscribers for the petition to uphold the Prayer Book.[32]

The most important question raised by this information is how genuine are the signs of support expressed for Prayer Book? To put it bluntly, were those who made their marks or signed their names simply caving in to pressure from above when they subscribed for the liturgy? It is argued here, based on the evidence from four parishes and one dependent chapelry, that the subscriptions for the Prayer Book represent a 'free-will offering'.

To begin with the male groups of those presumably most susceptible to 'social control': men receiving poor relief, those too economically insignificant even to be rated, and men rated for 1s or less. Taking the five communities together there are no clear trends of subscribers to non-subscribers; both groups appear to spread evenly across these economic categories. This is also true of the middling sort – the type of individuals who largely filled parish office. Again, those paying the subsidy were also fairly evenly divided.

Out of a group of five communities it is hard to generalise about the degree of influence exercised by the clergy. In three out of the five, the petition enjoyed support from the clergy: Frodsham (27%), Tilston (27%) and Wilmslow (69%). But there are no clear patterns. In Frodsham, where the vicar Rowland Heywood and his curate and parish clerk subscribed and where the incumbent was later ejected with great bitterness during the Civil War, 27% of adult males subscribed. Whereas in Tilston, which also had a subscription rate of 27%, the minister Essex Clark continued to serve the living until his death in 1654. The rector of Wilmslow, Thomas Wright, appears to have been a responsible and resident pastor and much regarded by his parishioners. In March 1645 when Sir William Brereton ejected Wright from his living with the use of parliamentary troops, the rector's neighbours rescued him from their hands and spirited him away. Such local regard may account for the high subscription rate of 69% but even a popular cleric like Wright did not absolutely control the religious sensibilities of his churchwardens, or even those receiving poor relief. The chapelry of Marbury produced a subscription rate of 29% – a rate similar to Tilston and Frodsham – without any apparent lead from the minister, one Thomas Orpe. Perhaps most striking of all is that Middlewich, with its notable nonconformist lecturer Thomas Langley and incumbent Robert Halliley, nevertheless produced a subscription rate of 41% of adult males in favour of the Book of Common Prayer.[33]

It is by examining the allegiances of parish officers that a pattern may be suggested. In Tilston, Wilmslow and Middlewich there was strong support among officers and leading parishioners for the Prayer Book petition. In Frodsham they were fairly evenly divided. Only in Marbury was there a clear majority of officers and leading parishioners who did not subscribe. Marbury at 29% is perhaps the strongest case of all for viewing the petition as an expression of individual consciences given the absence there of strong support from the gentry, clergy or church officers. In short, support for the lawful liturgy as expressed by signatures and marks on a petition appears to cut across the social spectrum of all five communities.[34] Several other questions need now to be briefly considered.

First of all, how is one to interpret *non*-subscription for the Prayer Book? Given that the Cheshire Root and Branch petition was never actually circulated in the county before being presented at Westminster – in sharp contrast to the petitions for episcopacy and liturgy – it is hardly surprising that no schedules of subscribers survive which would have allowed the comparison of places and individuals. Furthermore, we are left with a problem of interpretation that more usually dogs studies of conformity: is *failure* to subscribe an indication of opposition or apathy to the established Church? How do we judge the silence of the historical record? We may, however, be more sure of the *positive* nature of those who did subscribe as a legitimate expression of committed conformity.

Secondly, the historiographical questions concerning social control are put in a new light. Bearing in mind that it has only been possible to analyse five communities (although the five localities include nine hundred and seventeen individuals) nevertheless there was a tendency for the Prayer Book petition to enjoy support from the lay officers of the parish. But this support does not appear to have had a direct effect on the rate of subscriptions. These are just the sort of men who are often presented as the agents of the 'reformation of manners' and 'preciser protestantism'. It is suggested here, however, that such men could equally be agents for committed conformity, supporting the established Church not passively but actively. The men who held parish office, who signed the memoranda authorising rates, were individuals of local lay leadership and influence. That leadership, however, could be just as much for the maintenance of the religious settlement as for its reconstruction or complete transformation. For example, over a third of the parish officers in nine Cambridgeshire parishes put their weight behind a petition against Bishop Wren in particular, and episcopal government in general, in 1640–1. The men (and sometimes the women) who filled parish offices were, perhaps more than the clergy, the 'natural' local Church leaders. Their expressions of religious commitment could be on behalf of the established Church as against it, as the evidence from Cheshire and Cambridgeshire illustrates. Nevertheless, ordinary parishioners, even the poor, were capable of what appears to be a free expression of their own religious commitment. Even with strong local lay leadership generally only a minority of adult males subscribed. The Cheshire petition for the Book of Common Prayer reinforces the evidence from the Church courts that conformity was as 'sincere and genuine' a strand in parish religion as puritanism.[35]

V

We need to be more critical concerning the 'godly's' assessment of the quality of the religious lives of their conforming neighbours. Nonconformist innovations could drive people out of church as well as conformity to the Book of Common Prayer. Petitioners from Manchester complained of Ralph Kirk's innovations, 'whereby he hath driven a great number from the service of God'.[36] The godly were not always consistent about the multitude. Richard Baxter's famous description in his autobiography of a religiously and morally lazy Church of England in the 1620–30s should be weighed against another description of his on the religious activities of the people during the Commonwealth.

> The profane, ungodly, presumptuous multitude . . . are as zealous for crosses, and surplices, processions and perambulations, reading of a gospel at a cross way, the observation of holidays, and

fasting days, the repeating of the litany, or the like forms in the Common Prayer, the bowing at the naming of the word Jesus (while they reject his worship), the receiving of the sacrament when they have no right to it, and that upon their knees, as if they were more reverent and devout than the true laborious servants of Christ; with a multitude of these things which are only the tradition of their fathers; I say, they are as zealous for these, as if eternal life consisted in them.[37]

Even critics of the Church of England at times acknowledged the existence of enthusiasm for its worship and corporate liturgical life, however misguided they felt that support and affection to be. The time has come for historians of the Tudor-Stuart Church to acknowledge it as well. As to whether conformist enthusiasm was misplaced or not is a question which deserves greater even-handedness than it has received from historians heretofore.

6. The Clerical Estate Revitalised

ANDREW FOSTER

I

In 1640–1 Parliament was deluged with petitions critical of the clergy which went well beyond condemnation of Arminianism. It was claimed 'our bishops have so long played the governors, as they have forgotten how to play the priests'. Clergymen were accused of 'preaching divine authority and absolute power in kings' and also, paradoxically, of 'spoiling both the king and Parliament of their power'. Bishops were seen as 'labouring to overthrow or diminish the power of Parliament', whilst also encouraging their ministers 'to despise the temporal magistracy, the nobles, and gentry of the land, to abuse the subjects and live contentiously with their neighbours'. Apparently, 'the pride, the avarice, the ambition, and oppression, by our ill ruling clergy, is epidemical, it hath infected them all'.[1]

How should historians interpret such remarks? What do they reveal about changing clerical/lay relations between the 1590s and the 1640s? One stock response would be to invoke a tradition of 'anticlericalism' traceable back to the sixteenth century. Bills concerning 'scandalous clergy' were common in nearly all of the early Stuart Parliaments. This lay perspective would focus on common complaints about clerical ignorance and neglect, not to mention abuses related to drink and immorality. The accusations of the 1640s fit easily into a tradition of puritan complaints, from fellow clergymen as well as laymen. Latterly, some historians have been tempted to see ways in which such anticlericalism was 'activated' by the clergy, particularly when Laud took charge in the 1630s. This approach is complicated because for some historians much of the antipathy towards clergy can be explained by reference to

'Arminianism', with its exalted views of the priesthood, while for others, this controversial concept is unnecessary. Laud and his fellow clergymen became unpopular simply for the high-handed way in which they acted and for their subservience to Charles I. Both approaches place the initiative with the clergy, but one denies what the other emphasises, namely the importance of doctrine. The first scenario would highlight the 1590s as a critical decade of change; the second would fix on 1625 as the more decisive turning point.[2]

There is clearly no simple explanation for the virulent attacks made upon clergymen in the 1640s, but debates about puritanism, Arminianism and the origins of the Civil War may have confused matters. We need to take the views expressed above seriously. It is my contention that the laity did indeed have cause for concern about the growing assertiveness of the clergy, and that this can be dated earlier than the accession of Charles I in 1625. Doctrine did indeed play a part in key developments after that date, but this should not blind us to the full range of secular matters on which clergymen of *all* descriptions found themselves growing steadily at odds with the laity throughout this period. While there were many occasions on which the laity can be found attacking clerical rights and the Church, it was the clergy, with the assistance of Kings James and Charles, who were more often than not seizing the initiative after 1603. This interpretation helps to explain the range and venom of the criticisms voiced above, and accounts for why so many clergymen were condemned in the petitions of the 1640s, regardless of doctrinal positions.[3]

II

If clergymen really became guilty of 'meddling in secular affairs', 1603 surely marks the start of that process. Elizabeth treated her clergy notoriously badly and perhaps only Whitgift ever enjoyed her trust and affection. She left sees vacant with impunity and acted with little thought for the prestige and economic standing of her Church. All this changed dramatically under James I. After some initial alarms over the Hampton Court Conference, clergymen could be forgiven for thinking that God himself had descended to earth to aid them, and their eulogies about James frequently verged on the blasphemous. He was the 'breath of our nostrils' to quote one biblical phrase. James valued his bishops greatly and always kept several at court for company; the names of James Montagu, Richard Neile and Lancelot Andrewes spring quickly to mind.[4]

Thanks to Kenneth Fincham, we know that the number of bishops who remained for some time at court may not now be as great as was once thought, nor did they necessarily neglect their diocesan duties, nor can they be accurately depicted simply as courtiers in clerical clothing. Nevertheless, it is under James that we detect a big change from the reign of Elizabeth, as bishops were pulled into – and sought – more secular roles and authority than hitherto. Whitgift had been the sole cleric admitted to Elizabeth's Privy Council; he was retained on the accession of James I, but did not live to see six other Jacobean bishops serve on the Council – Bancroft, Abbot, Bilson, Andrewes, Montagu and Williams. The latter reached the exalted heights of Lord Keeper in 1621, no maverick decision, for Williams was not the only cleric considered for the post. James was happy to gain a clergyman as Lord Keeper, since that officer was regarded as the king's conscience. Just as we now see other decisions and appointments in the reign as more considered than was once supposed, so too the appointment of Williams can be seen as part of a plan whereby the king rectified what he saw as a loss of balance in the operation of the law courts. Clergymen were important 'interpreters' of the law of God and James declared that 'the law in this kingdom hath been too much neglected, and churchmen too much had in contempt'. In James, the clergy found a man who valued them enough to make them councillors, a patron who restored to them some degree of financial independence, and a king who spoke openly of their rights and place in society. This commanded support akin to adulation in return.[5]

The pattern continued under Charles I. Neile, Laud, Harsnett and Juxon served on his Privy Council before 1640, and there was another coup when William Juxon, Bishop of London, was appointed Lord Treasurer in 1636, the first cleric to hold that post since the reign of Henry VII, as William Laud proudly recorded in his diary. Where James had protected his clergy and given them space in which to rebuild their position, Charles actively encouraged them to think in even bolder terms. On Juxon's appointment Laud recorded 'now if the Church will not hold up themselves under God, I can do no more'. Abbot and Laud himself had both served as influential first commissioners of the Treasury, and Laud later claimed that had Juxon 'been left to himself, the king might have been preserved from most of those difficulties into which he fell for want of money'.[6]

The recent discussion of a 'British dimension' to the Civil War is a useful reminder that clergymen also gained important state offices in Scotland. Here the most celebrated appointment was that of John Spottiswood, Archbishop of St Andrews, who was made Chancellor of Scotland in 1634, but it is significant that James I (when VI of Scotland) had initiated the policy of employing bishops on his Scottish Privy Council as early as 1600. For a brief period before the Council was reconstituted in 1610, the entire Scottish episcopal bench of two archbishops and eleven bishops held rights to sit on the Council, though this never happened in practice. As the re-introduction of episcopacy into Scotland was hardly popular, the appearance of bishops on the Council was scarcely greeted with enthusiasm, yet both James and Charles persisted in such appointments in a more bold and reckless manner than they did in England. In 1635 ten members out of the fourteen-man episcopal bench (the see of Edinburgh having been created in 1633) sat on the Privy Council. Out of a total of thirty-six bishops who held office between 1600 and 1638, when they were abolished in Scotland, the staggering number of twenty-four had occasion to appear at Privy Council meetings. Bishops from as far away as the Isles and Orkney appear to have been diligent councillors; only those from Argyll missed out on the privilege altogether.[7]

It was not only in London and Edinburgh that bishops were exercising more secular power. They were representatives of central government in their dioceses, a role appreciated greatly by the king and Laud when bishops were instructed to remain resident in their dioceses rather than swarm around London and the court. Together with an army of unpaid J.P.s, bishops did the bidding of the Privy Council in all manner of ways, sitting on innumerable commissions of enquiry, dealing with petitions, monitoring the operation of the poor laws, and generally acting as the eyes and ears of the government. Some bishops were required to adopt rather strange roles, as when Richard Neile served as Lord Lieutenant of the County Palatine of Durham, thus effectively controlling the local militia. By virtue of this office, Neile has the odd distinction of being the only bishop to sit on a standing committee for defence in the House of

Lords in the 1620s. For the first time since the 1550s, clerical chancellors were appointed at Oxford University when Bancroft served after 1608 and Laud after 1630.[8]

The position of bishops in the House of Lords serves as an important barometer of the changing fortunes and status of the clergy during this period. The number of clergy entitled to sit in Parliament had been drastically cut at the Reformation. The now isolated bishops were frequently forced onto the defensive by the demands of a vociferous laity eager to have more say in matters of religion. Michael Graves has shown that the Elizabethan bishops were as conscientious as their predecessors, but owing to the large number of vacancies which Elizabeth permitted amongst her sees, 'there was never a full complement of bishops when Parliament met'. Moreover, bishops always figured amongst the 'backwoodsmen' who rarely attended Parliament, notably those from the north and 'incumbents of those remote Welsh fastnesses'.[9]

Once again the situation improved dramatically on the accession of James I. Twenty-six bishops (including two archbishops but excluding Sodor and Man) were qualified to sit in the House of Lords during the early seventeenth century. They were always outnumbered by lay peers, but James filled vacancies quickly and the bishops became very dutiful in their attendance and assumed a full range of committee work. In the Parliaments held between 1604 and 1621, there were generally twenty bishops in attendance, allowing for six absentees, some of whom did not sit and sent proxies. Recent research has shown that while three-quarters of the bishops generally attended the House, rarely half the lay peers were as conscientious. There could sometimes be more bishops in the House than lay peers, and even when outnumbered, they could probably give a good account of themselves by dint of superior intelligence and education![10]

A number of bishops became quite influential parliamentarians in this period. Richard Neile built up an impressive record of attendance and committee work during his sittings between 1610–1629. Apart from the Parliament of 1625, when he missed the session held at Oxford owing to illness, Neile's attendance record never dropped below 65%. Although it might have been politic to go off sick in 1614, he still put in 100% attendance in the 'addled Parliament'. His efforts peaked in the Parliaments of 1621 and 1624 when he attended 85% and 92% of the sessions respectively and sat on 53 committees in 1624, more than any other bishop.[11]

Effectiveness in the House of Lords was not, however, the prerogative of any one Church faction: Abbot, Harsnett, Morton and Lake all had good records for attendance and committee work. High attendance suggests most bishops valued their place in the Lords. The low-born Neile was particularly proud that 'here we are not called for the Church, but sit as lords and peers' to counsel the king. This earned a swift retort from the Lord Admiral that Neile might be a lord, but he was certainly no peer and could still be tried by a common jury! Despite this remark, and their generally low social origins, it is fair to say that the claims of bishops to sit in Parliament were fairly well defended until 1640, by which date it was the attitude of many clergymen towards Parliament which had become suspect.[12]

No doubt bishops felt under some pressure when the Commons was complaining about new canons, scandalous clergy, pluralities and other abuses in the early Parliaments of James. Yet there was growing evidence of clerical assertiveness during this same period. In 1604 John Thornborough, Bishop of Bristol, was deemed to have breached Parliamentary privilege by writing too openly in support of the king's plans for union with Scotland, while John Howson, future Bishop of Oxford, was reported to the Commons for 'some speeches of scandal and scorn to this house'. Debates in the Commons about the exercise of ecclesiastical jurisdiction, the recent canons and problems of non-residence clearly caused a stir in Convocation in 1606. In a letter to the Mayor of York, Christopher Brooke M.P. wrote angrily of how the debates did 'inflame and sharpen the Convocation house against us' and of how Dr Parker had used the platform at Paul's Cross in May 1606 to deliver 'an angry, scolding, irreverent and slanderous sermon particularly against that house of Parliament [the Commons]'. Apparently Parker 'took what could be collected, either out of all the holy writ, or profane authors against a tumultuous multitude, and that he applied to the Parliament'. Worse still, he did not do this 'in tropes and figures, but in plain English that the meanest might well understand his meaning'. King James was forced to mediate personally in this affair.[13]

In 1610 there was more acrimony. A prominent ecclesiastical lawyer, Dr John Cowell, had his book *The Interpreter* suppressed for passages in favour of royal absolutism. Bishop Harsnett of Chichester was attacked in the Commons for claiming that the king could levy taxes without the consent of his subjects. Senior divines at both universities criticised the Commons for impoverishing the ministry. At Cambridge, M.P.s learnt that they had been depicted as 'no better than Church robbers for our acts of reformation in the Church'. Whether in Convocation, at Oxbridge or from the pulpit, the clergy were beginning to make their voice heard. This spirit infected the bishops in Parliament, and the typically outspoken Bancroft blazed a trail for his colleagues in 1610, when he remarked scornfully of one bill on pluralities that 'I perceive in this bill a great deal of spleen against the clergy by those that profess a great deal of zeal'![14]

It was Bishop Neile's turn to be outspoken in 1614, when he warned that if the Lords met with the Commons to discuss impositions 'there would pass from them undutiful and seditious speeches unfit for us to hear'. This event became notorious and has been grossly exaggerated, but it was in 1614 that some in the Commons began to detect a pattern of hostility from bishops and other clergy towards them. Sir Henry Neville felt moved to advise that before future Parliaments, the Archbishop of Canterbury should issue orders 'to prohibit all books and invective sermons against the Parliament'. In 1614, links were not only drawn between Neile, Parker and Cowell, but memories stretched to recall Bishop Fisher's complaints about a rash of bills in 1535 'all to the destruction of the Church'. This was a far cry from the days when Queen Elizabeth had complained about her bishops colluding with the Commons against her on matters of religion.[15]

The most celebrated ways in which some clergy generally began to slight the power of Parliament can be found in a stream of sermons and publications in support of absolutism, and particularly the power of the king to tax his subjects. Examples of obsequiousness can be found in all ages, but some clergymen do seem to have relished eulogising their monarchs between the 1580s and the 1630s. Thomas Bilson asserted in 1585 that kings 'may justly command the goods and bodies of all their subjects, in time both of war and peace, for any public necessity or utility'. The theme has been well traced recently by Johann Sommerville through the sermons and writings of Saravia in 1593, Buckeridge in 1606, Bancroft and Harsnett in 1610, to the more famous cases of Sibthorpe and Manwaring in 1627. Whitelocke wrote scathingly of Sibthorpe's opinion 'that the king might make laws; and do whatsoever pleaseth him', noting sadly that Dr Manwaring 'preached the same divinity, and highly against the power of Parliaments'. Matters had clearly changed for the worst by this date.[16]

Under James, clergymen of all shades of opinion were happy to sing the praises of their king and speak warmly of his power. He in turn generally mediated with Parliament, as with Parker, when some clergymen overstepped the mark. Clergymen were encouraged to feel more confident about their position in society, and in 1621 it was claimed that 'His Majesty hath ever been a protector of religion and thinks that too much honour cannot be done to the clergy. And . . . the greatest advantage we can give our adversaries is to abase our ministry'. Earlier in the reign, Bancroft had observed that 'Henry VIII and the state disliked the clergy in anno 29. The King that now is, loveth his clergy as ever any'.[17]

The clergy found their feet again under James, but they were not allowed to make extravagant claims for power or property long lost to the laity. That situation changed dramatically under Charles I, and again the clergy took their cue from their king. When the Commons took the offensive against Richard Montagu in 1624 and 1625, over his controversial publications, bishops like Neile and Laud were quick to urge Buckingham and the king 'that if the Church be once brought down below herself, we cannot but fear what may be next struck at'. Richard Cust has recently drawn attention to William Laud's advice to the king against calling Parliament in 1628. Like Sibthorpe and Manwaring, Laud acknowledged that 'subsidies are due by the laws of God, nature and nations' and maintained that 'Parliaments have but deliberations and consents for manner of giving'. In the same memorandum, he urged that Parliaments should have restricted powers to discuss matters of religion, concluding 'the Church is too weak already. If it had more power, the king might have more both obedience and service'. It is hardly surprising that Laud was later accused of seeking to undermine Parliament![18]

In the 1630s some observers suspected that as a reward for their political support the clergy were cushioned against the full burden of Ship Money. Whitelocke recorded that 'great care was taken to favour the clergy', while 'all the rest of the people, except courtiers and officers, generally murmur at this tax'. Anthony Fletcher, and latterly Esther Cope, have drawn attention to the fact that the tax also sparked off a series of jurisdictional battles over cathedral closes. Chichester witnessed a typical dispute over who had the power to collect taxes from the cathedral closes: the city or the county? Such disputes fed into, and inflamed, existing tensions between cathedral chapters and town corporations. Moreover, the Ship Money cases seem to have lent the clergy a weapon which was by and large used to clinch matters of jurisdiction and precedence in their favour.[19]

Where James I had breathed new life into the old erastian formula that kingly and clerical power were inextricably linked, but the second subordinate to the first, Charles I allowed his clergy to flirt with the notion that they were an authority apart. When Prynne and others tried to drive a wedge between Charles and his clergy by pointing to examples of clerical pride, power and pretensions, particularly in relation to *jure divino* (divine right) theories of episcopacy, the king turned a blind eye. Where James could be portrayed as helping the clergy to defend themselves from lay attacks, Charles seems to have actively encouraged his clergy to take the offensive. Some of the friction in cathedral cities noted above arose because the king was permitting charter alterations which now openly favoured clerical rights where earlier James had been more circumspect. The growing assertiveness of the clergy is neatly caught in the number of disputes which now arose over matters of ceremonial like precedence in cathedral processions and seating arrangements.[20]

William Laud did not mince words when he claimed that 'the Bishops of England have been accounted, and truly been, grave and experienced men, and far fitter to have votes in Parliaments for the making of laws, than many young youths which are in either House'. Under Charles, the clergy came to see their role in the state as a secure right; they were also unashamed in their advice to the king on how to increase his and their power. Robert Chestlin openly conceded that in popular opinion 'the bishops and the clergy were the instruments for the king's intended tyranny' and acknowledged that 'this added to the name Baal's priests, and other such reproaches of the clergy . . . the new scoff of Caesar's friends'.[21]

There were many celebrated conflicts between clergymen (backed by their civil lawyers) and common lawyers in this period; Archbishops Bancroft, Abbot and Laud were all doughty defenders of Church interests, particularly over prohibitions and the rights of the Court of High Commission. To some, however, it must have seemed that the clergy were not only asking that Parliament and the laity should relinquish power to meddle in their business, but that the clergy were advancing claims of their own to have a say in secular justice. Drs Cockburn and Prest have identified an increased confidence on the part of clergy summoned to give assize sermons dating from about 1616. Preachers like Bartholomew Parsons, George Macey and Samuel Garey were all prepared to attack corruption, give advice and use their sermons to assert the rights of· the Church. In a sermon critical of clergymen holding pluralities, Thomas Scot rounded on lawyers who set themselves above the law and accused those who denied that tithes were *iure divino* of sacrilege. His easy solution for gaining harmonious Parliaments was to 'let the ministers prepare the people' for elections![22]

It is intriguing that in c. 1616–18, about the time when suffragan bishops made their reappearance on the Privy Council, that the numbers of clergymen on the commission of the peace also expanded. Of course, some clergy (most bishops and clerical vice-chancellors of the universities) did serve as J.P.s under Elizabeth I, but the scale and nature of Jacobean appointments were new. Divines were not slow to advance their claims: Humphrey Sydenham saw clergymen as obvious choices as J.P.s in view of their established role as mediators; and given James I's selection of Bishop Williams as Lord Keeper, it is perfectly possible that James shared this belief. So long as the numbers did not get out of proportion, and the clergymen selected were of a respectable and non-partisan character, why should there be problems? The noted Calvinist, Bishop Davenant, claimed that clergymen were well-qualified to exercise civil jurisdiction; 'it is no less expedient that clergymen should inflict one kind of chastisement rather than another'. The view that civil authority was prejudicial to the priestly function he dismissed as 'proud and unlawful'.[23]

In the late sixteenth century not all counties possessed clerical representation on the bench, partly because of Elizabeth's habit of leaving sees vacant. In 1604, eleven out of fifty-seven jurisdictions had no clerical J.P.s. A further nineteen areas had just one cleric, usually the bishop; and throughout England and Wales only ten clergymen below the rank of dean were magistrates. This is significant, for rarely may bishops have had the time or inclination to attend Quarter Sessions; their appointment, like so many of the aristocracy, was often honorary. Two developments stand out after 1604. First, the rising number of bishops selected for the bench; secondly, and more importantly, the great surge in representation from the lower ranks of the clergy. The figure of clerical J.P.s below the rank of dean jumped from ten in 1604 to seventy-eight by 1622, reaching ninety-one by 1625, before falling back to sixty-four in 1636.[24]

The high point of 1625 is deceptive, because after that date, Lord Keeper Coventry made sustained efforts to curb the size of commissions of the peace in the interests of efficiency. The proportion of clergymen who sat on the bench actually rose in the 1630s. It would be wrong, however, to exaggerate the importance of sheer numbers. At best, these figures meant that four or five clergymen found their way on to commissions averaging between thirty and seventy people in the 1630s. At no time were the clergy ever likely to dominate, except in certain areas and under special conditions. One rare example is Durham in the 1620s, where clerical J.P.s proved to be very diligent and may have occasionally outnumbered the gentry who bothered to attend.[25]

Detailed study of the records for Durham, Hampshire and Somerset suggests that the big jump in number of clerical representatives occurred around about 1617–18. In 1617 one lone clergyman was joined by three others in Hampshire; in 1618 the Bishop of Bath and Wells was joined by two colleagues in Somerset; and in the same year, the unusually high figure of six clerical justices for Durham was augmented by a further three, which helps explain some of the fears expressed in Parliament in 1621. Cambridgeshire, Kent, Ely and Durham seem to have been the best served areas as far as clergy were concerned. But the picture could be enhanced – as indeed was argued in Parliament – if one considers the presence of ecclesiastical lawyers and clerical relatives on the bench.[26]

Once appointed, ordinary clergymen usually proved to be energetic J.P.s. Between 1625 and 1640 Robert Kercher attended at least forty-eight out of a possible sixty-four sessions in Hampshire; his colleague Dean Young attended at least thirty-two. John Charlett attended one hundred and thirteen meetings associated with the Worcestershire Quarter Sessions between 1626 and 1638, second only to the performance of Sir John Bucke. Paul Godwin and Gerard Wood seem to have been active magistrates in Somerset. All this fits well with the judgement of T. G. Barnes in his pioneering study of Somerset: 'Doubtless the government appointed these clergymen-justices because they were above faction and had unique intellectual gifts needed in rural magistracy. Regular attenders at quarter-sessions, they were among the most active justices out of sessions'.[27]

One final indicator of a revitalised clerical estate relates to their economic status. Thanks to Peter Lake, we are familiar with the idea that many conformist clergy in the 1590s began to gain heart and define their position more positively, particularly against the presbyterian threat. Theories of divine right gained acceptance, not just with reference to bishops but also to tithes, which served to unite clergymen of all camps.[28]

Once again, the accession of James I in 1603 marks the critical watershed for the clergy, for at last they gained a monarch who valued his clergy. The economic spoliation of the Church was arrested in the very first Parliament of the reign. Bancroft was emboldened to defend Church interests at all levels, and the new atmosphere was quickly sensed by the lower clergy. In 1606 George Carleton dedicated *Tithes examined and proved to be due to the clergy by Divine Right* to Bancroft, confessing that he initially suppressed the work, but being 'persuaded of your grace's favourable acceptance, I have presumed to offer this as a pledge of my duty'. Carleton was actually the first clergyman to argue the case for tithes by divine right in print; his tract represents a breakthrough for the clergy, and he was now hopeful that 'by your grace's care the oppression of the Church may be mollified if not removed; that the malice of injurious customs and prescriptions against the Church may be abated'. Lancelot Andrewes had long held similar views, but had not dared to publish them. Now the gloves were off and clergymen felt able to print their views openly, encouraged by the knowledge that the king himself accepted the *iure divino* case for both bishops and tithes.[29]

Much has been made of the impact of John Selden's famous contribution to the tithes debate in 1618. His *History of Tithes* is usually regarded as further evidence of entrenched lay hostility, but it is more plausible to treat it as a defensive blow against clerical assertiveness. The book did indeed raise a storm, but it was one which Selden himself seems to have taken pains to avoid. In his preface (admittedly written later), Selden played down his aims: 'it is not written to prove that tithes are not due by the law of God; not written to prove that the laity may detain them . . . in sum, not at all against the maintenance of the clergy'. Selden conceded that the question of *iure divino* tithes had been handled 'so confidently by some of our late divines' that he dared not meddle with the matter. Selden was wise to tread warily: he was hauled before the king to explain his conduct, while a new spate of books by divines such as Richard Tillesley and Richard Montagu spat vitriol at his work.[30]

In a work published in 1590, Matthew Sutcliffe had lamented that rapacious laymen had 'devoured the late lands and abbeys; their stomachs are now so eager, that they can digest not only tithes, but also glebe and parish churches'. Thirty years later the clergy felt more secure under the protection of a beneficent monarch. Tillesley defended his reply to the king with the words 'to whom should the defence of the doctrine of tithes be dedicated, but to the defender of the faith?' James Sempill, a layman and the king's godson, wrote with full assurance that James accepted that tithes were due to the clergy *iure divino* in his *Sacrilege Sacredly Handled* of 1619. Where in the 1590s Hooker, Andrewes and Howson had defended tithes on practical grounds, mentioning expectations of clerical hospitality, the tone of works produced in the reign of James I was markedly more assured. Fulke Robarts prefaced his book on tithes, published in 1613, with a poem concluding:

So let him fear, who ere he be that dare
Purloin God's tribute and the churches share.

In a sermon of the same year, the puritan divine Richard Bernard spoke of 'church-robbing', a theme which clearly struck chords with clergymen of all shades of religious opinion.[31]

It is well known that Laud pursued various courses to regain tithes, impropriations and lost glebe property in the 1630s. It seems that his message was not entirely lost on the laity, and that his friend Viscount Scudamore was not the only one induced to make sacrifices. In 1637 Bartholomew Parsons dedicated a work on tithes to Sir William Doddington of Breamer in Hampshire with praise for some restored impropriations. There is confusion, however, as to how theory translated into practice in the localities. Bill Sheils has shown that tithe cases in the north were more likely to be brought by lay impropriators than clergymen, who were probably more fearful of the consequences and sensitive to pastoral obligations. Elsewhere, however, Helena Hajzyk has concluded that 'almost a third of Lincolnshire parishes were the subject of tithe causes between 1595 and 1641'. Tithe cases seem to have risen sharply over the period and Hajzyk felt that 'what the records suggest is that a significant proportion of clerical plaintiffs may have been making a stand over tithes as part of a general policy of self-assertion'. Such a policy would certainly follow logically from some of the arguments first published under James I.[32]

III

What effects did these stirrings amongst all ranks of the clergy have on the laity? How were they perceived before the 1640s? At what stage can we determine that they really began to cause problems?

It is fair to say that there was little overt criticism of the practice of employing bishops as Privy Councillors and officers of state during the reign of James I. They were resuming a traditional role which they had forfeited as recently as 1558, and all factions in the Church benefited from this resumption. It was the appointments of Charles I which really aroused concern. It was largely because Laud and Neile were prepared to endorse the king's 'new counsels' in Church and state that they became Privy Councillors in 1627, while Archbishop Abbot was temporarily removed from power. Sir John Holles was not the only one to express alarm at the influence of these 'counsellor-fixed clerics'. Charles was notably partisan in his choice of clerical councillors, and Abbot was only restored to the board in December 1628 in order to placate Parliament. High office was henceforth reserved for a very small coterie, and even a renowned Arminian such as Samuel Harsnett had to wait almost a year after his elevation to the archbishopric of York before he was admitted to the council.[33]

If there were qualms about appointments to political office under James, they surfaced with a vengeance under his son. The choice of Juxon as Lord Treasurer in 1636, the year in which he also became a councillor, signalled that there were few limits to the range of secular posts to which clergymen might now aspire. William Prynne wrote sourly that Juxon was 'the first prelate in our memory who relinquished the cure of souls and preaching of God's word to become a Lord Treasurer and sit as a publican at the receipt of custom'. Edward Hyde conceded that the appointment 'inflamed more men than were angry before, and no doubt did not only sharpen the edge of envy and malice against the archbishop . . . but most unjustly indisposed many towards the Church itself'. It was the same story for Scotland. Of Spottiswood's appointment as Chancellor, Bulstrode Whitelocke wrote that 'though he was a wise and learned man, and of good reputation and life, yet it gave great offence to many, that he being a clergyman, should be invested with that dignity; which they affirmed not to have been done before since the Reformation'.[34]

It matters not if the bishops in both England and Scotland were conscientious and diligent Privy Councillors, or that, as Hyde claimed, the king only appointed them in the hope that it 'would render them so much the more reverenced', for that policy clearly backfired. In England, the very presence of the bishops when the Privy Council sat as the Court of Star Chamber only served to bring that prerogative court into disrepute when it was seen to deal harshly with critics of the Church like Prynne, Bastwick and Burton. Not all the laity were hostile. In 1629, amid rumours that Lord Keeper Coventry was about to resign his office, Henry Aglionby regarded the Archbishop of York as a worthy candidate for the vacancy. Though common lawyers might regard it as 'spiritual wickedness in high places, yet methinks if the clergy cannot keep the office wholly as they were wont, yet it is equal that at the least it should be divided between the law and the gospel'. Yet such instances are hard to multiply, and the holding of high secular office was to prove a poisoned chalice for both the Scottish and English bishops.[35]

The work of bishops in the House of Lords stirred controversy over particular issues, like the power of Convocation in 1604, or clerical zeal for the royal prerogative in 1614, but it was not until 1640 that the floodgates were opened and charges of 'malignancy against Parliament' became common in petitions against the clergy. It was still not so much the presence of clergymen in Parliament which aroused concern, as the nature of the people, by and large, and the way in which they had achieved office. As early as 1610, Richard Martin had complained that the 'highway to get into a double benefice or to gain a higher dignity is to tread upon the neck of the common law'. By 1640 it was apparent to many that the clergy were now infected with Arminian views on theology and ceremonial, while they also neglected 'their studies and preaching to follow matters of state'. Whitelocke paraphrased Pym in claiming 'the ambitious and corrupt clergy preach divine authority and absolute power in kings to do what they will'.[36]

For Robert Chestlin and Peter Heylyn, it was an handful of puritans who were 'the true cause of the clergy-hatred among the people'. The status and economic power of the clergy had improved dramatically since 1603 and trouble could be laid at the door of jealous laymen, particularly lawyers. What Heylyn and Chestlin neglected to mention, however, was that much of the new found confidence, zeal and heightened sense of what was entailed in being a member of a sacramental priesthood, could be traced to English Arminianism. And Arminianism in an English context gave many clergymen a sense of the separate status of the clerical estate, and revived ideas that they could play a special role in secular government. It was this hallmark of Arminianism, as much as the stress on new ceremonial, which raised such real fears of a popish plot in the minds of so many in the 1640s.[37]

John Overall once noted that 'it hath been the manner of divines, from the apostles time almost to magnify and extol the worthiness and excellency of their own calling', adding defensively, that this was necessary, 'the ordinary contempt of the ministry considered'. But this had surely got out of hand when Nicholas Coleman of Preston called his parishioners 'blockheads and beetleheads that spoke against the cross in baptism'? In the petitions of the 1640s there were many complaints about the strict and haughty behaviour of ministers who refused to allow people to take communion unless they came and knelt at the rail. In a strident defence of this practice, Ephraim Udall had the nerve to claim 'it is a needless weariness put upon the ministers, to go up and down the church, reaching and stretching, rending and tearing themselves in long pews, to hold forth the elements, over four or five people'.[38]

The priestly claim to be able to grant absolution was a sensitive issue for many laity, and one given prominence by Arminians. At Donnington in Sussex in 1624, members of the congregation remonstrated with their minister, Thomas Harrison, about his interpretation of the Book of Common Prayer that 'whosoever would not believe that he could forgive sins was a fool, a knave and a villain'. This congregation clearly felt able to argue with a clergyman over complex matters of theology, but Harrison was making provocative claims that he could not only grant absolution, but also condemn a man 'that he shall never have salvation'. This was anathema to those who felt that the minister was simply God's messenger on earth, and that only God could forgive sins and determine salvation. The powers of the priest in this respect had been the subject of a controversial sermon by Lancelot Andrewes in 1600, but the idea became commonplace in the 1630s. Richard Neile had rejected the practice of confession as popish on taking his doctorate in 1600; by 1629 he happily acknowledged that 'it may be of great use in God's church'. For John Normington and Sylvester Adams, preaching openly in Cambridge in the 1630s, confession was a necessity.[39]

Education, a new feeling of superiority buttressed by ritual and ceremonial, and stress on different doctrines may have made some clergymen more confident and assertive. Arminian Church policies pursued in the 1630s certainly gave them opportunities to hector and clash with their parishioners. The introduction of altar rails, enforcement of the Book of Sports, and interference with parish customs like perambulations, all brought conflict between clergy and laity. Added to this, as Christopher Hill demonstrated long ago, Laud was seen to be 'trying to get back behind the Reformation, not only in ceremonies, but also in economics'. Whether true or not, many felt with Falkland in 1641, that 'some bishops and their adherents . . . encouraged all the clergy to suits'. Petitions of the 1640s often linked clerical support for royal absolutism with attempts to grasp more for themselves. While the godly minister was seen like Henry Hammond to be 'administering the sacraments, relieving the poor, keeping hospitality, reconciling of differences amongst neighbours, visiting the sick, catechising the youth', all too often, the petitions noted people like Mr Lidham of Leysdown, 'living very contentiously amongst us'. Only when we have more studies of the impact of Arminian policies at parish level will we be able to determine the truth or falsity of such charges.[40]

In a recent article on Laud, Lord Dacre has argued that 'it was not Laudianism that had ruined Charles I but Charles I who had ruined Laudianism'. In other words, the close identification of the work of the clergy with the state led to their downfall when he fell. The scenario may look attractive, but it underplays the importance of religious ideas. Moreover, it needs to be extended in turn, for surely the effects of close identification with the state damaged the clergy in general, not just the followers of Laud. And indeed, that process should be dated back at least to the reign of James I, rather than restricted to that of his son. What can be agreed upon readily, is that while James did manage to maintain a precarious balance between clerical and lay interests, that balance was lost on the accession of Charles I, owing to his partisan support for the Arminian faction within the Church of England.[41]

The importance of Arminianism is better discussed elsewhere, and it has already been acknowledged that controversy over this factor has distorted past analysis of the main theme of this article, namely the 'reality' behind fears about clerical pretensions in matters of state. The Arminian factor cannot be ignored, whether in dealing with appointments to high state office or those made at county level, but the critical thrust of this article has been to reveal grounds for fear about the spread of clerical influence at all levels of government, and to show that although these were heightened by Arminianism, they were also to some extent separate. Arminians formed only a small minority of the eighty-nine clergymen who served as J.P.s in the 1630s. Instances can be found when Arminians lobbied for their own kind to be appointed to the bench, as in the case of Christopher Dow for Sussex in 1640, but it was the number of clergymen who served in this capacity which did and should arouse comment.[42]

An enlarged role for the clergy on commissions of the peace was bitterly resented by the laity, however few the number and conscientious the personnel. The anonymous author of *Episcopal Inheritance*, writing defiantly in favour of bishops in 1641, depicted a long tradition of clergymen serving the state 'which is a thing that now many of our common people do much dislike, not well enduring a few justices of peace to be of the clergy'. Later in the tract, the author noted (correctly as it now seems) that 'there is not one hundred of the clergy employed throughout the whole kingdom, there being not above three or four justices of peace in a whole shire'. Such facts did not matter in the heated debates of 1641. A bill 'to restrain bishops and others in holy orders, to intermeddle with secular affairs' passed three readings easily in the House of Commons between 30 March and 1 May 1641. By that date many were prepared to agree with Lord Saye and Sele that holding temporal office hurt the clergy themselves by distracting them from their main function, namely preaching the word of God. Others, like Richard Bernard, saw the intrusion of clergy into secular posts as an insult to the aristocracy and gentry. Nathaniel Fiennes argued ingeniously that ministers dealt with souls through their minds and affections and that involvement in secular punishment would prejudice their work. Great fear of Roman law, possibly aggravated by recent experience of the work of Laud and his colleagues in High Commission, Star Chamber and metropolitical visitations, inclined Fiennes to pronounce that 'Ecclesiastical government will be no good neighbour unto the Civil, but will be still casting in of its leaven unto it, to reduce that also to a sole, absolute and arbitrary way of proceeding'.[43]

Important though the events of the 1630s may have been in fuelling this rhetoric of the 1640s, it is crucial to the argument of this article that we can register such fears much earlier. A bill for 'disburthening of clergymen of such affairs as hinder them in their divine callings and cures' was introduced into the Commons on 18 June 1604, which has the distinction of being the only bill to be rejected outright by the Lords during the early Parliaments of James I. The subject was raised briefly in 1614, when it gave Sir Henry Anderson the opportunity to remark that 'he lived in a country where the churchmen [are] the governors', an allusion to the lack of parliamentary representation for county Durham. Sir John Sammes, supported by Sir George Moore, backed a bill to prevent clergymen lower than bishops and deans from becoming justices, but it foundered on first reading.[44]

The issue surfaced again amidst some acrimony in 1621. The king was informed of debates concerning clerical justices in April and sent a message to the Commons that they should 'be tender in meddling with clergymen being justices of the peace'. The message led to some discussion of parliamentary privileges and attacks upon Neile, the Bishop of Durham, whom the Commons suspected of leaking information of their proceedings to the king. It was in this context that Sir Dudley Digges suggested that they should inform the king 'that in Durham, where but 12 in commission of the laity, there are 13 of the clergy, and dependents upon the clergy'. This was not the case, but may have been a correct reading of those who were regular attenders at Quarter Sessions. Digges and Sir Edward Coke combined at this stage to keep pressing for action to prevent parish clergy from becoming justices, but their efforts were in vain in the face of the royal pronouncement. It is noteworthy that this bill arose in 1621 when Parliament was so concerned with legal matters and the pursuit of corruption in the courts, somewhat surprising that little was said about the presence of civil lawyers on the bench, and intriguing that the bill should coincide with what seems to have been a fairly recent dramatic rise in the number of clerical appointments to the bench.[45]

No such bills were pursued in the next two Parliaments, but one 'that certain clergymen be not justices of the peace' went through three readings in the Commons quite smoothly by all accounts in March 1626, only to falter after two readings in the House of Lords. Easy passage in the Commons may have been helped by the presence of John Selden, Dudley Digges and Henry Anderson on the appropriate committee. An even more direct bill 'to disable clergymen to be justices of the peace' was put to the Commons in 1628 with the same result as above. There was time for one reading of a similar bill in the Short Parliament of 1640, before the matter was expedited by the Long Parliament one year later. At this date, of course, it was clear that all clergymen, of whatever rank, were included in the restrictions for, as was claimed in March 1641 'for bishops, or any other clergymen whatsoever, to be in the commissions of the peace, or to have any judicial power in the Star Chamber, or in any civil court, is a hindrance to their spiritual function, prejudicial to the commonwealth, and fit to be taken away.'[46]

It was on questions of secular power, apart from theological disputes over Arminianism, that we also detect evidence that some clergymen had doubts about the way things were going. In November 1631, Dr Hooke of Nettleham in Yorkshire was arraigned before the Court of High Commission because he had seen fit to challenge the right of his fellow clergymen to exercise temporal jurisdiction, either as J.P.s or as Privy Councillors. Needless to say, Bishops Neile and Laud took a dim view of this; Neile felt that Hooke was courting 'popularity' and that it was 'an assertion fit for an Anabaptist'. It is a tribute to the confidence of the authorities at this stage that Sir Nathaniel Brent felt able to justify 'temporal jurisdiction' by the clergy on the surprising grounds that 'the pope himself hath a great deal of temporal power'![47]

The later royalist, Edward Bagshaw, caused a furore in his Lent readings at the Middle Temple in 1639, when he suggested that bishops were unnecessary to Parliament. He also urged intriguingly, that before Edward VI 'the clergy were not put in commissions for temporal power,' but 'to persuade people to conformity, not to give judgement against them'. He argued that ministers could refuse such office if they felt it went against their conscience to exercise temporal power. Bagshaw was silenced for the moment, but pursued his case later in the Long Parliament. Many, like Whitelocke, recorded that in the 1630s they walked carefully 'because the spiritual men began in those days to swell higher than ordinary, and to take it as an injury to the Church that anything favouring of the spirituality should be within the cognizance of ignorant laymen'.[48]

IV

So we return to the complaints made about clergy in the Long Parliament. It looks as if there might be some substance in the fears expressed. We can see that some clergymen were taking on more secular roles in society, articulating their rights vis-à-vis the laity with greater clarity and assertiveness than in years before, and causing offence in the process. The clergy may have been encouraged to take on more secular roles in society first by the indulgence of James I and then, more notoriously, by his son Charles. Although some may have had doubts about the wisdom of such moves, there is evidence that the changes had been eagerly anticipated by many clergymen as early as the 1590s. What is more, the changes were embraced when they came initially under James by clergymen of all factions. Even when some of the work did become enmeshed in the policies of Arminians in the 1630s, there was no going back for the clergymen who served as J.P.s. All became tarred with the same brush.

The Long Parliament provided great scope for ventilation of grievances against clergymen. It has been demonstrated that the grounds for many complaints can be traced back to the 1590s. What made things worse by 1640 was the new doctrinal thrust of the clergy in power with their concern for outward ceremonies, and the willingness of Charles I to countenance what many regarded as even greater claims for clerical power than those permitted under James. While many laity might have been prepared to tolerate improvements in the status of clergymen under James, this became impossible when one faction within the Church appeared dominant after 1625. At the outset of the century the clergy had been content to argue against M.P.s and the laity meddling in their jurisdiction. By 1640, many were guilty of arguing that they could 'sway both swords'. Such an argument was not the product of the 1630s, however, but can be found much earlier as in Sydenham's sermon meant for the new king in 1625: 'Moses and Aaron you take too much upon you, was the cry of the Jew once, so 'tis now, who would manacle and confine them only to an ecclesiastic power, and divest them quite of any civil authority, though Moses here had both'. Clergymen had regained confidence in the reign of James I, so much so, that by 1640 many people agreed that 'these are bad divines and more ignorant statesmen'.[49]

7. The Laudian Style: Order, Uniformity and the Pursuit of the Beauty of Holiness in the 1630s

PETER LAKE

The early Stuart Church has always been the subject of controversy. In part this has been due to the reasons intrinsic to the subject and in part due to the perennial concern of historians with the origins of the Civil War. But where once scholarly attention was focused on an allegedly revolutionary or at least radical and radicalising puritanism, now the major object of discussion and study is an allegedly innovatory Arminianism.

On the one hand, Arminianism has been presented as a radical departure from a previously dominant reformed tradition, on the other the existence of Arminianism as a coherent ideological position has been denied and many of the factors and forces associated with its rise explained away as merely the results of an unconventionally zealous pursuit of the largely conventional conformist aims of uniformity, unity, order and obedience.[1]

Here, then, are two radically different visions of the phenomenon of Laudianism. Both, as will appear below, can claim considerable textual warrant in the writings of the Laudians themselves, but precisely because of that neither can provide a satisfactorily total or comprehensive characterisation of what I shall term Laudianism. I shall use that term rather than Arminian or anti-Calvinist because I want to shift the terms in which the discussion of these matters is conducted. At present the current debate is dominated by the single issue of predestination. Even those scholars who wish to assert the marginality of the doctrine to contemporary debate devote whole books and articles to the subject. In part this represents merely an amusing if extreme example of the tendency of polemicising historians to reproduce the structures of the argument they are trying to overthrow in their own discourse.[2] However, the resulting bizarre obsession with predestination is threatening to obscure what I take to be the real issues at stake in the current debate. Important though the theology of grace was to many contemporaries we will never understand why or how it was important and we will certainly never get to the bottom of the religious policies of the Personal Rule and their wider political, cultural and religious resonances if we focus exclusively on the issue of predestination. We desperately need a wider context in which the disputes about predestination can be set and it is to provide such a context, at least for the 1630s, that this essay is intended.

In using the term Laudian I do not mean to imply anything about the role of Laud in either originating or disseminating the views discussed here. I am employing it merely as a handy short-hand term for the policies and religious temper of the Personal Rule as those policies and that temper were legitimated and explained by the regime's apologists in court and visitation sermons and works of polemic and justification. Laudianism, I want to argue, did exist as a coherent, distinctive and polemically aggressive vision of the Church, the divine presence in the world and the appropriate ritual response to that presence.

What follows, then, is an attempt to capture the distinctive features of the Laudian style using the gloss on the policies and priorities of the Personal Rule produced by clerical spokesmen and supporters of the regime. In constructing or reconstructing that vision I shall be producing something like an ideal-type, a version of Laudianism, perhaps more rounded and coherent than anything to be found in at least some of the texts cited below. Such an enterprise has its drawbacks; it threatens to suppress differences of emphasis and opinion between individuals and groups, it may overestimate the coherence and/or radicalism of the opinions of the individual authors cited below, some of whom may have subscribed only to parts of the overall position being described here. Such an approach may, indeed, confer or seem to confer a false coherence on the position itself, privileging those strands which fit neatly together over those which do not, and thus creating an impression of a worked out programme or world-view where in reality there were only a number of positions, preferences, opinions, jumbled together, pushing their proponents this way and that and colliding, as always, with the demands of political prudence, personal ambition and the forces of court faction and royal whim.

The nature of the evidence certainly allows such a view of the matter. The great works delineating what is characterised here as the Laudian view of the world pre-dated the 1630s. The Personal Rule produced no classic statement of the position, no Laudian *summa* but instead a whole series of *livres de circonstances*, minor works by minor authors, individual pamphlets and sermons designed to defend or assert one strand of Laudian religion, one aspect of royal policy rather than another. The result is a patchwork of sources, uneven in their coverage of the polemical or theological ground, sporadic in their production. In what follows, however, I intend to argue that running through these individual works can be discerned certain larger patterns or trends, certain consistent associations or assemblages of themes, priorities and approaches which amount to a distinctive Laudian style. Moreover, without a proper sense of the coherence and contemporary resonance of that style, much about the nature of royal policy during the Personal Rule and the response to that policy will remain unintelligible.

The reader then is invited to eschew the illusory pleasures of an apparently rigorous nominalism for a more holistic approach. The term Laudian style has been adopted here to evoke the nature of this enterprise. For as we shall see below, scarcely any of the constituent parts of Laudianism as it is here discussed were novel in the 1630s and not all of them, viewed in isolation from the others, constituted exclusively Laudian opinions. The present essay should not, therefore, be regarded as an attempt to list a series of Laudian shibboleths, opinions or attitudes which wherever they occur betray the presence of 'Laudianism'. For what was distinctive about Laudianism – and this is true, too, about that other problematic term of religious categorisation, puritanism – was not so much any of the individual opinions that made up the whole but the overall package, the ideological synthesis, and the resulting style, the polemical orientation and aesthetic and argumentative tone of the whole position.

Certainly, given the current confusion which surrounds this sub-ject, the risks of over-simplification, inherent in too enthusiastic a process of pattern-making all seem well worth taking. Only thus will we be able to transcend that sterile oscillation between the mutually exclusive visions of Arminian innovation and radicalism, on the one hand, and of Laudian conservatism and moderation, on the other, with which the current historiography confronts us. In Laudianism we are, at bottom, dealing with an attempt to redraw, indeed, to redefine the line between the sacred and the profane, an attempt which cannot be reduced either to a series of numbered points about predestination nor an assemblage of conventional con-formist commonplaces about the need for order, obedience and uniformity. That is the choice that the current debate on this subject threatens to impose on us. It is a false choice and one that I hope to refuse, if not transcend, in this essay.

II

Let us start with the Laudian view of the divine presence in the world and more particularly of the divine presence within the church. According to a whole chorus of writers from the 1630s the church, conceived as a physical structure, a specific place or site of worship, was the house of God. As the place where 'our Lord God most holy most doth inhabit' it was, claimed Robert Skinner in 1634, 'his proper mansion or dwelling house'. For Skinner and John Browning the church was 'the house of God and the gate of heaven'. As Thomas Laurence told the University of Oxford in 1634 God's 'presence is indeed everywhere but his residence especially there and though his essence be diffused through heaven and earth in Jeremy, his glory in Exodus is peculiar to the tabernacle'.[3]

God's presence in the church suffused the whole structure and all the physical impedimenta used in his worship with an aura of holiness. While a physical object used in that worship could lay no claim to 'inherent sanctity' such objects were to be esteemed 'holy in relation to the holy use whereto it is assigned. And in this sense times, places, oil, bread and several utensils . . . when they be applied to divine worship are holy'. For Alexander Read even the cloth bags used to carry the communion bread into the church were special 'since the very bringing of it into the church to that use is

a taking of it out of the world, a promotion of it to more reverence
and a next step to consecration itself'. The act of consecration,
therefore, created holy or sacred objects and once conferred that
holiness was indelible – 'if it be once God's house tis always so',
concluded John Swan.[4]

Such a vision of the church as the house of God had certain very
practical consequences for the Laudians. For if God's presence in
the world was most intense and most manifest in the physical
building of the church, if that church really was the house of God,
it should be fitted out accordingly and humanity should conduct
itself within the church with the necessary reverence and respect.
The church should, in short, glow with the beauty of holiness.

To begin with this led the Laudians to deprecate any use of the
church building or the churchyard for secular purposes. It was not,
however, enough simply to separate the church off from the world.[5]
As one author pointed out if the church was the house of God we
should be able to 'behold his glory and majesty in the stateliness
and beauty of the building, in the richness of the sacred vessels and
ornaments, the numerous multitudes of his servants, the various
fruits of the blessed sacraments, the dignity, holiness and sacred
pomp of his ministers'.[6] Several Laudian authors cited the Old
Testament examples of the decoration of the temple and the tabernacle both as precedents for the lavish decoration of Christian
churches and as points of comparison for the lamentable state of
ecclesiastical decoration and ornament in contemporary England.[7]

Thus the status of the church as the house of God involved for
Laudians an intense concern with the material fabric of the church
and a heightened sense of the value of ecclesiastical ornament and
decoration.[8] But it also prompted an even greater stress on the
ceremonial and liturgical aspects of the beauty of holiness. God's
presence in his house demanded the utmost reverence from all who
approached that presence. The church should be a place of awe
and fear in the presence of God. That awe, fear and reverence had,
moreover, to take a directly physical form. Eleazor Duncon stressed
that God must be worshipped with both soul and body. Only those
'rapt with the manichaean fury', he claimed, were prepared to 'deny
our bodies to God'.[9]

What Fulke Robarts called the 'correspondency and sympathy
between the soul and the body' ensured both that outward ceremony
was a perfect vehicle for the expression of our inner reverence and

awe before the divine presence and that the mere repetition of the outward forms of reverence and holiness was a sure way to inculcate those very virtues or attributes into the souls of ordinary church-going Christians. Moreover, the believer's physical movements did not merely affect his or her own soul but the souls of others. 'How doth the visible and expressive devotion of one Christian beget and increase the same in another? And how powerfully shall the reverent behaviours and gestures of an whole congregation together work one upon another?' asked Robarts.[10]

All this made it possible for the Laudians to equate an active lay piety with mere assiduous attendance at and participation in the services of the established Church. 'We may not' wrote Edward Boughen, 'be like stocks and stones, like the pillars or pews in the church, always in one posture. Something or other we must be doing. We must be sometimes kneeling, sometimes standing, other-whiles bowing when and as we are commanded. . . . There is no idle time spared us in the house of God, no time for sleep and wandering thoughts.' While Boughen might thus exhort the laity to activity, their activism was completely contained within the structures of the liturgy; a liturgy which might leave ample room for this sort of routinised activism but which had no place for lay initiative. 'Here is nothing at all left to our discretion; nothing may be left undone, when and where we please.'[11] Boughen could retain a sense of this puppet-like obedience as a form of lay activism because of his typically Laudian insistence on the indissoluble link between the soul and the body outlined above. For Laudians the laity's outward, physical acts of reverence and piety, choreographed by the liturgy and performed at the promptings of the priest, served both to express and inculcate various spiritual qualities or habits of mind. It was in this sense that the ceremonies of the Church were visible sermons, ideally suited to teach the laity those feelings of reverence, humility and worship appropriate to the meeting between the individual and the divine presence which occurred each time a Christian believer attended divine service.

If God's presence demanded an outward reverence from all who came into the church, the collective ritual effects of that reverence became perhaps the most crucial and defining characteristics of the beauty of holiness. 'What a wonderful decency it is,' exclaimed Edward Boughen, 'when we behave ourselves in this place as in the presence of God; when every man begins with due obeisance to

God . . . and then fall down upon our knees. When the minister
like an angel of light appears in his white vestment behaving himself   •
with that gravity and reverence and decency which well befits his
calling and the religious duty he hath in hand. When the whole
congregation shall appear in the presence of God as one man,
decently kneeling, rising, standing, bowing, praising, praying
altogether . . . like men of one mind and religion in the house of
God'.[12]

The result of this vision of uniform and unified public worship
was a newly exalted view of the role of ceremonies in the life of the
Church and of the absolute necessity of ceremonial conformity if   ⸱
salvation were to be achieved. For John Browning 'not to perform
or retain any of the most necessary reverence in our churches' or
to 'lightly reckon of . . . God's reverence' was tantamount to apostasy; 'Oh dismal decay of Christianity! O apostating fall! O backsliding generation!' was his comment on the ceremonial laxity of
the contemporary English Church. According to John Yates 'to
worship before the lamb is without dispensation, and prostration
before him admits no prohibition. We perish if we do it not'. John
Featley expanded on the same point in a visitation sermon of 1635
in which he denounced moderate puritan ministers who 'will better
relish our doctrine than our discipline and will be content to obey
so they may not submit. Miserable men as they are, they would
fain go to heaven but they are loath to stoop low enough to enter
in at the gate'.[13]

In a remarkable passage in another visitation sermon of 1635
Edward Boughen equated 'the religion wherein we have been
trained up' with a particular pattern of outward worship, making
that pattern of outward worship or 'set discipline' a defining mark
of the Church and by implication excluding all those who refused
to comply with that discipline from the Church and hence from all
hope of salvation. This was to place external ceremony and worship
at the very centre of one's vision of true religion, of what the
visible church was for and how salvation could be achieved. Even
ceremonies otherwise individually legitimated by an entirely traditional rhetoric of things indifferent took on a heightened significance when viewed from this perspective. All this bespoke an attitude to ceremonial conformity very different from the *de iure*
insistence on subscription combined with the *de facto* toleration of

a certain variety of liturgical practice that had characterised the Church under James.[14]

III

If one element in the Laudian programme was a greatly enhanced stress on the importance of the beauty of holiness, defined in both material and liturgical terms, its concomitant was a similar re-evaluation of the role of both prayer and the sacraments particularly in their relation to preaching. For the Laudians, if the church was the house of God it was also, *par excellence*, the house of prayer. As Richard Tedder told the Norfolk clergy 'prayer is the end to which God's house is erected, *domus mea, domus orationis est*. Though there be many other religious duties to be exercised in God's house yet there is none other mentioned but prayer'.[15]

Many Laudians referred to the church as God's 'own house and presence chamber', 'the presence chamber on earth of the king of heaven and earth'. If in attending church Christians were seeking an audience with God, then prayer was the obvious means through which that audience could be conducted. But, for the Laudians, the church was not only a presence chamber it was also a temple. The temple of the Jews was 'but a type of our churches', claimed Walter Balcanquhall and in place of their literal sacrifices the Christians had their 'daily sacrifices of praise and prayer'. The Essex minister John Browning agreed; for him prayer was 'God's most peculiar service, our daily and continual sacrifice to which the apostles give, as fit is, the first place.'[16]

As several of these writers observed, the militant Church on earth was closest to the condition of the saints and angels in heaven when it was at prayer. In the word of Richard Tedder, 'the temple is then more like heaven and we more like angels of heaven when we are in the act of prayer. God hath commanded that his house on earth have as near a resemblance as may be to his house in heaven . . . and that is the work of prayer'. Of course, anyone could pray and they could pray anywhere, but these writers were agreed that it was public prayer which united Christians in the militant church with the saints and angels in the church triumphant.[17]

If these properties of public prayer were to yield their maximum return it was essential that the laity play an active part in the public

prayers of the Church. John Swan turned from the depressingly
desultory performance of his contemporaries to 'the primitive
Church' whose 'amen was like a clap of thunder . . . and their
hallelujah as the roaring of the sea'. Not only should the performance of the laity in public prayer be enthusiastic it should also be
frequent. John Browning hoped to have the sacrifice of public prayer
performed to God at least twice a day. According to Robert Shelford
'the oftener we beat upon God's word and repeat the Church prayers the more the son of God's light reflecteth upon us and the more
heat of devotion is stirred up in us'. As with the bodily ceremonies
and gestures which attended it, so with public prayer itself; the
more often Christian professors attended and repeated the forms of
public worship established in the Church the better Christians they
would become.[18]

On this view public prayer took its place close to the centre of
the Laudian vision of the beauty of holiness. Thus to enhance and
magnify the role and significance of prayer was almost inevitably
to diminish the relative significance of preaching. Many of the
passages lauding the church as the house of prayer went on immediately to point out that it was quite definitely not known as the
house of preaching.[19] As John Swan told the Cambridgeshire clergy
in 1638 'to prefer preaching before praying is to magnify the means
before the end'. Prayer, explained John Browning, was 'the proper
and peculiar service of God, absolutely necessary for all men and
times'; preaching on the other hand was a clerical function, most
necessary for the first planting of the Church. Prayer, Swan
explained, actually saved us, while preaching merely informed us
about God so that we knew how and to whom to pray. Thus, for
many Laudians, once the Church had been established, the main
task for preaching was to provide each generation with the basic
information necessary to pray properly and thereafter to perform
intermittent topping-up operations, designed to protect the Church
and commonwealth from lay immorality, heresy and schism. There
could scarcely be a starker contrast between these priorities and
the urgent, sermon-based evangelism that had characterised not
only puritan but Jacobean episcopal opinion, as Dr Fincham has
described it.[20]

Nor did the Laudians stop merely with this diminution of the role
of preaching in the Church, in the process they radically redefined
what preaching was. John Browning, for one, ridiculed the notion

that 'there is no hearing without a sermon'. For him the 'first and nearest degree in hearing' was to be had in listening to the scriptures themselves being read. After that came hearing 'the word of God applied either by general or particular Churches in their catechisms, their councils, confessions, their rituals, their homilies'. Only as a poor third did Browning mention 'the sermons or homilies of particular private men' which at best were subject to error and all too often were delivered by the ignorant, the careless, the seditious and the factious. Given that the Prayer Book, in line with the liturgies of the primitive Church, was composed mostly of the word of God, Browning was able to conclude that anyone anxious to hear the Word did not really need the services of a preacher at all. According to Robert Shelford 'the principal part of the minister's office is . . . the true understanding, distinct reading and decent ministry of the Church service contained in the Book of Common Prayer. This is the pith of godliness, the heart of religion . . . the backbone of all holy faculties of the Christian body'.[21]

If in Laudian eyes preaching was but a means to bring people to prayer, there was a real sense in which both prayer and preaching were in their turn but the means to bring people to the sacraments. According to one author the soul of a Christian was 'a temple of his God' created in and through the sacraments; 'it is dedicated and consecrated in baptism, it is re-edified by confirmation and the holy eucharist'. God's presence in the church was therefore most intense in the areas given over to the administration of the sacraments, the font and the altar and the life of the Christian could be construed as a journey from the one to the other.[22] According to John Swan 'our perfectest communion with God' 'begins indeed in baptism but ends in the Lord's Supper . . . and they are the best saints that are admitted to it'. Eleazor Duncon agreed; the benefits conferred by the font were considerable. 'All children or men', he claimed, 'if they hinder not themselves, being washed in the holy font do from thence obtain remission of sins, become sons of God and are made heirs of heaven.' But these benefits paled into insignificance when compared to those conferred by the eucharist, the reception of which represented the acme of the Christian's profession. Believers should prepare for it with prayer, fasting, meditation and alms deeds, for, John Browning claimed, 'by an obedient tendering of ourselves unto God in the blessed eucharist, receiving his body and blood, he living in us and we in him, we are made partakers of the divine nature'.[23]

This was to place the sacrament at the very centre of Christian piety and religion. The sacrament, said Yates, displayed 'God's more especial presence' in his church and represented 'our greatest communion with Christ'. 'It is the highest advancement a Christian hath to be fed at God's board and with Christ's very body.' Here, according to Eleazor Duncon, 'is the greatest perfection and consummation of the Christian religion.'[24]

IV

In the eyes of many Laudians such a view of the sacrament had immediate practical consequences. For if the church was the house of God, its status as such was conferred by the divine presence within it, but that presence was itself not evenly spread throughout the building. On the contrary, the intensity of the divine presence in and at the sacrament could not but lend a glow of holiness to the altar upon which the sacrament was administered. Thomas Laurence compared that glow to the aura of spiritual potency and holiness which attended the material objects used by Christ, the prophets and apostles in the working of miracles. 'Nor can any say,' Laurence claimed, 'this grace of his extraordinary residence and assistance or operation which we presume here is greater than ecclesiastical writers ordinarily ascribe to those parts our saviour in his humanity conversed principally in . . . no more than his garment had in St Mark or his spittle in St John; no more than the rod of Moses in Exodus, the mantle of Elijah or the bones of Elisha in the Kings; no more than the handkerchief of St Paul in the 19 of Acts or in the 5 the shadow of St Peter.' Of course, if the holiness of the altar and its attendant impedimenta was no greater than this, it was very great indeed. No wonder Alexander Read was so pernickety about the furniture and utensils used to prepare for and to administer the sacraments.[25] Such attitudes lay behind one of the central features of the Laudian programme during the 1630s, the attempt on the basis of the St Gregory's case to have moveable communion tables converted into altars, railed in at the east end of the church. Concomitant with this was a renewed concern with bowing towards the altar.

But if the Laudians were concerned to demarcate and exalt the physical site and liturgical impedimenta of the church as holy places and holy things they were almost equally insistent on the Church's power and obligation to create holy times. Here lay the roots of the other alleged Laudian innovation of the Personal Rule, the campaign against sabbatarianism. On the issue of the sabbath the Laudians constructed their position against what they took to be the simple-minded scripturalism of the puritans. The puritans wanted to base Sunday observance on the Jewish sabbath by construing the fourth commandment as simply part of the moral law and arguing that Christians under the New Testament as well as the Jews under the Old were bound to devote one day in seven to the worship of God and to rest for the entire day from all secular business and recreation. On this view, far from abrogating the sabbath Christ had merely transferred it from Saturday to Sunday. By thus elevating the Lord's day, as they insisted on calling it, to a uniquely scriptural status the puritans belittled the other holy days of the Church, in many cases explicitly denouncing them as merely human, indeed, popish superstitions. Thus they severely constricted the power of the Church to order the details of its own public worship and deprived the English Church of what for the Laudians was one of its important means of inculcating piety and reverence in the laity.

For their part the Laudians construed the fourth commandment as partly moral and partly ceremonial. The ceremonial part, which had been abrogated by Christ included the obligation to give a whole day to divine worship, to rest for the whole of that day from all secular activities and to devote the proportion of one day in seven to God. The moral part, which alone was still in force, simply contained the injunction to give due and convenient time to the worship of God. What constituted due and convenient time and the nomination of specific days and times for worship were matters for the relevant human authorities, the Church and the Christian magistrate, to decide.[26]

This position allowed the Laudians to repudiate what they took to be the superstition and Jewish servitude inherent in the sabbatarianism of the godly and to place the so-called sabbath on the same footing as the other holy days of the Church. Here therefore is a rounded vision of a Church able to define and demarcate holy places, objects and times. Here too is a vision of true religion centred on the capacity of the clergy to show forth and distribute throughout the social order the divine presence encapsulated within and conjured up through those places and times.

On this evidence it is surely impossible to agree with Christopher Hill, George Bernard and Kevin Sharpe that all that was involved here was a conventional conformist pursuit of uniformity and obedience.[27] No doubt Laud was concerned to stop dogs urinating on the altar but that was not all there was to the Laudian altar policy. It is certainly true that the Laudians could and did mobilise a traditional rhetoric of order, uniformity and obedience to the authority of the Church and Christian prince over things in themselves indifferent. But their intense emphasis on the religious charge and value of ceremonies and outward observance together with their deployment of scriptural and what they took to be immemorial, and hence essentially apostolic, Church customs to defend those claims placed an almost unbearable strain on the traditional conformist argument from adiaphora (or things indifferent).[28] Again their attitude to the sanctity of holy places and objects, their attendant revaluation of church decoration and devotional images and symbols flew in the face of what Professor Collinson and Margaret Aston have characterised as the iconoclastic indeed iconophobic temper of English protestantism. Again, while Dr Parker's picture of a simple consensus on sabbath observance in the period before the 1630s is clearly overdrawn, there can be no doubt that here as elsewhere Laudian priorities and principles diverged from assumptions and attitudes which were shared by far broader bodies of opinion than can usefully be described as puritan. Again, Dr Fincham's account of the evangelical, word-centred style of piety which characterised the majority of the Jacobean bench of bishops, and his attendant analysis of the predominant image of the prelate as a preaching pastor, both stand in marked contrast to Laudian attitudes to preaching and the role of the bishop as governor. Professor Collinson's analysis of English protestant treatments of the ministry has shown that those treatments were dominated by preaching to the virtual exclusion of all other ministerial functions. Again on Collinson's account the most common forms of lay activism and zeal centred on the repetition of the heads of sermons, the reading and exposition of scripture, household prayers, fasts and catechising – all activities centred on the word as the object and means of piety and on the conventicle and household as its social site. All this was in marked contrast to the Laudian obsession with the forms of public piety in the parish church, a piety centred on an intercessionary priesthood praying with and for the congregation and dispensing sacramental grace. Again, as Dr Tyacke has pointed out, Laudian attitudes to the sacraments as the prime source of a potentially saving grace, offered first in baptism and then in the eucharist to all members of the visible church implied a view of the theology of grace very different from the absolute predestinarianism which passed for orthodox among many educated English protestants.[29] In short, on a number of crucial issues Laudianism, as described here, diverged from, indeed, came into open conflict with, central features of what might best be termed the English reformed tradition, in both its moderate and more radical or puritan incarnations.

V

Nor were these novel aspects of Laudianism limited to the realm of formal theological debate. On the contrary, a great deal of what was central to Laudianism could be read off from the altar policy and the assaults on sabbatarianism, lectureships and afternoon sermons which characterised the Caroline Church. In the interiors of English churches as the altar policy envisaged them the sacrament's status as the acme of Christian piety, the highest form of union with the divine available in this life and its consequent superiority over the other divine ordinances (particularly preaching) was given tangible architectural form. John Browning claimed that the fact that 'in our churches the pulpits are placed below, the altar above or in the highest place' demonstrated that the word was a mere means or preparation for the sacrament; that, as he put it, 'we should first hear before we presume to offer'.[30]

Peter Heylyn took a similar line with John Williams, ridiculing Williams' insistence that in the Church at Milan altars were scattered all over the place, some even being located below the reading desk. This claim was false and Williams only made it 'because you said before that the pulpit and the reading pew might be called altars no less properly than the holy table; you would now show an altar near the reading desk in hope [that] the reading desk may one day become an altar'. This was a levelling tendency that Heylyn was determined to resist; for him the altar was 'more sacred than any material thing besides to the church belonging' and its position railed at the east end of the chancel was designed to reflect that.[31]

Again the nature of the Christian's journey from the font to the altar, via the service of God in repentance, prayer and praise, as set out in the Prayer Book and conducted in the body of the church, this too was figured in the church as arranged by the Laudians. Several Laudian authors cited the long, thin shape of most churches stretching away from the font at the west door to the altar railed in and perhaps raised up at the east end as a powerful inducement to lay piety. Fulke Robarts claimed that it was particularly fitting that the font should be located near the church door 'ready to receive and entertain' the neophyte. 'There is he made one of the company of those which have right and interest in the privileges of that part of the church where the font is placed viz. the water of baptism to wash away his sins, the word for his instruction and prayer whereby to communicate himself to almighty God until he be fitted to be further preferred to the holy table which is therefore elevated or set down upon an higher floor than the rest of the pavement to be the more in the eyes and view of the people, that so for their edification they may the better behold the behaviour of the priest, consecrating. And setting apart the elements to become the sacrament. And that the very sight of the holy table, at all times, may beget in the upholders an hunger and thirst after that blessed food.'[32]

Again the vindication of the round of holy days and Christian festivals which made up the English liturgical year implicit in the Laudians' opposition to sabbatarianism had a further religious resonance which reflected perfectly the emotional tenor and rhythms of Laudian piety. The great festivals of the Christian year both figured and extended to all believers the benefits conferred on fallen humanity by Christ's life, passion and resurrection. 'They which come to God's house upon the day of Christ's nativity (coming in faith and love as they ought) are,' argued Robert Shelford, 'partakers of Christ's birth; they which come upon the day of circumcision are with him circumcised from the dominion of the flesh . . . .' By observing saints' days and in dedicating 'temples to God in their names', Shelford continued, 'we have the blessed saints still living and dwelling amongst us.' It was this which allowed Shelford to conclude that the keeping 'of the holy feasts of the Church' was one of the main offices of holiness. Those who omitted it, he claimed, 'do as much as in them lies cut themselves from this holy communion [with the saints in heaven] and have a great loss which none can see but they that have spiritual eyes'.[33]

Here, therefore, in both the cycle of the great feasts of the Christian year and in the physical and liturgical progression from the font to the altar were figured the sacramental and emotional means – the cycles of repentance, praise and sacrifice – whereby the individual Christian could be integrated into the mystical body of Christ and through which the members of that body on earth could collectively worship their God through the rites and ordinances of the visible church. As a whole variety of Laudian authors emphasised, it was through the religious observation of the ceremonial duties attendant upon the feasts and sacraments of the church that the members of the visible church on earth came closest to the state of the members of the church triumphant in heaven.

Not only did the Laudian church interior encapsulate the Laudian view of true religion, it also figured their conception of the Christian community. For the extent to which different groups within the Christian community were granted access to the places of the greatest spiritual heat or divine presence could be taken to define their place within the Christian community. Here the most obvious division was that between the clergy and the laity. Given the overall balance of their style of piety it was inevitable that the Laudians should define and exalt the role of the clergy in terms of their monopoly over the ministration of the sacrament and of their control over access to the altar. Thus John Pocklington went to great lengths to emphasise that while all Christians could offer the spiritual sacrifices involved in praise, prayer and almsdeeds, 'the sacrifice of the altar . . . is the particular function of the priest to perform'. This fact was signified by the priest's sole right of access to the altar; only they could pass within the rails to 'the highest place of all, whereunto the priest ascended by certain steps and degrees and when they did so ascend were not psalms of degree sung . . . . Was it not the only place whither none but priests might be allowed to come to officiate? Was not the holy eucharist there and nowhere else consecrated? Durst the priests themselves ascend thither without doing lowly reverence three several times? Was not this holy altar and the mysteries thereof at sometime kept railed from the eyes of most men?' Joseph Mede, too, used the 'place of the clergy next to the altar' to establish the master division in Laudian social theory between the clergy and laity. On this view, Laudian clericalism was founded on, indeed could scarcely be distinguished from, their sacrament- and worship-centred view of the world. This is a basic point which writers like Christopher Hill overlook when they explain the apparent unpopularity of Laudianism as a simple anti-clerical backlash against a theologically neutral or commonplace clericalism no different from that of Whitgift or Bancroft. Used like this, 'clericalism' is too imprecise a notion adequately to capture the distinctive flavour of Laudian sacerdotalism.[34]

If the issue of proximity to the altar served firstly and most importantly to establish the master divisions between the laity and the clergy, between the communicants and the excommunicate, in the hands of some Laudians the same motif also served to establish an elaborately variegated vision of the social body of the church. Several of these authors maintained that the church should be seen as composed of a number of distinct component parts. These were defined in terms of their greater or lesser proximity to the altar and served both to express and enforce certain differences in status amongst the lay members of the Church. Thus Fulke Robarts explained in 1639 'as there be several ranks of people professing Church unity, so they have their places in their several distances. Some are unworthy to come within the doors of the church and therefore are to stand without. Some are fit to be received in, to be baptised; some to be instructed in the grounds of religion and to repair with the rest of the congregation. All which is done in the nave and body of the church. And as men profit in knowledge and a working faith, to discern the Lord's body, they are admitted into a higher room, where the sacrament of the body and blood of Jesus Christ is to be administered at the holy table in the chancel, which divideth it from the rest of the church'.[35]

There was general agreement on this point, but various authors disagreed on how precise the different distinctions and gradations both within the church and amongst the laity should be. The details of this arrangement, which was never proferred as normative for the English Church, but merely as a precedent 'agreeable with good reason, order and comeliness, free from any colour of superstition',[36] need not concern us. What is of interest, however, is the idealised vision it contains of a variegated or subdivided Christian community, stretching back from the rails of the altar to the church porch and beyond. The typical Laudian church interior, with the altar railed at the east end of the chancel, perhaps a screen erected between the nave and the chancel, and the obtrusive and irregular

private pews of the laity levelled as all signs of human status hierarchies were removed in the face of the divine presence, did indeed
present a picture, delineated in architectural or spatial terms, of
the Laudian view of the Christian community.

It was perhaps not without significance that the Laudian attitude
to Sunday sports ensured that this vision of the Christian community hierarchically ordered, under tight clerical control, in the
face of the divine presence of the altar, could, and in many parishes
would, be swiftly succeeded by and juxtaposed to an altogether
more relaxed, festive and self-consciously profane version of social
solidarity acted out on the village green. It might be possible to
argue that these two versions or visions of the social order represented two sides of the same coin; that they implied and confirmed
one another. The Laudians were redrawing the division between
the sacred and the profane in tight spatial and temporal terms.
The status of the physical confines of the church and indeed the
churchyard as sacred spaces unavailable at any time for any secular
or festive purpose and the holiness of the set days and times desig-
nated by the church was confirmed by the festive and secular
activities allowed by the Book of Sports *after* time of divine service
on the village green. In short the precision and strength of the
division being effected between the sacred and the profane was
reinforced by the proximity of the one to the other on the Laudian
Sunday. Having been suspended while the social body of the church
was strung out, ritually schooled and disciplined under the eyes of
the clergy in the church, normal social relations were reconstituted
in and through the festivities on the village green. Thus the potentially levelling effects of Laudian clericalism, whereby the laity were
reduced to an equality of subjection before the divine presence,
shown forth and distributed by the priest, were contained and
defused. In the Sunday service and Sunday sports as the Laudians
envisaged them, we are confronted with two different but complementary visions of social unity, the one achieved through sacred
means, the other through profane. This double-barrelled model of
social and religious unity was proferred in self-conscious opposition
to a view of the Church and the commonwealth radically divided
between the godly and the ungodly, a view which the Laudians
labelled puritan.

It is important to emphasise at this point that nearly all the
central features of Laudianism as they have been described here

were constructed against a countervailing image of puritan hetero-
doxy and subversion. On the Laudian's view, the puritans fatally
confused the sacred and the profane. On the one hand they denied
any aura of sanctity to the church building or the physical impedimenta of divine worship. They allowed the church to be used out
of service time for all manner of secular purposes. Moreover, they
tended to identify the notion of the Church with the congregation
or still worse the godly community, not with the physical, liturgical
and jurisdictional structures beloved of the Laudians.[37] On the
Laudian view puritans allowed the sacred or the holy to spill out
of the church and into the world, beyond clerical control, with all
sorts of subversive consequences. For the Laudians this slippage
was implicit and inherent in the basic structures of what they
labelled as puritan piety. To begin with, on the Laudian view, the
godly played down the role of the sacraments, public prayer and
the ceremonies which attended them in favour of a style of piety
centred solely on the word preached.[38] For them the central features
of public worship were the rantings and ravings – the extempore
sermons and prayers of the minister.[39] The master division which
separated the sacred from the profane was that between the godly
and the ungodly, a division which was underwritten for the godly
by the doctrine of predestination, which allowed them to equate
themselves with the elect and their lukewarm contemporaries and
enemies amongst the loyal and conformist clergy with the reprobate.
It was no accident that most Laudian discussions of predestination
during the 1630s took the form of excoriations of absolute predestinarian opinions produced in the course of denouncing the divisive
effects of puritan religion.[40] On the Laudian view, the godly came
to regard themselves as holy objects, their private meetings for the
repetition of sermons, conventicles, fasts and prayer sessions, in
private houses, barns and woods became the true locus of the holy
in the world rather than the meetings and public ordinances of the
national Church.[41] The spurious scripturalism of puritan sabbatarianism further allowed the sacred to escape from the confines of the
church and the structures of public worship to suffuse the whole of
the Lord's day. This not only gave the godly another occasion to
separate themselves off from the usual bonds of community and
neighbourhood through their pharisaical private devotions and
avoidance of all secular and lawful recreation, it also allowed them
to revile and ignore the genuine holy days proclaimed by the

Church. Small groups of self-selected godly persons then systematically gadded to sermons in other parishes, attended church only when a sermon was preached, arriving as the preacher started and leaving once he had finished. They would listen only to ministers who refused to use the ceremonies and shared both their view of the world and their own estimation of themselves as elect saints. All other loyal members of the Church of England they wrote off as mere conformists, time-serving careerists. The result was a generation of ambitious and factious ministers who played to the gallery in return for the applause of the people and the contributions and favour of the godly laity.[42] All this could not but undermine the authority of the clergy and the peaceful course of social relations in the community of Christians as the Laudians defined it. At stake was the unity and order of the Church and ultimately the stability of the entire Christian commonwealth.[43]

Laudian authors chose repeatedly and self-consciously to define themselves against the image of puritan deviance summarised above. It is only when the Laudian project is set over against this polemically constructed image of puritan deviance and subversion that the full polemical and political resonance of the Laudian project can be recovered and the Laudian style be properly integrated into a wider account of the Caroline style of the Personal Rule.[44] Certainly, when set against this backdrop Laudianism emerges as a coherent view of the Church and the Christian community; of the nature of the divine presence in the Church, of the ways in which that presence could be apprehended and communicated to the Church's members, of the relative value in the life of the Church of the word preached, prayer, the sacraments and of the liturgical and architectural frames in which those ordinances should be set. Here is a vision of the Christian community organised around the holy places and times delineated by the Church and centred in particular on the altar and on the sacerdotal powers of the priesthood. It is a vision well suited to the needs of an inclusive national Church, in which all members of the national community were assumed to be baptised members of the Church, subject both to the sacramental power of the clergy and the temporal authority of the Christian magistrate or prince.

It would be an error to claim either that this vision of the Church, true religion and order was novel in the 1630s or that it represented conventional wisdom. On the issue of novelty views like this had been canvassed amongst certain avant-garde conformist divines since at least the 1590s. If anyone has a claim to have invented this particular strain of English protestantism it was Richard Hooker, and it can be traced through the Jacobean period in the thought and writings of divines like Lancelot Andrewes and John Buckeridge and through the patronage network of Bishop Richard Neile.[45] However, the fact that such opinions had a history prior to the Personal Rule did not mean that they were simply conventional. On the contrary, as we have seen, many of the central tenets of the Laudian view of the world flew in the face of conventional Jacobean protestant wisdom. Even to quite moderate divines raised within what we might term the English reformed tradition, many features of Laudianism appeared at best worrying and at worst frankly popish.[46]

In the 1630s the view of the world that has been termed 'Laudian' in this article moved to a positon of dominance (if not monopoly) in the Church and became attached to a variety of official policies, the most notable of which were the altar policy and the suppression of sabbatarianism. This could not help but raise the stakes, transforming the significance of the ceremonies, practices and attitudes in question, rendering them, as we have seen, crucial characteristics of a properly reformed and refurbished Church. Such a revaluation of the role of the beauty of holiness in all its material and liturgical ramifications could not but in turn greatly increase the seriousness of any puritan lapse from full conformity as the Laudians understood it.

The Jacobean accommodation between evangelical protestant prelacy and moderate puritanism had been based on precisely the core of common attitudes and assumptions about the nature of the Church's mission, the role of the minister and the content of right doctrine summarised above. On that basis, many Jacobean bishops had gone out of their way to keep even quite notorious puritans like John Cotton within the pale of the Church. For their part even puritans with real scruples about conformity had been able to respect the bishops as honourable and orthodox men, essentially on the same side as themselves in the titanic struggle being waged between Christ and Antichrist, the light of the gospel and popular ignorance and irreligion.[47] With the fracture of that common core of assumption by Laudianism even moderate puritans who went through the motions of conformity appeared to Laudians as some sort of sinister fifth column dedicated to the overthrow of the Church from within. As Dr Fincham has shown, the main thrust of Jacobean policy had been towards the extraction of subscription from the clergy, a formal acceptance of conformity, often mitigated by a good deal of tolerance of practical non-conformity or laxity. Now that very policy came under the lash of Laudian tongues. To Laudians formal subscription unaccompanied by honest, punctilious, indeed, zealous obedience to the canons and formularies of the Church seemed if anything even more dangerous, because more difficult to root out, than overt non-conformity. The ordinary forms of puritan piety, formerly accepted even by many bishops as signs of zeal and orthodoxy, appeared to the Laudians to be sinister precursors to separation, seed beds of schism and the heresy that must inevitably follow any rent in the seamless garment of the Church's unity. In this scenario, the departure of puritans for the Low Countries or New England became a matter of self-congratulation.[48]

Increasingly the Laudians sought to characterise the choice facing the Church as one between their own vision of ecclesiastical order and the vision of puritan disorder, outlined above. The effect of this was inevitably to polarise religious opinion. The policies pursued during the Personal Rule and the Laudian gloss put upon them inevitably alienated all shades of puritan opinion. If conformity meant what the Laudians took it to mean then erstwhile puritan moderates, like John Davenport, who had been able to conform for the sake of their ministries now found any further truck with conformity impossible and moved to outright non-conformity and in Davenport's case semi-separatism and exile. At the same time the resulting confrontation between authority and newly-strident puritan dissent squeezed moderate evangelical Calvinist bishops between the demands of Laudian conformity on the one hand and the complaints and polemics of the godly on the other. In this way erstwhile puritan moderates like John Bastwick were forced to the left, while moderate bishops and Calvinist divines like Joseph Hall or Robert Sanderson ended up looking for all the world like Laudian fellow-travellers.[49]

To conclude, Laudian ceremonialism, the whole concern with the beauty of holiness, the altar policy, even the assault on sabbatarianism could be and often were defended simply in terms of the power of the Church and the Christian prince over things indifferent. However, this does not mean that Laudianism represented merely a traditional conformist insistence on order, decency and obedience nor that the constituent parts of the Laudian programme are best seen as a shopping list of isolated, piecemeal adjustments to the outward face of the English Church. On the contrary, behind those piecemeal adjustments and traditional conformist arguments lay a coherent view of true religion and ecclesiastical order, which while not, by the 1630s, conceptually novel was scarcely conventional by the standards of the English protestantism of the previous sixty years. Moreover, if the Laudians often chose to legitimate their policies and priorities in terms of a traditional conformist rhetoric of adiaphora, they also often chose to confer an aura of patristic, apostolic and even scriptural necessity upon their position which was in, at least potential, conflict with their more conventional insistence on things indifferent. A variety of authors cited scriptural texts on both the temple and tabernacle under the Old Testament as well as passages from Revelation and the Apocalypse on the practices of the church triumphant in order to justify both general Laudian positions on the church as the house of God and the beauty of holiness as well as more specific Laudian and conformist practices like kneeling in prayer, worshipping and bowing towards the altar or bowing at the name of Jesus. Even when their position claimed the warrant only of ecclesiastical custom, the customs involved were very often described as immemorial and thus apostolic in origin. There was, therefore, a maximum Laudian position based on scripture and patristic and apostolic precedent, as well as a minimum position based on the power of the Church and the Christian prince over things indifferent.[50]

Again, while the Laudians tended on the one hand to pass their policies and priorities off as both the product and vindication of an 'Anglican' essence, they often had difficulty in precisely locating that position in the foundation documents of the Elizabethan Church. Often they were reduced to viewing the position of the English Church through a grid composed of their own version of the practice of the Church fathers or the apostles in order to render the fit between the religion of the prayer book and their own preferences and practices the more complete.[51] Again, while they might claim that they were merely preserving some Anglican essence, located in a rather hazy golden age, in practice they were both anxious and proud to proclaim that the religious temper of the Personal Rule marked a sharp discontinuity from an immediate past typified at best by lay and clerical laxity and irreverence and at worst by sacrilege and semi-separation.[52]

Here their vision of the puritan threat came to their rescue. For, in the light of that threat, they could portray themselves on the one hand, as essentially conservative, restoring and refurbishing a Church fallen on hard times, according to a pattern of perfection located half in the Prayer Book and canons and half in a golden vision of the patristic past. On the other hand, however, when it suited them they could present themselves with equal cogency as a radical reforming force pushing back the corrupting, puritan tendencies and practices of the past forty or so years.

The result was an intensely ambiguous position, at once self-consciously conservative and innovative. Laudians were capable of a withering scepticism when confronted with the dogmatic doctrinal beliefs of their opponents (on such issues as predestination, assurance, the identity of the pope as Antichrist).[53] But they were also capable of an equally dogmatic assertion of the rights of the clergy, the authority of the Church, the demands of the beauty of holiness. Moreover in the defence of those things they could and did resort to a scripturalism almost as stark and uncompromising as that of the puritans. The mystery which sheathed and surrounded the divine will and the divine presence in the world, the church and the consecrated elements might serve to protect those subjects from the codifying rationalism of puritan predestinarian speculation. But that same mysteriousness also underwrote their own awe-struck approach to the divine presence and the outward forms of reverence and worship, which, they insisted, were an essential part of true religion and right worship. By concentrating on one aspect or another of the resulting ideological synthesis it is possible to produce a number of apparently mutually exclusive versions of what Laudianism was, each of which can claim considerable textual warrant in the writings of the Laudians themselves, but none of which, taken alone, can provide a convincing or comprehensive account of the phenomenon of Laudianism. Only an account of the Laudian view of the world which tries to accommodate all these diverse elements and attempts to come to grips with the relations between them can hope to do that. This essay is probably best approached as a crude and summary outline of what such a rounded picture of Laudianism would or might look like.

8. The Church of England, Rome, and the True Church: The Demise of a Jacobean Consensus

ANTHONY MILTON

Commentators have often noted that the key to comprehending the present condition of a society and its culture lies in understanding its perception of its own past. Recent historians of early modern England – most notably Peter Lake – have drawn attention to the importance of contemporary views of the pre-Reformation Church in influencing and expressing more general perceptions of the Church of England in the Elizabethan period. Attention has focused on the widely influential *Acts and Monuments* (or 'Book of Martyrs') of John Foxe, which gave an account of the survival of the true church during the Middle Ages, not through a succession of prominent Christian institutions, but through an 'underground' succession of a minority of true believers. In Foxe's schema, this tiny group of true Christians was seen in almost sectarian terms, as largely dissociated from the persecuting, antichristian medieval Church of Rome. It has been argued that this vision of the church proved difficult to reconcile with the situation in England after the Reformation, when the preachers of the established Church were called upon to extend this ideology of the 'saving remnant' to comprehend the whole national community, with its wide divergences in godly behaviour and belief.

Peter Lake has argued further that this Foxeian tradition of the 'saving remnant' was potentially undermined by the development within the English protestant conformist camp of the position that episcopacy was *iure divino* ('by divine right'), with its accompanying claim that the church had always been ruled by bishops. He has depicted Richard Hooker as the first divine to follow through the implications of a conformist position, which compelled him to vindicate the institutional church. While Hooker himself was studiously moderate on the point of *iure divino* episcopacy, he nevertheless developed a line of argument which also overthrew by implication the Foxeian position on the nature of pre-Reformation protestantism, by choosing to represent Rome as the true church of which the Church of England represented 'a reformed continuation', and by infusing the institutional Church and its ceremonies with a positive religious value, against Elizabethan Calvinism's emphasis on a form of individual piety centred on the Word preached.[1]

But what happened to these tensions in the Jacobean Church? Historians such as Patrick Collinson have emphasised the extent to which episcopacy was reconciled with more advanced forms of protestantism within a Jacobean 'consensus' which was essentially evangelical and Calvinist. Did this represent an effective rearguard action against Hookerian notions, or a qualified acceptance of them? If the latter was true, how far did Laud and his associates represent a break with the Jacobean position? This article attempts to answer these questions by focusing on the issue of the pre-Reformation Church, and the accompanying themes of visibility, succession and the true church. It will be argued that the Jacobean position represented an efficient though somewhat muddled compromise between different visions of the nature of the church. This compromise was eventually destroyed both by the Laudians' attempt to shake free from this composite structure those institutional elements which they preferred, and by the consequent determination of more puritan ministers to renounce these same elements as alien to the English protestant tradition. This meant the end of a Jacobean consensus which could only survive as long as such an incompatibility was denied.

II

Discussions of the doctrine of the church in this period revolved around the notions of the 'visible' and 'invisible' church. What did these terms mean? The moderate Calvinist John Davenant – Lady

Margaret Professor of Divinity at Cambridge and later Bishop of Salisbury – explained that there were two different senses in which the church could be said to be invisible. The first sense of 'invisibility' referred to the church of the elect – which comprised essentially the whole company of God's elect throughout history who alone were members of Christ's mystical body by an inward effectual calling. This church is invisible because the principal part of it is already triumphant in heaven, while even the part of this church which is militant on earth cannot be outwardly perceived. Where more radical puritan divines attempted to build forms of religious piety around the individual's ability to perceive his election and to move within the community of his fellow godly, a moderate Calvinist establishment figure such as Davenant emphasised that election could never be perceived. He therefore stressed the positive implications of the elect church's invisibility: all members of the visible institutional church should be assumed to be also members of the invisible church of the elect. Where conformist writers before Hooker had emphasised the inseparable distinction of the invisible from the visible church, Jacobean conformists such as Richard Field and John Prideaux attempted to infuse the visible, institutional Church of England with a more positive religious value by stressing that the distinction between the 'visible' and 'invisible' church simply referred to two different aspects of the same church.[2]

But this was not the only meaning of the term 'invisibility'. Davenant explained that the term could also be used to refer to the diminution of 'the true church' of orthodox believers in a time of corruption and oppression, in which sense it was applied to the protestant descent before Luther. But what is 'the true church'? Davenant explains that it is the sum of orthodox Christians, who are not guilty of heresy or schism, and are not necessarily coterminous with the church of the elect. On occasion, this 'true church' might be reduced to such an inferior degree of external eminence and conspicuousness, and to such a tiny minority, that it could be said for that time to have been, in a relative sense, 'invisible'. This concept of 'relative' invisibility offered a fundamental solution for early protestant reformers and later protestant polemicists to the problem of explaining away the predominance of the corrupt Roman Church in the medieval period. It did this by warning against identifying the outward *institutional* church of Christian history (which, for all its outward glory, had fallen prey to grevious heresy) with the church of true believers. Instead, these protestant writers emphasised the role of persecution in identifying the suffering 'saving remnant', and the perpetual visibility of the church, not through outward institutional greatness, but through the succession of true doctrine retained by this oppressed minority.[3]

This theme gained greater importance and prophetic meaning by its integral role in protestant apocalyptic expositions of the history of the medieval church and of the Reformation. The texts of 2 Thessalonians 2.4 and of Revelation 12.6 were central to this tradition: the former predicting the universal religious apostasy of the Middle Ages, and the latter – 'the woman fled into the desert' – the flight from persecution of the true church of pure believers during this period. Thus it was even claimed that Rome's outward 'visibility' in the past was itself a sign that she was *not* the true church, which instead was destined to suffer and flee from the world.[4]

The tradition of the relative 'invisibility' of the true church never implied that the succession of the Word and Ministry had necessarily been impaired, or that the true church had existed without them. It only meant that the church of true believers had not all been formally, visibly distinguished from the rest of the visible, institutional church. However, the apocalyptic tradition's stress on the eternal opposition of the true and false churches, and on the fact that the true church would be identified through its being persecuted, tended to emphasise the true church's alienation from the external church. Roman Catholic polemicists delighted in trying to embarrass their English protestant opponents by quoting the extreme apocalyptic formulations of radicals such as Napier, Fulke and Brocardo, that the true church had been completely invisible during the Middle Ages under the universal apostasy caused by the papal Antichrist, in order to reject English protestant claims of the church's perpetual visibility and the Church of England's episcopal succession. It is striking that, in reply, Jacobean protestant apologists such as Thomas Morton and Francis White refused to repudiate these writers or their arguments. Instead, they attempted to integrate them within arguments for ministerial succession and the perpetual visibility of the church's external forms by explaining their arguments in terms of the relative 'invisibility' of the true church.[5]

These related issues of visibility, succession and the true church came to a head when Romanist divines put to English protestants the perennial question – 'Where was your Church before Luther?' Faced with this question, mainstream Jacobean divines pointed to various groups. They looked to the primitive Church of the first five centuries, to those sounder members still in communion with the medieval Roman church, to medieval sects such as the Waldensians who separated from her communion and were persecuted by Rome, and also to national Churches of faithful Christians who rejected the pope's claims to universal jurisdiction, such as the Greek, Russian and Ethiopian Churches. They did this with no sense of contradiction or incompatibility.[6] Their first response was to deny that it was necessary to provide historical proof for an external visible succession of protestant professors through the ages: conformity with scripture was the only real test of a church's legitimacy, and it was also scripture which had promised that the Catholic faith would always remain. It therefore followed that, if the protestants held the Catholic faith, then they must necessarily have existed throughout the medieval period, even if patchy historical records did not reveal them. This point was argued even by those writers most diligent in compiling chronological successions of protestant believers. Nevertheless, they were prepared to meet their Romanist adversary on his own ground, and with his own weapon.[7]

In their search for medieval predecessors, English protestants' eyes inevitably came to rest upon the medieval heretical sects: the Waldensians, Albigensians, Lollards, Hussites and others. Here were manifest examples of unequivocal opposition to Roman doctrines and jurisdiction, driven into separation by popish abuses and persecution in the same way that protestants had been. The attraction of tracing the protestant church before Luther through these small persecuted sects derived in part from the ease with which they fitted into the protestant apocalyptic view of church history, with its stress on the persecution of the tiny spurned church of God's elect by the false church of Antichrist, and also from their clear manifestation of direct separation from a church to which Elizabethan and Jacobean protestants held themselves to be irreconcilably opposed. Throughout the Jacobean period, moderate puritan writers, while not denying the legitimacy of other routes, displayed a clear preference for this proto-protestant descent. However, the same period also saw a committed attempt by Calvinist episcopalians such as Ussher, Morton and Prideaux to clean up and dignify this line of descent by stressing the 'visibility' and institutional and doctrinal respectability of the various sects, renouncing those heresies historically ascribed to them as the hostile misreporting of their Romish enemies,[8] and increasingly focusing on their preservation of an outward and lawful ministry of the Word and Sacraments, and indeed an episcopal ordination and succession.[9]

A similar concern to emphasise visibility, continuity and respectability is clear in Jacobean developments regarding the next route of descent which the protestants identified. This was those Christians who made no clear separation from the Church of Rome during the medieval period, 'as not perceiving the mystery of iniquity which wrought in it, [but] did yet mislike the grosser errors, which at this day she maintaineth, and desired a reformation'.[10] Where Tudor writers had often spoken of this group in terms of an invisible elite, men such as Prideaux now chose to stress the visibility and distinctiveness of those before Luther who had opposed papal corruptions yet remained in communion with the Church of Rome.[11] While Foxe's list of witnesses in this category was mostly anti-clerical, this emphasis is mostly (and consciously) absent from Jacobean writings, where catalogues of witnesses to protestant doctrine commonly include many important clerics and members of the church hierarchy. This could result in strange anomalies: thus, Jean Gerson, St. Bernard and the Englishmen Thomas Gascoin and Thomas Netter were vehement opponents of the Hussites, Waldensians and Lollards respectively, but were all important protestant witnesses because they opposed popish abuses.[12] The protestant witnesses in these lists were commonly admitted to have had their errors, due to the veiling of the truth under the Roman tyranny, but it was argued that these errors were not fundamental and might be pardoned by a general repentance for all errors known and unknown, while in the crucial matter of justification by faith in Christ alone they were true protestants.[13]

This position was complicated, however, by the constant problem of protestant polemicists in explaining the fate of their natural forefathers (as opposed to their forefathers in faith) who died before the advent of true religion in the Reformation.[14] The basic response of Elizabethan and Jacobean divines was that those dying in times of ignorance might be pardoned by a judgement of charity for having sinned ignorantly in minor popish errors as long as they held on to the foundation of belief – salvation by faith in Christ's merits alone – and made a general repentance for sins known and unknown.[15] However, Foxe and others had maintained that justification by faith alone – the central protestant doctrine – had only been restored by Luther. The problem thus remained of how those who were ignorant of this fundamental doctrine before the Reformation could have been able to trust in Christ alone for their salvation. Richard Hooker ran into problems in his sermons at the Temple in 1586 when, in attempting to answer this question, he drew a distinction between overthrowing the faith directly and by consequent, and maintained that the Roman Church's doctrine of justification by inherent faith only did the latter. Thus, people might hold a popish doctrine of the merit of good works, yet without drawing the logical consequence that salvation could be earned by man, rather than being possible solely through Christ's merits. The problem was that such a distinction might easily imply the possibility of salvation for post-Reformation papists, and it was this which drew Walter Travers' fire and Archbishop Whitgift's careful reservations.[16]

This problem was effectively solved by Richard Field in his treatise *Of the Church*, and his solution gained acceptance among many writers in the Jacobean Church. Field's answer was to give a new positive emphasis to perceptions of the medieval Latin Church by arguing that the doctrine of justification by faith alone, and indeed the protestant position on all those points currently controverted between them and the Church of Rome, could be found being openly taught in all those western Churches under the Romish tyranny throughout the medieval period. Field presented a vision of the medieval Latin Church as an arena of far-reaching dispute between a corrupt 'papalist faction' – the Court of Rome – and the rest of the Church of Rome. In fact, he stressed that 'the Latin Church . . . continued the true Church of God even till our time'. The arguments for the salvation of protestants' forefathers and for the succession of the true church were essentially combined, as Field answered the customary question of the location of the church before Luther with the reply that 'it was where now it is. If they ask us, which? we answer, it was the known and apparent Church in the world, wherein all our fathers lived and died'. In fact, 'all those Christian Catholic Churches in the West part of the world, where the pope formerly tyrannized, and where our fathers lived and died, were the true protestant Churches of God'. This was because papist points of false doctrine and error were not constantly delivered nor generally received in the Latin Church, but only 'doubtfully broached and devised' by a faction until the Council of Trent (1545–63), convened after the Reformation had begun, where these errors were imposed as *de fide*, and thus the general doctrine of the Roman Church made damnable. The crucial point was that 'the Roman Church is not the same now that it was when Luther began'; 'formerly, the Church of Rome was the true Church, but had in it a heretical faction: now the Church itself is heretical'.[17]

Jacobean Calvinist writers from Bishops Morton, Carleton and Ussher to puritans such as Thomas Scot and Henry Burton all eagerly embraced the view that the papal religion only really began at the Council of Trent. Moderate writers could thus ensure the salvation of their forefathers and maintain institutional continuity, while more radical writers were happy to explore the further conclusion that, since the Council of Trent, Rome had ceased to be a Church at all, and had erected an anti-religion founded upon the pope's authority rather than that of scripture.[18]

The recapture of the medieval institutional church from Rome also found expression in the activities of vehement anti-papists such as Archbishop Ussher, William Crashaw and Richard Crakanthorp, who searched medieval liturgies, prayers, councils and scholastic authors for proof that protestant doctrine still flourished well into the later medieval period and (in some cases) right up to the Council of Trent itself. It also enabled apologists for the English Reformation to claim with more consistency that the Reformation did not erect a new church, but merely purified a corrupted old one.[19]

Here, clearly, were all the necessary ingredients for an alternative and self-sufficient answer to the question of the location of the protestant church before Luther based on the general medieval Christian community, which could easily jettison any need to appeal to Waldensians or to any notions of a godly elite of true worshippers within or outside the communion of the Church of Rome. However, it must be emphasised that this stream of thought was not necessarily developed in opposition to the sectarian, proto-protestant line of descent. Field's main concern was to stress that the true church before Luther should not be located *wholly* in men such as Wiclif and Hus, to the exclusion of others. He still occasionally used the language of the 'saving remnant' when talking of the anti-papal faction in the church, seeing those erring in the medieval church as 'the prevailing faction' and their anti-papist opponents as the only ones who were 'principally and in special sort' the church, who held a saving profession of truth in Christ, and to whom alone scriptural references to the church as a holy and undefiled paradise pertained. This blurring of language, in which definitions of the church of the elect and of the saving remnant of true believers seem to overlap in the Foxeian manner, along with Field's unequivocal denunciation of present Rome as 'the synagogue of Satan, the faction of Antichrist, and that Babylon out of which we must fly', kept him within earlier apocalyptic traditions.[20]

Similarly, in other writers such as Bishops Carleton and Ussher, this positive assessment of institutional churches in the time before Trent was usually tempered by a strong emphasis on Revelation 20.1–3 and 7 – the binding of Satan for a thousand years and his subsequent unleashing (in the eleventh century) – as holding the key to medieval chronology. Antichrist may have only been triumphant in the Council of Trent, yet those with the insight to flee Babylon far earlier were not to be criticised, even if popish errors were not then so transcendent.[21] Certainly, the resulting arguments were not always coherent (as Roman Catholic polemicists were not slow to point out). In Field and Ussher's works it is sometimes very difficult to tell exactly to which 'church' they are referring – whether to the elect, or to a saving remnant of true believers, or to the general Christian community – or whether when talking of the protestant 'church' before Luther they are in fact referring to protestant *doctrine*. But it was precisely this incoherence which made possible the multi-faceted Jacobean approach to the protestants' past, and allowed it to absorb many different arguments while disavowing none.

But that there were tensions beneath the surface is irrefutable. Daniel Featley and other radicals, while allowing that the visibility of the protestant church might be traced through 'the corrupt popish Church', felt this to be 'a slippery & dirty way . . . to seek the golden purity of the faith, amids the dung, and dross of Romish superstitions, and depravations in later ages', preferring the 'more excellent way' of the succession of sectarian, proto-protestant witnesses.[22] This potential division between moderate and radical Calvinists over the definition of the true church in terms of purity of doctrine, and the radicals' predisposition to treat the separation from Rome in absolute terms, was realised in the controversy which flared up in 1629 over Joseph Hall's short treatise *The Old Religion*, which will be discussed in more detail below. The compromise which the need to allow for the salvation of forefathers and to safeguard ecclesiastical continuity imposed upon the radical protestant desire to search for a true church of pure, orthodox believers was clearly in danger of breaking down in the 1620s.

While the Jacobeans left the potential for a view of the medieval church which traced the protestant descent solely through the Roman Church, it was under the Laudians that the final crucial break was made, and the Foxeian view of church history decisively rejected. Laud himself had no time for any search for catalogues of a minority of pure medieval believers: the traditional argument that 'the reformation of an old corrupted Church' was not 'the building of a new' was for him, and for other Laudian writers, the full and complete answer to the question of the protestants' origins, rendering all other arguments irrelevant. Richard Montagu opposed himself more directly to 'any lineal deduction from, and extraction out of, Wyclif, Huss, Albigenses . . . of a visible Church, though never so reverently preached or authoritatively printed', and Peter Heylyn inverted Featley's expressed preference by scornfully spurning the proto-protestant pedigree as 'so poor a shift'.[23]

Under the Laudians a clearer protestant succession thus emerged, which could be restricted wholly to independent, national episcopal churches. This tended to put a significant new emphasis upon the Church of England's continuity with the pre-Reformation Latin Church and its hierarchy. Where Jacobean writers had replied to Romanist questions by stating that the protestant church before Luther was 'where it is now' (thereby permitting an interpretation still based on ideas of a congregation of doctrinally pure believers), Laud could reply that 'it was just there, where *theirs* is now. One and the same Church still, no doubt of that; one in substance, but not one in condition of state and purity: their part of the same Church remaining in corruption, and our part of the same Church under reformation.'[24] A corrupt, impure church was thus for Laud a sufficient ancestor for the Church of England. Similarly, Montagu was not concerned to search for the succession of a pure church, or for an orthodoxy which might in any sense be invisible. There was no longer to be any confusion in the use of the word 'church' – it would now only refer to visible institutions, rather than to purity of doctrine.

This break from traditional English protestant thought on this issue, which even divided moderate and radical members of the Durham House Group (the circle around Bishop Richard Neile), may be observed most strikingly in the conferences conducted by Francis White and William Laud with the Jesuit Fisher in 1622. While White made great play in this conference with the concept of the 'relative' invisibility of the true church, and even seemed prepared to treat the proto-protestant sects as the only documentary evidence for the preservation of the true religion in the West before Luther,[25] his colleague Laud chose to make no use of this sense of the church. Laud also avoided any stress on the role of persecution, of the corruption of the church's hierarchy, or indeed of any idea of the succession of true doctrine and of the true church through a minority of despised, possibly exclusively lay, true believers.

For Richard Montagu, episcopacy itself was the key to the succession, and not just something that needed to be provided for within the terms of a succession of true doctrine. In rejecting the notion that ministers could (in case of necessity) be made without an episcopal ordination based upon the direct, personal succession, Montagu denied that any such case might arise, and applied to the local, episcopal succession Christ's promise to His church that He would be with it until the end of the world. This piece of scripture had always previously been applied to the guarantee of the preservation of an elite of true believers.[26]

When they looked back to the medieval church, the Laudians did not look back to a hidden succession of true believers, who had preserved the essence of right doctrine despite the persecution of a church hierarchy which reviled them as heretics. Instead, they concentrated almost exclusively upon the general Christian community in which their forefathers had participated, and upon the piety, devotion and reverence which the medieval church, for all its faults, had been able to instill. In Laudian times, medieval piety was more likely to be held up for unqualified emulation. Praise of the medieval church was shifting increasingly from a defence of the kernel of true doctrine which it had retained in the midst of popish superstitions, towards a celebration of its high standards of piety and its elaborate patterns of public worship.[27]

III

It was not until the 1630s that the Foxeian tradition of the 'saving remnant' was directly and publicly repudiated by Laudian writers such as Heylyn and Montagu. Earlier, while divines such as Laud and Montagu himself were clearly not in sympathy with the Foxeian vision of the protestants' ancestry, they yet chose (in the 1620s at least) to circumvent this tradition rather than to confront it head on in public. Nevertheless, it was in the 1620s, and most notably in Richard Montagu's notorious tracts the *New Gagg* and the *Appello Caesarem*, that the Foxeian vision was decisively undermined by the repudiation of two doctrines which lay at its very heart.

The first of these doctrinal changes was the Laudian rejection of the apocalyptic foundations of the Foxeian tradition – most strikingly, of the Elizabethan orthodoxy that the pope was the Antichrist foretold in scripture. While there had been murmurings of dissent in the universities from this point, beginning in Cambridge in 1599 with John Overall (the Regius Professor and friend of Lancelot Andrewes), the first clear assault on the consensus in print was mounted in Montagu's *New Gagg* and *Appello Caesarem* (1624–5). Montagu's chosen tactic was to stress the obscurity of the issue (as well as of other predestinarian doctrines), and to emphasise that the Church of England in her official formularies did not bind her members to any one view, and therefore not to commit himself to any single view on the issue. Nevertheless, he distanced himself and the Church of England from the 'private imaginations' and 'several fancies of men' who peremptorily affirmed the pope to be Antichrist, and argued that, not just a few, but all the scriptural prophecies might more fittingly be applied to the Turkish State and Tyranny. He thereby equipped his reader with all the evidence for an exclusive identification of Antichrist with the Turk. William Laud similarly had little time for the identification of the pope as Antichrist, dismissing it contemptuously as merely an example of the use of 'foul language in controversies'. Laud and Montagu wisely restricted themselves to the condemnation of those who 'peremptorily' asserted the pope to be Antichrist, and stressed the issue to be an area of impenetrable obscurity. By contrast, the Laudian polemicists Christopher Dow and Peter Heylyn (the latter in a book specifically commissioned 'by authority') showed less restraint in firmly rejecting the apocalyptic tradition, writing it off as the result of over-zealousness in the early years of the Reformation.[28]

Detailed alternative expositions of the Book of Revelation would not appear until Henry Hammond in the 1650s. Instead, efforts under Laud were directed more towards removing references to the Antichrist from protestant polemical writings, and discouraging speculation on these issues altogether. The doctrine's value was denied in the conversion of recusants: ignoring all previous thought on the issue, Laud simply denied 'that the calling of pope Antichrist did ever yet convert an understanding papist'. The doctrine of the papal Antichrist was clearly on the retreat in the 1630s. Joseph Mede, writing from Cambridge, clearly identified 'a party . . . [which] loves not the pope should be Antichrist', and was therefore reluctant to publish his own apocalyptical writings 'for fear of incurring . . . a dangerous prejudice by an overpotent opposition'.[29]

The second vital change stemmed from the Laudians' rejection of the notion of a 'relative' invisibility of the church. Laudian writers, with some exceptions, had no problems with the definition of the invisibility of the church of the elect, although they preferred not to refer directly to 'the elect' when talking of the invisible church, and generally side-stepped the issue. The single occasion on which Laud referred to the church of the elect in the whole corpus of his writings (and even then only in a footnote!) was in order to stress that it could only exist through the visible, institutional church.[30]

However, where Luther and Calvin were cited against him by the Jesuit John Fisher regarding their claims of the 'relative' invisi-bility of the true church during the Middle Ages, Laud interpreted them as referring wholly to the invisible church of the elect. While Richard Montagu was entirely orthodox in his definition of the invisible church of the elect, he had no time at all for the 'relative' invisibility of the true church. In his *New Gagg* he simply denied the existence of such a doctrine when his papist opponent tried to use it against him. Having described the invisibility of the church of the elect, he abruptly concluded: 'Otherwise then so, we do not speak of invisibility'. In his *Appello Caesarem*, he did acknowledge that some English writers did indeed talk of the invisibility of the true church on earth, but attributed this view only to 'Libertines and Brownists', and quite falsely claimed that it was repugnant to the basic point of the necessary visibility of the church on earth 'with visible cognisances, marks and signs to be discerned by' (such as the Word of God, the sacraments and the priesthood).[31] As has been explained above, the doctrine of the relative invisibility of the true church had in fact been held by many mainstream churchmen, and even bishops, who did not intend it to deny all forms of institutional succession.[32] This rejection of the occasional 'invisibility' of the true church only formed part of a more important rejection by the Laudians of the very notion of a 'true church' of orthodox believers, which we shall discuss shortly.

These doctrinal shifts among some Laudian divines carried profound implications for the way in which the medieval church and the separation from Rome were perceived. They also strongly influenced the way in which the contemporary Church of Rome was understood. By rejecting the identification of the pope as Antichrist and Rome as Babylon, most Laudian writers thereby removed a crucial qualification of Rome's status as a church, and also bypassed an important area of common ground with those puritans who denied that antichristian Rome could be accounted a church of Christ at all. It meant that Rome's errors were no longer seen in prophetic terms, as necessary heresies in a coherent programme which worked inevitably towards ever greater corruption. Those truths which she retained were no longer accidental to her nature and purpose. Jacobean writers had argued that the pope's status as Antichrist required that Rome be in some sense a church, as scripture related that Antichrist must sit in the Temple of God. Under the Laudians, some writers argued that, since Rome was a true church in professing the truths of Christianity, then she could not be Babylon and the pope could not be Antichrist.[33]

Mainstream Jacobean writers had generally accepted that Rome was a church *secundum quid*, in a certain sense, according to some aspects of her nature, noting that in retaining baptism and the scriptures she still had the means (however determinedly she attempted to corrupt them) whereby God could call forth His people to life and salvation in Christ. Nevertheless, any positive implications of this admission were heavily qualified by the emphasis on the fact that Rome's whole antiChristian religion was dedicated to undoing the efficacy of God's calling. Richard Field argued that Rome was only part of the church of God because 'it ministereth the true sacrament of baptism to the salvation of the souls of many thousand infants *that die after they are baptized, before she have poisoned them with her errors*'.[34]

When Laud and his associates spoke of the nature of the Church of Rome, such careful qualifications were ignored. Laud did not stress the distinction between Rome's position before and after the Council of Trent, but instead cited the arguments of Field, Prideaux, Archbishop Abbot and others for the preservation of true doctrine and the possibility of salvation in the pre-Reformation church, and then applied them to the *present* Church of Rome.[35] When Laud and Montagu spoke of Rome as being a true church 'in the verity of essence' (i.e. in its retention of baptism and of faith in Christ), although not a sound church due to her corruptions in doctrine and practice, they would not go so far as Joseph Hall or John Davenant in saying that, with respect to her doctrine, Rome was 'no church', or 'a false church'.[36] In their expositions, there is no sense that Rome's status as a church is simply dependent on which of her aspects is being considered, no distinction between a Christian face and an antichristian heart, no sense that Rome is only to be considered a church *secundum quid*. This perception of Rome as simply an erring, corrupt, particular church was supplemented by the increasing emphasis which Laud and Montagu placed on Rome's status as a member of the Catholic Church, and as thus on an equal par with other particular institutional churches.

If such a radical change did occur, it is important to study exactly how it was effected, and what implications this process has for historians' views of a 'Calvinist consensus' in the Jacobean Church, and of the nature of the Laudians' destruction of it. Firstly, it must be emphasised that the Laudians did not represent a *deus ex machina*. They introduced no radically new ideas, and did not need to do so. Rather, by rejecting other traditional aspects of English protestantism, they freed more institutionally-minded patterns of thought which were already becoming established within Jacobean protestantism, so that these elements could fulfil a radical potential. Their position was based upon a selective appropriation of elements from the Jacobean defence of the established Church. A variety of forces during the reign of King James were tending to give rise to more pacific justifications of the separation from Rome. These included the king's own pacific sensibilities, the particular requirements of the Oath of Allegiance controversy (attempting to separate moderate from radical papists), the need to condemn the growth of separatism from the Church of England, the defence of the episcopal succession, and the more general polemical requirement to claim the high ground of moderation. Increasing emphasis was placed on the themes of legality, canonicity, restraint and continuity in the Church of England's own Reformation, and the extent to which the Church of England shared Rome's doctrines. The classic example of this moderate approach, and of its purely polemical intent, is the puritan William Perkins' *A Reformed Catholike*. In this work Perkins studies the various controversies with the Roman Church and under each one describes the common ground which both Romanists and protestants shared before going on to describe those additional points on which the Church of Rome insisted and the protestants departed from her. A 'Reformed Catholic', Perkins explains, is 'any one that holds the same necessary heads of religion with the Roman Church: yet so, as he pares off and rejects all errors in doctrine whereby the said religion is corrupted'. One of the purposes of Perkins' work was to persuade papists to a better opinion of the protestant religion 'when they shall see how near we come unto them in sundry points'.[37] Yet it was quite explicitly *not* Perkins' intention to show that both churches shared the same foundation. Perkins consciously wrote to refute the opinion 'that our religion and the religion of the present Church of Rome are all one for substance'. In fact, he was adamant that 'they of the Roman Church have razed the foundation'. 'We are to make a separation from the present Church of Rome', he continued, 'in respect of the foundation and substance of true religion'. He began the book with an exposition of Revelation 18.3, and firmly maintained that Rome was not a church of Christ at all.[38]

Concerning the visibility and succession of the church, it was the Laudians' intention to free the positive aspects of this new emphasis on restraint in separation and on the necessary visibility of the church through the Word and sacraments, from the more traditional apocalyptic Elizabethan ideas of the absolute nature of the break with Rome, and the tendency to attach positive value to the invisible rather than the visible church. This was achieved by branding the latter position as the exclusive property of separatist sectarians, and as inherently incompatible with the defence of episcopacy.

The problem was, of course, that the absolute, apocalyptic ideas were still adhered to by moderate Calvinist episcopalian writers – indeed by men who were bishops themselves – who had struggled to defuse their radical potential by supplementing them with more moderate evaluations of the break with Rome. A vitriolic polemicist

such as Peter Heylyn sought to evade this problem by falsely claiming that the moderate Calvinist's position (in this case John Prideaux's) was itself exclusive, and limited entirely to the tracing of
the Church of England's pedigree through a succession of proto-
protestant heretical sects, thereby disguising the fact that it was
Heylyn's own vision of the protestant descent which was exclusive.[39]
More generally, however, Laudian writers preferred to enlist such
established divines for their cause by implying, through selective
quotation, that they did not support the Foxeian tradition. To
support their partial reading of the English protestant tradition,
Laudian writers selectively quoted those Jacobean writers most
carefully committed to dignifying the Foxeian tradition, making
Prideaux, Morton, Perkins, Abbot and Field speak against a tradition which they were in fact cautiously attempting to elaborate
and refine. Laud, as we have seen, misapplied Field, Prideaux and
Abbot's arguments to suit his purpose. Similarly, Montagu had
recourse to writers such as Thomas Morton and Francis White in
support of the necessary visibility of the church on earth, but
ignored the fact that they also asserted the relative *invisibility* of the
true church on earth.[40]

By enforcing this polarisation, by denying any middle ground,
Laudian writers were implicitly challenging such figures to renounce
any further adherence to more radical commentators, and thereby
effectively marginalising Elizabethan traditions by representing
them as the preserve of a radical, separatist fringe, and as inherently
incompatible with the defence of an established church polity.
Where Prideaux had advanced both the proto-protestant descent
and the argument that the Reformation did not erect a new church
but merely purified a corrupted older one, Heylyn attempted to
monopolise the latter argument and to present it as starkly contrary
to the former.[41]

The Jacobean consensus in action effectively worked through
confusion and blurred definitions, which attempted to build a
powerful defence of institutional continuity into a traditional frame
of argument which emphasised separation and the church as a
succession of a minority of true believers estranged from the institutional church. While these new elements of institutional continuity
may have introduced increasing complexities and discordances
within Jacobean protestantism, it would surely be premature to
claim that they were leading to the inevitable renunciation of the

Elizabethan protestant heritage. We should be wary of attempting to claim that writers such as Prideaux, Abbot, Field and even Perkins, may serve as representatives of an emerging 'Anglicanism' simply by their preparedness to pursue moderately-expressed arguments against Rome, to emphasise the appeal to patristic and medieval authors, and to stress the importance of the visibility of the institutional church. That is certainly how, for propaganda purposes, Laudian divines wished to represent them. But in the eyes of the more puritanical members of the Jacobean Church it was these writers' ability also to have recourse to apocalyptic arguments, to condemn Rome as the Synagogue of Satan, and to stress the opposition to her in terms of the most committed irreconcilability, which was most important, and which made their preparedness to embrace tactically moderate arguments easier for more radical spirits to swallow. It is an open question how far these Jacobean moderates were themselves happy with the composite picture of the church which they had created. It is possible to trace a development in the career of a former Perkins protégé such as William Bedell away from many of the radical protestant tenets regarding the nature of the church which he had imbibed in his youth. Nevertheless, the fact remains that writers such as Prideaux, Abbot, Hall, Morton and Davenant did not see themselves as in the same tradition as later Laudian divines, with whom their relations were often decidedly acrimonious.

Why did Laudian divines feel impelled to reject the moderate Jacobeans' truce with more radical protestant arguments? Part of the answer lies in the fact that, for the Laudians, the emphasis on the visible church, on institutional succession, and on the need to downplay the Church of England's separation from the Church of Rome and to emphasise points of agreement between them, were not merely effective tactical ploys in polemical argument with papists or separatists. Rather, these elements were truer expressions of Laudians' general predisposition (which Peter Lake identifies elsewhere in this volume) towards a piety more centred on the sacraments and public worship than on the Word, stressing the positive religious value of the rites and ceremonies of the Church of England and rejecting as 'puritan' the word-based piety of the Elizabethan and Jacobean Church. On the question of the location of the church before Luther, the essential issue for them was thus not the location of pure doctrine, but the preservation of an institutional succession, and especially that of an episcopal succession. The preoccupation with episcopacy arose in part due to further developments in the understanding of the nature of *iure divino* episcopacy during the Jacobean period, most notably in the Church of England's defence of her direct, linear episcopal succession. This had the approval of even the rigidly anti-papist Archbishop Abbot.[42] The necessity of an uninterrupted succession was increasingly emphasised by Laudian divines, but in their hands, combined with an insistence that episcopacy was not simply a different degree of the priesthood but a separate order altogether, it supplanted all other considerations when tracing the church before Luther.[43]

The new emphasis on the importance of the Church of England's episcopal succession was accompanied by the conviction that those promoting the form of 'relative' church invisibility were deliberately undermining it. Montagu stressed that the point of institutional visibility was especially important to the Church of England because she claimed and proved a succession 'and therefore needs a visibility from the time of the apostles. If any do think otherwise, or cannot do this, we undertake no patronage at all of them'. Heylyn argued that the proto-protestant line of descent 'utterly discontinueth that succession in the ecclesiastical hierarchy, which the Church of England claims from the very apostles'.[44]

The Laudians separated out the part which they wanted from the arguments of Calvinist episcopalian divines. Effectively clearing up, they were involved in producing a more internally consistent defence of the institutional Church of England, and thereby threw out much that, while peripheral to their view, was fundamental to the views of more advanced protestants. The whole vision of evangelical Calvinist episcopalianism became more difficult because Laudians denied the possibility of reconciling the defence of an established Church with advanced protestantism and apocalypticism. The denial of that reconciliation spelt the doom of the Jacobean Church.

IV

At the heart of all these disagreements lay a more fundamental issue. It concerned the very existence of 'the true church'. This was a phrase which had its roots in fundamental divisions of humanity, propounded by St Augustine and elaborated by later writers such as John Bale, which divided the world into the true church and the false. The precise identity of the false church was never entirely clear – it was not always related directly to Rome, and during the Elizabethan period this concept increasingly became the preserve of more radical puritans. The 'true church', however, remained at the centre of protestant ecclesiology, which became preoccupied with establishing its particular notes – these being chiefly the Word of God sincerely preached and the sacraments rightly administered – in opposition to the formal profession of Christianity and outward splendour of the Church of Rome. However, the true church was essentially defined in terms of the purity of its doctrine, and in this way Jacobean writers could talk of the true church existing *within* the Church of Rome (i.e. being the sum of true believers within but not of it). 'Relative' invisibility was thus merely an expression of the occasional state of the true church.

This was a vision which had been crucially challenged by Richard Hooker, who had chosen to define the church merely in terms of the outward (rather than the true, or pure) profession of Christianity. This perspective was by no means alien to general Elizabethan concepts of the church – most writers made allowance that the church might occasionally be spoken of in terms of Christian professors in general, and that in this way Rome might be allowed to be in some sense a church. Writers occasionally spoke in terms of the distinction between sound and unsound churches, thereby allowing Rome a certain standing as a church, but her status in this regard was largely seen in negative terms, meaning merely, as Whitgift commented, that 'the Church of Rome is not as the assemblies of Turks, Jews and Painims'.[45] But even this reflection was never developed in detail outside its application to particular areas of polemical argument. Hooker's novelty lay in the fact that he gave the admission that Rome was a church a positive emphasis, because in his analysis of the nature of the church he left no space for the 'true church' of orthodox believers – the whole concept was effectively abandoned. The 'true church' had thus been replaced in Hooker's vision by the visible church, which entailed as a consequence that all churches were essentially equal in nature.

The two visions were reunited by Hooker's friend Richard Field, who offered definitions both of the visible church in which all schismatics and heretics were included, and the true church of 'that more special number of them which communicate in all things wherein Christians should', and it was on this uneasy alliance that the Jacobean consensus was erected. While Hooker had replaced the 'true church' with the 'visible church', many Jacobeans took on Hooker's re-evaluation of the visible church, moderated through Field, by accepting both definitions, and applying them in different ways, using 'true church' definitions to attack Rome and 'visible church' definitions to attack separatist opponents. But there were constant tensions within this multi-dimensional ecclesiology, especially as the issues of episcopal continuity and the problem of separatism led to more committed defences of the visible church.

The incoherencies of this inclusive ecclesiology became most marked in the essentially dual vision of the nature of the Church of Rome. According to one line of argument Rome was a member of the church, yet another strand of the argument considered Rome to be fundamentally separated from it. These tensions came into open conflict in the controversy over Joseph Hall's tract *The Old Religion* in 1629. Here the point at issue was whether Rome could be considered a true church of God. Hall – with the support of moderate Calvinists Davenant, Prideaux and Morton – argued for a compound view of the Roman Church as having a Christian face and an antichristian heart. He still adhered to the conventional definition of the 'true church' of orthodox believers, but also sought to speak of Rome as being 'true' in the sense of retaining the fundamentals of Christianity (in the Bible, baptism and ministry). Hall's opponents Henry Burton and Thomas Spencer (and Daniel Featley) were unable to accept a view of the modern Church of Rome which attempted to describe it as concurrently both a true church (in its visible profession of Christianity) and Babylon (with relation to its errors). They remained firmly wedded to traditional notions of the 'true church'. While they did not seriously differ from Hall on the issue of salvation within the Roman Church, these writers had a more fundamental problem in grasping the concept of a heretical church which was still a church in a certain sense. Instead, they saw purity of doctrine as an essential mark of the church. Their persistent attempts to cite authors denying Rome to be *the* true church in order to deny it to be *a* true church display, not a basic confusion on their part, but rather the fact that for them the two terms meant essentially the same thing. If Rome was not a part of *the* true church, it was not a church at all.[46]

The Laudians resolved the Jacobean tension between the 'true church' and 'visible church' definitions by effectively rejecting the whole notion of 'the true church'. This point emerges clearly in Montagu's discussions of the succession of the church. Montagu was not concerned to search for the succession of a pure church, or for an orthodoxy which might in any sense be invisible. He declared unequivocally in a syllogism that 'the Church of Rome hath ever been visible. The Church of Rome is and ever was a true Church since it was a Church; therefore the true Church hath been visible'. He did not hereby intend to equate the Church of Rome with *the* true church: he went on to specify that he only meant it to be 'a true Church *ratione essentiae* [by reason of the essence] and Being of a Church, not a sound Church every way in their doctrine'. The essential point was that there was no room in his vision for 'the true church': any institutional church which retained the fundamentals of belief provided a sufficient descent. Montagu's syllogism shows, not a lack of ability in logic (as his opponents were swift to claim), but that for him the terms '*the* true church' and '*a* true church' mean essentially the same thing. If Rome is '*a* true church' then it must in effect be part of '*the* true church'. This reductionism may be paralleled with that of Hall's opponents: in abandoning the Jacobean compromise, at least, Laudians and their puritan opponents were in agreement.[47]

Thus, when some Laudian divines rejected the Foxeian tradition and the notion of relative church invisibility, they were, more fundamentally, abandoning the search for the 'true church', for congregations of pure and orthodox believers. Instead, as the visible church was now regarded simply as the collection of all those churches which upheld the fundamentals of Christian belief, so a corrupted church, with corrupt, unreformed members, was a sufficient ancestor for the protestant church. These were indications of a general shift away from protestant notions of the church as definable primarily in terms of true doctrine, and towards an emphasis on the sacraments as the primary concern in ecclesiology. Unlike doctrine, the sacraments did not permit easy distinctions according to the degree of purity with which they were held, but instead entailed an essential equality among the churches which left no room for any meaningful notion of a church composed solely of *orthodox* Christians.[48]

All these developments had profound implications for the way in which the Church of Rome was perceived. As Christopher Potter

noted, the depiction of Rome as simply an erring fellow-member of
the Catholic Church required that other churches must still in some
sense remain in communion with her.[49] The flight from ideas of
the role of true doctrine as being the essence of the church was
accompanied by a rejection of views of the separation from Rome
which found their justification merely in Rome's corruption of orthodox doctrine. Instead, the Reformation was increasingly depicted
as essentially representing the rediscovery by particular visible,
institutional churches of their right of self-reformation, the attention
shifting away from matters of doctrine towards matters of jurisdiction. Thus Richard Montagu based his defence of the Church of
England's separation from Rome on her ancient 'Cyprian Privilege'
to be governed by her own patriarch.[50]

The rejection of the notion of 'the true church' allowed divines
to follow through radically new perceptions of the relations between
particular visible churches. This amounted to far more than simply
a revival of the thought of Richard Hooker. The Laudians were not
merely freeing Hooker of the traces of Elizabethan fundamentalism
which had been allowed to remain awkwardly attached during
the Jacobean period. Hooker had only subscribed half-heartedly to
notions of *iure divino* episcopacy, and had been hesitant in breaking
fully with Calvinist doctrines of grace, or from the Foxeian tradition
(although he had abandoned it by implication). With a sympathetic
king to support them, Laudian divines could make a more decisive
break with previous modes of thought in following through the
implications of their doctrinal proclivities. Richard Montagu
embraced the re-assessment of the nature of the Church of Rome
by pursuing the goal of reunion with Rome in conversation with
the papal agent Panzani.[51] Other Laudian divines did not go so
far, but often adopted a more irenical posture on general Church
relations. One of the major casualties of this perspective was the
so-called 'protestant cause' – the agitation for a confessional and
bellicose foreign policy in support of the West European Calvinist
communities. This was the classic expression of a vision of the 'true
church' as an alliance of godly member churches, united by true
doctrine, in perpetual antipathy with the false church of the Roman
Antichrist. It is not surprising that no Laudian divines mustered
any enthusiasm for this cause. Nor is it unexpected that reformed
divines and Churches came in for more unqualified criticism in
England in the years of Laud's ascendancy than they had ever

known before, while the congregations of 'stranger churches' began to feel the weight of the archbishop's administrative hand.[52]

The demise of the Jacobean consensus in understandings of the nature of the church was thus profound in its consequences. This should not, however, lead us to assume that it was doomed from the moment Richard Hooker set pen to paper. Indeed, what is striking in the Jacobean period is the resilience with which more radical Elizabethan visions of the church were able to survive and co-exist with defences of the visibility and continuity of the church hierarchy. Moreover, it should be noted that some divines associated with Laud, while unequivocal in their departure from Calvinist doctrines of grace, still remained broadly within earlier traditions of thought regarding the nature of the church. Francis White and Thomas Jackson, while having departed from some traditional English protestant views, still expounded the apocalyptic interpretation of church history and adhered to notions of the 'true church'.[53] Nevertheless, the destruction of the Jacobean consensus was finally accomplished, not by the importation of totally new doctrines, but by the manipulation of inconsistencies which lay at its very heart.

9. The *via media* in the early Stuart Church

PETER WHITE

I

Sometime in 1630 Richard Johnson, a layman of the parish of St Laurence in Reading, left in his will £15 to buy 'a silver flagon and two bread plates of silver' to be used at the communion. 'And more I give unto them a fair pulpit cloth of silk and a fair cushion . . . and more I give unto them forty shillings in money towards the making of a wood fence for the communion table'.[1] Johnson can no doubt be added to the list of 'Arminians' who crept out of the ecclesiastical woodwork after 1625, for in that year, we are led to understand, the accession of Charles I destroyed a previously harmonious 'Calvinist' consensus in the English Church. By that revolution, it is claimed, the teaching of predestination was 'outlawed' and an alternative, sacramentally-centred, theology of grace enforced, the outward sign of which was the remodelling of church interiors by railing off altars at the east end. The enforcement of this policy, and the doctrinal novelty that lay behind it, are held to be crucial in explaining the English Civil War.[2]

All this, we may be sure, would have caused Johnson himself, whose will is one of the many examples of spontaneous lay initiative in the improvement of church furnishings, much astonishment. He fits awkwardly into current historiography, preoccupied as that is with the polarities necessary if church history is to be the tool of political explanation. That Richard Johnson was innocent of any preference of churchmanship is suggested by his bequest of ten shillings for the minister if he preached on the day of St John the Evangelist, for 'Arminians' (we are told) preferred prayer to sermons. Current historiography, however, has no interest in those churchmen it cannot categorise, and is bound on its own premises to ignore, if not altogether to deny, the existence of a middle ground. This should occasion no surprise, for in this as in so many other respects it reflects the outlook of William Prynne. It was Prynne who first claimed an Elizabethan 'Calvinist' consensus, evidenced both by the output of the printing presses and by university commencement theses; and it was Prynne who identified 'Arminian' novelty in the works of Richard Montagu.[3] It is from Prynne's perspective that establishment churchmen, conservative to the core, can be metamorphosed into revolutionaries.

An attempt will be made in the present chapter to offer an alternative matrix. It will be suggested that a spectrum offers a much better model, and that the doctrine of predestination was far from being a crucial determinant of that spectrum. While not of course denying the existence of polarities, it will attempt to balance them by exploring the limits of consensus, identifying some of those churchmen who pursued a moderating role under Elizabeth and James I, and who drew inspiration from the notion and practice of a *via media*. An attempt will thereafter be made to suggest in what senses, if any, the accession of Charles I disturbed the equilibrium.

II

The polarities in the early Stuart Church did not replace an earlier consensus, but were inherited from the earliest stages of the Reformation. The tension was between a protestantism of the right and a protestantism of the left, and it ran right through Europe. It was particularly acute in England because under both Henry and Elizabeth the Reformation impulse was carefully controlled by the crown, and conservatism was sustained first by the succession of Mary Tudor and thereafter by the claim of Mary Queen of Scots. Largely as a result, 'Elizabethan England was unique, in trying to find room within the borders of a single state, for the conservative (provided he were not too conservative) and the radical (provided he were not too radical)'.[4] Underlying the argument of the present chapter is the view that the Elizabethan settlement was intended to be as inclusive as possible of a people whose allegiances ranged from Marian conservative to 'the hotter sort of protestants'. The political pragmatism of the queen and her advisers set frustrating limits to the enthusiasm of clerical reformers. The result was a

Church that stood in an unmistakeably intermediate position between the more 'precise' Churches of the continent and the Church of Rome. The Thirty-nine Articles, the Book of Common Prayer and the Homilies represented a settlement of religion that was significantly different, both liturgically, doctrinally and in its Church polity, from other protestant Churches. The royal supremacy, and a diocesan episcopacy, both distinctive, guaranteed a fundamental continuity with the past, while a widespread conservatism, combined with the preferences of the queen, dictated the retention of rites and vestments elsewhere dispensed with. For similar reasons, the settlement of doctrine was less precise, the extent of permissible *adiaphora* (things indifferent) correspondingly wider, than in the continental reformed Churches.[5]

This contrast between the Church of England and the continental reformed Churches, above all with Geneva, was far from being, as has recently been claimed, the invention of Richard Hooker. It was widely recognised from the earliest years of the Elizabethan settlement. The reformers themselves were in no doubt about it, Calvin's gift of his commentaries on Isaiah to Elizabeth in January 1559 being coldly received, and Beza lamenting to Bullinger in 1566 that 'as to our own Church, it is so hateful to that queen . . . because we are accounted too severe and precise'. Some of the returned exiles were correspondingly apologetic about their Church in letters to their continental mentors. Others drew the same distinction only to applaud it. In 1562 a French professor of law praised the *moderatio* of the settlement as compared with the 'preciseness' of Zürich and Geneva. Similarly, the French ambassador, visiting Archbishop Parker in 1564, 'noted much and delighted in our mediocrity, charging the Genevans and Scottish of going too far in extremities'. Parker himself took considerable pride in that moderation, claiming that it resulted from a primitive orthodoxy and purity; and he made it a formidable tool of apologetic. In the preface to the Bishops' Bible, he buttressed it by appealing above all to English historians for evidence of the special origins of 'this Christian Catholic Church of England', and he told the story (originating in the *Liber Pontificalis* and later repeated by Bede, William of Malmesbury and Geoffrey of Monmouth), of the conversion of England in the second century under its first Christian king, Lucius. Lucius had appealed to Pope Eleutherus for teachers, whereupon the legates Eluanus and Medwinus had duly been sent.[6]

This legend was still taken seriously in the early Stuart Church: it was cited by both the 'prelatical' William Barlow and the 'puritan' Francis Hastings at the turn of the century in defence of the Church of England's right to call itself *Catholic*. Hastings went even further back, citing Gildas to the effect that Britain received the gospel in the time of Tiberius from Joseph of Arimathaea, sent by Philip the Apostle from France. The fact that Easter was kept according to the Eastern computation was also used as evidence of independence from Rome. Barlow appealed in addition to Joseph of Arimathaea to rebut the claim that Christianity in England dated only from St Augustine of Canterbury: in sending him Pope Gregory's aim 'was not to transmit the faith in its purity, but to adulterate it'.[7]

There were many clerics early in the reign of James I whose churchmanship reflected above all their awareness of the special character of the Church of England, and whose loyalties were above all to her polity and liturgy as established by law. Provided no more than that is read into the word, they are most appropriately described as 'Anglicans'. Although they were quite ready to accept an underlying unity of doctrine among the protestant churches, it did not tie them to a particular doctrine of predestination, and they cannot adequately be categorised as either 'Calvinist' or 'Arminian'. A brief study of four of them will enable the reader to construct a model of their central Jacobean churchmanship.

The first is Francis Mason (1566?–1621), Archdeacon of Norfolk. Against the papists he defended the validity of episcopal consecrations in the English Church so effectively as to earn himself the name *Vindex ecclesiae Anglicanae*. Against the puritans he preached in defence of the 'Church of England' and 'that holy Book of Common Prayer, a work of so great and admirable excellency'. Attempts to 'cut it up like an anatomy', opening every vein and ransacking every rubric, had only made it stronger. Although Mason spoke sympathetically of the Church of Geneva and the other reformed Churches, he argued explicitly that the Church of England was inherently different. In part that resulted from its dependence on an absolute monarchy, the canons being the 'king's ecclesiastical laws'; in part from its polity, modelled on 'purest and apostolical times', with its ministers not a popular parity but with bishops placed above the rest. There was also a difference in its doctrinal stance. Defending subscription to the Thirty-nine Articles and the Prayer Book, Mason argued that those who so much admired foreign Churches should compare the Church of England with that of Geneva: Geneva required it of the common people where the Church of England limited it to ministers; where the Church of England merely required acceptance that her rites were not contrary to the word of God, Geneva 'will have her discipline received in a more high and glorious manner'; and finally, where the Church of England required only subscription, Geneva was 'more peremptory', 'requiring a solemn oath'.[8]

Mason commended preaching, and lamented that too many patrons failed to make provision for it, preferring 'a golden purse before a golden wit'; but he reminded ministers that the Homilies were available as an alternative to preaching, and following the Homilies he taught that above all a church was a house of prayer. He praised the order of Holy Communion, in which 'we repent and pray; we rejoice and pray, we thank God and pray; we confess our sins and pray; we preach and pray; we receive the sacraments and pray'. As to ceremonies, he asked God to bless the reformed Churches which had rejected them, but 'why should we be bound to their example'? Again quoting the Homilies, 'we condemn no other nations, nor prescribe anything but to our own people only'. Those who objected to the surplice, church music, the reading of psalms, the Litany, thanksgiving after childbirth, kneeling at Holy Communion and, above all, to the use of the cross in baptism overlooked that Churches varied in their needs in matters indifferent, and that diversity of rites was not harmful if there was unity of faith. The logic of their position was that we should pull down our churches because they had been built by papists, and they forgot (a palpable hit) that the Church of England had not, like Geneva, enforced wafer cakes![9]

Another Jacobean 'Anglican' was John Boys (1571–1625), a Dean of Canterbury patronised in turn by Whitgift, Bancroft and Abbot. 'From my youth up, I did ever esteem as a second Bible the Book of Common Prayer'. 'Every tittle' was grounded upon scripture. The liturgy was threatened on both sides, 'crucified between two malefactors: on the left hand the papists, on the right schismatics'. 'Against the Romanist I use a sword, against the novelist a buckler'. His published works were commentaries on the Book of Common Prayer, and he was a staunch supporter of the establishment. 'Except we have the Church for our mother, we shall never have God for our father.'

There is no doubt of Boys' protestantism. He made many references to the elect and the reprobate, but offered no formal treatment
of the doctrine of predestination, affirming that exact knowledge to
discuss curious points is not required of a Christian. On the doctrine
of justification, he recommended Luther on Galatians and Robert
Abbot's *Defence* of Perkins' *Reformed Catholic* – 'my conscience was
never more quieted than in reading the one, and my curiosity never
satisfied more than in examining the other'. He strongly believed
in preaching, and wrote of 'ministers', 'pastors' and the 'Lord's
table'. Yet 'we protest, and that unfeignedly, that no Church ought
further to depart from the Church of Rome, than she is departed
from herself in her flourishing estate'. Grace was conveyed both by
the preaching of the word and by the administration of the sacraments, of which there were only two, baptism and the Lord's
Supper. The former is a sacrament of initiation, and therefore the
font is placed at the church door; the latter is a sacrament of
confirmation, and therefore 'the Lord's table by good order is placed
in the best and highest room of the church'. Boys was not afraid to
use the word 'priest', or to speak of the Communion as in some
respects a sacrifice (above all as representative and commemorative
of Christ's).[10]

Another important moderate was Arthur Lake (1569–1626), a
Bishop of Bath and Wells admired both by the Dort delegate
Samuel Ward and by Laud's biographer Peter Heylyn. Like Boys,
he was exercised equally by threats from the right and the left. On
the one hand, the papists had 'bred up the people in an ignorant
devotion and bid them rest content with an implicit faith, and rest
their souls upon the authority of the Church; they offend *in Parum*
('by asking too little') in over-scanting the people's knowledge'; on
the other, 'the separatists run to the other extreme, they offend *in
Nimium* ('by asking too much') attribute too little to the Church,
and exceed in knowledge, or fancies, which they suppose to be
divine knowledge'. Lake was an assiduous preacher, but his preaching often had a sacramental emphasis. He preached at St Paul's
Cross at the beginning of James's reign that 'God's mercy is double
to his justice', and that 'the first grace that fails us is a good
conscience'. Far from predestination being the foundation of his
view of Christian doctrine, he invariably expounded it in the light
of the Church's teaching about the sacraments. In an attempt to
include him within the 'Calvinist consensus' he has been described

as a 'hypothetical universalist', but his universalism was in reality pragmatic or sacramental, as in a notable sermon in which he identified the 'elect' with members of the Church through baptism, and in which the whole emphasis is on the need for prayer 'or else they [the elect] shall not have what God doth purpose them'.[11]

The last example is Richard Field (1561–1616). 'He did not make use of his parts for the increase of controversies but rather for the composing of them'. It is said that King James wanted to send him on a mission to bring about a reconciliation between the Calvinists and the Lutherans, and planned to give him the see of Salisbury which in the event went to Robert Abbot. Abbot was Regius Professor at Oxford, and Field had been deeply disturbed by what he thought would be the harmful consequences for the Church of England of Abbot's lectures attacking the Arminians. As far as Field was concerned the dispute was a matter of opinion and not of faith, and 'in points of such extreme difficulty he did not think fit to be too positive'.[12]

Jacobean churchmen, it has been said, can be divided into 'two sides, the members of which knew who each other were and disliked each other heartily',[13] but Mason, Boys, Lake and Field do not naturally fall into either category, nor do many others. Printed works are not necessarily adequate evidence, for by definition moderate churchmen were less likely to enter the lists of Jacobean polemical theology. Nor should we be too influenced by competition for preferment, which has always tended to sharpen rivalries and provoke abrasive churchmanship. Even the model of a spectrum should not be taken too literally. Both conservative and radical protestantism were heterogeneous. Doctrinal preference did not necessarily correspond with liturgical taste. Men, especially thinking men, develop. For all these reasons it is not always possible neatly to categorise individual churchmen. As the Church developed, moreover, the defence of the existing settlement required a flexible response to new challenges. The *via media* was exactly that, implying movement as well as moderation.

The foundations of the Jacobean *via media* were laid at the Hampton Court Conference. Lay observers had no difficulty in identifying two sides, but there is no reference in the contemporary records to the 'Calvinists' and 'Arminians' of modern historiography. On the contrary, the disagreement was between the 'prelates' unwilling to contemplate even moderate reforms and 'puritans' who arrogated to themselves the names of 'zealous' and 'reformed' and whose chief passion was the imitation of foreign Churches. As Francis Bacon wrote, 'The truth is, here be two extremes: some few, would have no change; no, not reformation. Some many, would have much change, even with perturbation', and Dudley Carleton observed 'these two companies as they differ in opinions so do they in fashions, for one side marches in gowns and rochets, and th'other in cloaks and night-caps'. Bacon rejoiced that the king was 'disposed to find out the golden mediocrity in the establishment of that which is sound, and in the reparation of that which is corrupt and decayed'.[14] Accounts of the Conference repeatedly suggest moderation and equilibrium. It was evident, even before it started, in the proclamation of 24 October 1603, where the Church of England was claimed not only to be 'near to the condition of the primitive Church' but also to be 'agreeable to God's word': the appeal to antiquity was deliberately balanced by an appeal to scripture obviously mindful of the puritan emphasis on holy writ.[15]

There is no real substitute for Barlow's account of the proceedings,[16] and it too repeatedly offers variations on the theme of balance. In the discussions on baptism, for example, there was no question either that the king doubted the necessity of the sacrament, or that private baptism would not continue: yet James was firm that the sacrament should be administered by a lawful minister, and that the rubric should be made explicit to rule out baptism by midwives and laymen. Similarly, in the discussions on predestination, the king 'wished that the doctrine might be very tenderly handled, and with great discretion, lest on the one side, God's omnipotency might be called in question . . . or on the other, a desperate presumption might be arreared, by inferring the necessary certainty of standing and persisting in grace'. When Rainolds suggested that the 'nine orthodoxal assertions concluded at Lambeth' be added to the Thirty-nine Articles, the king made it clear that he was against any extension of doctrinal tests. 'Curious questions' should be determined only in the universities, and avoided 'in the fundamental instruction of the people': it is clear that for King James, predestination was not part of that basic doctrine.[17]

One example of the *via media* propounded at Hampton Court struck at the very heart of puritanism. The immediate point at issue was the use of the cross in baptism. To make it binding, Rainolds had suggested, was an impeachment of Christian liberty. The king's rebuttal was uncompromising. As far as he was concerned, the appeal to private conscience, in essence an appeal to individual illumination by the Holy Spirit, 'smelled very rankly of Anabaptism' and 'therefore I charge you never to speak more to that point (how far you are bound to obey) when the church hath ordained it'. For the king, however, the point at issue was far from being merely the right of the Church to order obedience in matters indifferent. As he went on to explain, it involved the very cornerstone of the Church's defence against the papist charge of novelty, which was to tell them 'that their abuses are new, but the things which they abused we retain in their primitive use, and forsake only the novel corruption'. According to the puritan principle, we should have to renounce even the doctrine of the Trinity, because the papists abused it, or ('speaking to Dr Rainolds merrily') go around barefoot because they wore hose and shoes. A further exchange showed that the king agreed with Bancroft that too much emphasis was being placed on preaching, 'which motion his majesty liked very well, very acutely taxing the hypocrisy of our times, which placeth all religion in the ear, through which there is any easy passage; but prayer, which expresseth the heart's affection, and is the true devotion of the mind, as a matter putting us to overmuch trouble'. This representation of the king's standpoint was by no means clerical wishful thinking. Bacon had made the same point before the Conference, warning the king of the excessive elevation of preaching by those who had forgotten that 'my house is a house of prayer'. James himself subsequently returned to the same theme.[18]

One important decision at Hampton Court illustrates the error of supposing that when Hooker emphasised the sacraments as means of grace he was 'attacking Calvinist piety',[19] for Calvin too had a strong doctrine of the sacraments, and at Hampton Court it was the puritans' spokesman Rainolds who suggested 'that there might be a more perfect catechism, made for the instruction of all sorts, as well in the mysteries of the Lord's Supper, as of baptism, and all other things needful, whereunto it was readily yielded'. The outcome was the addition of a section on the sacraments to the Prayer Book catechism. It taught that two sacraments only, those of baptism and the Lord's Supper, were 'generally necessary to salvation'. The inward and spiritual grace received in baptism was defined as 'a death unto sin, and a new-birth unto righteousness: for being by nature born in sin, and the children of wrath, we are hereby made the children of grace'. Whatever their differences on predestination, agreement on that sacramental doctrine united Rainolds and Overall. By contrast, the addition quickly drew a protest from Stephen Egerton that it was a change for the worse: he complained that the wording savoured of 'the popish doctrine, if not of seven sacraments, yet of more than by our Church hath always been acknowledged'.[20] Hooker's target was not Calvin but the distortion by puritans like Egerton of Calvin's teaching.

The agreement to arrange for a new translation of the Bible was a further stage in the evolution of the *via media*. As is well known, the most popular English translation was the Geneva, dating from early in the reign of Elizabeth. It had no official standing, but its superior scholarship had ensured that it rapidly superseded the Great Bible of 1538. The Bishops' Bible of 1568, although authorised by the canons of 1571, had never won the universal acceptance that Parker had hoped for it. Since then, publication of the Roman Catholic Rhemish version, along with detailed criticisms of the Bishops' Bible, made a new translation desirable. In spite of Bancroft's objections, King James agreed, the more so because he thought the Geneva the worst of all the English translations, taking particular exception to its marginal notes.

It was agreed that the new version should be the joint work of the flower of English linguistic scholarship, irrespective of churchmanship. Instructions to the translators required them to base their work on the Bishops' Bible, and failing that the older English versions; in cases of ambiguity they were to follow the consensus of the ancient fathers. In practice, however, the translators were not inhibited from following the Rhemish version where they thought fit. As a result, it has been deservedly said that the Authorised Version is 'even in the minutest details the translation of a church and not of a party. It differs from the Rhemish version in seeking to fix an intelligible sense on the words rendered: it differs from the Genevan version in leaving the literal rendering uncoloured by any expository notes. And yet it is most worthy of notice that these two versions, representing as they do the opposite extremes of opinion, contributed most largely of all to the changes which the revisers introduced'. That the catholicity of design was no accident is demonstrated by the notes left by one of the revisers, which suggest that the translators deliberately sought a rendering which left the version open to a range of meanings.[21]

III

James I's comments at Hampton Court show how seriously he took the claim to true catholicity. That claim went back to Jewel's *Apology*. The *Apology* was republished in 1609 and a copy ordered to be in every parish church. A preface by Overall emphasised that the object of Jewel's works had been to show 'that this is and hath been the open profession of the Church of England, to defend and maintain no other Church, Faith and Religion than that which is truly Catholic and apostolic, and for such warranted, not only by the written word of God, but also by the testimony and consent of the ancient and godly fathers'. Overall adduced the canon of 1571, that preachers and pastors 'should never teach anything, as matter of faith religiously to be observed, but that which is agreeable to the doctrine of the Old and New Testaments, and collected out of the same doctrine by the ancient fathers and Catholic bishops of the Church'. The canon was sufficient refutation of the popish calumny 'that our faith, church and religion is new, and lately upstart from Luther's time, and not ancient Catholic and apostolic'.[22]

The claim to true Catholicity was given a contemporary significance by James's relations with the Roman Church. In his speech to the first Parliament of his reign he revealed his hopes for a reconcilation. Again, the concept of the *via media* made its appearance

> I could wish from my heart that it would please God to make me one of the members of such a general Christian union in religion, as laying wilfulness aside on both hands, we might meet in the midst, which is the centre and perfection of all things. For if they would leave, and be ashamed of such new and gross corruptions of theirs, as themselves cannot maintain, nor deny to be worthy of reformation, I would for mine own part be content to meet them in the mid-way . . .

Such a union, James believed, might be achieved through an ecumenical council summoned by the pope, and he let it be known that if the pope agreed he would use his influence with heads of state in northern Europe.[23] He stressed his reverence for antiquity, and said he was even prepared to contemplate a common order of divine worship. Although Pope Clement VIII received James's proposals coldly, they were not altogether lost sight of in the controversy which followed over the Oath of Allegiance. James defended his orthodoxy and that of the Church of England in the *Premonition* addressed to European heads of state in 1609. The criterion he chose was the Vincentian canon: 'I will never refuse to embrace any opinion in divinity necessary to salvation which the whole Catholic Church with an unanimous consent has constantly taught and believed even from the apostles' days'. Returning to the idea of a reunion of the churches, James repeated his view that it would have to come by means of a General Council held on neutral ground, attended by all which 'believe and profess all the ancient grounds of the true, ancient Catholic and apostolic faith'. Again, the *via media* made its appearance. 'All the incendiaries and novelist firebrands on either side should be debarred, as well Jesuits and puritans.'[24]

Theologians from both home and abroad supported the king's defence of his orthodoxy. Lancelot Andrewes was engaged to write against Bellarmine. 'Our appeal is to antiquity yea even to the most extreme antiquity. We do not innovate; it may be we renovate what was customary with some ancients but with you has disappeared in novelties.' In limiting what the Church of England believed to the creeds and the first four councils, Andrewes denied that the points rejected were of the faith. Whatever was clouded by controversy was not part of fundamental truth, for whatever was necessary God had made plain, and whatever was not plain was not necessary. The name protestant, which Bellarmine claimed had not been heard of for the first fifteen hundred years of the church's history, was defended by Andrewes as a temporary convenience. It was intended to last only so long as the Roman abuses remained unreformed. In the English Church, religion was reformed, not formed anew. The Church of England was in the position of an appellant, waiting for a genuinely general council, but meanwhile she had not cut herself off from Catholicism, for she had preserved the apostolic succession, and her faith was that of the universal Church. She trod a middle way. 'We follow neither Calvin nor the pope, where either has forsaken the footsteps of the fathers.'[25]

Two foreign theologians, both of whom had been welcomed to the Jacobean court, added their defence of the Church of England to that of Andrewes. Isaac Casaubon, who had come to England in 1610 because he was attracted by the reputation of the English Church for patristic studies and because it offered a middle way between Rome and Geneva, echoed Andrewes and Overall. 'The authors of the Reformation here, had no purpose to erect any new Church (as the ignorant and malicious do cavil), but to repair the ruins of the old', and Casaubon instanced that was no denial of auricular confession, merely a concern to guard against abuses and dangers. Casaubon praised the 'godly moderation' of the Church of England on the real presence, the eucharist as the commemoration of a sacrifice, prayer for the dead and invocation of the saints. It was only abuses, like private masses and communion in one kind, that the king rejected. Similarly Antonio de Dominis refuted Suarez, who had portrayed the English Reformation as if all the churches had been destroyed and 'the Reformation . . . nothing but a devastation'. In fact, many most beautiful churches had survived, and de Dominis commented on the abundance of stained glass portraying the crucified Christ, the virgin, the apostles and martyrs, but nothing idolatrous. In both towns and villages, crosses shone as signs of Christianity. It was one thing to remove an abuse, another to destroy religion; one to reform and cleanse it, another to change it.[26]

It would be hard to overestimate the importance of this Jacobean apologetic against Rome. It is there we should look (and not to Arminius) if we are seeking the theological basis of Laudianism. When Francis White was asked to examine Montagu's *Appello Caesarem*, and certify its orthodoxy, his method was to compare it with the Thirty-nine Articles and the Prayer Book, and then to consider 'what antiquity professed', and he justified that method by reference to what James himself, Andrewes, Casaubon and de Dominis had written. By contrast 'modern and novel divines . . . do multiply questions and by subtle and curious disputations make many things of very good use generally before these times established dubious and uncertain.[27]

IV

The centrality of the apologetic of true catholicity also helps to explain the relations between the English Church and the Netherlands. The king was under strong pressure from his Archbishop,

George Abbot, to take the lead in condemning the Remonstrant followers of Arminius. Supporters of the Remonstrants, however, were convinced, on the basis of the king's patronage of Andrewes, Casaubon and Overall, and his known moderation on the doctrine of predestination, that they could secure his support against the Contra-Remonstrants (the extreme Calvinists).[28] The full story of James's involvement in the events which culminated in the condemnation of the Remonstrants at the Synod of Dort cannot be told here,[29] but the primary aim of the king and of the British delegates was the preservation of peace. James would not allow either side to monopolise his support without qualification. In 1613 he wrote that 'we find neither the one nor the other so wide of the mark that they cannot be reconciled both with Christian truth and the salvation of souls'.[30] In 1614 he suggested that a ban on polemical preaching was preferable to a national synod, provided that it was acceptable to both parties, and the resulting draft was submitted to him for approval. Only after the ban had failed to resolve the dispute did James become reconciled to the need for a synod.[31]

The conduct of the delegates at Dort demonstrates that throughout their aim was to bring peace if they could. They saw themselves as representatives of the king and as apologists of the English Church rather than as defenders of 'Calvinist' orthodoxy. In the debates on doctrine, their influence was invariably towards moderation. Notwithstanding the contrary efforts of George Abbot, they heard from John Young that their stance had pleased the king. 'His Majesty likes very well of your *media via*'. Balcanquhall was justified in claiming that the British *Suffrage* was 'most just and equal, condemning the rigidity of some of the Contra-Remonstrants' opinions, though not by that name, as well as the errors of the Pelagians, the Semi-Pelagians, and the Remonstrants'.[32]

However eirenic the role of the British delegation, one result of the condemnation of the Remonstrants at Dort was to polarise opinion in the English Church. Tensions were further inflamed by the outbreak of the Thirty Years' War. Abbot hoped that James would intervene to secure the *dénouement* that militant protestant theology expected. Instead he had to stomach the opening of negotiations for a Spanish Match for Prince Charles, a development which shocked even moderate protestant opinion abroad. A number of preachers found themselves in prison for protesting against it. Anti-Arminian sermons at Paul's Cross were matched by provoca-

tive anti-Calvinist sermons at both Oxford and Cambridge: the
debate, it has been rightly pointed out, was 'fully in the public
domain long before Montagu appeared on the scene'.[33] The Directions to Preachers of 1622, issued on the king's personal authority,
required all under the rank of bishop or dean to restrict their
sermons to the Articles of Religion and the Homilies and to avoid
predestination altogether. Bitter invectives against either papists or
puritans were to be avoided.[34] However unpalatable to the archbishop, this represented no change of view by James, whose dislike
of the finer points of predestinarian teaching being aired in popular
preaching had been evident since the Hampton Court Conference.

The puritan and parliamentary attack on Montagu's anti-Calvinism has tended to obscure the fact that the *New Gagg* was a piece
of anti-Roman apologetic of the type that the king had been long
promoting. Aggressive as indeed he was, Montagu too believed in
a middle way: he said he 'wanted to stand in the gap between
popery and puritanism, the Scylla and Charybdis of ancient piety'.
Even unsympathetic observers agreed. 'Such', said Fuller, 'was the
equability of the sharpness of his style he was unpartial therein, be
he ancient or modern writer, papist or protestant, that stood in
his way', while Prynne criticised him for being a 'neuter'. Many
churchmen, especially those who liked to assimilate the English
Church to the reformed Churches, were of course incensed at his
distinction between the moderation of the doctrines of the Church
of England compared with the extreme ones of 'doctrinal puritans',
but Montagu did not invent the phrase, for it had been used by
Roman writers since at least the turn of the century.[35]

King James provoked not only the writing but the publication of
the *Appello Caesarem*.[36] Montagu had throughout been confident of
his backing, but he was unsure how Charles would react. Historians
content to follow Prynne and Rushworth in associating the 'rise of
Arminianism' with Charles and Laud have written that 'the
accession of Charles I in 1625 meant the overthrow of Calvinism',[37]
but the facts are that the new king did all he could to satisfy
Montagu's critics without abandoning the middle way. Although
Charles, supporting the right of Convocation to judge doctrine,
made Montagu his chaplain (to protect him from proceedings in
Parliament), he was far from committing himself to approval of his
books. Clergy of all shades of opinion pressed him to inhibit further
doctrinal debate. Although some (like Ussher) argued that 'Armini-

anism' alone should be suppressed, others (Laud, yes, but Joseph Hall too) argued that both sides should be silenced.[38] The draft of the 1626 *Proclamation for Peace and Quiet in the Church of England* was in fact anti-Arminian, but the final version, approved by a committee under the chairmanship of Abbot and at least seven other bishops (Davenant and Felton among them) was, as even Tyacke concedes, 'neutral'.[39] Its impartiality is evident both in the fact that Prynne ignores it altogether, and that Samuel Fell launched an inflammatory attack on it in an address at Oxford. 'To cry peace, peace where there is no peace is the voice of Jacob but the hand of Esau . . . a middle way between God and Baal was always pernicious . . . .'[40]

The publication of Fell's address is one example of Calvinist defiance of the 1626 Proclamation, but there are several others.[41] By contrast, the only 'Arminian' authors Prynne could cite in 1630 were Montagu (who did not publish after the Proclamation) and Thomas Jackson, whose *Treatise of the Divine Essence and Attributes* appeared in 1628. To that extent it might be plausible to argue that the Declaration prefixed to the Thirty-nine Articles of 1628 was intended to redress the balance. This, however, would be to ignore the thrust of royal policy at the time, determined decisively by the king's hopes for an amicable relationship with his third Parliament: accordingly Abbot was restored to his jurisdiction, and Dudley Carleton appointed Secretary of State. As with the 1626 Proclamation, it was Abbot who was asked to chair a group of bishops who met at Lambeth to approve it. Incredibly, it has been argued that the Declaration 'abandoned the neutrality of the Proclamation' and that 'Charles glossed the Thirty-nine Articles in favour of the Arminians and their doctrine of universal grace'.[42] It did nothing of the sort. It tried to heal divisions by pointing out that 'both sides' appealed to the Articles: it therefore required that in future everybody should accept them 'in the plain and full meaning thereof, and shall not put his own sense or comment to be the meaning of the Article'. The so-called Arminian gloss is a literal quotation from the final paragraph of the article in question.

For the next four years Abbot was responsible for enforcing the Declaration. Montagu's *Appello Caesarem* was withdrawn by royal proclamation early in 1629.[43] Enforcement under Laud was even-handed, but Calvinism was not suppressed. The works of William Perkins were in print throughout the 1630s. There was no alteration

to official formularies, no propagation of new doctrines, no promul-
gation of new definitions. Of course it is understandable that those
who were committed to 'Calvinism' feared that their rivals of
'Durham House' (the circle around Bishop Richard Neile) would
be given free licence to propagate 'Arminianism', but that is not
what happened. Laud was widely recognised to have acted even-
handedly. It is not enough merely to concede that he took action
against 'extreme' Arminians like Tooker of Oriel College, for even
moderates were discouraged from disturbing the precarious harmony. As archbishop, Laud wrote to Samuel Brooke, who had
written a treatise which tried to steer a middle course on the disputed points, saying that he doubted whether the king would be
willing to have them 'any further stirred, which now, God be
thanked, begin to be more at peace'. Yet the notion lingers among
historians that in subtle and insidious ways Laud tried to insinuate
a new heresy into the seventeenth-century Church. There is simply
no evidence to support them.[44]

V

What happened in 1625–9 then? Not the propagation of Arminianism by the king and Laud, but the redefinition of Arminianism by
Pym. From being a particular doctrine of predestination, it became
a 'bridge to usher in popery' and a plot to impose arbitrary government.[45] Laud was charged with it not because of any doctrinal
statement, but because he was believed (incorrectly) to have
licensed Sibthorpe's and Manwaring's sermons. Neile was also
accused, but much more for 'popery' than for Arminianism.
Harsnett, by contrast, was not charged: his influence was independent of either Neile or Buckingham, and he had supported the
Petition of Right. For the future of the *via media*, the decisive change
was the political ascendancy of Durham House, which dates not
from 1625 but from 1617. The controversy over Montagu threatened
rather than consolidated that ascendancy, but it was reinforced by
the appointment of Neile and Laud to the Privy Council and by
Abbot's sequestration.

With the rise of Durham House, conservative churchmanship (of
the sort that James I liked, to judge by his *Meditation on the Lord's
Prayer*) was triumphant. But if in some cases (Wren's and Cosin's,

for example) that churchmanship was aggressive, from Laud's point of view it was still determined by the ideal of a *via media*. Like his 'old master' Aristotle, he 'did ever believe that truth lies betwixt two extremes'.[46] The Church of England, as he told Charles, was 'in a hard condition', condemned by the Romans for novelty in doctrine and by the separatist for an antichristian discipline. 'The plain truth is, she is between two millstones, and unless your majesty look to it, she will be ground to powder.' Laud justified his preoccupation with the 'external worship of God in the Church' on the grounds that 'no one thing hath made conscientious men . . . more apt and easy to be drawn aside from the sincerity of religion professed in the Church of England than the want of uniform and decent order in too many churches; and the Romanists have been apt to say, the houses of God could not be suffered to lie so nastily, as in some places they have done, were the true worship of God observed in them'. Decency and order could not be had without ceremonies, 'and scarce anything hath hurt religion more in these broken times than an opinion in too many men, that because Rome had thrust . . . some superstitious ceremonies upon the Church, therefore the Reformation must have none at all; not considering that ceremonies are the hedge that fence the substance of religion from all the indignities which profaneness and sacrilege too commonly put upon it'.[47]

Such was the rationale of the 'altar policy', a misleading term unless it is remembered that it was part of a much wider movement of emphasis on the visual and sacramental aspects of Prayer Book worship which had its origins deep in Elizabeth's reign. Churchwardens' accounts demonstrate that parochial religion was marked from the 1570s onwards both by more frequent communions and by improved buildings and church furnishings. There is space here only to remove a few common misconceptions. In the first place, not only the Injunctions of 1559 but also the canons of 1604 envisaged the east end of the chancel as the normal position for the communion table at times other than during a communion.[48] It remains true, however, that it was not *enforced* generally until the 1630s. Secondly, that programme of enforcement was not, and on the whole was not perceived as, 'anti-Calvinist': some 'Calvinist' churchmen imposed the changes with less hesitation than Laud.[49] A canon imposing the east end position was adopted without protest by the Irish Church under Archbishop Ussher in 1634, by a Convocation which refused to accept bowing at the name of Jesus. Thirdly, the vast majority of English parishes railed their communion tables off at the east end without significant resistance. Destruction of altar rails in the early 1640s (by no means universal) was often the work of disaffected minorities and it dismayed parishioners.[50] In most parishes the Restoration was followed by their spontaneous replacement and the permanent removal of the communion table to the east end.

Other aspects of the Personal Rule were more contentious, but it is a mistake to conclude that the *via media* as Boys or Mason understood it disappeared under Charles I. The 1630s was the peak decade in the seventeenth century for sales both of Authorised Versions of the Bible and Books of Common Prayer. Between 1630 and 1639, for example, there were seventy editions of the Prayer Book, compared with an average of twenty per decade under Elizabeth and thirty-three per decade under James I. The predominance of small bindings suggests popular demand. Wider use of the Prayer Book is also suggested by the growing number of catechisms devoted to the exposition of the enlarged 1549 catechism.[51]

It was not so much the novelty of policy but its vigour that distinguishes the 1630s. The canons of 1604 were enforced systematically for the first time.[52] Insistence on the wearing of the surplice, the use of the sign of the cross at baptism, bowing at the name of Jesus and the licensing of lecturers could be contrasted with what seemed the appeasement of papists. 'The neglect of punishing puritans breeds papists', Charles told Neile in 1634. The thrust of policy was inevitably misrepresented. The imposition of the Book of Sports was portrayed as an attempt to muzzle preachers. The suppression of the Feoffees for Impropriations and the controls on the stranger churches looked like a betrayal of the Reformation. It is understandable that Sir Benjamin Rudyerd should tell the House of Commons in 1640 that 'under the name of puritans, all our religion is branded . . . . The great work, now is, their masterpiece, to make all those of the religion to be the suspected party of the kingdom'.[53] It was all so different from the days of good Queen Bess, when penal laws had been for papists.

There was one sense in which the middle way as it had been understood under both Elizabeth and James I was abandoned under Charles I, and that was in its careful balance of clerical and lay interests. Where James I is reported to have been suspicious of

Laud's 'schemes of reformation in his own brain', Charles upbraided his bishops for not giving the church a higher profile in Parliament, and expressed his readiness to 'promote the cause of the Church'. Laud, who 'ever hated a palsy in religion', and for whom Church and state were but one Jerusalem, was only too glad to preach in Council and before Parliament, and rejoiced when Juxon was appointed Treasurer. 'Now if the Church will not hold up themselves under God I can do no more'.[54] One result was that the public perception of the Church became inextricably linked to the external face of the Caroline court, including the Catholic household of Henrietta Maria. Ironically, Laud's political influence was limited.

The downside was that the very survival of the Church came to depend on the king's own skills as a monarch. James, who understood only too well that politics was the art of the possible, was succeeded by Charles who (more cleric than king) could neither defend a bad cause nor yield in a good one. The difference was evident above all in their respective policies towards Scotland. James had learned to abandon his scheme for a union, and in Church policy finally rested content with the Five Articles of Perth. Charles was determined to do better. James had said 'No bishop, no king'. Under Charles, it was more a case of no king, no bishop.

List of Abbreviations

AO	*Alumni Oxonienses . . . 1500–1714*, ed. J. Foster (4 vols, Oxford, 1891–2)
BI	Borthwick Institute, York
BIHR	*Bulletin of the Institute of Historical Research*
BL	British Library
Bodl.	Bodleian Library, Oxford
CCAL	Canterbury Cathedral Archives and Library
CRO	Cheshire RO
CSPD	*Calendar of State Papers, Domestic*
CUL	Cambridge University Library
DDCM	Durham Dean and Chapter Muniments
DNB	*Dictionary of National Biography*
DRO	Devon RO
EHR	*English Historical Review*
GDR	Gloucester Diocesan Records
GL	Guildhall Library
He.RO	Hereford County RO
HJ	*Historical Journal*
HLC	Huntington Library, California
HLRO	House of Lords RO
HMC	Historical Manuscripts Commission
HRO	Hampshire RO
HWRO	Hereford and Worcester RO
JBS	*Journal of British Studies*
JEH	*Journal of Ecclesiastical History*
LAO	Lincolnshire Archives Office
Laud, *Works*	W. Laud, *Works*, eds J. Bliss and W. Scott (7 vols, Oxford, 1847–60)
LPL	Lambeth Palace Library

NNRO	Norfolk and Norwich RO
NRO	Northamptonshire RO
OCRO	Oxfordshire County RO
P and P	*Past and Present*
PDR	Peterborough Diocesan Records
PRO	Public Record Office
RO	Record Office
SRO	Somerset RO
STC	*Short-Title Catalogue of Books . . . 1475–1640*, eds A. W. Pollard, G. R. Redgrave and K. F. Pantzer (3 vols, 1976–91)
TRHS	*Transactions of the Royal Historical Society*
WCRO	Wiltshire County RO
Wing	*Short-Title Catalogue of Books . . . 1641–1700*, ed. D. Wing (3 vols, 1945–51)
WSRO	West Sussex RO

Bibliography

The place of publication for books is London, unless otherwise stated.

INTRODUCTION

We await a comprehensive study of the early Stuart Church. In the meanwhile, sound introductions are available in H. G. Alexander, *Religion in England 1558–1662* (1968) and C. Cross, *Church and People 1450–1660* (1976); and more recently, in A. Hughes, *The Causes of the English Civil War* (Basingstoke, 1991), ch. 2 and C. Russell, *The Causes of the English Civil War* (Oxford, 1990), chs 4–5, which provides an important British dimension.

On theological development, especially in the universities, contrast N. Tyacke, *Anti-Calvinists: the Rise of English Arminianism c.1590–1640* (Oxford, 1987) with P. Lake, 'Calvinism and the English Church 1570–1635' *P and P*, 114 (1987) and both with P. White, *Predestination, Policy and Polemic* (Cambridge, 1992).

For the richest and most incisive work on Jacobean puritanism, see P. Collinson's collection of essays, *Godly People* (1983) and his *The Religion of Protestants* (Oxford, 1982); C. Hill, *Puritanism and Society in Pre-Revolutionary England* (1964) remains a stimulating read. N. Tyacke, *The Fortunes of English Puritanism 1603–1640* (Dr Williams's Library Lecture, 1990) is an important essay reinstating the radical edge of puritanism. On millenarian thought, see W. M. Lamont, *Godly Rule: Politics and Religion 1603–60* (1969).

The experience of English Catholics, rather neglected in this set of essays, can be traced through J. Bossy, *The English Catholic Community 1570–1850* (1975), J. C. H. Aveling, *The Handle and the Axe: the Catholic Recusants in England from the Reformation to Emancipation* (1976) and C. Hibbard, 'Early Stuart Catholicism' *Journal of Modern History* (1980).

For any investigation of popular religion, K. Thomas, *Religion and the*

Decline of Magic (1971) is indispensable. Local studies can be illuminating: for rather different approaches, and conclusions, compare M. Spufford, *Contrasting Communities: English Villagers in the Sixteenth and Seventeenth Centuries* (1974) with K. Wrightson and D. Levine, *Poverty and Piety in an English Village: Terling, 1525–1700* (1979). The view that protestantism was unpopular and widely resisted in Tudor England has obvious implications for this period, and is rehearsed in C. Haigh, 'The Church of England, the Catholics and the People', in C. Haigh (ed.), *The Reign of Elizabeth I* (Basingstoke, 1984).

1. THE ECCLESIASTICAL POLICIES OF JAMES I AND CHARLES I

James's kingcraft is best approached through J. Wormald, 'James VI and I: two kings or one?' *History*, 68 (1983); see also M. Lee, *Great Britain's Solomon: James VI and I in his three kingdoms* (Urbana, Ill., 1990).

For important work on his attitude to puritans, see F. Shriver, 'Hampton Court Revisited: James I and the Puritans' *JEH*, 33 (1982) and B. W. Quintrell, 'The Royal Hunt and the Puritans 1604–5', ibid., 31 (1980); towards Rome, see W. B. Patterson's two articles, 'King James I's call for an Ecumenical Council' in *Studies in Church History*, 7, eds G. J. Cuming and D. Baker (Cambridge, 1971) and 'King James I and the Protestant Cause in the Crisis of 1618–22' *Studies in Church History*, *18*, ed. S. Mews (Oxford, 1982). Studies of Jacobean court bishops have illuminated ecclesiastical politics during the reign. See S. B. Babbage, *Puritanism and Richard Bancroft* (1962), and P. A. Welsby's *Lancelot Andrewes* (1958) and *George Abbot* (1962). For a recent attempt to rehabilitate Abbot, see K. Fincham, 'Prelacy and Politics: Archbishop Abbot's defence of Protestant Orthodoxy' *Historical Research*, 61 (1988).

C. H. McIlwain (ed.), *The Political Works of James I* (Cambridge, Mass., 1918), contains speeches as well as published writings; and for a good insight into both James's role as mediator, and the range of issues dividing his leading churchmen, see N. Cranfield and K. Fincham (eds), 'John Howson's answers to Archbishop Abbot's accusations at his "trial" before James I . . . 1615' in *Camden Miscellany XXIX* (Camden 4th series, 34, 1987).

There is less to recommend on Charles I, a result of royal reticence and the production in the nineteenth century of Laud's *Works*, in seven volumes, which has distracted attention from his supreme governor. However, some important research has been published recently on the political and religious values of Charles and his court: K. Sharpe, 'The image of virtue: the court and household of Charles I' in D. Starkey (ed.), *The English Court* (Harlow, 1987); C. Russell, *The Causes of the English Civil War* (Oxford, 1990), ch. 8; R. M. Smuts, *Court Culture and the Origins of a Royalist Tradition in Early Stuart England* (Philadelphia,

1987); and C. Hibbard, *Charles I and the Popish Plot* (New Chapel, NC, 1983). Dr Sharpe has a major study of the Personal Rule forthcoming (1992) from Yale.

G. Albion, *Charles I and the Court of Rome* (1935) contains valuable accounts of Charles I's conversations with successive papal agents; G. Donaldson, *The Making of the Scottish Prayer Book of 1637* (Edinburgh, 1954) offers evidence of Charles's directing hand: K. Sharpe has championed Charles I as the architect of religious policy in the 1630s, in his *Politics and Ideas in Early Stuart England* (1989), pp. 108–9, 123–8. Readers may draw their own conclusions by consulting one important source, the royal annotations on the annual reports on the Church between 1633 and 1640, printed in W. Laud, *Works*, ed. J. Bliss and W. Scott (7 vols, Oxford, 1847–60), reprinted 7 vols in 5, Olms, New York, 1977), vol. 5.

2. ARCHBISHOP LAUD

There is no modern full-length study of Archbishop Laud. Still useful, however, is H. R. Trevor-Roper, *Archbishop Laud, 1573–1645* (3rd edn 1988), which should be supplemented by the essay 'Laudianism and Political Power' in his *Catholics, Anglicans and Puritans: Seventeenth-Century Essays* (1987), ch. 2. Another valuable essay is J. S. McGee, 'William Laud and the Outward Face of Religion', in R. L. DeMolen (ed.), *Leaders of the Reformation* (1984), ch. 11. A more general overview of the subject is provided by C. Carlton, *Archbishop William Laud* (1987). K. Sharpe, 'Archbishop Laud', *History Today*, 33 (August 1983), 26–30, stresses the ordinariness of Laud, but compare A. Foster, 'Church Policies of the 1630s', in R. Cust and A. Hughes (eds), *Conflict in Early Stuart England: Studies in Religion and Politics, 1603–1642* (Harlow, 1989), ch. 7. For a Marxist restatement, readers may consult C. Hill, 'Archbishop Laud's Place in History', in his *A Nation of Change and Novelty: Radical Politics, Religion and Literature in Seventeenth-Century England* (1990), ch. 4.

The doctrinal context is analysed by N. Tyacke, *Anti-Calvinists: the Rise of English Arminianism, c.1590–1640* (Oxford, 1990). For a different view see P. White, 'The Rise of Arminianism Reconsidered', *P and P*, 101 (1983), 34–54, and the subsequent debate in the same journal, especially nos 114 (1987), 32–76, and 115 (1987), 201–29, as well as J. E. Davies, 'The Growth and Implementation of "Laudianism" with special reference to the Southern Province', Oxford D. Phil. thesis (1987).

Attitudes towards stipendiary lectureships and sabbatarianism are discussed separately by P. Seaver, *The Puritan Lectureships: the Politics of Religious Dissent, 1560–1662* (Stanford, 1970) and K. L. Parker, *The*

English Sabbath: a Study of Doctrine and Discipline from the Reformation to the Civil War (Cambridge, 1988). The socio-economic problems of the English Church are treated by C. Hill, *Economic Problems of the Church from Archbishop Whitgift to the Long Parliament* (Oxford, 1956), and more recently by R. O'Day and F. Heal (eds), *Princes and Paupers in the English Church, 1500–1800* (Leicester, 1981).

3. EPISCOPAL GOVERNMENT 1603–40

Biographies of bishops and diocesan studies abound for the early Stuart Church, although there are few general interpretations of episcopal government. Contrast, however, H. R. Trevor-Roper, 'King James and his Bishops' *History Today* (September 1955), reprinted in his *Historical Essays* (1957) with P. Collinson, *The Religion of Protestants* (Oxford, 1982), ch. 2, and K. Fincham, *Prelate as Pastor: the Episcopate of James I* (Oxford, 1990). For the 1630s, see N. Tyacke, *Anti-Calvinists* (Oxford, 1987), ch. 8; A. Foster, 'Church Policies of the 1630s' in R. Cust and A. Hughes (eds), *Conflict in Early Stuart England* (Harlow, 1989); and H. T. Blethan, 'Bishop Williams, the Altar Controversy and the Royal Supremacy 1627–41' *Welsh History Review*, 9 (1978). Julian Davies's *The Caroline Captivity of the church: Charles I and the remoulding of Anglicanism* (Oxford, 1992), will be important and controversial.

The most useful episcopal biographies (often as articles) are listed in Fincham, *Prelate as Pastor*, 343–7. Most are stronger on personality than the nature of the episcopal office or the supervision of diocesan work. The best studies of court bishops are discussed above on 234; while the most ambitious integration of court and diocesan activity remains unpublished: A. Foster, 'A biography of Archbishop Richard Neile' (Oxford D. Phil. thesis, 1978), though see his article on Neile in R. O'Day and F. Heal (eds), *Continuity and Change: Personnel and Administration of the Church in England 1500–1642* (Leicester, 1976). Among diocesan studies, see the articles by Haigh (on Chester) and Sheils (on Peterborough), both in *Continuity and Change*; R. A. Marchant, *The Puritans and the Church Courts in the Diocese of York 1560–1642* (1960); A. Fletcher, *A County Community at Peace and War: Sussex 1600–1660* (1975), ch. 4; M. Tillbrook, 'Arminianism and County Society in County Durham, 1617–42', in D. Marcombe (ed.), *The Last Principality* (Nottingham, 1987); and J. Fielding, *Conformists and Puritans: the Diocese of Peterborough 1603–42* (1994). M. Stieg, *Laud's Laboratory: the Diocese of Bath and Wells in Early Seventeenth-Century* (East Brunswick, NJ, 1982) should be used with caution.

Work on the episcopate's economic position and social relations provide much of the context for their pastoral work: most valuable here is C. Hill, *The Economic Problems of the Church from Archbishop Whitgift to the Long Parliament* (Oxford, 1956); P. Hembry, *The Bishops of Bath and Wells 1540–1640: Social and Economic Problems* (1967); and R. O'Day and F. Heal (eds), *Princes and Paupers in the English Church 1500–1800* (Leicester, 1981).

The most authoritative guides to the church courts are R. A. Marchant, *The Church under the Law* (Cambridge, 1969); R. A. Houlbrooke, *Church Courts and the People during the English Reformation 1520–1570* (Oxford, 1979); and M. Ingram, *Church Courts, Sex and Marriage in England, 1570–1640* (Cambridge, 1987).

4. ARMINIANISM IN THE LOCALITIES: PETERBOROUGH DIOCESE 1603–1642

The best guides to the background and development of Arminianism in general are N. Tyacke, *Anti-Calvinists: the Rise of English Arminianism c.1590–1640* (Oxford, 1987) and P. Lake, 'Calvinism and the English Church, 1570–1635' *P and P*, 114 (1987).

For accounts of the Jacobean Church see P. Collinson, *The Religion of Protestants. The Church in English Society, 1559–1625* (Oxford, 1982), K. Fincham and P. Lake, 'The Ecclesiastical Policy of King James I', *JBS*, 24 (1985), and K. Fincham, 'Prelacy and Politics: Archbishop Abbot's defence of Protestant Orthodoxy', *Historical Research*, 61 (1988). The best recent introduction to the religious developments of the 1630s is A. Foster, 'Church Policies of the 1630s' in R. Cust and A. Hughes (eds), *Conflict in Early Stuart England: Studies in Religion and Politics 1603–42* (Harlow, 1989).

Several local studies have dealt with religion from the puritan side: for the purposes of comparison the best of these is probably R. C. Richardson, *Puritanism in north-west England: a regional study of the diocese of Chester to 1642* (Manchester, 1972). Fewer local studies contain much information on the Arminians. R. Marchant, *The Puritans and the Church Courts in the Diocese of York, 1560–1642* (1960) sees the Arminians as simply efficient administrators in a conservative tradition; more useful is A. J. Fletcher, *A County Community in Peace and War: Sussex 1600–1660* (1975), ch. 4.

Little attention has been paid to moderate Calvinist reactions to the policies of the 1630s: two exceptions to this rule are P. Lake, 'Serving God and the times: the Calvinist conformity of Robert Sanderson', *JBS*, 27 (1988) and M. Todd, 'An "act of discretion": evangelical conformity and the Puritan dons', *Albion*, 18 (1986).

Finally, for an introduction to the political climate see the volume of essays edited by Cust and Hughes, cited above, and R. Cust, *The Forced Loan and English Politics, 1626–28* (Oxford, 1987).

5. 'BY THIS BOOK': PARISHIONERS, THE PRAYER BOOK AND THE ESTABLISHED CHURCH

Nonconformity both within and without the established Church – as well as 'from above' and 'from below' – has been well serviced by historians. For the view 'from above' taking the 'Anglican vs. puritan' approach see: J. H. New, *Anglican and Puritan, The Basis of Their Opposition 1558–1640* (Stanford, 1964); Horton Davies, *Worship and Theology in England*, vols I, II (Princeton, 1970, 1975); Richard Greaves, *Religion and Society in Elizabethan England* (Minneapolis, 1981); J. Sears McGee, *The Godly Man in Stuart England: Anglicans, Puritans, and the Two Tables, 1620–1670* (New Haven, 1976). Among the best of the great number of studies of the Reformation 'from below' are Margaret Spufford, *Contrasting Communities: English Villagers in the Sixteenth and Seventeenth Centuries* (Cambridge, 1974) for Cambridgeshire, and Christopher Haigh, *Reformation and Resistance in Tudor Lancashire* (Cambridge, 1975).

More recently the views of conformist clergy and bishops have received some fresh and serious attention such as Patrick Collinson, *The Religion of Protestants* (Oxford, 1982); Kenneth Parker, *The English Sabbath: a Study of Doctrine and Discipline from the Reformation to the Civil War* (Cambridge, 1988); Peter Lake, *Puritans and Anglicans? Presbyterian and English Conformist Thought from Whitgift to Hooker* (1988); Kenneth Fincham, *Prelate as Pastor: the Episcopate of James I* (Oxford, 1990). The role of 'Anglicanism' in the creation of royalism on the eve and during the period of the Civil War is well explored by Anthony Fletcher, *The Outbreak of the English Civil War* (1981) and John Morrill, 'The Church in England in the 1640s', *Reactions to the English Civil War 1642–1649*, ed. J. Morrill (1982) and 'The Attack on the Church of England in the Long Parliament, 1640–1642', *History, Society and the Churches: essays in honour of Owen Chadwick*, (eds) Derek Beales and Geoffrey Best (Cambridge, 1985). The case that Anglicanism may have had some popular appeal, though perhaps primarily for its anti-puritanism, in the early Stuart and Commonwealth period is put forward in David Underdown, *Revel, Riot, and Rebellion: Popular Politics and Culture in England 1603–1660* (Oxford, 1985).

We await, however, a major published study of conformity which places its emphasis of the religious views of the laity – particularly of those below gentry level. In the meantime several essays in *Parish, Church and People: Local Studies in Lay Religion* (1988), ed. Susan Wright make important contributions in this neglected area, in particular those by Nick Alldridge on the period 1540–1640 in the city of Chester, Susan Wright on young people and preparation for communion and confirmation, and Donald Spaeth on attachment to the Prayer Book in Restoration Wiltshire. D. M. Palliser presents a view of lay religion which includes conformity in *The Age of Elizabeth: England under the Later Tudors 1547–1603* (1983). Margaret Spufford in 'Can we Count the

"Godly" and the "Conformable" in the Seventeenth Century?', *JEH*, 36 (1985) offers a sharp and challenging critique of the bias towards 'the godly' on the part of many historians working in the field. Eamon Duffy too has questioned the objectivity of the 'godly's' view of the multitude in 'The Godly and the Multitude in Stuart England', *The Seventeenth Century*, 1 (1986). Both Ian Green in 'Career Prospects and Clerical Conformity in the Early Stuart Church', *P and P*, 90 (1981) and Martin Ingram, *Church Courts, Sex and Marriage in England, 1570–1640* (Cambridge, 1987) (especially ch. 3) provide more balanced use of the Church courts as a source for the study of conformity as well as nonconformity. Christopher Haigh's controversial 'The Church of England, the Catholics and the People', *The Reign of Elizabeth I*, ed. C. Haigh (1984) presents one view of 'parish Anglicanism' discussed in my article in this volume. His 'The recent historiography of the English Reformation', *The English Reformation Revised*, ed. C. Haigh (Cambridge, 1987) is a stimulating and helpful introduction to problems of approaching the Reformation 'from above' or 'from below'. An excellent starting point for all students of the Reformation in England. Another helpful introduction to the complex historiography of this field for students can be found in Borden W. Painter, 'Anglican Terminology in Recent Tudor and Stuart Historiography', *Anglican and Episcopal History*, 56 (1987).

Familiarity with the Book of Common Prayer itself has been made easier by the availability of a modern edition of the 1559 Prayer Book edited by John Booty, *The Book of Common Prayer 1559* (Washington, D.C., 1976) which unfortunately modernises the spelling of the Elizabethan Common Prayer Book but nevertheless provides an accessible text and includes a helpful short history of the Prayer Book.

The complex and shadowy area of what the experience of church-going was actually like for Tudor-Stuart Christians and the inter-relationship between worship, theology and environment has not yet been superseded by G. W. O. Addleshaw and F. Etchells, *The Architectural Setting of Anglican Worship* (1948) though it begins to show its age. Nicholas Temperley, *The Music of the English Parish Church* (Cambridge, 1979) offers much fascinating information on a crucial area of lay piety almost totally neglected by Church historians, but suffers from an over-simplified 'Anglican vs. puritan' model. John Phillips, *The Reformation of Images: the Destruction of Art in England 1535–1660* (Los Angeles, 1973) imaginatively explores, albeit only among elites, the complex mixture of attitudes towards the visual in worship held by English protestants.

Although I have been critical in some respects of the work of both Patrick Collinson and Keith Thomas it would be inappropriate not to mention either Collinson's *Elizabethan Puritan Movement* (1967) and Thomas's *Religion and the Decline of Magic* (New York, 1971). Both books undoubtedly broke new ground, significantly altered our view of Tudor-

Stuart religion, inspired a generation of new research and therefore remain the most important contributions to the field in this century.

6. THE CLERICAL ESTATE REVITALISED

Ian Green and Rosemary O'Day have made the subject of the role of parish clergy their own. Green's 'The persecution of "scandalous" and "malignant" parish clergy during the English Civil War', *EHR*, 94 (1979) is important for teasing out why so many clergy were unpopular by the 1640s; his ' "Reformed Pastors" and *Bon Cures*: The Changing Role of the Parish Clergy in Early Modern Europe' is to be found in the excellent collection *The Ministry: Clerical and Lay*, eds W. J. Sheils and D. Wood, *Studies in Church History*, 26 (Oxford, 1989) and provides both a European context and an antidote to some of the more extravagant claims of O'Day, *The English Clergy: The Emergence and Consolidation of a Profession 1558–1642* (Leicester, 1979). For a comprehensive account of the ideal ministry against which to judge events related in my article see P. Collinson, 'Shepherds, Sheepdogs, and Hirelings: The Pastoral Ministry in Post-Reformation England', also in *The Ministry: Clerical and Lay*.

Valuable works on the problems of the clergy by the 1640s include: J. Morrill, 'The attack on the Church of England in the Long Parliament, 1640–1642', in D. Beales and G. Best (eds), *History, Society and the Churches* (1985); J. Morrill, 'The Religious Context of the English Civil War', *TRHS*, 5th series, 34 (1984); J. Sharpe, 'Scandalous and Malignant Priests in Essex: the Impact of Grassroots Puritanism', in C. Jones, M. Newitt and S. Roberts (eds), *Politics and People in Revolutionary England*, (Oxford, 1986).

Christopher Hill, *Economic Problems of the Church from Archbishop Whitgift to the Long Parliament* (Oxford, 1956) and *Society and Puritanism in Pre-Revolutionary England* (1964) justifiably stand as classic works on economic and social issues relating to the Church of England. For important new work on the matter of tithes see W. J. Sheils, ' "The Right of the Church"; The Clergy, Tithe, and the Courts at York, 1540–1640', in W. J. Sheils and D. Wood (eds), *The Church and Wealth, Studies in Church History*, 24 (Oxford, 1987). For the work of Laud and his associates see F. Heal, 'Archbishop Laud revisited: Leases and Estate Management at Canterbury and Winchester before the Civil War', in R. O'Day and F. Heal (eds), *Princes and Paupers in the English Church 1500–1800*, (Leicester, 1981).

The character and significance of 'anticlericalism' is hotly disputed; contrast C. Haigh, 'Anticlericalism and the English Reformation', *History*, 68 (1983) with M. Schwarz, 'Some Thoughts on the Development of a Lay Religious Consciousness in Pre-Civil War England', in G.

Cuming and D. Baker (eds), *Popular Belief and Practice, Studies in Church History, 8* (Cambridge, 1972).

Conrad Russell, *Parliaments and English Politics 1621–1629* (Oxford, 1979) remains vital to understanding debates about religion in Parliaments; E. R. Foster, *The House of Lords, 1603–1649* (Chapel Hill, N.C., 1983) provides context, while E. Cope, 'The Bishops and Parliamentary Politics in Early Stuart England', *Parliamentary History*, 9 (1990), and K. Fincham in *Prelate as Pastor* provide badly needed specific material in print on the work of the bishops in the House of Lords.

The more mundane matters of local government are well covered by J. H. Gleason, *The Justices of the Peace in England 1558–1640* (1969) now complemented by Anthony Fletcher's excellent *Reform in the Provinces. The Government of Stuart England* (1986). For a list of essential sources see T. Barnes and A. Hassell Smith, 'Justices of the Peace from 1558 to 1688 – a Revised List of Sources', *BIHR*, 32 (1959). To place such works in context see good examples of local studies such as T. G. Barnes, *Somerset 1625–1640* (Oxford, 1961) and A. Fletcher, *A County Community in Peace and War: Sussex 1600–1660*, (1975).

7. THE LAUDIAN STYLE

For background to the Laudian style see P. Lake, *Anglicans and Puritans? Presbyterianism and English Conformist Thought from Whitgift to Hooker* (1988), esp. ch. 4; 'Lancelot Andrewes, John Buckeridge and *avant garde* conformity at the court of James I' in L. L. Peck (ed.) *The Mental World of the Jacobean Court* (Cambridge, 1991); K. Fincham, *Prelate as Pastor* (Oxford, 1990), esp. chs 7–8.

On the 1630s themselves there is surprisingly little of value. N. Tyacke, *Anti-Calvinists* (Oxford, 1987), ch. 8 is the best account. There is still much useful material in G. Addleshaw and F. Etchells, *The Architectural Setting of Anglican Worship* (1948) and G. Addleshaw, *The High Church Tradition* (1941). Also see Sears McGee, 'William Laud and the Outward Face of Religion' in R. DeMolen (ed.), *Leaders of the Reformation* (Susquehanna University Press, 1984). On the university *avant garde* see D. Hoyle, 'A Commons Investigation of Arminianism and Popery at Cambridge on the eve of the civil war' *HJ*, 29 (1986). For an outstanding study of a leading lay Laudian see I. Atherton, 'Viscount Scudamore's "Laudianism"; the religious practices of the first Viscount Scudamore', *HJ*, 34 (1991). For other aspects of Laudian thought and activity during the 1630s see P. Lake, 'The Laudians and the Argument from Authority' in B. Y. Kunze and D. D. Brautigam (eds), *Court, Country and Culture*, (Rochester, N.Y., 1992) and Anthony Milton's *Catholic and reformed: the Roman and Protestant Churches in English Protestant thought, 1600–1640* (Cambridge, 1993).

8. THE CHURCH OF ENGLAND, ROME AND THE TRUE CHURCH

Early Stuart religious thought has (until recently) received little attention from historians, and the doctrine of the church has suffered its fair
share of neglect. The late Elizabethan period is now well served by
Peter Lake's excellent *Anglicans and Puritans?* (1988). The conclusion to
this book, and Lake's article 'Presbyterianism, the Idea of a National
Church and the Argument from Divine Right' in P. Lake and M.
Dowling (eds), *Protestantism and the National Church in Sixteenth-Century
England* (1987) provide useful guides for the early Jacobean period. The
most comprehensive general survey remains H. F. Woodhouse, *The
Doctrine of the Church in Anglican Theology 1547–1603* (1954), which contains a brief survey of developments 1603–49 in ch. 12, although this
account is now showing its age. Paul Avis, *The Church in the Theology of
the Reformers* (1981) highlights many important issues, but his analysis
is poor, and his interpretation of Hooker and Field faulty. Individual
ecclesiological issues have received more attention. On issues of church
visibility and succession, Jane Facey's article 'John Foxe and the
Defence of the English Church' in Lake and Dowling (eds), *Protestantism
and the National Church* provides a useful summary of the Foxeian position, while T. H. Wadkins, 'The Percy-"Fisher" Controversies and the
Ecclesiastical Politics of Jacobean Anti-Catholicism, 1622–1625', *Church
History*, 57 (1988) provides useful information on the Fisher controversy.
On apocalyptic issues Richard Bauckham's *Tudor Apocalypse* (Abingdon,
1978) provides an excellent analysis of Elizabethan material, but we
still lack a detailed study of the general output of the English presses
on this subject during the early Stuart period. Useful summaries are
provided by B. Capp 'The political dimension of apocalyptical thought'
in *The Apocalypse in English Renaissance Thought and Literature*, (eds.) C.
A. Patrides and J. Wittreich (Manchester, 1984), and in Christopher
Hill's *Antichrist in Seventeenth-Century England* (Oxford, 1971): revised
paperback edn (1990).

There is still surprisingly little in print concerning the protestant/
Roman Catholic controversy during this period. It has been calculated
that over five hundred works on this issue were published in the Jacobean period alone by approximately one hundred and fifty different
protestant and Romanist authors, and the vast majority of these works
(and therefore the main bulk of controversial writings of the period)
remain virtually unread. A useful summary is provided in G. R. Cragg,
Freedom and Authority (Philadelphia, 1975), ch. 6, while P. Millward,
Religious Controversies of the Jacobean Age (1978) is a helpful bibliographical
guide. Peter Lake's 'Anti-Popery: the Structure of a Prejudice' in R.
Cust and A. Hughes (eds), *Conflict in Early Stuart England* (Harlow,
1989) provides a lucid and incisive account of the more radical anti-
Roman position, but he describes an ideal type drawn partly from

converts' accounts, and it remains unclear how far and in what ways this paradigm was held by more moderate churchmen.

9. THE *VIA MEDIA* IN THE EARLY STUART CHURCH

The view of Church history which I have ventured to criticise is most accessible in C. Russell (ed.), *The Origins of the English Civil War* (1973), especially in the introduction and in N. Tyacke's chapter, 'Puritanism, Arminianism and Counter-Revolution'. Modifications and extensions of their approach may be found in Russell, *The Causes of the English Civil War* (Oxford, 1990), and N. Tyacke, *Anti-Calvinists: the Rise of English Arminianism c.1590–1640* (Oxford, 1987). For my earlier criticisms, see 'The Rise of Arminianism Reconsidered' in *P and P*, 101 (1983) and Tyacke and White, 'Debate: The Rise of Arminianism Reconsidered' ibid., 115 (1987). See also my *Predestination, Policy and Polemic: Conflict and Consensus in the English Church from the Reformation to the Civil War* (Cambridge, 1992).

Readers who find themselves in sympathy with the approach taken in this chapter, and who would like to know more about the Elizabethan background, will enjoy H. C. Porter, 'Hooker, the Tudor Constitution, and the *Via Media*' in *Studies in Richard Hooker. essays preliminary to an edition of his Works* (1972) ed. W. Speed Hill. A good general introduction to Hooker is still F. Paget, *An Introduction to the Fifth Book of Hooker's Treatise* (1907). For a broader perspective, see also G. W. Bernard, 'The Church of England c.1529–c.1642' *History*, 75 (1990).

On the Hampton Court Conference, M. H. Curtis, 'The Hampton Court Conference and its aftermath', *History*, 46 (1961) should be weighed against F. Shriver, 'Hampton Court Revisited: James I and the Puritans' *JEH*, 33 (1982).

On James I generally, K. Fincham and P. Lake, 'The Ecclesiastical Policy of King James I' *JBS*, 24 (1985), argue that James pursued a *via media* by attempting to isolate both puritan and Roman Catholic extremists through concessions to moderates. James I's *Premonition to All the Most Mighty Monarchs, Kings, Free Princes, and States of Christendom* (1609) is printed in C. H. McIlwain (ed.), *The Political Works of James I* (Cambridge, Mass., 1918).

On the Synod of Dort, the account in Tyacke, *Anti-Calvinists*, ch. 4, should be contrasted with J. Platt, 'Eirenical Anglicans at the Synod of Dort' in D. Baker (ed.), *Studies in Church History, Subsidia 2: Reform and Reformation: England and the Continent c.1500–c.1700* (Oxford, 1979).

On Laud, W. H. Hutton, *William Laud* (1895) includes perspectives ignored in H. R. Trevor-Roper, *Archbishop Laud* (2nd edn, 1962). Also valuable is C. Hill, *Economic Problems of the Church from Archibishop Whitgift to the Long Parliament* (Oxford, 1956). For more recent assessments see H. R. Trevor-Roper, *Catholics, Anglicans and Puritans* (1987), and K. Sharpe, 'Archbishop Laud and the University of Oxford' in H. Lloyd Jones, V. Pearl and B. Worden (eds), *History and Imagination* (1987).

Notes and References

INTRODUCTION *Kenneth Fincham*

The author thanks Andrew Foster, Peter Lake and Nicholas Tyacke for their comments on an earlier version of this chapter.

1. D. MacCulloch, *The Later Reformation in England 1547–1603* (Basingstoke, 1990), chs 3–4; P. Collinson, 'Andrew Perne and his times' in D. McKitterick (ed.), *Andrew Perne: Quatercentenary Studies*, Cambridge Bibliographical Society Monographs no. 11 (1991), 7–10; P. Collinson, *Archbishop Grindal 1519–1583* (1979), 233–52.

2. C. Hill, *Society and Puritanism in Pre-Revolutionary England* (1964); J. F. H. New, *Anglican and Puritan: the Basis of their Opposition 1558–1640* (Stanford, 1964). See also J. S. McGee, *The Godly Man in Stuart England: Anglicans, Puritans and the Two Tables 1620–1670* (1976).

3. H. Trevor-Roper, *Archbishop Laud 1573–1645* (1940), 41–2, 435–6; id. *Historical Essays* (1957), 130–45; P. A. Welsby, *George Abbot: the Unwanted Archbishop 1562–1633* (1962), 37–8.

4. For recent defences of the term, see R. Greaves, 'The Puritan-Nonconformist Tradition in England, 1560–1700' *Albion*, 17 (1985), 453, who uses it to describe 'non-Puritans'; D. Hirst, *Authority and Conflict: England 1603–1658* (1986), 68–9 who applies it to 'protestant, yet ceremonial' members of the Church; P. Lake, *Anglicans and Puritans? Presbyterianism and English Conformist Thought from Whitgift to Hooker* (1988), 4–6, 159–60, 227–8, who sees Hooker as the founding-father of the *via media* between Rome and Geneva in doctrine, polity and liturgy, though its advocates were few in number until the 1620s; and against Lake, by P. White, above 214–17.

5. P. Collinson, *The Elizabethan Puritan Movement* (1967); id. *English Puritanism* (Historical Assoc. pamphlet, 1983); P. Lake, 'Puritan Identities' *JEH*, 35 (1984), 112–23; id. 'Matthew Hutton – a Puritan Bishop?' *History*, 64 (1979), 182–204; N. Tyacke, 'Puritanism, Arminianism and

Counter-Revolution' in C. Russell (ed.), *The Origins of the English Civil War* (1973), 123.

6. K. Fincham, *Prelate as Pastor: the Episcopate of James I* (Oxford, 1990), 28, 139–40, 220, 303.

7. Tyacke, 'Puritanism', 119–43; id. *Anti-Calvinists: the rise of English Arminianism c.1590–1640* (Oxford, 2nd edn 1990); id. 'Debate: The Rise of Arminianism Reconsidered' *P and P*, 115 (1987), 201–16. See also his 'Arminianism and English Culture' in A. C. Duke and C. A. Tamse (eds), *Britain and the Netherlands*, 7 (The Hague, 1981), 94–117.

8. Collinson, *Archbishop Grindal*, 283–93; id. *The Religion of Protestants* (Oxford, 1982), 79–91; id., *The Birthpangs of Protestant England* (Basingstoke, 1988), 140–1.

9. G. W. Bernard, 'The Church of England c.1529–c.1642' *History*, 75 (1990), 183–206; C. Hill, 'Archbishop Laud's place in English History' in his *A Nation of Change and Novelty* (1990), 56–81; K. Sharpe, *Politics and Ideas in Early Stuart England* (1989), 30, 123–8, 142–3; P. White, 'The Rise of Arminianism reconsidered', *P and P*, 101 (1983), 34–54, and 'A Rejoinder', ibid. 115 (1987), 217–29. See also I. M. Green, ' "England's Wars of Religion"? Religious Conflict and the English Civil Wars' in J. van den Berg and P. G. Hoftijzer (eds) *Church, Change and Revolution* (Brill, 1991), 100–21.

10. For Tyacke's response to his critics, see *Anti-Calvinists*, vii-xv.

11. Ibid., 53–6; M. Todd, ' "An act of discretion": Evangelical Conformity and the Puritan Dons', *Albion*, 18 (1986), 594 n. 57. See also Fincham, *Prelate as Pastor*, chs 7–8.

12. N. Tyacke, 'The "Rise of Puritanism" and the legalizing of Dissent, 1571–1719' in O. Grell, J. Israel and N. Tyacke (eds), *From Persecution to Toleration: The Glorious Revolution and Religion in England* (Oxford, 1991), 21–4; *Commons Debates 1628*, eds R. C. Johnson, M. F. Keeler, M. J. Cole and W. B. Bidwell (New Haven, 1977–83), iii. 515–20; Elton, quoted in C. Russell, *Parliaments and English Politics 1621–1629* (Oxford, 1979), 26–32.

13. N. Tyacke, *The Fortunes of English Puritanism, 1603–1640* (1990); Bodl., Rawlinson Letters 89 fo. 4; C. Russell, *The Fall of the British Monarchies 1637–1642* (Oxford, 1991), 22.

14. Collinson, *The Religion of Protestants*, 242–83; J. H. Primus, *Holy Time: Moderate Puritans and the Sabbath* (Macon, Ga., 1989), 61, 65–6, 156, 162; K. Parker, *The English Sabbath* (Cambridge, 1988); A. Milton in *JEH*, 41 (1990), 492–3; for Bernard, see above 83.

15. R. T. Kendall, *Calvin and English Calvinism to 1649* (Oxford, 1979), 8–9 and *passim*; P. Lake, 'Calvinism and the English Church 1570–1635' *P and P*, 114 (1987), 38–40.

16. Kendall, *Calvin and English Calvinism*, 79–80; Tyacke, *Anti-Calvinists*, 16, 32, 93–5; Lake, 'Calvinism', 54–9; Fincham, *Prelate as Pastor*, 261, 269; D. Wallace, *Puritans and Predestination* (Chapel Hill, N. C.

1982), 81; B. Donagan, 'The York House Conference Revisited: Laymen, Calvinism and Arminianism' *Historical Research*, 64 (1991), 312–30; *pace* Bernard, 'Church of England', 196. Conformist Calvinists could be 'experimentalists', as Tyacke has observed for both George Abbot and Toby Matthew. In neither case, however, did this perception seem to dominate their style of piety as archbishops (*Anti-Calvinists*, ix, 18–19).

17. For Abbot, see Francis Manson, *Of the Consecration of the Bishops of the Church of England* (1613), dedicatory epistle; STC, 39; for Abbot and Lake, see Fincham, *Prelate as Pastor*, 269–70. See also P. Lake, 'The Significance of the Elizabethan Identification of the Pope as Antichrist' *JEH*, 31 (1980), 161–78.

18. J. E. Davies, 'The Growth and Implementation of "Laudianism" with special reference to the southern province' (Oxford D.Phil. thesis, 1987), ch. 7; Tyacke, *Anti-Calvinists*, 210–12. For the normative status of *iure divino* episcopacy in the reign of James I, see J. P. Sommerville, 'The Royal Supremacy and Episcopacy *Iure Divino* 1603–1640' *JEH*, 34 (1983), 548–58.

19. For a different view, see P. Collinson, 'Shepherds, Sheepdogs and Hirelings' in W. J. Sheils and D. Wood (eds), *Studies in Church History, 26* (Oxford, 1989), 186. For studies of conformist Calvinists, see J. M. Atkins, 'Calvinist Bishops, Church Unity and the Rise of Arminianism' *Albion*, 18 (1986), 411–27; Todd, 'Evangelical Conformity and the Puritan Dons', ibid., 581–99; P. G. Lake, 'Serving God and the Times: the Calvinist Conformity of Robert Sanderson' *JBS*, 27 (1988), 81–116; Fincham, *Prelate as Pastor*, 260–1.

20. Tyacke, *Anti-Calvinists*; Lake, *Anglicans and Puritans?*, 145–230; Fincham, *Prelate as Pastor*, 231–40.

21. Tyacke, *Anti-Calvinists*, 60, 110; Lake, *Anglicans and Puritans?*, 182–97; P. A. Welsby, *Lancelot Andrewes 1555–1626* (1958), 20–9; Primus, *Holy Time*, 173–4.

22. Collinson, 'Andrew Perne', 15; D. MacCulloch, *Suffolk and the Tudors* (Oxford, 1986), 210–11. See also Tyacke's comments on Bishop Young, above 54.

23. HRO, A1/31 fo. 13v; *STC*, 4644, 18037; Tyacke, *Anti-Calvinists*, 155–6.

24. S. B. Babbage, *Puritanism and Richard Bancroft* (1962), chs 4–8; T. Cogswell, *The Blessed Revolution: English Politics and the Coming of War 1621–1624* (Cambridge, 1989), 20–35; Collinson, *Birthpangs*, 127–55; D. Underdown, *Revel, Riot, and Rebellion* (Oxford, 1987), 44–72.

25. The phrase is from Tyacke, 'Puritanism', 121.

26. Sampson Price, *A Heavenly Proclamation to Fly Romish Babylon* (Oxford, 1614), 34.

27. BL, Add. MS 25278 fo. 136r; P. Lake, 'Anti-Popery: the Structure of a Prejudice' and T. Cogswell, 'England and the Spanish Match',

both in R. Cust and A. Hughes (eds), *Conflict in Early Stuart England* (Harlow, 1989), 84–92, 116–19; R. Cust, 'Charles I and a draft declaration for the 1628 Parliament' *Historical Research*, 63 (1990), 143–61.

28. All cited above, n. 9.

29. Tyacke, *Anti-Calvinists*, esp. 248–65.

30. Russell, *The Fall of the British Monarchies*, 23.

31. Collinson, *Birthpangs*, 115–21; M. Aston, *England's Iconoclasts* (Oxford, 1988), 450–1, 461–2; H. R. Trevor-Roper, *Catholics, Anglicans and Puritans* (1987), 82, 84; P. Croft, 'The Religion of Robert Cecil' *HJ*, 34 (1991), 787–9; T. Watt, *Cheap Print and Popular Piety* (Cambridge, 1991), 173; C. J. H. Fletcher, *A History of the Church and Parish of St. Martin, Oxford* (Oxford, 1896), 70.

32. See also A. Milton, 'The Laudians and the Church of Rome c.1625–1640' (Cambridge Ph.D. thesis, 1989); W. J. Tighe, 'William Laud and the Reunion of the Churches: some evidence from 1637 and 1638' *HJ*, 30 (1987), 717–27; C. Russell, *The Causes of the English Civil War* (Oxford, 1990), 197–8; and D. Hoyle, 'A Commons Investigation of Arminianism and Popery in Cambridge on the eve of the Civil War' *HJ*, 29 (1986), 419–25.

33. Lake *Anglicans and Puritans?*, ch. 4; Tyacke, *Anti-Calvinists*, 267; C. Hibbard, *Charles I and the Popish Plot* (Chapel Hill, N. C., 1983), 57; Laud, *Works*, ii. pp. xiii-xvi; PRO, SP 16/259/78; John Cosin, *Works*, ed. J. Sansom (5 vols, Oxford, 1843–55), i. 95–6.

34. Laud, *Works*, v. 610–11, vi. 42; Bodl., Tanner MS 68 fo. 221. It is striking how few references there are to Bancroft in Laud's *Works*.

35. Russell, *The Fall of the British Monarchies*, 16–17; M. L. Schwarz, 'Lay Anglicanism and the Crisis of the English Church in the Early Seventeenth Century' *Albion*, 14 (1982), 1–19.

36. William Gouge, *The Sabbaths Sanctification* (1641), sig. A2v. For typical puritan reactions to religious developments in the 1630s, see P. S. Seaver, *Wallington's World* (Stanford, 1985), 158–63; J. Fielding, 'Opposition to the Personal Rule of Charles I: the diary of Robert Woodford 1637–41'; *HJ*, 31 (1988), 769–88.

37. Tyacke, *Anti-Calvinists*, xii-xiv, 184–5, 248–65. The four are: Richard Bernard, *A Threefold Treatise of the Sabbath* (1641), sig. a2v-a3r; John Ley, *Sunday A Sabbath* (1641), sig. A3iv; William Twisse, *Of the Morality of the Fourth Commandement* (1641), 38 (*recte*, 42) and Bodl., Tanner MS 65 fo. 83; George Walker, *The Doctrine of the Holy Weekly Sabbath* (1641), sig. A2v (originally published in 1638 at Amsterdam). See also George Abbot, *Vindiciae Sabbathi* (1641), sig. A2iiv-iiir; William Gouge, *The Sabbaths Sanctification* (1641), sig. A2r.

38. *The Diary of Thomas Crosfield*, ed. F. S. Boas (1935), 89; BL, Add. MS 70002 fo. 81r; *STC*, 19910. I owe the latter two references to Dr J. Eales. S. Lambert, 'Richard Montagu, Arminianism and Censorship', *P and P*, 124 (1989), 61–8.

39. For Burgess, see *DNB*; Joseph Hall, *Works*, ed. P. Wynter (10 vols, 1863), i. p. xivi. For his diocesan rule, see above 86.

40. Bodl., MS Top Oxon c 378, pp. 228, 283, 284, 314.

41. Atkins, 'Calvinist Bishops', 411–27; Lake, 'Serving God and the Times', 100–3.

42. Tyacke, *Anti-Calvinists*, 213; Russell, *The Fall of the British Monarchies*, 18 n. 65; PRO, LC 5/134 fo. 6, a reference I owe to Nicholas Cranfield.

43. Green, ' "England's Wars of Religion"?', 107; I. Green, ' "For Children in Yeares and Children in Understanding": the Emergence of the English Catechism under Elizabeth and the Early Stuarts' *JEH*, 37 (1986), 397–425; R. O'Day, *The English Clergy: the Emergence and Consolidation of a Profession* (Leicester, 1979); Collinson, *The Religion of Protestants*, 92–140; Fincham, *Prelate as Pastor*; M. Ingram, *Church Courts, Sex and Marriage in England, 1570–1640* (Cambridge, 1987), 323–74. On literacy, see D. Cressy, *Literacy and the Social Order: Reading and Writing in Tudor and Stuart England* (Cambridge, 1980), which demonstrates low levels of literacy (judged by ability to write) even by 1642. Other historians have suggested that ability to read, the more crucial aptitude for the transmission of protestantism, was a good deal higher: see M. Spufford, *Small Books and Pleasant Histories* (1981), 19–37; K. Thomas, 'The Meaning of Literacy in Early Modern England' in G. Baumann (ed.), *The Written Word: Literacy in Transition* (Oxford, 1986), 97–131.

44. K. V. Thomas, *Religion and the Decline of Magic* (1980), 179–206.

45. C. Haigh, 'Puritan Evangelism in the Reign of Elizabeth I' *EHR*, 92 (1977), 30–58; C. Haigh, 'The Church of England, the Catholics and the People' in Haigh (ed.), *The Reign of Elizabeth I* (Basingstoke, 1984), 195–219.

46. M. Spufford, 'Can We Count the "Godly" and the "Conformable" in the Seventeenth Century?', *JEH*, 36 (1985), 428–38; C. Haigh, *Reformation and Resistance in Tudor Lancashire* (Cambridge, 1975); Ingram, *Church Courts*, 84–124; J. Boulton, *Neighbourhood and Society: A London Suburb in the Seventeenth Century* (Cambridge, 1987), 275–85; Collinson, 'Shepherds, Sheepdogs and Hirelings', 199–203.

47. K. Wrightson and D. Levine, *Poverty and Piety in an English Village: Terling 1525–1700* (1979); W. Hunt, *The Puritan Moment: The Coming of Revolution in an English County* (Cambridge, Mass., 1983); Underdown, *Revel, Riot, and Rebellion*.

48. M. Ingram, 'Religion, Communities and Moral Discipline in Late Sixteenth- and Early Seventeenth-Century England: Case Studies' in K. von Greyerz (ed.), *Religion and Society in Early Modern Europe 1500–1800* (1984), 177–93; J. A. Sharpe, 'Crime and Delinquency in an Essex Parish 1600–1640' in J. S. Cockburn (ed.) *Crime in England 1550–1800* (1977), 90–109; N. Tyacke, 'Popular Puritan Mentality in Late Elizabethan England' in P. Clark, A. Smith and N. Tyacke (eds),

The English Commonwealth 1547–1640 (Leicester, 1979), 77–92. See also M. Spufford, *Contrasting Communities: English Villagers in the Sixteenth and Seventeenth Centuries* (Cambridge, 1974), chs 6–10, 13.

49. Ingram, *Church Courts*, 354–5, 365; Collinson, *Religion of Protestants*, 189–241. For a qualified endorsement of this point, see R. von Friedeburg, 'Reformation of Manners and the Social Composition of Offenders in an East Anglican Cloth Village: Earls Colne, Essex, 1531–1642' *JBS*, 29 (1990), 347–85.

50. Ingram, 'Religion, Communities and Moral Discipline'; see also M. Spufford, 'Puritanism and Social Control' in A. Fletcher and J. Stevenson (eds), *Order and Disorder in Early Modern England* (Cambridge, 1985), 41–57; K. Wrightson, 'Alehouses, Order and Reformation in Rural England, 1590–1660' in E. and S. Yeo (eds), *Popular Culture and Class Conflict 1590–1914* (Brighton, 1981), 1–27.

51. J. R. Kent, 'Attitudes of members of the House of Commons to the regulation of "personal conduct" in late Elizabethan and early Stuart England', *BIHR*, 46 (1973), 41–71; Lake, 'Serving God and the Times', 101–2; K. Sharpe, 'Archbishop Laud and the University of Oxford' in his *Politics and Ideas in Early Stuart England*, 128–46; P. Slack, *Poverty and Policy in Tudor and Stuart England* (Harlow, 1988), 148; Hunt, *The Puritan Moment*, 250.

52. For 1641–2, see Lake, 'Anti-Popery', 93–6.

53. Spufford, 'Can We Count the "Godly"?'; E. Duffy, 'The Godly and the Multitude in Stuart England' *The Seventeenth Century*, 1 (1986), 31–55.

54. Watt, *Cheap Print and Popular Piety*.

55. Haigh, 'The Church of England', 216–19 and in *JEH*, 35 (1985), 400. See also J. J. Scarisbrick, *The Reformation and the English People* (Oxford, 1984), 187.

56. J. Morrill, 'The Church in England, 1642–9' in J. Morrill (ed.), *Reactions to the English Civil War 1642–1649* (1982), 89–114.

57. Bernard, 'The Church of England', 199.

58. J. S. Morrill, 'The Religious Context of the English Civil War' *TRHS*, 5th series, 34 (1984), 155–78, presents the conflict as 'the last of the Wars of Religion'. See also A. J. Fletcher, *The Outbreak of the English Civil War* (1981), 407–19.

59. Russell, *Causes of the English Civil War*, 109–30, 220–6.

60. J. Eales, *Puritans and Roundheads: the Harleys of Brampton Bryan and the Outbreak of the English Civil War* (Cambridge, 1990), 198–201.

61. D. L. Smith, 'Catholic, Anglican or Puritan? Edward Sackville, Fourth Earl of Dorset and the Ambiguities of Religion in Early Stuart England' *TRHS* (1992). I am very grateful to Dr Smith for a sight of his argument. See also J. P. Sommerville, *Politics and Ideology in England 1603–40* (Harlow, 1986), 221–4; A. Hughes, *The Causes of the English*

Civil War (Basingstoke, 1991), 114–16; Green, ' "England's Wars of Religion"?', 108–17.

62. B. Manning, *The English People and the English Revolution 1640–1649* (1976), ch. 3.

63. Russell, *The Fall of the British Monarchies*, 347–8, 527; id., 'Why did Charles I fight the Civil War?' *History Today* 34 (June 1984), 31–4; id., *Unrevolutionary England, 1603–1642* (1990) 165–76.

1. THE ECCLESIASTICAL POLICIES OF JAMES I AND CHARLES I *Kenneth Fincham and Peter Lake*

The authors thank Simon Adams, Jackie Eales, Andrew Foster, Conrad Russell, Kevin Sharpe and Nicholas Tyacke for their helpful comments on an earlier draft of this essay.

1. L. J. Reeve, *Charles I and the Road to Personal Rule* (Cambridge, 1989), 292–6; P. Donald, *An Uncounselled King: Charles I and the Scottish Troubles 1637–1641* (Cambridge, 1990), 6–15, 320–7; C. Russell, *The Causes of the English Civil War* (Oxford, 1990), 45, 107, 185–219.

2. R. Ashton, *The English Civil War: Conservatism and Revolution* (1978), 110; P. Collinson, *The Religion of Protestants* (Oxford, 1982), 90; J. Morrill, 'The Religious Context of the English Civil War' *TRHS*, 5th series, 34 (1984), 155–78. These views, with which he would not necessarily agree, represent an extrapolation from the seminal and nuanced work of Nicholas Tyacke. See his 'Puritanism, Arminianism and Counter-Revolution' in C. Russell (ed.), *The Origins of the English Civil War* (1973), 119–43; *Anti-Calvinists: the Rise of English Arminianism c.1590–1640* (Oxford, 1987).

3. P. White, 'The Rise of Arminianism Reconsidered', *P and P*, 101 (1983), 34–54; K. Sharpe, *Politics and Ideas in Early Stuart England* (1989), 108–9, 123–8; C. Hill, 'Archbishop Laud's place in English History' in his *A Nation of Change and Novelty* (1990), 56–81; G. W. Bernard, 'The Church of England c.1529–c.1642' *History*, 75 (1990), 183–206.

4. What follows on James I is an abbreviated and amended version of our article, 'The Ecclesiastical Policy of King James I', *JBS*, 24 (1985), 169–207.

5. See, for example, *A Meditation upon the Lord's Prayer written by the Kings Maiestie* (1619), 5–12, 17.

6. *The Political Works of James I*, ed. C. H. McIlwain (Cambridge, Mass., 1918), 6–8, 23–4. From its use by puritans, see BL, Add. MS. 8978 fos 2v–3v and LPL, MS 933, no. 23; by conformists, see Thomas Sparke, *A Brotherly Perswasion* (1607) and John Denison, *Beati Pacifici* (1620), sig. A4r.

7. M. H. Curtis, 'Hampton Court Conference and its Aftermath', *History*, 46 (1961), 9–12; William Barlow, *The Summe and Substance of the*

Conference (1604), 91–2, 99–101. For the enforcement of subscription in the dioceses, see above 75–6. James followed a similar tactic when introducing the Articles of Perth (1618) in Scotland: see Russell, *Causes of the English Civil War*, 49.

8. K. Fincham, *Prelate as Pastor: the Episcopate of James I* (Oxford, 1990), 214–16, 225–8, 307–8; B. W. Quintrell, 'The Royal Hunt and the Puritans, 1604–5' *JEH*, 31 (1980), 41–58; *Les Reportes del Cases in Star Chamber 1593 to 1609*, ed. W. P. Baildon (1894), 341. For Cotton's puritan ministry at Boston, see C. Holmes, *Seventeenth-Century Lincolnshire* (Lincoln, 1980), 52–3, 95–6.

9. F. Shriver, 'Hampton Court revisited: James I and the Puritans' *JEH*, 33 (1982), 61–4; D Wilkins, *Concilia Magnae Britanniae et Hiberniae* (1737), iv. 413–14, 440–2; Fincham, *Prelate as Pastor*, 307–8; *Lords' Journals*, ii. 658.

10. Tyacke has noted that no work versus puritanism was licensed for publication between 1611 and 1618 ('Puritanism', 125). Thomas Ball, *The Life of the Renowned Doctor Preston*, ed. E. W. Harcourt (Oxford, 1885), 68–9, 98.

11. W. B. Patterson, 'King James I's Call for an Ecumenical Council' in *Studies in Church History, 7*, eds G. J. Cuming and D. Baker (Cambridge, 1971), 267–75; *Political Works of James I*, 149–50; *Spain and the Jacobean Catholics*, vol. 2, *1613–24*, ed. A. J. Loomie, Catholic Record Society, 68 (1978), 146.

12. *Political Works of James I*, 71–2, 275, 323, 341; A. Dures, *English Catholicism 1558–1642* (1983), 45–51; for the expulsion of radicals, see *Stuart Royal Proclamations*, ed. J. F. Larkin and P. L. Hughes (2 vols, Oxford, 1973–83), i. 70–3, 142–5, 245–50, 591–3. For the vagaries of Jacobean enforcement of the oath, see PRO, SO 3/6 fo. 6r where Henry James forfeited his property for refusing the oath. It was then granted to his son, who was dispensed from taking the oath! We owe this reference to Conrad Russell.

13. Dures, *English Catholicism*, 40–54; J. C. H. Aveling, *The Handle and the Axe* (1976), 124–5; A. J. Loomie, 'A Jacobean Crypto-Catholic: Lord Wotton' *Catholic Historical Review*, 53 (1967), 328–45; L. L. Peck, *Northampton* (1982), 55, 57; *State Trials*, eds T. B. and T. J. Howell (34 vols, 1816–28), ii. 268. A further reason for the limited impact of Jacobean theory was, as recent research has demonstrated, the fact that royal officials saw the recusancy issue almost entirely in financial terms. See M. C. Questier, 'Recusancy and the phenomenom of conversion, 1570–1640' (Sussex Ph.D. thesis, 1991), ch. 5.

14. W. R. Foster, *The Church before the Covenants* (1975), 11; M. Lee, 'James VI and the revival of Episcopacy in Scotland 1596–1600' *Church History*, 43 (1974), 50–64; G. Donaldson, *Scotland: James V to James VII* (1965), 188–9, 193–4; P. Collinson, *The Elizabethan Puritan Movement*

(1967), 243–88, 403–31; A. Pritchard, *Catholic Loyalism in Elizabethan England* (1979), 120–9.

15. Thomas Fuller, *The Church-History of Britain* (1655), x. 45–6; Tyacke, 'Puritanism', 125; Fincham, *Prelate as Pastor*, 22–34.

16. *Pace* White, 'Arminianism Reconsidered', 41–5. J. P. Sommerville, 'The Royal Supremacy and Episcopacy *Iure Divino*, 1603–1640' *JEH*, 34 (1983), 548–58; C. Grayson, 'James I and the Religious Crisis in the United Provinces, 1613–19' in *Studies in Church History: Subsidia 2*, ed. D. Baker (Oxford, 1979), 195–219. For James's belief in *iure divino* episcopacy, see *Political Works of James I*, 126.

17. Tyacke, *Anti-Calvinists*, 21–4, 41–5; Fincham, *Prelate as Pastor*, 25, 37, 49; P. Lake, 'Lancelot Andrewes, John Buckeridge and "avant garde" conformity at the court of James I' in L. L. Peck (ed.), *The Mental World of the Jacobean Court* (Cambridge, 1991).

18. K. Fincham, 'Prelacy and Politics: Archbishop Abbot's Defence of Protestant Orthodoxy' *Historical Research*, 61 (1988), 44–8.

19. N. Cranfield and K. Fincham, 'John Howson's Answers to Archbishop Abbot's Accusations at his "Trial" before James I at Greenwich, 10 June 1615', *Camden Miscellany XXIX* (Camden 4th series, xxxiv, 1987), 320–41; Lancelot Andrewes, *Works*, eds J. P. Wilson and J. Bliss (11 vols, Oxford, 1841–54), iii. 32.

20. K. Brown, *Bloodfeud in Scotland 1573–1625* (Edinburgh, 1986), 116–21, 144–73; N. Cuddy, 'The revival of the entourage: the Bedchamber of James I, 1603–1625' in D. Starkey (ed.), *The English Court* (Harlow, 1987), 173–225.

21. *Stuart Royal Proclamations*, i. 495–6, 519–21; PRO, SP 14/118/39, 120/13, 122/46, 123/105, 129/35–6; Wilkins, *Concilia*, iv. 465–6.

22. Anthony Weldon, *The Court and Character of King James* (1651), 217–18; P. Welsby, *George Abbot* (1962), 108–10.

23. Andrewes, for example, was enthusiastic enough to be considered as an envoy to Spain in 1616, and it was he who answered Hakewill's claim in 1621 that all papists were idolaters: T. Birch (ed.), *The Court and Times of James the First* (2 vols, 1848), i. 447; PRO, SP 14/122/46.

24. R. Montagu, *A Gagg for the New Gospell? No: A New Gagg for an Old Goose* (1624), 110, 157–72; S. Lambert, 'Richard Montagu, Arminianism and Censorship' *P and P*, 124 (1989), 42–50.

25. Fincham, *Prelate as Pastor*, 28–9; T. Cogswell, 'England and the Spanish Match' in R. Cust and A. Hughes (eds), *Conflict in Early Stuart England* (Harlow, 1989), 126.

26. BL, Harl. MS 159, fo. 136v; T. Cogswell, *The Blessed Revolution: English Politics and the Coming of War 1621–1624* (Cambridge, 1989), 283–5.

27. Sir Philip Warwick, *Memoirs of the Reigne of King Charles I* (1701), 70. See, for example, R. Cust, 'Charles I and a draft declaration for the 1628 Parliament' *Historical Research*, 63 (1990), 143–61.

28. Tyacke, *Anti-Calvinists*, 154, 166-8; Laud, *Works*, iii. 159, 178, 180, 196, 205-6.

29. Ibid., 160, 186-8, 189, vi. 249; Tyacke, *Anti-Calvinists*, 48-9; *Stuart Royal Proclamations*, ii. 90-3.

30. *Pace* Bernard, 'The Church of England', 198. George Coke of Bristol and later Hereford is usually regarded as a Calvinist, but only on the grounds of having a Calvinist brother, the secretary of state. For the new ritualism, see above Chapter 7.

31. PRO, LC 5/134. Conrad Russell has suggested that Davenant's role at the Caroline court as a 'tame Calvinist' was almost comparable to that of Andrewes, the 'tame Arminian', at James's court. Yet Andrewes possessed great influence over James, while Charles and Davenant were never close, and in 1646 Charles spoke slightingly of his memory: C. Russell, *The Fall of the British Monarchies 1637-1642* (Oxford, 1991), 18; *The Workes of King Charles the Martyr* (1662), 178.

32. P. Collinson, 'The Jacobean Religious Settlement' in H. Tomlinson (ed.), *Before the English Civil War* (1983), 35-6; Lambert, 'Richard Montagu', 42-56.

33. Laud, *Works*, iii. 180; T. Birch (ed.), *The Court and Times of Charles the First* (2 vols, 1848), i. 449, 451, ii. 3, 5; Tyacke, *Anti-Calvinists*, 169; *Stuart Royal Proclamations*, ii. 218-20; BL, Add. MS 35331 fos 26r, 27v; William Cobbett, *Parliamentary History*, ii. (1807), 457-8.

34. R. Cust, *The Forced Loan and English Politics 1626-1628* (Oxford, 1987), 14-15, 51-2, 72-85; Tyacke, *Anti-Calvinists*, 168-9; Henry Leslie, *A Sermon preached before his Majesty at Wokin* (1627).

35. C. Russell, *Causes of the English Civil War*, 194-6; Bodl., Tanner MS 290 fos 86r-7r.

36. Bodl., MS Jones 17 fo. 303.

37. BL, Add. MS 20065 fos 9r-10v, 37v-8r, 39r, 87r-8r, 159v; John Prideaux, *Certaine Sermons* (Oxford, 1636), esp. 'Heresy's Progress'.

38. PRO, SP 16/140/37, 142/75, 151/41; Bodl., MS Top. Oxon c 378 p. 253; *Stuart Royal Proclamations*, ii. 248-50.

39. C. Hill, *Economic Problems of the Church* (Oxford, 1956), 275-337; A. Foster, 'Church Policies of the 1630s' in *Conflict in Early Stuart England*, 208; LPL, CM 8/46; A. I. MacInnes, *Charles I and the Making of the Covenanting Movement 1625-1641* (Edinburgh, 1991), chs 3-4; Charles I, *A Large Declaration* (1639), 6-11 and *passim*.

40. Warwick, *Memoirs*, 82; *Workes of King Charles*, 449; HMC, *45 Buccleuch and Queensberry*, iii. 387; R. F. Rimbault (ed.), *The Old Cheque-Book or Book of Remembrance of the Chapel Royal 1561-1744* (Camden 2nd series, iii. 1872), 155; Bodl., MS Eng. Hist. c 28 fo. 4v; G. Donaldson, *The Making of the Scottish Prayer Book of 1637* (Edinburgh, 1954), 257-333.

41. G. Ormsby (ed.), *Correspondence of John Cosin* (Surtees Society, 2 vols, lii and lv, 1869-70), i. 216; HMC, *Appendix to 4th Report*, 130, 144; Bodl., Tanner MS 70 fo. 103r.

42. Laud, *Works*, v. 609–11, vii. 23–4, 27–8, 33–4; *Workes of King Charles*, 164.

43. Walter Balcanquhall, *The Honour of Christian Churches* (1633), 1; Robert Skinner, *A Sermon preached before the King at White-Hall* (1634), 35–6.

44. Peter Heylyn, *Antidotum Lincolniense* (1637), 84–5; George Vernon, *The Life of the Learned and Reverend Dr Peter Heylyn* (1682), 89–90.

45. *Workes of King Charles*, 165, 175; Elias Ashmole, *The Institution, Laws and Ceremonies of the most noble Order of the Garter* (1672), 496. How often the ceremony was performed in the 1630s at present remains an open question. For a pessimistic view, see J. Richards, ' "His Nowe Majestie" and the English Monarchy: the kingship of Charles I before 1640', *P and P*, 113 (1986), 86–93; for a more positive assessment see H. Farquhar, 'Royal Charities' *British Numismatic Journal*, 12 (1915), 112–13, 132; Bodl., MS Jones 17 fo. 300r.

46. Reeve, *Charles I*, 118–71; LPL, CM 8/46 fo. 7r; Heylyn, *Antidotum*, 40–1; S. R. Gardiner, *History of England . . . 1603–1642* (10 vols, 1883–4), ix. 142–3.

47. Ashton, *The English Civil War*, 110; S. Foster, *Notes from the Caroline Underground* (Hamden, Conn., 1978), xiv-xv, 69–70; Sharpe, *Politics and Ideas*, 108–9.

48. PRO, SP 16/248/12; Donaldson, *Making of the Scottish Prayer Book*, 52. We are indebted to Jackie Eales for this second reference.

49. Laud, *Works*, vii. 213, 288; G. Albion, *Charles I and the Court of Rome* (1935), 177.

50. Laud, *Works*, v. 319, 321, 338, vi. 349–50.

51. LPL, MS 943 p. 619; Laud, *Works*, v. 360. Similarly, in 1631, Laud protected Cosin and Lindsell against Bishop Howson of Durham by drawing the dispute to Charles's attention and securing a royal reprimand for Howson. See *Correspondence of John Cosin*, i. 202–7.

52. PRO, SP 16/499/42; Nottingham University Library, Clifton MSS, Francis Cheynell to Sir Gervase Clifton, c. June 1636.

53. P. Lake, 'Anti-Popery: the Structure of a Prejudice' in *Conflict in Early Stuart England*, 84–7; K. Sharpe, 'The Image of Virtue: the Court and Household of Charles I, 1625–1642' in *The English Court*, 226–60; M. Smuts, *Court Culture and the Origins of a Royalist Tradition in Early Stuart England* (Philadelphia, 1987); E. Veevers, *Images of Love and Religion. Queen Henrietta Maria and Court Entertainments* (Cambridge, 1989).

54. An important perception which we owe to Kevin Sharpe: *Politics and Ideas*, 47–8.

55. Fulke Robarts, *Gods Holy House and Service* (1639), 91; John Swan, *Profanomastix* (1639), 58; Joseph Mede, *The Reverence of God's House* (1638), 11; Skinner, *A Sermon*, 12.

56. Peter Heylyn, *The Historie of St George* (1633), 268–9.

57. Albion, *Church of Rome*, 261; Russell, *Causes of the English Civil War*, 197–8.

58. J. Morrill, 'The National Covenant in its British Context' in J. Morrill (ed.), *The Scottish National Covenant in its British Context* (Edinburgh, 1990), 8–9; Russell, *Causes of the English Civil War*, 44–52, 109–116; *Workes of King Charles*, 178.

2. ARCHBISHOP LAUD   *Nicholas Tyacke*

1. A. Grey, *Debates in the House of Commons from the year 1667 to the year 1694* (1769), I.112–13. For the post-Restoration position of the communion table, see N. Yates, *Buildings, Faith and Worship: the Liturgical Arrangement of Anglican Churches, 1600–1900* (Oxford, 1991), 32.

2. H. R. Trevor-Roper, *Archbishop Laud, 1573–1645* (1940), 2–3, 7, 12–22; C. Carlton, *Archbishop William Laud* (1987), 1, 152–3, 228; E. C. E. Bourne, *The Anglicanism of William Laud* (1947).

3. P. Heylyn, *Cyprianus Anglicus* (1668), 50–3, and *Historia Quinqu-Articularis* (1660), pt.III, 74. There appears no evidence, contrary to what is often said, that Heylyn was ever chaplain to Laud.

4. K. Sharpe, 'Archbishop Laud', *History Today*, 33 (August, 1983), 26–30, and 'The Personal Rule of Charles I', in H. Tomlinson (ed.), *Before the English Civil War* (1983), 62–3; J. E. Davies, 'The Growth and Implementation of "Laudianism" with special reference to the Southern Province', Oxford D.Phil. thesis (1987), Ch. 7. For the role of Archbishop Laud's vicar-general, Sir Nathaniel Brent, see above 78–9.

5. K. Sharpe, 'Archbishop Laud and the University of Oxford', in H. Lloyd-Jones, V. Pearl and B. Worden (eds), *History and Imagination* (1981), 161; P. A. Welsby, *George Abbot: the Unwanted Archbishop* (1962), 3, 37–8; K. Fincham, 'Prelacy and Politics: Archbishop Abbot's Defence of Protestant Orthodoxy', *Historical Research*, 61 (1988), 36–64; *CSPD, 1611–18*, 533.

6. N. Tyacke, 'The Rise of Arminianism Reconsidered', *P and P*, 115 (1987), 202–3, 207–8, 215 fn. 94; N. Tyacke, *Anti-Calvinists: The Rise of English Arminianism, c.1590 – 1640* (2nd edn Oxford, 1990), Chs 2–3 and Appendix I. Whether Heylyn was correct in his assessment of the Elizabethan settlement is a question which I plan to pursue elsewhere. Suffice it to say for the moment that English protestantism had received a major injection of Reformed theology even before the Marian exile.

7. Laud, *Works*, III. 131; D. Lloyd, *Memories of the Lives . . . of Excellent Persons that suffered for Allegiance to their Sovereign* (1668), 225–6.

8. J.Young, *A Sermon* (1576), sigs C4v-C5v; S. Clarke, *The Lives of Thirty-Two English Divines* (1677), 38–42. These are my identifications and there is some dispute over the evidence concerning Buckeridge

being a prebendary of Rochester. J. Le Neve, *Fasti Ecclesiae Anglicanae,
1541–1857*, III, Canterbury, Rochester and Winchester Dioceses, comp.
J. M. Horn (1974), 67n.

9. W. Bradshaw, *A Myld and Just Defense of Certeyne Arguments* (1606),
44–5; G. Powell, *A Rejoynder unto the Mild Defense* (1607), 118–19; H.
C. Porter, *Reformation and Reaction in Tudor Cambridge* (Cambridge, 1958),
chs 15–17.

10. Laud, *Works*, IV. 309; Heylyn, *Cyprianus Anglicus*, 54; Tyacke,
Anti-Calvinists, 70–1, 266–70.

11. W. H. Stevenson and H. E. Salter, *The Early History of St. John's
College Oxford* (Oxford Hist. Soc., N.S. i, 1939), 197, 353, 356–7.

12. J. Buckeridge, *A Sermon Preached at Hampton Court* (1606), 41–2;
J. Strype, *Annals of the Reformation* (Oxford, 1824), I, i. 540–1; Tyacke,
Anti-Calvinists, 250.

13. C. Coates, *The History and Antiquities of Reading* (1802), 411; PRO,
PROB: 11/9, fo. 117b; R. O'Day, *The English Clergy: the Emergence and
Consolidation of a Profession, 1558–1642* (Leicester, 1979), Ch. 13.

14. G. Abbot, *The Reasons which Doctour Hill hath brought for the Uphold-
ing of Papistry* (Oxford, 1604), 26–71; Heylyn, *Cyprianus Anglicus*, 53; A.
Clarke (ed.), *The Register of the University of Oxford* (Oxford Hist. Sóc.,
X, 1887), II, i 206.

15. Laud, *Works*, V.117, VI.704; Tyacke, *Anti-Calvinists*, 11–12, 14.

16. Laud, *Works*, I.26, VI.689–91; Tyacke, *Anti-Calvinists*, 70–1,
110–13.

17. Laud, *Works*, I.5–6, 63–4, VI.57, 119–20.

18. Laud, *Works*, I.55–7. See also Tyacke, *Anti-Calvinists*, Appendix
II.

19. Laud, *Works*, I.56; O. Chadwick, *John Cassian* (2nd edn Cambridge, 1968), ch. 4. Writers on Laud have strangely neglected this
sermon and in particular the vital Cassian reference.

20. The St John's copy of the *Collationes* is a 1606 Lyons edition. I
am grateful to Miss A. Williams, the assistant librarian of St John's
College, Oxford, for supplying this information.

21. J. P. Kenyon, *The Stuart Constitution* (2nd edn Cambridge, 1986),
128–30; K. Fincham and P. Lake, 'The Ecclesiastical Policy of King
James I', *JBS*, 24 (1985), 202–6.

22. Laud, *Works*, IV.233–4, VI.57, 239–41; Tyacke, *Anti-Calvinists*,
71, 116–17; C. Oman, *English Church Plate, 597–1830* (Oxford, 1957),
71, 205, 226 and plate 80.

23. PRO, PROB. 11/160, fos. 16b–17; J. Buckeridge, *A Sermon . . . to
which in added a Discourse concerning Kneeling at the Communion* (1618), 68,
96; Laud, *Works*, IV.441–2.

24. Laud, *Works*, III. 74–5.

25. Laud, *Works*, III. 196; L. Andrewes, *XCVI Sermons* (1635), sig.
Rrrrr5 and 'A Table of the Principal Contents'.

26. L. Andrewes, *XCVI Sermons* (1629), pt. I, 299–308. Historians using the nineteenth-century edition of Andrewes's collected works have assumed wrongly that this sermon dates from 1593/4 as opposed to 1594/5, the Old Style year beginning on 25 March. Compare, for example, Porter, *Reformation and Reaction*, 352. My redating allows this sermon by Andrewes to be fitted into the sequence of events unfolding at Cambridge, between February and April 1595. P. Lake, *Moderate Puritans and the Elizabethan Church* (Cambridge, 1982), 201–4.

27. Tyacke, *Anti-Calvinists*, 45; L. Andrewes, *Works*, eds J. P. Wilson and J. Bliss (Oxford, 1841–54), VI.296, XI. pp. xcvii,c, and *The Preces Privatae*, ed. F. E. Brightman (1903), 121.

28. *The Sarum Missal in English* (trans.), F. E. Warner (1911), pt i, 17–19. Compare *The Orthodox Liturgy* (Oxford, 1982), 5–14. The language of these prayers is much more extreme than anything to be found in the English Prayer Book.

29. Laud, *Works*, III.160, 196. This revises my earlier argument that up to then Richard Neile was the 'Arminian candidate for Canterbury'. Tyacke, *Anti-Calvinists*, 123.

30. J. Hacket, *Scrinia Reserata* (1693), pt i, 63–4; Heylyn, *Cyprianus Anglicus*, 85–6, 100–1; Laud *Works*, II.144, 147, 194–5, III.138–9. I owe the St Jerome reference to Dr Peter Lake.

31. Laud, *Works*, VI.245–6.

32. Tyacke, *Anti-Calvinists*, 48–51, 76–81, 149; J. Strype, *The Life and Acts of . . . John Whitgift* (Oxford, 1822), II.260–1.

33. Laud, *Works*, I.71, VI.11–12, 133; Tyacke, *Anti-Calvinists*, 182, 249, 263–5.

34. Laud, *Works*, IV.274, V.307–9, VI.23–34; Bodl., Rawlinson MS A.127, fo. 73a-b. I owe this last reference to the work of Dr Julian Davies.

35. Tyacke, *Anti-Calvinists*, 18–19, 21, 49; Laud, *Works*, IV.303; I. M. Calder (ed.), *Activities of the Puritan Faction of the Church of England* (1957); N. Tyacke, *The Fortunes of English Puritanism, 1603–1640* (1990), 14.

36. Tyacke, *Anti-Calvinists*, 199–209, 222–3; K. L. Parker, *The English Sabbath: a Study of Doctrine and Discipline from the Reformation to the Civil War* (Cambridge, 1988), ch. 7.

37. PRO, SP 16/485, fo. 252. The attitude of Laud on this issue has been much debated, but the passage quoted is his own retrospective account of what he recommended. Compare, however, J. E. Davies, thesis cit., ch. 7.

38. Laud, *Works*, V.204–7, 624–6, VI.59.

39. Tyacke, *Anti-Calvinists*, xiii, 184–5, 198, 216–18.

40. Laud, *Works*, III.335–7, 356–7; G. Donaldson, *The Making of the Scottish Prayer Book of 1637* (Edinburgh, 1954), 200–1.

41. Laud, *Works*, III.341.

3. EPISCOPAL GOVERNMENT 1603–1640   *Kenneth Fincham*

I am grateful to Andrew Foster, Peter Lake and Nicholas Tyacke for their comments on an earlier version of this chapter.

1. G. W. Bernard, 'The Church of England c.1529-c.1642' *History*, 75 (1990), 202–3.

2. K. Fincham, *Prelate as Pastor: the Episcopate of James I* (Oxford, 1990); Laud, *Works*, vii. 102, 168.

3. H. R. Trevor-Roper, *Historical Essays* (1957), 130–45. For the Jacobean episcopate, see Fincham, *Prelate as Pastor, passim*; I intend to document these claims about their Caroline successors elsewhere. J. E. Davies, 'The Growth and Implementation of "Laudianism" with special reference to the Southern Province' (Oxford D.Phil. thesis, 1987), contains much valuable evidence of episcopal activities in the 1630s.

4. Fincham, *Prelate as Pastor*, 135–6, 241; E. Cardwell, *Documentary Annals of the Reformed Church of England* (Oxford, 1839), ii. 120–8.

5. For Barlow, Charles Richardson, *A Workeman that needeth not to be ashamed* (1616), 29; LAO, LC/3; SRO, D/D/Vc 21 (Montagu), 78, 80, 82 (Lake); GL, MS 9537/10 (Ravis); GDR 115 pp. 1–151, WCRO, D1/53, He.RO, Vis. Call Bk 5 (all for Abbot), Call Bk 7 (Bennett); Samuel Crook, 'The ministeriall husbandry and building' in *Three Sermons* (1615), dedicatory epistle and 122–3, 127; Richard Carpenter, *A Pastoral Charge* (1616), 55.

6. Smith of Gloucester and Thornborough of Bristol then Worcester were probably infrequent preachers. Fincham, *Prelate as Pastor*, 82–91, 178–83, 188–98.

7. Ibid., 253–68; BI, Prec. Bk 4 p. 122.

8. Fincham, *Prelate as Pastor*, 140, 165–76; SRO, D/D/Ca 185 fo. 235.

9. For terriers, see Fincham, *Prelate as Pastor*, 139–40; for church fabric, see WSRO, Ep.I/17/13 fos 85v–113v; GDR 125; Gloucs. RO P329 CW2/1 pp. 167–220 (regular surveys of Tewkesbury Abbey); PDR Church Survey Books I–III (1606–19); DDCM, SJB/8 fos 5r–40r.

10. For enforcement of the Three Articles before 1603, see LPL, Carte Misc. XIII nos 59, 61; LAO, Reg. XXX fo. 74ff.; for their neglect, see CRO, EDA 1/4; DRO, C 151a pp. 1–85; WCRO, D5/9/1 fos 1r–6v; at Chichester in the 1590s Bishop Bickley pressed for conformity, while his successor Watson was less vigorous: WSRO, Ep.I/17/7–10.

11. Fincham, *Prelate as Pastor*, 213–15, 323–6.

12. S. B. Babbage, *Puritanism and Richard Bancroft* (1962), 81–4, 113–15; Fincham, *Prelate as Pastor*, 219, 225–7.

13. BI, Bk I fos 98r, 114v (for Cooke), 76r, 91v, 254v, 284r, 289v (for other examples).

14. GDR 97, 111, 120; GL, MS 9537/11 fos 133r–61r. See also GDR

115 p. 391 for reference to 'a most notable sermon for conformitie' preached at an episcopal visitation in Gloucestershire in 1616.

15. Fincham, *Prelate as Pastor*, 9–13, 250–75. For a classic evocation of this churchmanship, see Daniel Featley's consecration sermon of 1619 in his *Clavis Mystica* (1636), 133–44.

16. N. Tyacke, *Anti-Calvinists: The Rise of English Arminianism c.1590–1640* (Oxford, 1987), 106–24; Fincham, *Prelate as Pastor*, 231–7, 277, 279, 283–4, 288; Laud, *Works*, vi. 42.

17. Fincham, *Prelate as Pastor*, 238–46.

18. LAO, Add. Reg. 3 fo. 197; WSRO, Ep. II/11/3 fo. 73r; GDR 189 fos 8v–9r; PRO, SP 16/485/118.

19. BL, MS Egerton 784 fo. 105r; WSRO, Ep. II/11/3 fo. 73r; Laud, *Works*, v. 609–13.

20. Ibid., iv. 121, v. 360, vi. 60; CCAL, Z.4.6. fo. 127r; Davies, 'The Growth and Implementation of "Laudianism"', 230.

21. Laud, *Works*, v. 624–6; *The Diary of John Young STP*, ed. F. R. Goodman (1928), 108–9; PRO, SP 16/291/16, 474/80; Richard Montagu, *Articles of Enquiry and Direction for the diocese of Norwich* (1638), sig. Bv.

22. Laud, *Works*, vi. 193.

23. He.RO, AL 19/16 i. p. 449; K. Parker, *The English Sabbath* (Cambridge, 1988), 199, 217; George Vernon, *The Life of . . . Dr Peter Heylyn* (1682), 88.

24. Laud, *Works*, vi. 57, 59; Bodl., Tanner MS 68 fo. 221r.

25. *The Speech of Dr Robert Skinner, Lord Bishop of Bristol, at the Visitation at Dorchester, September 18 1637* (1744); BL, Add. MS 20065 fos 37r–44r.

26. I intend to substantiate this point in a forthcoming volume entitled *Visitation Articles and Injunctions of the Early Stuart Church* (1993).

27. HMC, *45 Buccleuch and Queensberry MSS*, i. 275; for the enforcement of subscription, see, for example, DRO, C 150, 151a; OCRO, Oxf. Diocesan Papers e 13; *The Subscription Book of Bishop Tounson and Davenant 1620–40*, ed. B. Williams, Wiltshire Record Society, 32 (1977), 32–86.

28. Fincham, *Prelate as Pastor*, 229, 263–4; SRO, D/D/Ca 299 fos 56v–8r; 75v, 309 fo. 52r; Richard Bernard, *A Threefold Treatise of the Sabbath* (1641), sig. a2v–3r.

29. A. Hughes, *Politics, Society and Civil War in Warwickshire 1620–1660* (Cambridge, 1987), 79–80, 85–87; PRO, SP 16/274/12, 293/128; H. Smith, *The Ecclesiastical History of Essex* (Colchester, 1932), 44, 53.

30. The two were Humphrey Chambers and William Thomas: SRO, D/D/B Reg. 20, D/D/Ca 294 fos 60r, 61v, 120v, D/D/Ca 412.

31. A. Foster, 'Church Policies of the 1630s' in R. Cust and A. Hughes (eds), *Conflict in Early Stuart England* (Harlow, 1989), 206–7; PRO, SP 16/345/85. I; Laud, *Works*, v. 340, 347; R. J. Acheson, 'Sion's Saint: John Turner of Sutton Valence' *Archaeologia Cantiana* 99 (1983), 189.

32. Laud, *Works*, v. 319, 334; S. Palmer (ed.), *The Nonconformists' Memorial* (3 vols, 1803), i. 231; SRO, D/D/Or Box 5 (note on reverse of citation dated 19 February 1639); Bodl., Tanner MS 68 fo. 92; Hughes, *Warwickshire 1620–1660*, 71–9; HWRO, BA2648/10(ii) p. 83.

33. Joseph Hall, *Works*, ed. P. Wynter (10 vols, 1863), i. p. xlvi; BI, Sub. Bk 2; SRO, D/D/Vc 40; Fincham, *Prelate as Pastor*, 205; NNRO, REG/16/23, fos 154r–84v; Bodl., Tanner MS 68 fo. 9v.

34. HRO, 24M82 PW2 (1636–7); 49M67/PR1 fo. 16; 75M72/PW1 p. 93; A1/31 fos 8r, 45r; *DNB, sub* William Page; *STC*, 19096; Bodl., Carte MS 77 fo. 350v; J. R. Bloxam, *A Register of the Presidents, Fellows, Demies . . . of Saint Mary Magdalen College . . . Oxford* (8 vols, 1853–85), ii. p. xcv.

35. Bodl., MS Top Oxon c 378 p. 314; *Proceedings principally in the county of Kent . . . 1640*, ed. L. B. Larking (Camden 1st series, 80, 1862), 87; BL, Add. MS 35331 fo. 56v; OCRO, Ms Oxf. Dioc. Papers c 27 fo. 15r; Woodstock Borough MSS 79/1 (3 May 1631 – 1 Oct. 1633); Laud, *Works*, v. 330.

36. PRO, SP 16/474/80; Montagu, *Articles of Enquiry* (1638), sig. A3v; J. A. W. Bennett and H. R. Trevor-Roper (eds), *The Poems of Richard Corbett* (Oxford, 1955), xxviii-xli; Laud, *Works*, v. 334, 339–42.

37. Tyacke, *Anti-Calvinists*, 211–13; Hall, *Works*, i. p. liii.

38. For audience court, see DRO, C 57 fos 7r–11v, CC 178, CC 6A Box 19, CC 6B, CC 190, Halberton PW2 (15 June 1636); Zeal Monachorum PW1 fo. 11r; for visitation charge, John Bury, *The Moderate Christian* (1631), sig. A3v; for lectures, C 764 fos 84v, 125r; C/45/16; Chudleigh PW1 pp. 564–95; Thomas Bedford, *A Treatise of the Sacraments* (1639), 'To the Courteous Christian Reader'.

39. DRO, Awliscombe PW6; Chudleigh PW1 p. 574 and *passim*; Dartington PW2 p. 473 and *passim*; Honiton PW1 fo. 137v and *passim*; Kilmington PW2 (1634–5); Lapford PW1; North Tawton PW1 (1636–7); Zeal Monachorum PW1 fo. 16r and *passim*.

40. Foster, 'Church Policies of the 1630s', 198–203; A. Fletcher, *A County Community in Peace and War: Sussex 1600–1660* (1975), 85–7; M. Tillbrook, 'Arminianism and Society in County Durham, 1617–42' in D. Marcombe (ed.), *The Last Principality* (Nottingham, 1987), 212–16; PRO, SP 16/274/12; *The East Anglian* (1st series, 1864), i. 70–1.

41. Hall, *Works*, i. p. li, v. 465–86, 518, 535, x. 1–44; DRO, C 217–18, C 43 pp. 296–8, C. 57 fo. 11r.

42. BL, Egerton MS 784 fo. 83v; Bodl., MS Top Oxon c 378 p. 307; Peter Studley, *The Looking-Glass of Schisme* (1635), 285–6; 'A Speech spoken in the House of Commons by . . . Robert Lord Bishop of Coventry and Litchfield . . . 1641', *Harleian Miscellany*, vi. (1745), 257; J. Latimer, *Annals of Bristol in the Seventeenth Century* (Bristol, 1900), 124.

43. Thomas Warmstry, *A Convocation Speech* (1641), 13–16; John Ley, *Sunday A Sabbath* (1641), sig. b3v-b3ir.

44. Peter Heylyn, *The Parable of the Tares* (1659), 311–36. See also the rather similar line taken by John Cosin in his consecration sermon of 1626 in *Works*, ed. J. Sansom (5 vols, Oxford, 1843–55), i. 95–6. A similar re-evaluation is implicit in some parochial sermons by Caroline apologists. See, for example, Edward Boughen, *A Sermon concerning Decencie and Order* (1638), 1.

45. *Articles of Accusation and Impeachment . . . against William Pierce* (1642), 3; Laud, *Works*, vi. 193; J. Wickham Legg (ed.), *English Orders for consecrating churches* (Henry Bradshaw Society, 41, 1911), 104, 136, 144, 167, 309; Bodl., Tanner MS 314 fo. 158r.

46. *Poems of Richard Corbett*, xxxvi; BL, Add. MS 25278 fo. 139v; Tyacke, *Anti-Calvinists*, 156.

47. S. L. Ollard, 'Confirmation in the Anglican Communion' in *Confirmation and the Laying On of Hands by various writers* i. (1926), 104–37; Fincham, *Prelate as Pastor*, 123–9.

48. Huntingdon County RO, Manchester Papers, Box 28 bundle 4, a reference I owe to Conrad Russell; P. Lake, 'Serving God and the Times: the Calvinist Conformity of Robert Sanderson', *JBS*, 27 (1988), 81–116; *Diary of John Young, passim*.

49. Tyacke, *Anti-Calvinists*, 140–2, 192–4; I. Atherton, 'Viscount Scudamore's "Laudianism": the religious practices of the First Viscount Scudamore' *HJ* 34 (1991), 567–96; L. G. Wickham Legg (ed.), *A Relation of A Short Survey of 26 Counties . . . begun on August 11 1634* (1904); 'Relation of a Short Survey of the Western Counties' *Camden Miscellany XVI* (Camden 3rd series, 52, 1936); BL, Stowe MS 184 fo. 10r.

50. Bodl., Tanner MS 68 fos 220–1; *STC*, 3406, 3919, 7551, 23513, 23515, 23857.7; Wing, S2340, S5986; for Ancketyll, see SRO, D/D/Ca 297 (10 Dec. 1634); M. Stieg, *Laud's Laboratory: the diocese of Bath and Wells in the early seventeenth century* (East Brunswick, N.J. 1982), 297. By December 1634 Ancketyll was Piers' chaplain (BL, Add. MS 39535 fo. 45r).

51. Bodl., Tanner MS 68 fos 45r, 164r, 220r, 309r; Fulke Robarts, *Gods Holy House and Service* (1639); Thomas Newhouse, *Certaine Sermons* (1614), 143; NNRO, Norwich Court Book/16 fo. 171; Tyacke, *Anti-Calvinists*, 99–100, 148–9.

52. Hall, *Works*, i. p. xlvi; Humphrey Sydenham, *Sermons upon Solemne Occasions* (1637), 269.

4. ARMINIANISM IN THE LOCALITIES: PETERBOROUGH DIOCESE
1603–1642   *John Fielding*

1. N. Tyacke, *Anti-Calvinists: the Rise of English Arminianism c.1590–1640* (Oxford, 1987), *passim*; J. Morrill, 'The attack on the Church of Eng-

land in the Long Parliament 1640–2' in D. Beales and G. Best (eds), *History, Society and the Churches* (Cambridge, 1985), 105–25.

2. R. T. Kendall, *Calvin and English Calvinism to 1649* (Oxford, 1979), 1–13; P. G. Lake 'Calvinism and the English Church 1570–1635', *P and P*, 114 (1987), 32–76.

3. Ibid.

4. For ecclesiastical patronage in the diocese see A. J. Fielding, 'Conformists, Puritans and the church courts: the diocese of Peterborough 1603–42' (University of Birmingham Ph.D. thesis, 1989), 12–56.

5. BL, Sloane MS 271, fos 20r–22r.

6. K. Fincham, 'Prelacy and politics: Archbishop Abbot's defence of Protestant orthodoxy', *Historical Research*, 61 (1988), 40 n.20; PDR, C[orrection] B[ook] 38, fo. 24r; BL, Sloane MS 271, fos 25r-v, 23r-v.

7. Fielding, op. cit., 62–4.

8. PRO, SP 14/12/69; 12/74; 77/90; long quotation from SP 14/12/96.

9. PRO, SP 14/122/55, 56.

10. Robert Bolton, *Works*, I (1635), 163; Joseph Bentham *The society of saints* (1630), 151.

11. PDR, CB41, fo. 412.

12. Tyacke, *Anti-Calvinists*, 209; HMC, *Duke of Buccleuch and Queensberry MSS*, I, 214; III, 207–12, 208 (quotation of Williams), 210 (Throckmorton).

13. John Hacket, *Scrinia Reserata: a memorial offered to the great deservings of J Williams . . . Archbishop of York* (1693), 37; W. Notestein and F. H. Relf (eds), *Commons debates in 1621* (1935), VI, 473; PRO, SP 14/122/55, 56; *DNB*, 'Montagu, Edward'.

14. K. Fincham and P. Lake, 'The ecclesiastical policy of King James I', *JBS*, 24 (1985), 198–202; PRO, SP 14/122/55.

15. John Pocklington, *Altare Christianum or the dead vicar's plea* (1637), 57–8; Francis Dee, *Articles to be enquired of throughout the whole diocese of Peterborough* (1634), section 6, art. 1; John Towers, *Articles to be enquired of throughout the whole diocese of Peterborough* (1639), section 1, art. 7; Pocklington, *Altare*, 175 (quotation), 61–2; HLRO, Main Papers, 6 Dec. 1641; 15 Dec. 1640; William Piers, *Articles to be enquired of within the diocese of Peterborough in the first triennial visitation of . . . William Lord Bishop of Peterborough* (1631), 3; Augustine Lindsell, *Articles to be enquired of within the diocese of Peterborough in the first triennial visitation of Augustine Lord Bishop of Peterborough* (1633), section 4, arts 3–7, 11–13; Dee, *Articles* (1634), section 3, art. 4.

16. Dee, *Articles* (1634), section 2, art. 3; Tyacke, *Anti-Calvinists*, 199–204.

17. PDR, church survey 1637; HLRO, Main Papers, 6 Feb. 1641; PRO, SP 16/261/fos 298v–299v; 370/51; 393/92; 395/79; Tyacke, *Anti-Calvinists*, 204.

18. NRO, 55P/68 (Burton Latimer churchwardens' accounts 1636–40), disbursements 1635; 241P/42 (St Sepulchre, Northampton churchwardens' accounts), disbursements 1637; E. C. Rouse, *The wall paintings in Passenham church* (1989), *passim*; Dee, *Articles* (1634), section 2, art. 3.

19. Bodl., Tanner MS 71, fos 186–7, Nicholas Estwick to Samuel Ward, 23 Jan. 1633.

20. PRO, SP 16/531/135; HMC, *Buccleuch*, I, 275; New College, Oxford, MS 9502, pp. 344, 361; Laud, *Works*, v. 349, 368–9; PDR, CB-A57 (unfoliated), under 'All Saints, Northampton'; PRO, SP 16/308/52.

21. Edward Reynolds, *A sermon touching the peace and edification of the church preached at the second triennial visitation of Francis, Bishop of Peterborough, at Daventry July 12 1637* (1638), *passim*; HLC, Stowe MSS (unfoliated), Robert Sibthorpe to Sir John Lambe, 24 April 1639; 5 May 1639; William Prynne, *Canterbury's doome* (1646), 378–80.

22. R. P. Cust, *The forced loan and English politics 1626–8* (1987), 62–5, 248, 250; PRO, SP 16/317/46; 318/6; 417/47; T. B. Howell and T. J. Howell (eds), *State Trials* (34 vols, 1816–28), III, 1380; HLC, Stowe MSS, Sibthorpe to Lambe, 30 May 1639.

23. Daniel Cawdry, *Superstitio superstes* (1641), 'to the reader' and 4, 14; New College Oxford, MS 9502 pp. 93, 197, 226; PRO, SP 16/308/52, 251/25, 370/57, 302/16, 406/102; PDR, church survey 1637, fo. 99v, CB-A63 fo. 181; HLC, Stowe MSS, Sibthorpe to Lambe, 7 June 1639; Bedfordshire RO, St John (Bletso) MS 1361; Towers, *Articles* (1639), section 2, art. 17.

24. Bodl., Tanner MS 71, fo. 186v.

25. Reynolds, *A sermon*, 25.

26. PRO, SP 16/489/15, 465/8, 12, 45, 375/82; Cust, *Forced Loan*, 310, 301, 233–4, 178–80, 166; for Woodford, see my 'Opposition to the Personal Rule of Charles I: the diary of Robert Woodford, 1637–41' *HJ*, 31 (1988), 778–88.

5. 'BY THIS BOOK': PARISHIONERS, THE PRAYER BOOK AND THE ESTABLISHED CHURCH *Judith Maltby*

1. Henry Barrow, *A Briefe Discoverie of the False Church* in *The Writings of Henry Barrow 1587–1590*, ed. Leland Carlson (1962), 362. I am grateful to Dr Kenneth Fincham, Professor Caroline Hibbard and Dr Andrew Pettegree for their helpful criticism and advice on this chapter. It is based on work from my 'Approaches to the Study of Religious Conformity in late Elizabethan and early Stuart England' (University of Cambridge Ph.D. thesis, 1991).

2. John Morrill, 'The Church in England in the 1640s', *Reactions to*

the English Civil War 1642–1649, ed. J. Morrill (1982), 91; Patrick Collinson, 'A Comment: Concerning the Name Puritan', *JEH*, 31 (1980). For the 'Anglican vs. puritan' approach see the works by New, Davies, Greaves and McGee listed in the bibliography; and Patrick Collinson, *The Puritan Character: Polemic and Polarities in Early Seventeenth-Century English Culture* (Los Angeles, 1989), 27. For his more favourable view of popular religion elsewhere, see *The Religion of Protestants* (Oxford, 1982), ch. 5.

3. Keith Wrightson, *English Society 1580–1680* (1982), 213, see also 206–21; Keith Thomas, *Religion and the Decline of Magic* (New York, 1971), ch. 6, esp. 159–66. For challenges to the 'economic determinist' view of religious identity see Margaret Spufford, *Contrasting Communities: English Villagers in the Sixteenth and Seventeenth Centuries* (Cambridge, 1974), ch. 13, and Collinson, *The Religion of Protestants*, ch. 5. For a sensitive treatment of issues of conformity, see Spufford, 'Can We Count the "Godly" and the "Conformable" in the Seventeenth Century?', *JEH*, 36 (1985); and Martin Ingram, *Church Courts, Sex and Marriage in England 1570–1640* (Cambridge, 1987), 94, see also ch. 3 *passim*.

4. Christopher Haigh, *Reformation and Resistance in Tudor Lancashire* (Cambridge, 1975), 306–7; 'The Church of England, the Catholics, and the People', *The Reign of Elizabeth I*, ed. C. Haigh (1984), 206–9, 211, 217–19. Ian Green, 'Career Prospects and Clerical Conformity in the Early Stuart Church', *P and P*, 90 (1981), 111–12. See also Haigh's stimulating article 'The recent historiography of the English Reformation', *The English Reformation Revised*, ed. C. Haigh (Cambridge, 1987).

5. CRO, EDC.5/1604 misc. (Manchester); Haigh, *Reformation and Resistance*, 209, 214, 217, 218–19, 220; see F. R. Raines, *The Rectors of Manchester and Wardens of the Collegiate Church* (Chetham Society, v. vi, 1885); *The Fellows of the Collegiate Church of Manchester* (Chetham Society, xxi, 1891); R. C. Richardson, 'Puritanism in the Diocese of Chester to 1642' (University of Manchester Ph.D. thesis, 1969), 55–61. For more of Kirk's activities see R. C. Richardson, *Puritanism in north-west England: a regional study of the diocese of Chester to 1642* (Manchester, 1972), 23, 27, 29, 40, 41, 81, 185.

6. LAO, 58/1/5; Ch. P/6 fol. 27; 58/2/67; C. W. Foster, *The State of the Church in the Reigns of Elizabeth and James I as illustrated by documents relating to the Diocese of Lincoln* (Lincoln Record Society, xxiii, 1926), 217, 290; CRO, EDC.5/1639/129; *The Book of Common Prayer 1559*, ed. John Booty (Washington, D.C., 1976), 248–9. All references to the Prayer Book are taken from this edition. Nesta Evans, 'The Community of South Elmham, Suffolk, 1550–1640' (University of East Anglia M.Phil. thesis, 1978), 170–71. Claire Cross, 'Lay Literacy and clerical misconduct in a York parish during the reign of Mary Tudor', *York Historian* (1980), 10, 12, 14. That ordinary villagers were willing and

able to use both the ecclesiastical and secular courts to present their grievances in the early modern period has been demonstrated for an Essex community. See Keith Wrightson and David Levine, *Poverty and Piety in an English Village: Terling, 1525–1700* (New York, 1979), 113–14.

7. Professor Collinson cites in support of the 'church papist' argument the example of Wye in Kent where parishioners objected to the puritan practices of the vicar. Wye probably had the highest number of recusants in East Kent. He does not say, however, what percentage of the population were recusant or whether any of those presented for their Catholicism were involved in the presentations against the minister. Patrick Collinson, 'Shepherds, Sheepdogs, and Hirelings: the Pastoral Ministry in Post-Reformation England', *The Ministry: Clerical and Lay*, eds W. J. Sheils and Diana Woods (*Studies in Church History*, 1989), 208n. 74, see also 207–11; Richardson, thesis, 55–68; Earl of Clarendon, *Selections from the History of the Rebellion and The Life by Himself*, eds G. Huehens and H. R. Trevor-Roper (Oxford, 1978), 103.

8. CRO, EDC.5/1628 misc. (Bruera Chapelry, St Oswald, Chester).

9. Thomas Morton, *A Defence of the Innocencie of the Three Ceremonies of the Church of England* (1618), 44. The rubrics direct: 'Then shall the minister receive the communion in both kinds himself . . . and after to the people in their hands kneeling'. *1559 BCP*, 263–4. See also Spufford, 'Can we count the "godly"?'. LAO, 58/1/5; BL, Add. MSS 36913, fo. 140. See also CRO, QJB 1/6/87v–88; QJF 71/4/23–4; EDC.5/1639/ 129; Haigh, 'The Church of England', 219; CRO, EDP.263/5; James Hart, 'The House of Lords and the Reformation of Justice 1640–1643' (University of Cambridge Ph.D. thesis, 1985), 99–105, 121, 225–6, 231. I am grateful to Dr Hart for bringing these cases in the Lords to my attention.

10. LAO, 58/1/5; CRO, QJF 71/4/23; George Herbert, *A Priest to the Temple*, ed. Edward Thomas (London, 1908), 246; CRO, EDC.5/1612 misc. (St Bridget's, Chester); *1559 BCP*, 257.

11. LAO, 69/1/23; 69/1/14; 69/2/15; CRO, QJF 71/4/24. Dr Haigh has commented on the neglect of 'sacrament-gadding' in contrast to 'sermon-gadding' in our view of post-Reformation lay religion. Haigh, 'The Church of England', 218.

12. Cited in Richardson, *Puritanism*, 28; LAO, 69/1/23; Herbert, 256; *1559 BCP*, 277. The Prayer Book also makes it clear that baptism normally should take place as part of the main worship on Sunday: 'And then the godfathers, godmothers, and the people with the children must be ready at the font either immediately after the last Lesson at Morning Prayer, or else immediately after the last Lesson at Evening Prayer, as the curate by his discretion shall appoint', *1559 BCP*, 270. It has been argued that high rates of infant mortality and particular views of providential theology made parents less bereaved at the deaths of their children than in the modern period. See Lawrence Stone, *The*

Family, Sex and Marriage in England 1500–1800 (1977), 206–15. Arguing against this view are Linda Pollock, *Forgotten Children: Parent-child relations from 1500 to 1900* (Cambridge, 1983), 124–8, 134–7, 140–2; Ralph Houlbrooke, *The English Family 1450–1700* (1984), 202–7, 215–22. See also John Bossy, *Christianity in the West 1400–1700* (Oxford, 1985), 14–19, 26–34, on baptism and death.

13. Failure to perform, or objections to the sign of the cross in baptism has been used as evidence of 'puritanism' in, e.g., Richardson, *Puritanism*, 26–8, 79–80; Ronald A. Marchant, *The Puritans and the Church Courts in the Diocese of York 1560–1642* (1960), 225–317, *passim*; W. J. Sheils, *The Puritans in the Diocese of Peterborough 1558–1610* (Northamptonshire Record Society, 30, 1979), 68, 69, 78, 84; Patrick Collinson, *The Elizabethan Puritan Movement* (1967), 367. Dr Haigh has emphasised the conformist element in disputes over the sign of the cross in baptism. Haigh, *Reformation and Resistance*, 306.

14. LAO, 69/1/14; Herbert, 256.

15. CRO, QJF 71/4/24. See the *Visitation Articles* for Chester diocese of Richard Vaughan (1604, no. 30) and Thomas Morton (1617, no. 40). See also Vernon Staley (ed.), *Hierurgia Anglicana* (3 vols, 1902–1904), ii, 195–6; Claire Gittings, *Death, Burial and the Individual in early modern England* (1984), 133–5. CRO, EDC.5/1630, misc. (Bunbury). There were sentences of scripture appointed to be read while the body was carried to the church yard gate to the grave. *1559 BCP*, 309. CRO, EDC.5/1628 misc. (Bruera Chapelry, St Oswald's, Chester).

16. LAO, 69/1/24. 'The priest meeting the corpse at the church stile, shall say or else the priests and clerks shall sing, and so go either unto the church, or toward the grave "I am the resurrection and the life" ', *1559 BCP*, 309.

17. LAO, 69/2/15; 69/1/23; see also 69/2/14; CRO, EDC.5/1604 misc. (Macclesfield). The churchwardens of Apethorpe, Northamptonshire complained that they had no curate to perform clerical offices, so that 'for want of a priest, they have been compelled to bury the dead bodies themselves', neither had they service read, nor sermons preached. Cited in Sheils, *Puritans*, 91.

18. David E. Stannard, *The Puritan Way of Death: a Study in Religion, Culture and Social Change* (New York, 1977), 101, 103–1044; Thomas, *Decline of Magic*, 603; Barrow, *A Brief Discoverie*, 458; Collinson, *Movement*, 370–1. See Natalie Zemon Davies' discussion of these issues in 'Some Tasks and Themes in the Study of Popular Religion', *The Pursuit of Holiness in Late Medieval and Renaissance Religion*, eds C. Trinkaus and H. Oberman (Leiden, 1974).

19. LAO, 58/1/5. Nicholas Tyacke, *Anti-Calvinists: the Rise of English Arminianism c.1590–1640* (Oxford, 1987).

20. *The Short Parliament Diary (1640) of Sir Thomas Aston*, ed. Judith Maltby (Camden Fourth Series, xxxv, 1988). William Abbott, 'The

Issue of Episcopacy in the Long Parliament: the Reasons for Abolition' (University of Oxford D.Phil. thesis, 1981); John Morrill, 'The attack on the Church of England in the Long Parliament, 1640–1642', *History, Society and the Churches: essays in honour of Owen Chadwick*, eds Derek Beales and Geoffrey Best (Cambridge, 1985), 105–108 and *passim*; Anthony Fletcher, *The Outbreak of the English Civil War* (1981), esp. chs 3, 9.

21. John Nalson, *An Impartial Collection of the Great Affairs of State* (2 vols, 1682), ii. 720–2, 726.

22. Nalson, ii. 726–7; David Underdown, *Somerset in the Civil War and Interregnum* (Newton Abbot, 1973), 22–8; John Webb, *Memorials of the Civil War* (1879), i, 85–6; BL, Thomason Tracts E.150 (28), p. 41; Derek Hirst, 'The Defection of Sir Edward Dering, 1640–1641', *HJ*, 15 (1972), 193; Anthony Fletcher, 'Petitioning and the outbreak of the civil war in Derbyshire', *Derbyshire Archaeological Journal* (1973), 33–44.

23. Gloucs. RO, D2510/13; BL, Thomason Tracts E.150(28), p. 41, Alan Everitt, *The County of Kent and the Great Rebellion* (Leicester, 1966), 92; Hirst, 'Defection', 201; David Underdown, *Revel, Riot and Rebellion: Popular Politics and Culture in England 1603–1660* (Oxford, 1985), 140; Fletcher, *Outbreak*, 194.

24. Abraham Cowley, *The Civil War*, ed. A. Pritchard (Toronto, 1973), 77; *CSPD, 1640–41*, 529; John Morrill, *Cheshire 1630–1660: County Government and Society during the 'English Revolution'* (Oxford, 1974), 51–3; Fletcher, *Outbreak*, 302–306.

25. *Buller Papers*, Buller Family (1895), 31, 33–4; Clive Holmes, *Suffolk Committee for Scandalous Ministers 1644–1646* (Suffolk Record Society, 1970), 54, 69; J. W. F. Hill, 'The Royalist Clergy of Lincolnshire', *Lincolnshire Architectural and Archaelogical Society Reports and Papers* (ii, 1938), 45, 49, 53, 54; BL, Add. MSS 39614, fo. 211; 36913, fos 131–2v; Fletcher, *Outbreak*, 195–6, 209, 302–307; BL, Thomason Tracts E.150(28), [pp. 41–2]; BL, Add. MS 11055, fols 130v–131. Discussed in greater detail in Chs 3 and 4 of my Cambridge Ph.D. thesis.

26. Hirst, 'Defection', 206 n.57.

27. Sir Thomas Aston, *A Collection of Sundry Petitions* (1642), 42; Nalson, ii, 720–2, 758; BL, Thomason Tracts E.151(11), pp. 6–7.

28. *Buller Papers*, 33–4.

29. LAO, 69/2/15.

30. HLRO, Main Papers, Feb. [27], 1640/1; 20 Dec. 1641.

31. The methods applied to produce the economic and population statistics presented here are fully discussed in ch. 5 of my Cambridge Ph.D thesis.

32. The Cheshire gentry, as in other parts of the country appear to have developed a rota system among themselves for spreading out the burden of payment. Such a system helps to explain why most of the self-styled gentlemen among the subscribers fail to appear in the 1640–1 subsidies. Henry Best, *Rural Economy in Yorkshire in 1641* (Surtees Society,

xxxiii, 1857), 87. Graham Kerby, 'Inequality in a Pre-Industrial Society: A Study of Wealth, Status, Office and Taxation in Tudor and Stuart England with Particular Reference to Cheshire' (University of Cambridge Ph.D. thesis, 1983); Spufford, *Contrasting Communities*, 233–4. Subsidies used: PRO, E179/85/135; E179/85/131; E179/85/136.

33. 'Loans, contributions, subsidies, and ship money, paid by the clergy of the diocese of Chester in the years 1620, 1622, 1624, 1634, 1635, 1636, and 1639', ed. G. T. O. Bridgeman in *Miscellanies relating to Lancashire and Cheshire* (Lancashire and Cheshire Record Society, xii, 1885), 78, 92, 100, 115, 120; Frodsham: John Walker, *The Sufferings of the Clergy*, ed. and revised A. G. Matthews (Oxford, 1948), 91; G. Ormerod, *History of Cheshire* (3 vols, 1882), ii, 58; *AO*; Tilston: *AO*; Ormerod, ii, 697. Wilmslow: *AO*; Ormerod, iii, 595; J. P. Earwaker, *East Cheshire* (2 vols, 1877), i. 91, ii, 91–3; *Minutes of the Committee for the Relief of Plundered Ministers* (Lancashire and Cheshire Records Society, xxviii, 1893), 146–7. Marbury: *AO*; Walker, 305, 306; Raymond Richards, *Old Cheshire Churches* (Didsbury, revised and enlarged edn, 1973), 227; William Urwick (ed.), *Historical Sketches of Nonconformity in Cheshire* (Manchester, 1864), 150. Middlewich: *Plundered Ministers*, 173–4; Urwick, 7, 62, 151, 164–7, 201, 213–14; Ormerod, iii, 185.

34. See ch. 5 of my Cambridge Ph.D. thesis.

35. Margaret Spufford, 'Puritanism and Social Control?', *Order and Disorder in early Modern England*, eds A. Fletcher and J. Stevenson (Cambridge, 1985), *passim: Contrasting Communities*, 232–3, 267–71; 'Can we Count the "Godly"?', 434, 437n. 20. Cf. Collinson, *Puritan Character*, 27.

36. CRO, EDC.5/1604 misc. (Manchester).

37. Richard Baxter, *The Saints Everlasting Rest* (1650), 342, 344.

6. THE CLERICAL ESTATE REVITALISED *Andrew Foster*

I am grateful to Peter Lake, Wilfred Prest, Conrad Russell, Pauline Croft, John Hawkins, Louise Yeoman, Jackie Eales and Judith Maltby for advice and encouragement whilst preparing this article. An earlier working paper on this theme received trenchant criticism at the Reformation Studies Colloquium held at Bangor in April 1990 for which I thank members of that group. Most thanks should, however, be reserved for the editor of this volume, Dr Kenneth Fincham, who has supplied inspiration, references, constant encouragement and advice – and waited patiently for results.

1. *Journal of Sir Symonds D'Ewes*, ed. W. Notestein, (New Haven, 1923), 431; B. Whitelocke, *Memorials of the English Affairs During the Reign of Charles I* (1732 edition), 38; extract from Root and Branch petition of December 1640 quoted in J. Kenyon, *The Stuart Constitution,*

(Cambridge, 1966), 174; *A Petition presented to the Parliament from the County of Nottingham complaining of grievances under the Ecclesiastical Government of Archbishops, Bishops, etc.*, (1641), 6; extract from Root and Branch petition, *op. cit.*, 172; Sir Edward Dering's speech in parliament of 13 January 1641 as quoted in *Proceedings, principally in the County of Kent, in connection with the Parliament called in 1640 . . .* , ed. Rev. L. B. Larking, Camden Series, 80, (1862), 27. John Morrill agrees with W. Shaw that probably eight hundred parishes petitioned in the first two years of the Long Parliament to denounce their ministers: J. Morrill, 'The attack on the Church of England in the Long Parliament, 1640–1642', D. Beales and G. Best (eds), *History, Society and the Churches. Essays in Honour of Owen Chadwick*, (Cambridge, 1985), 107.

2. Anticlericalism is well documented in C. Hill, *Society and Puritanism in Pre-Revolutionary England*, (1964), *passim*, C. Hill, *Economic Problems of the Church*, (Oxford, 1956), *passim* and latterly in J. Sommerville, *Politics and Ideology in England, 1603–1640*, (1986), ch. 6. For the debate over Arminianism see: N. Tyacke, *Anti-Calvinists: the Rise of English Arminianism c.1590–1640*, (Oxford, 1987); K. Sharpe, 'Archbishop Laud', *History Today*, 33, (Aug. 1983), 26–30; P. White, 'The Rise of Arminianism Reconsidered', *P and P*, 101, (1983), 34–54; and N. Tyacke and P. White, 'Debate: the rise of Arminianism reconsidered', *P and P*, 115, (1987), 201–29.

3. I. Green, 'The Persecution of "scandalous" and "malignant" parish clergy during the English Civil War', *EHR*, 94, (1979), 507–53; J. Sharpe, 'Scandalous and malignant Priests in Essex: the impact of grassroots Puritanism', C. Jones, M. Newett and S. Roberts (eds), *Politics and People in Revolutionary England*, (1986), 253–73.

4. Phrase used constantly in the 1640s: *Two Diaries of the Long Parliament*, ed. M. Jansson, (Gloucester, 1984), 105; *Two Speeches spoken in the House of Lords*, Lord Viscount Newarke, May 1641, 5; Hill, *Economic Problems of the Church*, part 1; Lamentations, IV, 20: used by Richard Neile in answer to a question by James I, introduction to *Poems*, E. Waller, (1712), vi, and in the sermon preached at the execution of Charles I by William Juxon, W. Marsh, *Memoirs of Archbishop Juxon and His Times*, (Oxford 1869), 200; K. Fincham and P. Lake, 'The ecclesiastical policy of King James I', *JBS*, 24, (1985), 169–207.

5. K. Fincham, *Prelate as Pastor: The Episcopate of James I*, (Oxford, 1990); H. Trevor-Roper, 'King James and his Bishops', *History Today*, 5 (Sept. 1955), 571–81; Bancroft (1605–10), Abbot (1611–33), Bilson (1615–16), Andrewes (1616–26), Montagu (1617–18), and Williams (1621–5); Richard Neile was apparently also considered for the post of Lord Keeper; PRO, SP 14/267/121; G. Thomas, 'James I, Equity and Lord Keeper John Williams', *EHR*, 91, (1976), 506–28, also notes Abbot and Andrewes in running for the job; *The Political Works of*

James I, ed. C. H. McIlwain, (New York, 1965), 330 – speech in Star Chamber, 20 June 1616.

6. Neile (1627–36), Laud (1627–45), Harsnett (1629–31) and Juxon (1636–49); Laud, *Works*, III, 226, VI, 176.

7. C. Russell, 'The British Problem and the English Civil War', *History*, 72, (1987), 395–415; for more fully developed case see: C. Russell, *The Causes of the English Civil War*, (Oxford, 1990); Whitelocke, *Memorials*, 23; *Registers of the Privy Council of Scotland*, ed. D. Masson, (Edinburgh, 1884), VI, xxxi; VIII (1887), xxii; VI (second series, 1905), vi; M. Lee Jr, *The Road to Revolution: Scotland under Charles I, 1625–1637*, (Urbana and Chicago, 1985), 154–7, 185.

8. Kenyon, *Stuart Constitution*, instructions of 1633, 159; Fincham, *Prelate as Pastor*, 96–111; A. W. Foster, 'A Biography of Archbishop Richard Neile (1562–1640)' (Oxford University D.Phil. thesis 1978), 95–107, 139–40.

9. M. Graves, *The Tudor Parliaments, Crown, Lords and Commons 1485–1603*, (1985), 132, 135.

10. Fincham, *Prelate as Pastor*, 58–64; A. Britton, 'The House of Lords in English Politics 1604–1614' (Oxford D.Phil. 1982), 23.

11. Foster, 'Richard Neile', 108–63; see also E. Cope, 'The Bishops and Parliamentary Politics in Early Stuart England', *Parliamentary History*, 9, (1990).

12. Fincham, *Prelate as Pastor*, 58–64; *Proceedings in Parliament 1610*, ed. E. R. Foster, 2 vols, (New Haven, Conn., 1966), I, 136–7.

13. *Proceedings in Parliament 1614*, ed. M. Jansson, (Philadelphia, 1988), 345, n. 33; *Commons Journals*, I, 235; York City Archives, Corporation House Book 33, fo.24v; D. H. Willson (ed.), *The Parliamentary Diary of Robert Bowyer, 1606–1607*, (1971), 181.

14. *Proceedings in Parliament 1610*, I, 71, II, 59–60; Sommerville, *Politics and Ideology*, 121–7, 132; T. Birch (ed.), *The Court & Times of James I*, 2 vols, (1848), I, 129.

15. *HMC Hastings MSS*, IV, (1947), 253; *Proceedings in Parliament 1614*, 251, 342, n.21; G. R. Elton, *The Parliaments of England 1559–1581*, (Cambridge, 1986), 199.

16. J. Sommerville, 'Ideology, Property and the Constitution', R. Cust and A. Hughes (eds), *Conflict in Early Stuart England*, (Harlow, 1989), 50–1; Whitelocke, *Memorials*, 8.

17. *Commons Debates 1621*, eds W. Notestein, F. Relf and H. Simpson, 7 vols, (New Haven, 1935), II, 333; *Proceedings in Parliament 1610*, I, 221.

18. Laud, *Works*, VI, 245; R. Cust, *The Forced Loan and English Politics 1626–1628*, (Oxford, 1987), 79–80; W. Prynne, *Canterbury's Doome* (1646), 25–28.

19. Whitelocke, *Memorials*, 22–3; A. Fletcher, 'Factionalism in Town and Countryside: The significance of Puritanism and Arminianism', D.

Baker (ed.), *The Church in Town and Countryside*, Studies in Church History, 16, (Oxford, 1979), 297–300; E. Cope, *Politics without Parliament. 1629–1640* (1987), 109–12; WSRO, Cap. I/23/3; A. Foster, 'Church Policies of the 1630s', Cust and Hughes (eds), *Conflict in Early Stuart England*, 208–9.

20. William Prynne supplied evidence for attacks made on John Cosin in the parliamentary session of 1629: W. Prynne, *A Brief Survey and Censure of Mr Cozens his Couzening Devotions*, (1628); *Commons Debates for 1629*, eds W. Notestein and F. Relf, (Minnesota, 1921), 35–46; Peter Smart of Durham also chipped in with material on Cosin: W. Longstaffe (ed.), 'Acts of the Court of High Commission at Durham', *Surtees Society*, 34, (1858), 199; Fincham, *Prelate as Pastor*, 91–96 covers corporation disputes under James I.

21. Laud, *Works*, VI, 194; R. Chestlin, *Persecutio Undecima*, (1648), 9 (but note confused pagination in Ch 5).

22. J. S. Cockburn, *A History of English Assizes 1558–1714*, (1972), 231; W. Prest, *The Rise of the Barristers*, (1986), 224; T. Scot, *The Highwaies of God and the King*, (1623), 87.

23. H. Sydenham, *Moses and Aaron or the Affinitie of Civill and Ecclesiasticke power*, (1626), 10; Anon., *Episcopall Inheritance*, (Oxford, 1641), 48–51.

24. BL, Add. Ms. 3813, fos 108–177v (Liber Pacis 1604); PRO, C 193/13/1 (Liber Pacis 1622); T. Rymer, *Foedera*, 18, (1726), 566–625 (Liber Pacis 1625); PRO, SP 16/405 (Liber Pacis 1636). D. Mullan, *Episcopacy in Scotland. The History of an Idea 1560–1638*, (Edinburgh, 1986), 173, notes that in 1634 all Scottish bishops were appointed as J.P.s

25. J. Gleason, *The Justices of the Peace in England 1558–1640*, (Oxford, 1969), 68–82; A. Fletcher, *Reform in the Provinces. The Government of Stuart England*, (1986), 1–11; M. James, *Family, Lineage & Civil Society*, (Oxford, 1974), 163–4; *Commons Debates 1621*, III, 111–12; *Commons Journals*, I, 599; A. Foster, 'The Struggle for Parliamentary Representation for Durham, c.1600–1641', D. Marcombe (ed.), *The Last Principality*, (Nottingham, 1987), 186; Durham County RO, Q/S/BO 1.

26. Durham County RO, Q/S/BO 1; HRO Q1/1–2; Rev. E. Bates (ed.) 'Quarter Sessions Records for the County of Somerset', *Somerset Record Society*, 23, (1907); over twenty civil lawyers regularly sat as J.P.s during this period.

27. HRO, Q1/1–2; *Worcestershire County Records. Calendar of the Quarter Sessions Papers, Vol. 1 1591–1643*, ed. J. Willis Bund, (Worcester, 1900); *Somerset Record Society*, 23, (1907); T. G. Barnes, *Somerset 1625–1640*, (Oxford, 1961), 46.

28. Peter Lake, 'Conformist Clericalism? Richard Bancroft's Analysis of the Socio-Economic roots of Presbyterianism', W. Sheils and D. Wood (eds), *The Church and Wealth*, Studies in Church History, 24, (Oxford, 1987), 219–29; P. Lake, 'Presbyterianism, The Idea of a

National Church and the Argument from Divine Right', P. Lake and
M. Dowling (eds), *Protestantism and the National Church in Sixteenth Century
England*, (1987), 193–224; Lake, *Anglicans and Puritans?, passim.*

29. Hill, *Economic Problems of the Church*, 32; G. Carleton, *Tithes Examined and Proved to be due to the Clergy by Divine Right*, (1606), dedication;
P. Lake, 'Presbyterianism', 211–13; L. Andrewes, *Of the Rights of Tithes*,
(1647).

30. Hill, *Economic Problems of the Church*, 77–131; M. Schwarz, 'Some
Thoughts on the Development of a Lay Religious Consciousness in
Pre-Civil War England', G. Cuming and D. Baker (eds), *Popular Belief
and Practice*, Studies in Church History, 8, (Cambridge, 1972), 176–7;
J. Selden, *The History of Tithes*, (1618) preface; R. Tillesley, *Animadversions upon Mr Selden's History of Tithes and his review thereof*, (1619); R.
Montagu, *Diatribe Upon the First Part of the Late History of Tithes*, (1621).

31. M. Sutcliffe, *A Treatise of Ecclesiastical Discipline*, (1590), espistle to
reader; R. Tillesley, *Animadversions*, (1619); J. Sempill, *Sacrilege Sacredly
Handled*, (1619); Lake, *Anglicans and Puritans?*, 223, 245–50; F. Robarts,
*The Reverence of the Gospel is Tythes. Due to the Ministerie of the Word, by
that Word*, (1613), frontispiece; R. Bernard, *Two Twinnes*, (1613), 49.

32. F. Heal, 'Archbishop Laud revisited: Leases and Estate Management at Canterbury and Winchester before the Civil War', R. O'Day
and F. Heal (eds), *Princes and Paupers in the English Church 1500–1800*,
(Leicester, 1981), 129–51; B. Parsons, *Honus & Onus Levitarum or Tithes
vindicated to the Presbyters of the Gospel*, (1637); W. J. Sheils, ' "The Right
of the Church"; the Clergy, Tithe, and the Courts at York, 1540–1640',
in *The Church and Wealth*, 231–55; Helena Hajzyk, 'The Church in
Lincolnshire c.1595–c.1640', (Cambridge University Ph.D. thesis,
1980), 215; R. O'Day, *The English Clergy*, (Leicester, 1979), 190–206,
noted a general increase in tithe cases, but felt that the evidence against
clergy in particular was inconclusive; see also P. Collinson, 'Shepherds,
Sheepdogs, and Hirelings: the Pastoral Ministry in Post-Reformation
England', W. Sheils and D. Wood (eds), *The Minstry: Clerical and Lay*,
Studies in Church History, 26, (Oxford, 1989), 213.

33. P. Seddon (ed.), 'Holles Letters, Vol. II (1587–1637)', *Thoroton
Record Society Series*, XXXV, (1983), 351–3.

34. W. Prynne, *The Antipathy of the English Lordly Prelacie. Both to Regall
Monarchy and Civill Unity*, (1641), 240; Edward Hyde, Earl of Clarendon,
The History of the Rebellion and Civil Wars in England, 3 vols, (1705 edition),
I, 99; Whitelocke, *Memorials*, 23.

35. Clarendon, *History of the Rebellion*, 87; H. Phillips, 'The Last Years
of the Court of Star Chamber, 1630–41', *TRHS*, 4th series, 21, (1939),
103–131; Bodl., MS Rawlinson D1104, fo.17v.

36. *Proceedings in Parliament 1610*, II, 328–9; Anon, *Prelacie is Misery*,
(1641), 8; Whitelocke, *Memorials*, 38.

37. Chestlin, *Persecutio Undecima*, 5; for discussion of Arminian views of the priesthood see Peter Lake's article in this volume.

38. *Bishop Overall's Convocation Book, MDCVI Concerning the Government of God's Catholick Church and the Kingdoms of the Whole World*, (1690), 290; Clive Holmes (ed.), 'The Suffolk Committees For Scandalous Ministers 1644–1646', *Suffolk Record Society*, XIII, (1970), 55; E. Udall, *Communion Comlinesse*, (1641), 9.

39. WSRO, Ep. I/15/2/19; L. Andrewes, *Works*, ed. J. Bliss, (1841–54), V. 82–103; Prior's Kitchen, Durham, Hunter MS. 67/14/7–9; Tyacke, *Anti-Calvinists*, 222; Trevor-Roper, *Catholics, Anglicans and Puritans*, 107.

40. The question of how far education may have 'alienated' the clergy from their flocks has become quite controversial: O'Day, *The English Clergy*, 191–206; C. Haigh, 'Anticlericalism and the English Reformation', *History*, 68, (1983), 391–407; I. Green, ' "Reformed Pastors" and *Bon Cures*: The Changing Role of the Parish Clergy in Early Modern Europe' and P. Collinson, 'Shepherds, Sheepdogs, and Hirelings', both to be found in *The Ministry: Clerical and Lay*; for the campaigns of the 1630s see: Foster, 'Church Policies of the 1630s', 192–223; Hill, *Economic Problems of the Church*, 332, 328. Typical of the mood of the 1630s was the rumour recorded by Thomas Crosfield in December 1636 that the king was planning to take all lay patronage into his own hands, 'but this is supposed too good to be true' – F. S. Boas (ed.), *The Diary of Thomas Crosfield*, (1935), 82; John Fell, *Life of the Rev. H. Hammond*, (Oxford edn, 1806), 162–3; Larking (ed.), *Proceedings, principally in the County of Kent*, 159; Collinson also notes the importance of the 'peacemaking' function of the clergy for the godly in *The Religion of Protestants*, (Oxford, 1982), 108–10.

41. Trevor-Roper, *Catholics, Anglicans and Puritans*, 118.

42. See article in this volume by Peter Lake and work of Tyacke; figures gained from analysis of PRO, SP/16/212, C193/13/2, and SP/16/405; Fletcher, *Reform in the Provinces*, 10.

43. Denis Bond of Dorset wrote in his diary of collections for St Paul's Cathedral in 1632 and of how some were 'enforced to give, by the active clergy, then put in justices of the peace' – Dorset RO, D53/1, 24 – a reference I owe to Dr Kevin Sharpe; Anon, *Episcopall Inheritance*, (1641), 18, 27; *Commons Journals*, II, 114, 115, 122, 124–5, 127, 131; Lord Saye and Sele, *Against the Supremacy of Bishops and their power in Civil Affairs and Courts of Justice*, (1642), 2–3; R. Bernard, *A Short View of the Praeliticall Church of England*, (1641), 11–12; *Speech of the Honourable Nathaniel Fiennes*, (1641) 15, 18.

44. *Commons Journals*, I, 241; Britton 'The House of Lords', 235; *Proceedings in Parliament 1614*, 216.

45. *Commons Journals*, I, 599; *Commons Debates 1621*, III, 111–12.

46. *Commons Journals*, I, 832, 834, 836, 841; 884, 886, 888, 891, 899;

Commons Debates 1628, (eds) M. Keeler, M. Cole and W. Bidwell, (New Haven, 1978), 6 vols, II, 507, 512, 521; III, 3, 7, 9, 430, 433, 437; V, 531, 533–6; *Commons Journals*, II, 16; 99, 102, 110, 114–15, 122, 124–5, 127–31; E. Cope and W. Coates (eds), 'Proceedings of the Short Parliament 1640', Camden 4th series, XIX, (1977), 273–4; M. Jansson (ed.), *Two Diaries of the Long Parliament*, (Gloucester, 1984), 106.

47. S. R. Gardiner (ed.), *Reports of Cases in the Courts of Star Chamber and High Commission*, Camden new series, 39, (1886), 253–9; it is interesting that even Archbishop Abbot thought that to say 'that no clergy man be so much as a Justice of the Peace, this is fantastical', 259.

48. Whitelocke, *Memorials*, 33, 23.

49. H. Sydenham, *Moses and Aaron*, 10; *Proceedings of the Short Parliament 1640*, 142.

7. THE LAUDIAN STYLE   *Peter Lake*

1. Contrast N. Tyacke, 'Puritanism, Arminianism and Counter-Revolution' in C. Russell (ed.), *The Origins of the English Civil War* (1973) and the more recent and comprehensive *Anti-Calvinists* (Oxford, 1987) with P. White 'The Rise of Arminianism Reconsidered' *P and P*, 101 (1983) and White's more recent *Predestination, Policy and Polemic* (Cambridge, 1992). For variations on the same theme see G. W. Bernard, 'The Church of England, c.1529-c.1642' *History*, 75 (1990) and K. Sharpe, 'Archbishop William Laud and the University of Oxford' in his *Politics and Ideas in early Stuart England* (1989).

2. The first statement of the rise of Arminianism thesis was almost a perfect inversion or negative image of its Hillian predecessor. Now it was the Arminians who were the real revolutionaries, overthrowing the dogmatic certainties of Calvinist predestinarianism and anti-popery, allied in cultural terms with the baroque *avant garde* of the Caroline court and, in the universities, with the rise of rationalist scepticism and empirical science. Such a view fitted perfectly with a revisionist account of the Civil War as an essentially conservative reaction against a centralising, innovating court. For the enlistment of Dr Tyacke's work to support such a view see R. Ashton, *The English Civil War; conservatism and revolution* (1978) and more subtly C. Russell, *The Causes of the English Civil War* (Oxford, 1990). For a recent example of these sort of inversionary tactics see H. Trevor-Roper, *Catholics, Anglicans and Puritans* (1987), esp. ch. 2 and the works by White and Bernard cited above.

3. Robert Skinner, *A sermon preached before the king at Whitehall* (1634), 'published by his majesty's command', 21–2; John Browning, *Concerning public prayer and the fasts of the church* (1636), 23; Thomas Laurence, *Two sermons* (Oxford, 1635), 20–1. The first of these sermons was an Act

sermon preached at Oxford on 13 July 1634, the second a visitation sermon preached at Salisbury during Laud's metropolitical visitation of 1634. Laurence was also a royal chaplain. Also see W. Balcanquhall, *The honour of Christian churches* (1633), 12–3. This was a court sermon preached before the king at Whitehall on 8 December 1632 and 'published by his majesty's special commandment.'

4. Fulke Robarts, *God's holy house and service* (1639), 3; Alexander Read, *A sermon preached April 8 1636 at a visitation at Brentwood in Essex* (1636), *passim*; J. Swan, *Profanomastix* (1639), 22, 57; also see R. Tedder, *A sermon preached at Wymondham in Norfolk at the primary visitation of . . . Matthew Wren* (1637), 8–9; T. Laurence, *A sermon preached before the King's majesty at Whitehall, 7 February 1636* (1637), 'published by the King's special command', 15, 'wheresoever a consecration is there God especially is by a peculiar dispensation of his gracious and merciful presence'. This attitude had a special relevance to revenues and property dedicated to ecclesiastical use. The alienation of such revenue and property was regarded by the Laudians as sacrilege and helped to fuel their concern with impropriated tithes and church property. For further discussion of this see I. Atherton, 'Viscount Scudamore's "Laudianism": the religious practices of the first Viscount Scudamore', *HJ*, 34 (1991).

5. For diatribes against the use of churches for secular purposes see Balcanquhall, *The honour of Christian churches*, 16–17; Swan, *Profanomastix*, 58–60; J. Browning, *Concerning public prayer* (1636), 53–4.

6. R. T., *De templis, a treatise of temples, wherein is discovered the ancient manner of building, consecrating and adorning churches* (1638), 111–2; also see Skinner, *A sermon*, 29.

7. R. T., *De templis*, 177–8; Balcanquhall, *The honour of Christian churches*, 6; R. Shelford, *Five pious and learned discourses* (Cambridge, 1635), 11–12; Swan, *Profanomastix*, 5, 26–7; Robarts, *God's holy house and service*, 14–6, 47–8.

8. On the value of external decoration with 'all kind of ornaments that might add glory and grace . . . as curious paintings, hangings, gilding, sumptuous vestments, rich gifts in money, chalices, plate' see for instance R. T., *De templis*, 177.

9. Balcanquhall, *The honour of Christian churches*, 12–3; Skinner, *A sermon*, 10; Robarts, *God's holy house and service*, sig. *3r; Eleazor Duncon, *Of worshipping towards the altar* (London, 1660) [an English translation of the original Latin act lecture in 1633], 4–5, 9–13.

10. Robarts, *God's holy house and service*, sig.*3r; also see Browning, *Concerning public prayer*, 25.

11. E. Boughen, *A sermon concerning decency and order in the church* (1638), 6–7, 8.

12. Ibid. 10–11; also see Tedder, *A Sermon*, 9–10, for a long passage

on the uniform public worship of the primitive Church as a model for contemporary practice.

13. Browning, *Concerning public prayer*, 29–30; J. Yates, *A treatise of the honour of God's house* (1637), section headed 'the danger of an altar in the name and use', sig.*3v; J. Featley, *Obedience and submission* (1636), [a visitation sermon preached at St Saviour's Southwark], 24; also see Tedder, *A Sermon*, 17–18, for a passage claiming that those opposed to ceremonies 'would take the light out of the church', an interesting contrast to the rhetoric of the light of the gospel, which had become almost a protestant cliché since the early Reformation.

14. E. Boughen, *Two sermons, the first preached at Canterbury at the visitation of the Lord Archbishop's peculiar in St Margaret's church April 14 1635. The second preached at St Paul's Cross, 18 April 1630* (1635), first sermon, separately paginated, 21–3.

15. Tedder, *A Sermon*, 11; also see J. Swan, *A sermon pointing out the chief causes and cures of such unruly stirrs as are not seldom found in the church of God* (1639) [a visitation sermon preached at Sawston at the Archdeacon of Ely's visitation 19 September 1638], 14; Balcanquhall *The honour of Christian churches*, 21.

16. Robarts, *God's holy house and service*, 30; Balcanquhall, *The honour of Christian churches*, 10–1; Browning, *Concerning public prayer*, 113, from a visitation sermon preached at Dunmow, in Essex, 11 September 1634.

17. Tedder, *A sermon*, 16; Swan, *A sermon*, 15; Browning, *Concerning public prayer*, 125. On the superiority of public over private prayer see, for instance, Swan, *A sermon*, 14.

18. Swan, *Profanomastix*, 54–5; Browning, *Concerning public prayer*, 127; Shelford, *Five pious and learned discourses*, 40.

19. Swan, *A sermon*, 14, Swan called the 'sermon bell' rung to tell people when the sermon was about to start 'a true token that there is some schism in the church' since it allowed the godly to hear the sermon and miss public prayer; Tedder, *A sermon*, 11, 15, 'preaching must give place to prayer in the temple. God himself hath said it and Christ hath said it again'.

20. Swan, *A sermon*, 14; J. Browning, *Concerning public prayer*, 55, 103.

21. Ibid. 48–51; Shelford, *Five pious and learned discourses*, 35.

22. R. T., *De templis*, 132; Shelford, *Five pious and learned discourses*, 15.

23. Swan, *Profanomastix*, 39; Duncon, *Of worshipping toward the altar*, 21; Browning, *Concerning public prayer*, 58. As Dr Tyacke has pointed out Laudian attitudes to the grace vouchsafed to all believers in the sacraments played a central role in their critique of Calvinist doctrines of absolute predestination, see below n. 29.

24. Yates, *Treatise of the honour of God's house*, 62–3; Duncon, *Of worshipping toward the altar*, 22; in the same vein also J. Pocklington, *Altare Christianum* (1637), 118 where Pocklington cited a passage from Chrysostom on the presence of angels at the reception of the sacrament,

a sight fit to lead devout recipients to 'conceive heaven itself to be open to us'.

25. Laurence, *A sermon*, 20; Read, *A sermon*; also see Swan, *Profanomastix*, 40. 'Although the Lord be present in all his holy ordinances yet here [in the sacrament] more specially insomuch that the holy table or altar must upon necessity be evermore taken as the great sign of his presence as carrying with it the highest relation thereunto.'

26. On puritan scripturalism see F. White, *An examination and confutation of a lawless pamphlet* (1637), 33–4 and F. White, *A treatise of the sabbath day* (1635), dedicatory epistle. For the sabbatarian assault on other holy days see John Pocklington, *Sunday no sabbath* (1636), 7 and P. Heylyn, *The history of the sabbath* (1636), pt 2, 254–5. On the absence of any hint of sabbatarian doctrine in natural law see J. Prideaux, *The doctrine of the sabbath* (1634), sig. C r-v, from the translator's preface by Heylyn. On the grounding of the sabbath in divine positive law, viz. the Mosaic Law see C. Dow, *A discourse of the Lord's day* (1636), 21–5; for the abrogation of the ceremonial Law of Moses, including the obligation to observe the sabbath, by Christ see F. White, *A treatise*, 63, 160; for the partly moral and partly ceremonial status of the fourth commandment see Heylyn, *The history of the sabbath*, pt 2, 162–3 and G. Ironside, *Seven questions of the sabbath*, (Oxford, 1637), 69. For the dependence of Sunday worship on ecclesiastical authority and its inherent mutability see Heylyn, *A history of the sabbath*, pt 2, 94–5.

27. C. Hill, *A nation of change and novelty* (1990), ch. 4 and Bernard and Sharpe, cited above n. 1.

28. See my article 'The Laudians and the argument from Authority' B. Y. Kunze and D. D. Brautigam (eds), *Court, Country and Culture* (Rochester, N.Y., 1992).

29. K. Parker, *The English Sabbath* (Cambridge, 1988) and for a corrective also see J. H. Primus, *Holy Time* (Macon, Ga., 1989) and the reviews of Parker's book by Anthony Milton in *JEH*, 41 (1990) and by N. Tyacke in *EHR*, 106 (1991); M. Aston, *England's Iconoclasts* (Oxford, 1988) and P. Collinson, *The birthpangs of English protestantism* (1988), ch. 4; K. Fincham, *Prelate as Pastor* (Oxford, 1990), *passim*; P. Collinson, 'Shepherds, sheepdogs and hirelings: the pastoral ministry in post-reformation England', in W. J. Sheils and D. Wood (eds), *Studies in church history*, 26 (Oxford, 1989); P. Collinson, 'The English conventicle' in W. J. Sheils and D. Wood (eds), *Studies in church history*, 23 (Oxford, 1986) and *The religion of protestants* (Oxford, 1982); Tyacke, *Anti-Calvinists*, 175–7, 197–9, 246–7.

30. Browning, *Concerning public prayer*, 46; also see Yates *A treatise of the honour of God's house*, 62–3 on the reasons why 'the pulpit, font, desk etc' were not 'as holy as the table'; Duncon, *Of worshipping God towards the altar*, 21.

31. P. Heylyn, *Anti-dotum Lincolniense or an answer to a book called the holy table name and thing* (1637), section II, 86, 121; section III, 40.

32. Robarts, *God's holy house and service*, 45; also see R. T., *De templis*, 190–1.

33. Shelford, *Five pious and learned discourses*, 26–7.

34. Pocklington, *Altare Christianum*, 104, 117; J. Mede, *The name altar* (1637), 36; Hill, *A nation of change and novelty*, ch. 4.

35. Robarts, *God's holy house and service*, 41; also see Heylyn, *Anti-dotum Lincolniense*, section II, 79; R. T., *De templis*, 55–7; Pocklington, *Altare Christianum*, 25–7, 50–1.

36. Robarts, *God's holy house and service*, 41.

37. For puritan attitudes to the 'holiness' of churches see, for instance, Tedder, *A sermon*, 8; Swan, *Profanomastix*, 1; William Strode, *A sermon preached at a visitation held at Lynn in Norfolk, June 24th, 1633* (1660), 28–9; Heylyn, *Anti-dotum Lincolniense*, section I, 48; for the liturgical consequences of this attitude see J. Elborow, *Evodias and Syntyche or the female zealots of the church of Philippi . . . set forth in a sermon at Brentwood in Essex February 28th 1636/7* (1637) 12; on the puritans' tendency to equate the church with the godly community as they defined it see, for instance, Skinner, *A sermon*, 30.

38. On the puritan obsession with preaching see Balcanquhall, *The honour of Christian churches*, 22; Browning, *Concerning public prayer*, 2, 53, 112; Shelford, *Five pious and learned discourses*, 47; Strode, *A sermon*, 2–3.

39. On extempore preaching, see Browning, *Concerning public prayer*, 51; Read, *A sermon*, 17; G. Wall, *A sermon at the Lord Archbishop of Canterbury his visitation metropolitical, held at All Saints in Worcester . . . June 3 1635* (1635), 10, 12; on extempore prayer, see Browning, *Concerning public prayer*, 93–4 where extempore prayer in public worship was denounced as a harbinger of division and schism; Skinner, *A sermon*, where the contents of such prayers were characterised as 'seditious', 'ridiculous' and 'blasphemous'; Tedder, *A sermon*, 14–15, where extempore prayer was termed 'babbling not praying' and 'raw and extempore preaching' blamed for driving out 'common prayer' from the church and putting all religion into 'a consumption' thereby.

40. On Laudian discussions of predestination in the context of a critique of divisive and sacrilegious puritan religion see, for instance, Laurence, *Two sermons*, 10–11, 22–3, 27–40; for the rhetoric of mystery, reverence and restraint applied against both speculative theologising and puritan profanity see Swan, *A sermon*, 16–17.

41. On puritan conventicles see, for instance, Laurence, *Two sermons*, 22–4, subjugating lay devotions to public worship conducted by the priest in church; Laurence, *A sermon*, 11–2, denouncing those who 'make merchandise of the word of God by the peck and the pound', preferring 'ware houses before churches' and making no difference between 'the pulpit and the tables end, the belfry and the altar'; Yates, *A treatise of*

the honour of God's house, section headed 'the danger of an altar in the name and use', sig. § 3v.

42. On the puritans' liking for only their own kind of preacher see J. Fisher, *The priests duty and dignity, preached at the triennial visitation in Ampthill 1635, August 18* (1636), 32–6; Boughen, *Two sermons*, first sermon, separately paginated, 4–5; on 'popular' preachers playing up to the people see S. Hoard, *The church's authority asserted in a sermon preached at Chelmsford at the metropolitical visitation of the most reverend father in God, William Lord Archbishop of Canterbury . . . March I, 1636* (1637), 32; Laurence, *Two sermons* second sermon, separately paginated, 26–7, where the puritans' disturbance of the 'peace of the church' was attributed to 'missing an honour in it' and grounded on the preachers' desire 'to be honoured before the people'; P. Heylyn, *A coal from the altar* (1636), 58, where the puritan argument from the need to avoid the offence of the brethren was described as 'a trick to please the people and put the reins into their hands'; M. Wigmore, *The meteors, a sermon preached at a visitation* (1636), 13–4, denouncing men who will 'come and croak for a piece of silver' as 'dissembling parasites, glavering parasites, trencher chaplains that will . . . become all things to all men so that they may please some men'.

43. On the inextricable link between secular and spiritual, civil and ecclesiastical order see, for instance, Browning, *Concerning public prayer*, 67; Boughen, *Two sermons*, first sermon, 4–5, 'difference of religion breeds a disunion in affection'. These, of course, were commonplaces. What rendered them less so in Laudian hands was their characterisation of the whole 'puritan' sermon-centred, predestinarian and sabbatarian style of divinity summarised here as inherently divisive, a staging post on a road that led inevitably to heresy and schism.

44. See above ch. 1; also M. Smuts, *Court culture and the origins of a royalist tradition in early Stuart England* (Philadelphia, Pa., 1987), esp. ch. 8.

45. For Hooker see my *Anglicans and puritans? English conformist thought from Whitgift to Hooker* (1988), chs 4 and 5; and on Andrewes and Buckeridge see my article 'Lancelot Andrewes, John Buckeridge and *avant-garde* conformity at the court of James I' in L. L. Peck (ed.), *The mental world of the Jacobean court* (Cambridge, 1991).

46. Even in court sermons of the 1630s John Prideaux was prepared to lament the role of proud prelates in manufacturing or provoking puritan error and to murmur darkly about the spread of Pelagian and Socinian heresies. See, for instance, his sermons 'Heresies' Progress' and 'A plot for preferment' both in *Certaine sermons* (Oxford, 1636). In the first he vindicated the 'efficacy of God's grace and the perverseness of man's will' against our 'new Pelagians' (15, 21) and called on the governors of Church and state to unite against the threat of heresy. 'The heaviest doom perchance would light on superiors who are not

only accountable for themselves but others and they betray them that
soothe their security and take not all fair opportunity according to their
places and callings to mind them of it' (19). In the second he denounced
'the causelsss strangeness and stateliness of some . . . to their meaner
and weaker brethren'. Such *hauteur*, 'so different from apostolical
humility', had 'made more schismatics and (as we call them puritans)
than all the vantages that could be ever taken against the sacred
order of our reverend bishops or any part of our Church discipline or
ceremonies' (12–13). In private he was a good deal less eliptical and
openly denounced various Laudian ceremonies like bowing to the altar.
See Sheffield University Library, Hartlib MS 29/2, fo. 48r, a passage
from Hartlib's 1634 Epemerides that reports that 'Prideaux is writing
a treatise proving the unlawfulness of cringing or bowing to the tables
et says rather die than do it et that the martyrs die for far less matters'.
I owe this reference to the kindness of Anthony Milton.

47. Fincham, *Prelate as Pastor*, chs 7–8; for Cotton see Larzer Ziff,
The career of John Cotton (Princeton, 1962), ch. 2.

48. See Hoard, *The church's authority asserted*, 52–3; Boughen, *Two
sermons*, first sermon, 22–3; W. Quelch, *Church customs vindicated in two
sermons preached at Kingston upon Thames, the one at the primary visitation
of . . . Richard [Neile] late Lord Bishop of Winton, anno 1628. The other at the
first metropolitical visitation of . . . William . . . Lord Archbishop of Canterbury,
July 9, 1635* (1636), 24–5; for diatribes against those who subscribed
with reservations or subscribed and then only partially or half-heartedly
conformed see W. Hardwick, *Conformity with piety requisite in God's service,
delivered at a visitation sermon at Kingston-upon-Thames, September 8, 1638*
(1638), 16–7; Strode, *A sermon*, 22–5; for thanks to God for the flight
into exile of various puritans see Featley, *Obedience and submission*, 10.

49. For Bastwick see F. Condick *The life and works of Dr John Bastwick*
(University of London Ph. D. thesis, 1983), *passim*; for Davenport see
I. M. Calder, *The letters of John Davenport: Puritan Divine* (New Haven,
1937); more generally for ministers going to New England see Theodore
Dwight Bozeman, *To live ancient lives* (Chapel Hill, N.C. 1988), ch. 3;
on Sanderson, see my 'Serving God and the times: the Calvinist conformity of Robert Sanderson' *JBS*, 27 (1988).

50. This paragraph summarises my 'The Laudians and the Argument
from Authority'.

51. For the difficulties experienced by Heylyn in justifying the altar
policy in terms of the Edwardian history of the Prayer Book see his *A
coal from the altar*, 39 and *Anti-dotum Lincolniense*, section 1, 116–28, for
the attempt to explain the changes from the first to the second Edwardian prayer books in terms of the sinister power of laity in the Church
and the meddling influence of foreign reformed divines. For similar
attempts to suppress any hint of 'puritan' sabbatarianism in the homi-

lies, see White, *An examination*, 34; Heylyn, *History of the sabbath*, pt 2, 242–9.

52. For the explanation of the apparent novelty of some Laudian policies in terms of the laxity of the immediate past see Robarts, *God's holy house and service*, sig. *4r; for Laud and Wren as reformers, see ibid., sig. *2v.

53. For the language of mystery and reverent awe before the divine presence and will, deployed in relation both to predestination and the divine presence in the sacrament, and also to underwrite a humble outward reverence in church, see Laurence, *Two sermons, passim*; BL, Add. MS 20065 fo. 11r (Skinner preaching before Charles I, 27 Dec. 1631).

8. THE CHURCH OF ENGLAND, ROME AND THE TRUE CHURCH: THE DEMISE OF A JACOBEAN CONSENSUS   *Anthony Milton*

I am grateful to Julia Merritt, Peter Lake and Kenneth Fincham for their comments on an earlier draft of this article.

1. P. Lake and M. Dowling (eds), *Protestantism and the National Church in Sixteenth-Century England* (1987) (especially articles by J. Facey and P. Lake); P. Lake, *Anglicans and Puritans?* (1988) (esp. 155–62, 177–82, 220–2); Conrad Russell, *The Causes of the English Civil War* (Oxford, 1990), 89–91.

2. John Davenant, *Determinationes Quaestionum quarundam Theologicarum* . . . 2nd edn (Cambridge, 1639), 156, 216; idem, *Expositio Epistolae D. Pauli ad Colossenses* 3rd edn (Cambridge, 1639), 145, cf. 8–9, 93–5; Richard Field, *Of the Church* 4 vols (Cambridge, 1847–52), 1. 27, 31–2; John Prideaux, *Viginti-duae lectiones de totidem religionis capitibus* 3rd edn (Oxford, 1648), 130, cf. 141.

3. Davenant, *Determinationes*, 57–8; Field, *Of the Church* 1. 33; Richard Bauckham, *Tudor Apocalypse* (Abingdon, 1978), 118–22.

4. Bauckham, *Tudor Apocalypse*, 119–21; George Abbot, *A Treatise of the Perpetuall Visibilitie, and Succession of the True Church* (1624), 28–9.

5. Bauckham, *Tudor Apocalypse*, 118–22; Thomas Morton, *A Catholike Appeale* (1610), 70, 72–3; Francis White, *The Orthodox Faith and Way to the Church* (1617), 324; idem, *A Replie to Jesuit Fisher's answere* (1624), 7, 56–7, 60–2, 67, 96–7, 104.

6. E.g. Thomas Morton, *The Grand Imposture of the (now) Church of Rome* 2nd edn (1628), 398; Abbot, *Treatise*, 93–7; Prideaux, *Viginti-duae lectiones*, 136–43; Simon Birckbek, *The Protestants Evidence* (1635), ii. 150–1; Anthony Cade, *A Justification of the Church of England* (1630), 138–204.

7. Daniel Featley, *The Fisher Catched in His Owne Net* (1623), 21; Edward Chaloner, *Credo Ecclesiam Sanctam Catholicam* (1625), 83; John

Prideaux, 'Perez-Uzzah, Or the Breach of Uzzah', 12 in idem, *Certaine Sermons* (Oxford, 1636); Birckbek, *Protestants Evidence*, 19–20; Henry Rogers, *The Protestant Church Existent* (1638), 42, 114–15; Humphrey Lynde, *Via Tuta* 4th edn (1630), sig A3v.

8. James Ussher, *Works*, 17 vols (Dublin, 1847–64), 11. 169–91, 231–80, 316–413; Abbot, *Treatise*, 84–6, 100–13; Richard Bernard, *Looke beyond Luther* (1624), 23; Prideaux, *Viginti-duae lectiones*, 138–9; idem, 'Perez-Uzzah', 17.

9. Prideaux, *Viginti-duae lectiones*, 140, 142; idem, 'Perez-Uzzah', 16; Chaloner, *Credo Ecclesiam*, 94; Ussher, *Works*, 11. 387–8.

10. Chaloner, *Credo Ecclesiam*, 91, 94.

11. Prideaux, *Viginti-duae lectiones*, 130–37.

12. J. Facey, 'John Foxe and the Defence of the English Church' in Lake and Dowling (eds), *Protestantism*, 175–7; Francis Godwin, *A Catalogue of the Bishops of England* (1601), 'Address to the Reader'; Field, *Of the Church*, IV. 286–7, 304–5, 354–82; John Panke, *Collectanea, Out of St. Gregory and St. Bernard against the papists* (Oxford, 1618); Abbot, *Treatise*, 91–3; George Carleton, *Consensus Ecclesiae Catholicae contra Tridentinos* (1615), 224–6; Morton, *Catholike Appeale*, 458–60; Prideaux, *Viginti-duae lectiones*, 137.

13. Morton, *Catholike Appeale*, 458–60; Abbot, *Treatise*, 93–4.

14. Morton, *Grand Imposture*, 414; Ussher, *Works*, XV. 91–2.

15. R. J. Bauckham, 'Hooker, Travers, and the Church of Rome in the 1580s', *JEH*, 29 (1978), 45–7.

16. Ibid., 46–7.

17. Field, *Of the Church*, I. 165–7, 171, 359–60; II. 1–387; IV. 522–6.

18. Carleton, *Consensus*, 18, 226–7; idem, *Directions to know the True Church* (1615), 32–55, 50–2, 57, 60–5, 67–8, 79, 81–3; Thomas Scot, *A Tongue-Combat*, 86 in *the Workes of . . . Mr. Thomas Scot* (Utrecht, 1624); Morton, *Grand Imposture*, 418; Cade, *Justification*, 202–3; Henry Burton, *Babel no Bethel* (1629), 5; Ussher, *Works*, II. 167; 111, 90, 118, 176. See also White, *Orthodox Faith*, 324; idem, *Replie*, 168–9.

19. Prideaux, *Viginti-duae lectiones*, 136; Ussher, *Works*, II. 213–14, 492, III. 572–9; Richard Crakanthorp, *Vigilius Dormitans* (1631), Epistle Dedicatorie, sigs A2v-A4r, 1; William Crashaw (ed.), *Manuale Catholicorum* (1611).

20. Field, *Of the Church*, I. 171–2; IV. 522–5, 535, 572.

21. Ussher, *Works*, II. 1–21 see 74–98, 158–64 and *passim*; Carleton, *Consensus*, 1–4.

22. Daniel Featley, *The Romish Fisher Caught and Held in His Owne Net* (1624), sig. K3*r.

23. Laud, *Works*, II. p. xiii; G. Ornsby (ed.), *The Correspondence of John Cosin*, 2 vols *Surtees Society*, 52, 55 (1868–72), i. 45–6; Peter Heylyn, *A Briefe and Moderate Answer* (1637), 72; idem. *Examen Historicum* (1659), 214.

24. Laud, *Works*, II. p. xii (my italics).

25. White, *Replie*, 104.

26. Richard Montagu, *THEANTHROPIKON*, (1640), ii. 464.

27. E.g. F. R. Goodman (ed.), *The Diary of John Young* (1928), 98 n. 4; Peter Hausted, *Ten Sermons* (1636), 176–8; John Pocklington, *Altare Christianum* (1637), 11–12; Walter Balcanquhall, *The Honour of Christian Churches* (1633), 11; Richard Tedder, *A Sermon preached at Wimondham* (1637), 5.

28. CUL, MS Gg/1/29 fols 39–42r, 67v, 102–5; LPL, MS 2550 fo. 105; PRO, SP 14/80 fol. 177v; John Prideaux, *Ephesus Backsliding* (1614), 36; Richard Montagu, *New Gagg* (1624), 73–5; idem, *Appello Caesarem* (1625), 143–61; Laud, *Works*, IV. 308–9, 313; Heylyn, *Briefe Answer*, 127–9; Christopher Dow, *Innovations unjustly charged* . . . (1637), 53.

29. B. W. Ball, *A Great Expectation* (Leiden, 1975), 72–4; Laud, *Works*, IV. 309; Joseph Mede, *Works* (1672 edn), 796, (1664 edn), 1017.

30. Montagu, *Appello*, 134–5; idem, *New Gagg*, 49–50; idem, *Apparatus ad origines ecclesiasticarum* (Oxford, 1635), 3–4; idem, *The Acts and Monuments of the Church before Christ Incarnate* (1642), 71; Francis White, *Replie*, 49–50; Laud, *Works* II. 155 note n.

31. Laud, *Works*, II. 155–6; Montague, *New Gagg*, 49–50; idem, *Appello*, 133–6; Thomas Choun, *Collectiones Theologicarum* (1635), 31–4.

32. See above, 189–90.

33. Heylyn, *Briefe Answer*, 128–9; Robert Shelford, *Five Pious and Learned Discourses* (Cambridge, 1635), 296.

34. Richard Crakanthorp, *Defensio Ecclesiae Anglicanae* (Oxford, 1847), 78; Joseph Hall, *Works*, 10 vols (Oxford, 1863), VIII. 742; Field, *Of the Church*, IV. 527 (my italics).

35. Laud, *Works*, II. pp. xiii–xiv note q (quoting Field), 314–15 and note f (quoting Prideaux and Abbot).

36. Ibid., II. 143–4; Montagu, *New Gagg*, 'To the Reader'; idem, *Appello*, 139; Hall, *Works*, VIII. 719, 721, 729, 742.

37. William Perkins, *A Reformed Catholike* (1634 edn), sigs. A3v–A4r.

38. Ibid., sigs. A2r, A3v, 1–9, 290–1, 293–4.

39. Contrast Heylyn's account of Prideaux's views in his *Examen Historicum*, 214–15 with Prideaux's wide-ranging argument in *Viginti-duae lectiones*, 136–40.

40. Montagu's citation of Morton was especially fraudulent, as in asserting that protestants and Romanists differ only in the application, and not in the sense, of church invisibility. Morton was talking wholly in terms of the relative invisibility of the true church – a concept which Montagu was claiming did not exist; Montagu, *Appello*, 138–9; Morton, *Catholike Appeale*, 659–71.

41. Prideaux, *Viginti-duae lectiones*, 136–7; Heylyn, *Briefe Answer*, 71–2.

42. It was Abbot who instructed his chaplain Francis Mason to write a detailed description and defence of the canonicity of the consecration

of the Elizabethan bishops; see Francis Mason, *Of the Consecration of the Bishops of the Church of England* (1613), Epistle Dedicatory.

43. John Yates, *Treatise of the Honour of Gods House* (1637), 21–2, 35, and ch. 7; John Pocklington, *Sunday No Sabbath* (1636), 47; Dow, *Innovations*, p. 175; Bodl., Rawlinson MS D. 853 fos 174–5.

44. Montagu, *New Gagg*, 49; Heylyn, *Examen Historicum*, 214.

45. Richard Hooker, *Works* 3 vols (Oxford, 1888), I. 65.

46. Henry Burton, *Babel no Bethel* (1629), 15, 37–8, 74, 129; idem, *The Seven Vials*, (1628), 44–5 – cf. Daniel Featley, *A Second Parallel* (1626), ii. 79, 93–4.

47. Montagu, *Appello*, 139–40; John Yates, *Ibis ad Caesarem* (1626), iii. 14.

48. William Page (tr. and ed.), *The Imitation of Christ* (Oxford, 1639), 'To the Christian Reader' [unpaginated]; Walter Curle, *A Sermon preached at White-Hall* (1622), 28.

49. Christopher Potter, *Want of Charitie* (Oxford, 1633), i. 56, 74–5.

50. CUL, MS Gg/1/29 fo. 101r (from back).

51. G. Albion, *Charles I and the Court of Rome* (Louvain, 1935), 183–5.

52. O. P. Grell, *Dutch Calvinists in Early Stuart London* (Leiden, 1989), 224–48; H. R. Trevor-Roper, *Archbishop Laud 1573–1645* 3rd edn (1988), 197–204.

53. Thomas Jackson, *Works*, 12 vols (Oxford, 1844) II. 23–4, 26–7; White, *Orthodox Faith*, 265–6; *Replie*, 104–5, 130, 139.

9. THE *VIA MEDIA* IN THE EARLY STUART CHURCH   *Peter White*

I am indebted to Kenneth Fincham, Ian Green and Suzanne Fagence for comments on earlier drafts of this chapter.

1. Berkshire RO, Parish Documents, DP 97/5/9, p. 6.

2. N. Tyacke, 'Puritanism, Arminianism and Counter-Revolution' in C. Russell (ed.), *The Origins of the English Civil War* (1973), 119–43; N. Tyacke, *Anti-Calvinists: The Rise of English Arminianism, c.1590–1640* (Oxford, 1987).

3. William Prynne, *Canterburies Doome* (1646), 155–61, followed by John Rushworth, *Historical Collections*, i, 1618–1629 (1659), 62, 173–4, 413.

4. G. Nuttall and O. Chadwick, *From Uniformity to Unity 1662–1962* (1962), 5–6.

5. For a contemporary statement of this view, see Edwin Sandys, *Europae Speculum, or A View or Survey of the State of Religion in the Western Parts of the World* (1605), 213.

6. P. Lake, *Anglicans and Puritans? Presbyterianism and English Conformist Thought from Whitgift to Hooker* (1988), 159–60. *Zürich Letters* (2 vols, Parker Society, Cambridge, 1842–5), ii, 34–6, 127–35; i, 55, 71–2, 129,

133–4, 220–1; *The Correspondence of Matthew Parker* (Parker Society, Cambridge, 1853), 215; 'A Preface unto the Bible following', sig *11v. In view of Dr Tyacke's claim that the Bishop's Bible was doctrinally calvinist, it is worth pointing out that Parker's preface emphasised that 'to all belongeth it to be called unto eternal life . . . No man, woman or child is excluded from this salvation'. (sig. *1r) Among the 'observations respected of the translators' was 'to make no bitter notes upon the text, or yet set down any determination in places of controversy': Parker to Cecil, 5 Oct. 1568.

7. Francis Hastings, *An Apologie or Defence of the Watchword* (1600), 192–3; William Barlow, *A Defence of the Articles of the Protestants' Religion* (1601), 20.

8. F. Mason, *Of the Consecration of Bishops in the Church of England* (1613); idem, *The Authority of the Church in making Canons and Constitutions* (1607) sig. A3r, 9, 15–17, 23–4.

9. Ibid., 18, 25, 29, 57–8, 38.

10. John Boys, *Workes* (1629), 6, 14, 23, 40–1, 61, 184, 207–9.

11. Arthur Lake, *Sermons* (1629), 81, 531–47. Preaching about the eucharist, Lake wrote, 'Would any man be sure that he is of God's family? What better evidence can he have than that he is fed at God's table?'. Ibid., 167. *Ten Sermons* (1640), 16.

12. Nathaniel Field, *Some Short Memorials concerning the Life of . . . Richard Field*, ed. J. Le Neve (1716–7), esp. 15, 21–2.

13. P. Lake, 'Calvinism and the English Church, 1570–1635', *P and P*, 114 (1987), 49–50.

14. J. Spedding, *The Letters and Life of Francis Bacon*, (1861–74), iii, 73–4; vii, 36ff, 43–6, 54, 63. PRO, SP 14/6/21, quoted by F. Shriver, 'Hampton Court Revisited: James I and the Puritans' in *JEH*, 33 (1982), 59. For the hostility of the clerical establishment, see *The Answer of the Vice Chancellor, the Doctors, both the Proctors and the other Heads of House in the University of Oxford . . . to the Humble Petitions of the Ministers of the Church of England* (Oxford, 1603).

15. Shriver, 'James I and the Puritans', 53–4.

16. William Barlow, *The Summe and Substance of the Conference . . . at Hampton Court* (1605), printed in E. Cardwell, *A History of Conferences . . .* (Oxford, 1849), 167–212. The arguments of M. H. Curtis, 'The Hampton Court Conference and its aftermath' in *History*, 46 (1961), 1–16 against its reliability, and in favour of the alternative anonymous version printed in R. G. Usher, *The Reconstruction of the English Church* (2 vols, 1910) ii, 341–54 from BL, Harleian MS 828 fo. 32f. have been critically considered in Shriver, 'James I and the Puritans'. As I argue elsewhere, on the doctrinal issues the incoherence of Harl. 828 means that there is on the whole no substitute for Barlow's version.

17. Barlow, *Summe and Substance*, 172, 175–6, 181, 185.

18. Ibid., 198–9, 191; Bacon, *Works*, vii, 58. For James I, see *A*

Meditation upon the Lord's Prayer (1619), 4–6, where the king complains that the puritans 'will have us hunt for hearing of sermons without ceasing, but as little prayer as ye will . . . turning the commandment of the Apostle from *Pray continuously* to *Preach continually*'.

19. Lake, *Anglicans and Puritans?*, 182ff., 240.

20. Usher, *Reconstruction*, ii, 345; S. B. Babbage, *Puritanism and Richard Bancroft* (1962), 79.

21. B. F. Westcott, *A General View of the History of the English Bible*, 3rd edn, revised by W. Aldis Wright (1905), 112–5, 256–7; G. W. Bernard, 'The Church of England, c.1529–c.1642' in *History*, 75 (1990), 189.

22. J. Jewel, *Works*, (1609), preface, sig. q2r–3r.

23. W. B. Patterson, 'King James I's Call for an Ecumenical Council', in C. J. Cuming and D. Baker (eds), *Studies in Church History, VII* (Cambridge, 1971), 267–8.

24. C. H. McIlwain (ed.), *The Political Works of James I* (Cambridge, Mass., 1918), 110–68. The Vincentian canon was a threefold test of catholicity laid down by St Vincent of Lerins (d. before 450) in his 'Commonitorium' (II. 3), viz. *quod ubique, quod semper, quod ab omnibus creditum est* ('what has been believed everywhere, always, and by all'). By this triple test of ecumenicity, antiquity and consent the Church was able to differentiate between true and false traditions.

25. Lancelot Andrewes, *Tortura Torti* (Oxford, 1851), 96; *Responsio ad Apologiam Cardinalis Bellarminum* (Oxford, 1851), 25–6, 69, 216–7.

26. Mark Pattison, *Isaac Casaubon, 1559–1614* (1875) 299–300, 328; *The Answer of Mr Isaac Casaubon to the Epistle of the most illustrious and most reverend Cardinal Peron* (1612), esp. 4, 13, 16, 20, 25, 29, 32, 33–43; Antonio De Dominis, *Ostensio Errorum quos adversum fidem Catholicam Ecclesiae Anglicanae conatus est defendere* in *De Republica Ecclesiastica* (1617) esp. 891–3, 902, 910–5.

27. Bodl., MS Rawl. C 573, fos 1v, 4r-v.

28. For Remonstrant hopes, see Grotius to Casaubon, 7 Jan. 1612; *Briefwisseling van Hugo Grotius*, eds P. C. Molhuysen and B. L. Meulenbroek (11 vols, The Hague, 1928–81), i, 192–3; for Abbot's perspective, K. Fincham, 'Prelacy and Politics: Archbishop Abbot's Defence of Protestant Orthodoxy' *Historical Research*, 61 (1988), 36–64.

29. The best short accounts of British involvement are C. Grayson, 'James I and the Religious Crisis of the United Provinces, 1613–19' in D. Baker (ed.), *Studies in Church History, Subsidia 2: Reform and Reformation, England and the Continent, c.1500–c.1750*, (Oxford, 1979), 195–219, and J. Platt, 'Eirenical Anglicans at the Synod of Dort', ibid., 221–43.

30. The French text of James's letter is printed in *Praestantium ac Eruditorum Vivorum Ecclesiasticae et Theologicae* (2nd edn, Amsterdam, 1684), 351.

31. Jan Den Tex, *Oldenbarnevelt* (trans. R. B. Powell, 2 vols, Cambridge, 1973), ii, 547ff.

32. Bodl., Tanner MS 74 fo. 196, John Young to Samuel Ward, 25 Feb. 1619. Balcanquhall to Dudley Carleton, 25 Apr. 1619: *The Golden Remains of the. Ever-Memorable Mr John Hales of Eton College: Letters from the Synod of Dort* 2nd edn (1673), 145–6.

33. S. Lambert, 'Richard Montagu, Arminianism and Censorship', *P and P*, 124 (1989), 51.

34. The Directions to Preachers are printed in J. P. Kenyon, *The Stuart Constitution* (2nd edn, Cambridge, 1986), 128–30.

35. R. Montagu, *A Gagg for the New Gospell? No, a New Gagg for an Old Goose* (1624), 179. J. S. Macauley, 'Richard Montague, Caroline Bishop, 1575–1641' (Cambridge Univ. Ph.D. thesis 1964), 73, 192–3; W. Prynne, *The Perpetuity of a Regenerate Man's Estate* (1626), 250–1.

36. Lambert, 'Richard Montagu', 43–4.

37. Tyacke, *Anti-Calvinists*, 8.

38. Laud, *Works*, vi. 249; *The Works of Joseph Hall*, 10 vols (Oxford, 1863) ed. P. Wynter, ix, 498; *The Works of James Ussher*, 17 vols (Dublin, 1847–64) ed. C. R. Elrington, xv, 348–9, 351.

39. For *A Proclamation for the establishing of the Peace and Quiet of the Church of England*, see P. L. Hughes and J. F. Larkin (eds), *Stuart Royal Proclamations*, (Oxford, 1983) ii, 90–1. The draft is PRO, SP 16/29/79.

40. Samuel Fell, *Primitae sive Oratio habita Oxoniae None Novembris et Concio Latina ad Baccalaureos Die Cinerum* (Oxford, 1627), 9–16. Cf. Lake's claim that 'both sides were addicted to the language of moderation', 'Calvinism and the English Church', 69.

41. New editions of Prynne's *Perpetuity of a Regenerate Man's Estate*, of Carleton's *Examination* of Montagu's *Appello Caesarem* and of Rous's *Testis Veritatis* were all published in defiance of the proclamation. Lambert, 'Richard Montagu', 59.

42. Tyacke, *Anti-Calvinists*, 50.

43. Hughes and Larkin (eds), *Stuart Royal Proclamations*, ii. 218–9.

44. Laud, *Works*, v, 15; vi, 292.

45. H. Schwarz, 'Arminianism and the English Parliament, 1624–29' in *JBS*, 12 (1973), 41–68.

46. Laud, *Works*, vi, 85.

47. Ibid., ii. pp. xiii-xvi. Cf. George Herbert, 'not . . . as putting a holiness in the things, but as desiring to keep the middle way between superstition and sloveliness'. *English Works of George Herbert*, ed. G. H. Palmer, 3 vols (Boston, Mass., 1915), i. 248.

48. R. Bancroft, *Articles to be enquired of, in the first Metropolitical Visitation of the Most Reverend Father in God Richard . . .* (1605), 15. I hope to argue this point in more detail elsewhere.

49. As will be evident from J. E. Davies, *The Caroline Captivity of the Church: Charles I and the Remoulding of Anglicanism* (Oxford, 1992).

50. A. Fletcher, *The Outbreak of the English Civil War* (1981), 109–20.

51. I am grateful to Dr Ian Green for these figures, which will be finalised in his *Religious Instruction in Early Modern England, c. 1540–1740* (Oxford, forthcoming).

52. Julian Davies, 'The Growth and Implementation of 'Laudianism' with special reference to the Southern Province', (Oxford University D. Phil. thesis, 1987).

53. Bodl., Tanner MS 65, fo. 179.

54. Laud, *Works*, iii, 189, 226.

Notes on Contributors

JOHN FIELDING studied history at the University of Birmingham. He has published an article on the puritan diarist, Robert Woodford of Northampton, and his doctoral thesis, *Conformists and Puritans: the Diocese of Peterborough 1603-42*, is to be published shortly.

KENNETH FINCHAM is Lecturer in History at the University of Kent. He was educated at Oxford and London Universities, and was Head of History at Wellington College from 1987 to 1989. His first book, *Prelate as Pastor: the Episcopate of James I*, was published by Oxford University Press in 1990.

ANDREW FOSTER is Senior Lecturer in History at West Sussex Institute of Higher Education. He studied History at the University of Kent at Canterbury before moving to Balliol College, Oxford, where he undertook research on Archbishop Richard Neile. He has published several articles on early modern ecclesiastical and regional history, and is currently working on churchwardens' accounts as a key source for understanding parish religion in early Stuart England.

PETER LAKE is Professor in History at Princeton. He has written *Moderate Puritans and the Elizabethan Church* (Cambridge, 1982) and *Anglican and Puritans? Presbyterianism and English Conformist Thought from Whitgift to Hooker* (1988) as well as numerous articles. He is currently working on conformist thought from Hooker to Laud, and on funeral sermons.

JUDITH MALTBY has been Tutor in Church History at Salisbury and Wells Theological College since 1987. Previously she taught history at Wesley College, Bristol and was a Research Fellow of Newnham College, Cambridge. She is the editor of *The Short Parliament (1640) Diary of Sir Thomas Aston* (Camden series, 35, 1989).

ANTHONY MILTON is Lecturer in History at Sheffield University. He was a Lightfoot Scholar in Cambridge 1987-90, during which time he completed his Ph.D. thesis under the supervision of Dr John Morrill and was also a Research Fellow at Clare Hall. He is currently completing a monograph, *Catholic and Reformed: the Roman and Protestant Churches in English Protestant Thought, 1600–1640*, to be published by Cambridge University Press.

NICHOLAS TYACKE is Senior Lecturer in History, University of London. Author of *Anti-Calvinists: the Rise of English Arminianism, c. 1590–1640* (2nd edn. Oxford, 1990) and joint editor of *From Persecution to Toleration: the Glorious Revolution and Religion in England* (Oxford, 1991). He is also author of *The Fortunes of English Puritanism, 1603–1640* (Dr Williams's Library Lecture, London, 1990).

PETER WHITE is a graduate of Cambridge in History and Theology and until 1992 taught at Wellington College. He has published articles in *Theology* and *Past and Present*, and a book, *Predestination, Policy and Polemic: Conflict and Consensus in the English Church from the Reformation to the Civil War* (Cambridge, 1992).

Index